From Daedalus to Desert Storm, Balloons to Baghdad and beyond—a spellbinding history of Army Aviation, the how, what, when, where and why. This is the rest of the story, some never told and certainly not always understood. Jim Williams' research and academic diligence bring fascinating history to life. He tells how this 21st Century formidable fighting force came to be in spite of technological challenges, roles and missions, personalities and pundits. He traces aviation successes over many decades through the American spirit and the leadership and ingenuity of our fighting soldiers. Paramount are his treatments of combat evolutions and weapons capabilities, how Army Aviation was born into the warrior brotherhood on the battlefields of Europe, Korea, Vietnam, Iraq and countless other nameless places. A critical gap in the third dimension of land combat has now been filled. This is a story that has begged to be told, long, yet very complex, but only now complete, with sources and substance heretofore missing from similar accounts. Historians, military scholars, and aviators, yet unborn, will rely on this work for years yet to come.
Carl H. McNair, Jr.
Major General, U.S. Army (Retired)

"Soldiers, scholars, and aviation enthusiasts alike can learn much from this comprehensive examination of Army Aviation, a volume that successfully blends lively and insightful historical narrative with astute analysis. Williams' deft interweaving of the evolution of Army Aviation branch doctrine, technology, and organization, continuously illuminated by the operational experiences of generations of committed and highly professional aviators and the support personnel who kept them flying, produces an unfailingly honest assessment of Army Air's many contributions to our national defense."
Carol Reardon, Associate Professor of History, Pennsylvania State University author of—*Launch the Intruders: A Naval Attack Squadron in the Vietnam War*

In this first comprehensive history of Army aviation, U.S. Army Aviation Center Historian Jim Williams provides a welcome overview of the evolution of aviation from its inception in 1907 as the Aeronautical Division of the Signal Corps into an indispensible part of the modern, combined-arms fighting machine. He charts the maturation of Army aviation from its limited early roles of observation platform and messenger service into a multicapable asset providing medical evacuation, transportation, air assault capability, aerial attack, and support for special operating forces. During this evolutionary process, the aviators never lost sight of their reason for being—to support the Soldier on the ground. Williams discusses how Army aviation did so in America's wars, and operations other than war, from the 1916 Punitive Expedition through Operation IRAQI FREEDOM, highlighting the ingenuity and bravery of pilots and aircrew in the process. He goes beyond operational history, however, to address important aspects often overlooked, such as maintenance, training, personnel management, research and development, doctrine, and safety. His objective assessments go beyond the success stories to include the problems and failures, such as the abortive Comanche helicopter program, the Apache helicopter fratricide incident during Operation DESERT STORM, and the downing of two Black Hawk helicopters by friendly fighter aircraft in northern Iraq in 1994. Despite such problems and failures, the story of Army aviation is a positive one that the country, the Army, and the aviators themselves can be proud of. Williams does an admirable job of telling that story.

Dr. Peter Kindsvatter, author of—*American Soldiers: Ground Combat in the World Wars, Korea, and Vietnam*

"This is worth a good read…a welcome and long overdue history of Army Aviation."

Joseph L. Galloway senior military correspondent, Knight Ridder Newspapers and co-author of—*We Were Soldiers Once…and Young*

Jim Williams tells the whole story of Army Aviation concisely by addressing seven key themes. His crisp prose and well-chosen illustrations keep the reader flipping pages with heightened interest. This old ground-pounder owes his life to the fast-movers of the Air Force and Navy and to the brave crews of Army birds that flew low and slow and never said no when there was no hope. God bless Army Aviation, and thank you, Jim Williams.

Henry Gole, Ph.D. Colonel (RET) US Army, author of *Soldiering*

In general, United States military aviation history focuses on the development of the Air Force. In this tightly written and focused work, Dr. Jim Williams reminds us that combat aviation is also a key component of the Army. He provides us with an expansive work which traces the aviation branch from its inception through two world wars, the loss of a major portion to the new Air Force, its reconstitution, continuous development and modernization, and utilization up through its current role in the Global War on Terror. This is a well written and vital work, and required reading for anyone who desires to understand the genesis and rationale for Army aviation.

Darrel Whitcomb, author of—*The Rescue of Bat 21*, and *Combat Search and Rescue in Desert Storm*

A History of Army Aviation

A History of Army Aviation

From Its Beginnings to the War on Terror

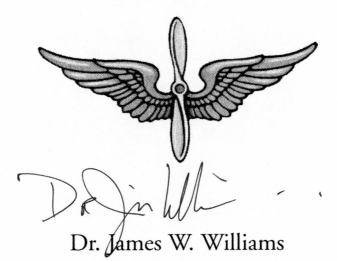

Dr. James W. Williams

Historian, U.S. Army Aviation Center

iUniverse, Inc.

New York Lincoln Shanghai

A History of Army Aviation
From Its Beginnings to the War on Terror

iUniverse books may be ordered through booksellers or by contacting:

iUniverse
2021 Pine Lake Road, Suite 100
Lincoln, NE 68512
www.iuniverse.com
1-800-Authors (1-800-288-4677)

ISBN-13: 978-0-595-36608-8 (pbk)
ISBN-13: 978-0-595-67396-4 (cloth)
ISBN-13: 978-0-595-81036-9 (ebk)
ISBN-10: 0-595-36608-2 (pbk)
ISBN-10: 0-595-67396-1 (cloth)
ISBN-10: 0-595-81036-5 (ebk)

Printed in the United States of America

Table of Contents

Chapter 3: 1945–1961—Toward an Air Fighting Army 45

Chapter 5: 1970s Through Operation Desert Storm (ODS)—the New Generation 173

Chapter 6: 1990s and Beyond 275

List of Illustrations

A History of Army Aviation

CPT Charles D. Chandler, chief of Signal Corps Aeronautical Division, 1912

Chapter 1: Introduction

The Army Aviation Branch today reflects a long, complex interplay among people, their ideas, and the technology to turn ideas into reality. The Army Aviation Branch is also only one piece of a larger picture of military aviation in the U.S. armed forces. That larger picture includes the U.S. Air Force, naval and Marine aviation, and bits of aviation and related functions located in other parts of the Army. Army Aviation today is also only a waypoint on a journey that goes back to the Civil War and that stretches over the horizon.

Seven major themes

Seven major themes, interweaving through the past to the present, go far to explain why events turned out as they did. These themes also suggest the path ahead into the unknown future.

Ideas

The idea of flying is old. The Greek myth of Icarus and Daedalus goes back about 3500 years. That myth contains several insights still true today. One is that flight, by its very nature, is hazardous. His technology limits man's flight. He must stay within those limits to survive. Another is that wisdom, often acquired by experience, is important. The father, Daedalus, carefully instructed the son not to fly too high or the wax holding the feathers together would melt. Excitement in flight overcame Icarus. He momentarily forgot the instructions and flew too high. The sun melted the wax, and Icarus fell into the sea. Thus, Icarus not only became one of the first two aviators but also the first flight fatality. For modern aviators, two lessons are clear: Always listen to your instructor pilot, and a moment's lapse of attention in the cockpit can kill you.

People

The myth of Daedalus and Icarus highlights something about people in aviation. Daedalus was exceptionally talented and able. He was a famous architect of his day, brought to Crete to design the Labyrinth for King Minos. Minos confined

Daedalus and his son as punishment for other activities while in the royal court. This situation led Daedalus to devise this new technology as a means of escape. A less talented person would have stayed in prison. The nature of aviation still requires talented people. It takes a special combination of physical and mental abilities to do the job. So aviators are a cut above average. They will often find ways to overcome the limits of their situations. This fact makes them, especially in the aggregate, a force to be reckoned with. As with Daedalus and Minos, aviators can become a problem for those in charge. Aviators are often fertile with new ideas, which they then want to put into practice. The history of Army aviation often shows this effect. Repeatedly progress in Army aviation occurred because someone or a group of aviators defied or bypassed those in charge to achieve what seemed like a better idea. The balance between obedience and loyalty to what seems right has often been tricky. The line between delinquent and hero has sometimes been narrow. Sometimes the label depended entirely on who was making the call.

Technology

Ideas are good but have no reality without technology. Sometimes a great idea has had to wait centuries for the technology to arrive. The helicopter is an example. About the time Columbus was discovering the New World, Leonardo da Vinci sketched a design for a vertical-flight aircraft. Over the next several centuries, others tried to make one fly. A Baltimore inventor in 1828 devised an 'inverted windmill'—a true rotor system. He even made an internal combustion engine to power it. It failed. The only metals around were too heavy and the best fuel around was too weak to give a thrust-to-weight ratio that could get the device off the ground. Igor Sikorsky tried to fly his first helicopter in 1909. Lack of an adequate power plant made him fail. During the next three decades, metallurgy and chemistry crossed thresholds that allowed an adequate combination. On 14 September 1939 Igor Sikorsky flew his first practical helicopter. Suddenly what was impossible for centuries became reality. Within three years, Sikorsky produced a helicopter that worked successfully in combat during World War II. The pace of change from an unproven idea to successful combat use is a near miracle that parallels the Manhattan Project to build the atomic bomb.

A constant, driving force in Army aviation has been matching ideas with technology and creating new technology, if lacking. Sometimes the technology has come along too slowly. Then an idea and an aircraft to express it were obsolete before it could reach the field. As discussed later, this situation spelled death to the AH-56 Cheyenne in 1972. The Cheyenne was the premier development project of Army aviation. It was also one of the whole Army's highest-priority systems. The program started with some key pieces of technology missing. By the time all the vital technology existed, the operating environment had changed to make it obsolete. A similar fate befell the RAH-66 Comanche in 2004. Sometimes a reverse relationship has prevailed. Someone takes an old technology and applies it to a current problem with a revolutionary result. The Sopwith Camel of World War I is an example. The builder, Thomas Sopwith, created an aviation fuel pump by putting a windmill on a wing strut. So doing overcame the limits on maneuver that came from depending on gravity to pull fuel into the engine. This change let Sopwith pilots maneuver freely and claim the largest number of kills of any fighter aircraft in World War I. Sopwith's idea swept the aviation industry worldwide. Ever since, almost no aircraft lacked a pressurized fuel system of some sort. Even today, some commercial airliners have a tiny windmill as a backup source of emergency electrical power.

Organization

To understand Army aviation demands understanding how people have organized to express ideas and use technology. The Army is an organization about doing things on the ground. Aviation is about doing things in the air. So a natural mismatch exists. From the Civil War to the present, the Army has taken two basic approaches to reconcile this mismatch. One was to create a separate, specialized organization, focused on aviation. In its history the Army has had the Balloon Corps, the Air Service, the Air Corps, the Army Air Forces, and now the Aviation Branch. Out of the stream of Air Service, Air Corps and Army Air Forces came a completely separate service—the United States Air Force. The other basic approach was to put aviation people and technology into existing branches of the Army. This approach started with Army Aeroplane Number 1 in 1909. That aircraft went into the Signal Corps, whose functions of reconnaissance and communication that technology would serve. The Army revived that approach on 6 June 1942. On that date the War Department created Organic Army Aviation within Artillery to provide observation and fire adjustment. This event occurred because of conflicts between air and ground people over what were the best ideas and technology to meet combat needs. This new start came largely because the first generation of Army airmen had, as was often said, 'flown away' from the ground Soldier and his fight. The approach of having aviation integrated within existing organizations continued until 1983, when the current Aviation Branch was born. The integrated approach led to diffusion of aviators and aviation technology through many organizations. Today this pattern persists in the independent United States Air Force, the Army Aviation Branch, along with specialized aviation in the Army Medical Department for medical evacuation and Military Intelligence, and under Special Operations Command.

Support to the Ground Commander

In the different organizations are differences in technology. The Air Force has always been committed primarily to fixed-wing aircraft. While the Army retains fixed-wing aircraft for some uses, the Army became heavily invested in helicopters. The differences reflect a basic difference in relationships between these organizations and ground commanders or ground Soldiers. The main purpose of Army Aviation today, as well as aviation in the other Army branches, is direct support to the ground commander and to Soldiers on the ground. From the time balloons left the battlefield, fixed-wing technology was the only way to meet these needs until helicopters appeared in World War II. Even then, helicopters played a minor part until after the Korean War. The advantage of light, fixed-wing aircraft such as Organic Army Aviation adopted in World War II and of helicopters was their ability to live and work directly with the ground troops. This ability translated into responsiveness to the ground commander's needs. Responsiveness was and remains the key that distinguished the path that led to the Air Force from the stream that became Army Aviation. The ideas and technology associated with the Air Force today did not meet the needs of Army ground commanders—at least, not as ground commanders saw their needs. Technology characterized by high speed, high altitude, and long distance had little immediate value to a Soldier in a close fight. This difference in ideas and technologies, along with disagreements about the priority between close support and long-range missions, was the root of conflicts that produced two separate streams of aviation development in the Army. Even after the separation of an independent Air Force, the struggle continued. Over the decades advances in technology have changed the relationships among speed, altitude, and participation in ground events. Even today, though, occasions arise where there is no substitute for the helicopter's ability to hover—thus, providing an immediacy and persistence that changes the situation on the ground.

Adaptability and Flexibility

Responding to immediate needs on the ground has often meant going beyond the limits of existing ideas and technology. Repeatedly Army aviators have adapted technology designed for something else to meet an emergency. This adaptability and flexibility has been a hallmark of Army aviation. This capacity reflects the high quality of people in Army aviation. They have had both willingness and ability to respond past the written doctrine and design limits of their equipment. In some cases, this adaptive response has created a new mission and new technology for the Army. An example was impromptu aerial medical evacuation in Korea. Success in that arena led to the Army's acquiring the mission and to acquiring new technology—the UH-1 Iroquois, or "Huey"—as an air ambulance. In some cases, this adaptability and flexibility has cost the lives of aviators who tried to respond. A common pattern in Army aviation is people working one mission beyond the design of the systems available to meet the need.

Army Values

Over the decades, Army aviators and those associated with them have lived the Army Values, however codified at the time. Their leadership, moral and physical courage, commitment to serving those on the ground, and pursuit of skill in their special areas have commonly exceeded the norm. They have answered the call of their country, sometimes under the most extreme conditions. They have been loyal to each other and those they served and supported. They have argued passionately among themselves and with others for what they believed to be right. Thousands have given their lives in combat. Tens of thousands are living and proud to have served. This book is largely about and for those who are serving now and those who have served, whether living or dead. The nation owes them all a great debt.

Roadmap

Following this introduction are several chapters about Army aviation's development. Each chapter deals with a specific era. Within that era, certain concerns and events dominated. The outcomes in each era set the conditions for the next era. Often things that were unnoticed in the focus on larger issues and events loomed up to dominate the next era. Although each chapter has a major focus, there are also minor aspects that overlap the breaks in chapters.

A word on conventions used in the text

There are some deviations here from normal practices of capitalization. As directed in 2004, the word Soldiers is capitalized to highlight the importance of those who serve. The word Aviation is capitalized where it refers to Army aviation, as distinct from general aviation and the air arms of the other services.

Acronyms and abbreviations, used to shorten the text, have been expanded the first time used. Those used recurrently also appear in the Acronym Glossary.

In cases where I have quoted material quoted in other sources, those words appear in single quotation marks. The exact source can be found by consulting the unabridged draft of this book.

BG William (Billy) Mitchell and Vought Bluebird, 1920

Chapter 2: Early Years through World War II

Earliest years through the Balloon Corps—death by logistical tail

In 1783 the first hydrogen-filled balloon ascended in Paris, France. Ten years later the French army used balloons to observe enemy positions and direct artillery.

On 12 April 1861 the attack on Fort Sumter, South Carolina, began the Civil War. On 20 April Thaddeus Sobieski Constantine Lowe—a civilian scientist interested in weather—landed a balloon just west of Unionville, South Carolina. He told the crowd that surrounded him that he had just flown from Cincinnati, Ohio—more than 500 miles away. The crowd thought he was a Union spy but let him go to Columbia. His reputation as a balloonist let him return North, but Lowe's observations convinced him that a long war was starting. On 11 June Lowe met with President Abraham Lincoln, proposed to demonstrate his balloon, and raised the possibility of increasing the value of reconnaissance through aerial telegraphy. On 17 June Lowe and representatives of the American Telegraph Company rose to 500 feet and sent the world's first aerial telegram. This effected a marriage between aviation and command, control, communication, and intelligence (C3I).

The next few weeks showed both value and vulnerability of military aviation. Lowe was only one among balloonists wanting to serve the nation. On 21 July John Wise, chosen to accompany the Union army, lost the honor of being the first aerial observer for the Army. Balloons could not be filled in the field. Wise inflated his using the gas main in downtown Washington. Dragging his inflated balloon to the field, teamsters ripped it in trees. Later that day Lowe ascended at Falls Church and saw the Union army fleeing the first Battle of Bull Run. Confederate success caused a panic in Washington. Lowe helped calm public fears by proclaiming that no aeronaut in the South could perform aerial reconnaissance as the North had. So Aviation's first military value was psychological, not tactical.

Lowe and other balloonists began reconnaissance and observation for the Union army. On 25 September the Secretary of War created a Balloon Corps. Lowe became Chief Aeronaut, a civilian position. Thus, the pattern was established of civilian contractors on the battlefield as an essential part of Aviation. The high point for the Balloon Corps was the Battle of Fair Oaks, Virginia, in May-June 1862. Frequent ascents with telegraph equipment helped the Union win. Confederate artillerists tried to shoot down the balloons, which were too small a target for the gunnery of the day.

The Balloon Corps lasted only another year. Inadequate logistical support frustrated balloonists and limited their ability to work. Balloonists' egos frustrated commanders, who differed on how valuable aerial reconnaissance was. In June 1863 the War Department disbanded the Balloon Corps. Timing was unfortunate. A balloon at Gettysburg the next month might have given the Union a decisive victory, shortening the Civil War by two years.

The logistical burden of supporting aerial vehicles in the field was key to the Balloon Corps' short life. To operate a single balloon took extra equipment, exotic supplies, special skills, and time. At Fort Monroe, John LaMountain asked for sixty gallons of sulfuric acid, three and one-half tons of metal filings, and special equipment to produce the gas he needed. Failure to convince enough key commanders that the battlefield returns justified these costs killed the Balloon Corps. Aviation's existence ever since has depended on similar cost-benefit decisions.

Rise of Signal Corps aviation and powered flight

It took another 30 years for the Army again to see a need for aviation. In 1892 Brigadier General (BG) Adolphus W. Greeley, Chief Signal Officer, created the Balloon Section in the Signal Corps. At least one balloon from this first, truly-military aeronautical organization saw combat. The "Santiago" supported the assault on San Juan Hill in the Spanish-American War.

Signal Corps aviation—technology, organization and first Army pilots

Aviation within the Army stayed tied to the Signal Corps through its next phase. On 1 August 1907 BG James Allen, Chief Signal Officer, issued a memo establishing an Aeronautical Division of his office. On 23 December 1907, this division advertised for a heavier-than-air flying machine. The machine was to have no gas bag, be built so that it could be moved in a standard Army wagon, and be simple enough so that 'an intelligent man' could quickly master it. It would carry two men 125 miles without landing, and sustain 40 miles per hour in still air. Its acceptance test included a flight of "at least one hour without touching the ground. During that time it had to be 'steered in all directions without difficulty and at all times under perfect control and equilibrium.' The contract included training two pilots.

The Signal Corps also experimented with other types of aircraft. In August 1908 a non-rigid dirigible built by Baldwin successfully completed trials, and the Aeronautical Division sent three young officers to Baldwin for training. Lieutenants (LT) Frank P. Lahm, Benjamin D. Foulois and Thomas E. Selfridge had all volunteered.

These officers and their interests eventually flowed into the Army's use of powered flight. On 19 May 1908 Selfridge became the first U.S. officer to solo in a powered aircraft, Alexander Graham Bell's 'White Wing.' Selfridge's flying had a bad end. Just two days after the Army acquired the Baldwin airship, the Wright brothers arrived at Fort Myer with their airplane. On 3 September they began flights for the Army and stayed aloft two minutes longer than the contract required. On 17 September Orville Wright took Selfridge up for familiarization. At 150 feet Wright lost control and crashed. Selfridge became the first fatality in a heavier-than-air machine.

On 2 August 1909 the Army accepted a redesigned Wright aircraft as Army Aeroplane Number 1. On 8 October lieutenants Lahm and Frederic E. Humphreys began training, becoming the first Army pilots. Humphreys and Lahm both returned to regular duties. So First Lieutenant (1LT) Benjamin D. Foulois, who began training 20 October, became the first Army pilot who stayed involved with aviation. Orville Wright chose Foulois for the final acceptance flight because Foulois was short, slender, and could read a map. In November 1909, before completing his instruction, Foulois took the Army's only airplane to

Fort Sam Houston, Texas. There he finished his aeronautical instruction by mail. Such was the sophistication of flight training.

At the same time the Wrights were instructing Foulois, BG Allen was wrestling large issues of organization that guided development of Aviation over the next three decades. In 1909 Allen noted that other countries were forming 'aerial fleets' and said the U.S. should immediately start. In August 1913, the same year Allen had to retire because he reached the age limit of 64, Congress called for an aeronautical branch as part of the line Army. This action eventually produced the independent United States Air Force in 1947. Thus, the pattern seen in the Balloon Corps of creating a specialized aviation organization, as opposed to integrating aviation into existing organizations, reappeared.

Experiments and innovations

Experiments and innovations of all kinds marked these early years. The pace was fast and possibilities expanded rapidly. Consider just the summer of 1910. In June, Charles Keeney Hamilton won $10,000 for flying from New York City to Philadelphia. On 17 July Walter Brookins set an altitude record of 6000 feet. On 10 August, Foulois and mechanic O. G. Simmons converted the landing gear on the Army's Wright flyer from skids to a wheeled, tricycle gear. On 20 August Second Lieutenant (2LT) Jacob E. Fickel fired two shots with a rifle at a ground target. On 27 August James McCurdy sent and received messages using an air-to-ground radio. Before 1910 ended Glenn Curtiss dropped dummy bombs on the outline of a battleship, Charles K. Hamilton conducted the first documented night flight, and Eugene Ely flew off the USS Birmingham.

In 1912 experiments of special importance to ground forces occurred. During October and November the Army conducted its first tests coordinating aircraft with artillery. At Fort Riley, Kansas, 2LT Henry H. Arnold and a LT Bradley sent messages down to a firing battery. Like Benjamin Foulois, "Hap" Arnold became a major figure in events leading to the modern Air Force.

Inauspicious beginnings of a brilliant career—LT Hap Arnold

Mechanical troubles sometimes made flight nerve-wracking. During the artillery tests, Hap Arnold had a mishap that almost ruined a great career. On 5 November, Arnold's aircraft inexplicably went out of control during a normal landing. Arnold wrote his superiors: 'At the present time my nervous system is in such a condition that I will not get in any machine.' He asked about shipping the airplanes. The other pilot did not want to fly to Leavenworth alone. Arnold regained his composure. On 21 December 1944 Arnold became the only airman ever promoted to five-stars.

First Army combat aviation—the Punitive Expedition and 1st Aero Squadron

Before the U.S. entered World War I, Aviation gained its first combat experience and, along with it, a new organization. In early 1916 the Mexican Revolution spilled into New Mexico. On 15 March the Army formed the 1st Aero Squadron, with Captain (CPT) Foulois commanding, as part of the Mexican Punitive Expedition. The squadron incidentally achieved the Army's first use of trucks in a combat operation. The Aero Squadron had trucks to support the aircraft. Mechanical unreliability of the aircraft in the hot climate caused trouble. Both Foulois and 1LT Herbert A. Dargue had to be rescued after forced landings in Mexico. Curiously, in Dargue's case, an angry crowd stood by quietly while someone took a photo of pilot and airplane.

1LT Herbert A. Dargue and Curtiss 'Jenny' in Mexico

World War I

The U.S. finally entered World War I in April 1917, two and a half years after the European powers. This war was the first where science and warfare tightly intertwined. There were four major efforts to use technology to break the stalemate on the Western Front—the tank, chemical warfare, the submarine, and aviation. Of these, aviation had the greatest, long-term potential.

Logistical limitations—U.S. industrial unreadiness

The war showed serious deficiencies in American industry, which could produce neither quantity nor quality to meet some requirements. When the U.S. entered the war, fewer than a thousand airplanes of all types had been built in the U.S. In May 1917 the French asked the U.S. to provide 4500 aircraft, 5000 pilots, 50,000 mechanics, and supporting services within a year. Major (MAJ) Foulois, who headed a planning group, proposed a program for over 22,000 aircraft supported by spares. American manufacturers' maximum effort produced 78 airplanes in July 1917.

Within the next year, reorganization came, trying to speed and improve wartime production. On 21 May 1918 President Wilson merged the Bureau of Aircraft Production and Division of Military Aeronautics. He put both directly under the Secretary of War. On 24 May the Army recognized the Bureau of Aircraft Production and Division of Military Aeronautics as a single agency, called the Air Service—independent of the Signal Corps.

When the war ended in November 1918, only one type of U.S. aircraft had actually reached the front. This was a light/reconnaissance bomber, the DH-4—not so fondly nicknamed 'a hearse with two wings.' The total number of DH-4s at the front was 417. The most numerous aircraft was the Curtiss JN-4 or Jenny, used only as a trainer. As a result U.S. aviators were largely trained by their allies and flew allied aircraft. Over 8000 American pilots and observers trained in France. In the last year of the war alone, the French delivered 4800 aircraft to the Air Service. The Army could never provide its own maintenance training. British-trained mechanics supported at least 15 U.S. squadrons in France.

Early flight simulator

World War I aircraft production did lay the basis for later success. When the war ended, the Jenny was sold at surplus. Thousands turned barnyards and pastures into private airfields. This dispersal spawned a new generation eager to become aviators, laying the foundation for the huge expansion of U.S. air forces in World War II.

Dangers of flying, flight training, and aggressive tactics

Flight was hazardous during World War I. Training itself was dangerous. The British and French took different approaches. The British put students in more powerful aircraft sooner and had higher fatality rates. The least dangerous training came first, killing only one student out of every ninety. Advanced training overall killed one in fifty. Most dangerous was single-seat, pursuit training. That killed one in nine. A common problem was students flying the aircraft too slow to stay in the air. This fact gave special meaning to the phrase, the quick and the dead. It likely fed airmen's lasting enthusiasm for bigger, higher and faster.

Individual aircraft posed special hazards. The Sopwith Camel was the most successful pursuit aircraft in World War I and accounted for 1294 enemy kills. Because of its small size and high torque of its rotary engine, the Camel could turn the fastest of any aircraft of its day. The same features meant it could quickly spin out of control on a novice pilot or one whose attention lapsed for a second. Construction of aircraft also created risk. Some tended to come apart in the air. The Nieuport, another pursuit plane widely used by U.S. pilots, commonly shed the fabric on its wings during a dive.

Tactical innovations increased risks. CPT Edward Rickenbacker, the most famous U.S. ace, was relentless in his efforts to bring down the enemy. Once, all else failing, Rickenbacker used his tailskid to tear off his opponent's wing.

Beginnings of aviation medicine

Among more successful efforts to make flight both safer and more effective were developments in aviation medicine. The key figure in the U.S. Army was MAJ Theodore C. Lyster, the first Chief Surgeon of the Aviation Section of the Signal Corps. Lyster had joined the Army as a private and got his medical degree in 1899. With the wartime expansion of aviation, he rose rapidly. In March 1918 Lyster became a brigadier general. From watching British experience during the first years of war, Lyster made two key contributions to the efficiency and safety of flying. First he stressed physical standards for pilots. The British had cut their flying fatalities from sixty percent to twenty percent just by screening pilots for medical defects. Lyster went further. He championed a research program under a board that established the first laboratory of its kind. This laboratory gave aviation medicine a sound scientific basis in the U.S. Lyster also made key changes in how medicine was organized for aviation. He insisted on making aviation surgeons part of the squadrons they served. This meant that surgeons already familiar with aviation deployed with flying units rather than having them part of a larger medical organization that would respond more slowly to the needs. The result was the concept of the flight surgeon. Lyster created a school for flight surgeons. On 8 May 1918 CPT Robert J. Hunter became the first graduate from Lyster's School of Aviation Medicine, located at Hazelhurst Field.

Technological impulse to break friction with the ground— and with ground forces

While the major technological innovations of World War I were about breaking a stalemate on the ground, Army aviators ideas about how best to use their technology veered away from the front lines and the ground Soldier. A huge gap became obvious between speeds of maneuver and potential effects. This mismatch affected both tanks and aircraft, but the huge difference even between those technologies made the problem much more acute for aviation. Compounding the situation was the visionary aspect of some airmen and their associates. To them, it made little sense to tie a ninety-mile-per-hour aircraft to a four-mile-an-hour infantryman.

The idea of airpower as an independent, decisive combat arm

As BG Allen had noted, even before the World War I started, enthusiasts foresaw air armies operating independently and decisively by destroying the enemy's ability to fight. Key among these people was Italian army CPT Giulio Douhet, who began writing as early as 1909. Douhet's ideas were so unpopular with his superiors that they imprisoned him. His ideas reached the Army Air Service, where others quite likely developed the same ideas independently.

Defining strategical and tactical aviation—Billy Mitchell's 'General Principles'

Army aviators tried to employ such ideas before the war ended. In November 1917 newly-commissioned MAJ Raynal C. Bolling, prominent in civil aviation, sought to give production of bombers priority over observation and pursuit aircraft. Meantime in France, Colonel (COL) William (Billy) Mitchell, published "General Principles Underlying the Use of the Air Service in the Zone of Advance, A.E.F." Mitchell commanded the Air Service in the Zone of Advance of the American Expeditionary Force (AEF).

More temperate than some air advocates, Mitchell said that no arm could achieve victory by itself. The Air Service's role was to help the other arms achieve the goal. Mitchell did clearly define two types of aviation. Tactical aviation worked immediately near ground troops. It included observation, pursuit and tactical bombardment. "Strategical" aviation worked beyond the reach of the other arms and had an independent mission. That was to destroy the enemy's means to fight. Mitchell identified strategical targets as enemy aircraft, air depots, air defense organization, other depots, factories, lines of communication, and personnel. Mitchell's "General Principles" was the first formal statement of what eventually emerged as the core doctrine of Airpower and basis for an independent Air Force.

In the last months of the war, these ideas became reality. In September 1918 Mitchell mounted the first thousand-plane raid during the St. Mihiel offensive. These events and conclusions air enthusiasts drew from them established dominant thinking among Army airmen for subsequent decades.

Mitchell's idea for a decisive, coordinated air/ground campaign— including air assault

The Great War ended on 11 November 1918. Mitchell later said he regretted that because it robbed air enthusiasts of final proof of their ideas. Had the war gone into 1919, Mitchell thought that large bombing raids into Germany, combined with a parachute invasion behind the German lines, would have given decisive victory. Notably, Mitchell's vision of the decisive campaign was not pure air forces acting independently. Instead, he described a coordinated, joint, air-ground campaign. A later generation would call the ground piece of that an air assault. Many air advocates lost that piece of that vision.

First aviation Medals of Honor

Army aviators displayed real heroism during the war. Some posthumously received the Medal of Honor. In September 1918 2LT Frank Luke, who had shot down 18 enemy balloons and four aircraft during a two-week period, was killed, resisting capture after being shot down over Germany. On 6 October 1918 lieutenants Harold E. Goettler and Erwin R. Bleckley were shot down and killed on their second mission dropping supplies to the entrapped 77th Division.

The 1920–30s—rise of Airpower

The end of 'The War To End All Wars' dramatically ended military support in the U.S. Foulois' experience returning from Europe was symbolic. When his ship reached New York, Brigadier General Foulois walked down the gangway and became Captain Foulois when his foot touched the dock. The effect on aviation across the board was similar. With the urgency of wartime gone and any real commercial value yet to be shown, aviation in the U.S. largely lost steam. The general loss of support for serious aviation led to a strange mixing of military and civilian activities through the next decade. This became a time of increasing conflict between Army aviators and senior Army leaders. A similar conflict existed with advocates of tanks like George Patton and Dwight Eisenhower. Tank advocates quickly toed the line when tanks were subordinated to the Infantry.

Aviators—most notably, Billy Mitchell—proved openly rebellious. Along with various activities tied to civil aeronautics, aviators' rebellion drew public attention and fed movement toward an independent air branch.

Postwar experiments and demonstrations

During the 1920s advocates and skeptics loudly and publicly argued the military potential of aviation. U.S. armed forces conducted some tests to settle the disputes. One test in July 1921 powerfully influenced future courses. Billy Mitchell and his aircrews dropped 2000-pound bombs on a former German battleship, Ostfriedland. Navy brass disputed the real value of the demonstration, stacked to favor airmen. The ship was anchored. There were no damage control parties onboard. No one was shooting back. Success even in this limited case raised questions about a Navy built around battleships and showed a potential of airpower. The results served to strengthen the hand of aviation advocates within the Navy. On 20 March 1922 the USS Langley, a converted coal ship, became the U.S. Navy's first aircraft carrier.

Bombing of the Ostfriedland

Pioneers pressing the envelopes—Jimmy Doolittle

Army aviators pioneered many aspects of aviation. Among the most important pioneers was James H. (Jimmy) Doolittle. Doolittle had a reputation for feats bordering on insanity. Doolittle acknowledged that one of his most valuable skills was knowing how to crash, but his success left little to chance.

Doolittle's approach was meticulous, analytical, repetitive, and cumulative. In 1929 he helped develop a system for blind, instrument landings. He made hundreds of blind approaches and landings with a section of railroad track as a target and gauge of accuracy. No aspect of aviation was too small or farfetched for him. In 1925 he received one of the first American doctorates in aeronautical sciences for studies of wind effects on aircraft performance. His work in chemistry had huge strategic value in World War II by producing fuels that drastically reduced Allied logistics burdens compared to Axis powers. Much of his work depended on commercial sponsorship, and he left active duty for some time to work for Shell Oil Company.

Pioneers versus existing organizations and ideas—the Billy Mitchell court martial

Lack of government support to aviation led to the most famous clash of the era. Within a few days in September 1925 the Navy lost both an aircraft and an airship in crashes. The Secretary of the Navy pronounced that these mishaps proved that aircraft could not attack the U.S. Billy Mitchell had just reverted to the rank of colonel after his assignment as Assistant Chief of the Air Service expired. Related frustration was possibly present in his publicly condemning the Navy and War Departments for 'almost treasonable administration of our national defense.'

The Army convened a court martial, which Mitchell and his allies made into a major spectacle. They informed the public about their views and what they saw as the wrong-headedness of military leadership. Mitchell was convicted and resigned from the Army. As a civilian Mitchell hoped more freely to advocate for aviation, but he was disappointed. Onset of the Depression in 1929 largely obscured Mitchell and his ideas. He died in 1936 before events vindicated at least some of his views.

Mitchell's ideas took firm root among Army aviators, as shown in the motto of the Army Air Corps Tactical School, established in 1920: 'Progress uninhibited by tradition.' Tradition meant the ground Army and any who failed to see the vision of decisive airpower. When it became a separate service in 1947, the Air

Force adopted this motto. In 1926 the school began teaching high-altitude, precision bombing. In 1928 the school produced "The Doctrine of the Air Force," claiming that air power alone might subdue the will of the enemy. This was the most extreme extension of Mitchell's ideas. It was also the view that prevailed within the Air Corps' successor organizations. It was also the view that—to create an alternative, meeting the ground commander's needs—gave birth to Organic Army Aviation in 1942.

Lack of synchronization among ideas, technology, and needs—precision bombardment

Technology seriously lagged the ideas of Mitchell and his supporters. In 1923 the Air Service began acquiring the Keystone bomber and, later, Curtiss Condors. Both bombers were open-cockpit, twin-engine biplanes. They could carry 2500 pounds of bombs up to 800 miles, but below 17,500 feet and slower than 130 miles per hour. The first, even minor improvement came with the Martin B-10 in 1932—an all-metal monoplane with fully enclosed cockpit and rotating gun turret. The first aircraft with any real capability was the B-17. That began trials in 1935. By then the Air Corps Tactical School was teaching a full-blown theory of high-level, daylight bombardment of pinpoint, strategic targets.

Civil-military cooperation in promoting the idea of aviation

Effective interest in aviation got at least two boosts within a few months after Mitchell resigned from the service. On 20 May 1926 President Calvin Coolidge signed the Air Commerce Act of 1926 into law. The act instructed the Secretary of Commerce to foster air commerce. Promotion included establishing airways, navigational aids, licensing pilots, issuing airworthiness certificates for aircraft, and investigating accidents. Soon after, the Air Corps Act of 2 July 1926 renamed the Army Air Service as the Army Air Corps and created a new position of Secretary of War for Air. This position created a powerful spokesman at the War Department. The following day, Congress gave the Army a special role in developing civilian aviation. The President could detail officers of the Army Air Corps to the Commerce Department to help promote civil aviation.

The costly pursuit of records as publicity

Army aviators participated in a host of activities designed to promote interest. These included air races, long-distance flights, and the pursuit of altitude records. Army aviators, including Jimmy Doolittle, set, broke, and rebroke a host of records. A few examples of other exploits will suffice. In May 1923 two lieutenants made the first nonstop flight across the U.S. In September 1924 four Army aircraft completed the first around-the-world flight. On 2 May 1927 President Calvin Coolidge presented the first awards of the newly-created Distinguished Flying Cross to four Army aviators from a 22,000-mile Pan American Tour. Among these four were two future generals—Ira Eaker and Muir Fairchild. On New Year's Day 1929 an aircraft named The Question Mark took off from Los Angeles to show how long it could stay aloft. Three of its five crewmembers became general officers: Carl ("Tooey") Spaatz, Ira Eaker, and Elwood (Pete) Quesada.

These efforts, often almost solely for publicity, were dangerous. In 1920 MAJ Rudolph Schroeder passed out from lack of oxygen when he flew his plane to a world-record 33,143 feet. He revived after falling five miles. Others were less lucky. In 1927 CPT Hawthorne Gray died from hypoxia while descending from setting a world's record of 42,470 feet in a balloon. More died in races.

Practical uses and bad results—flying the mail, 'legalized murder'— and reorganization

Among less glamorous but valuable involvements of Army aviators in civil aeronautics was flying mail. In 1926, when William P. MacCracken, Jr.—an Army pilot in World War I—became the first Assistant Secretary of Commerce for Aeronautics and head of the Aeronautics Branch. Secretary of Commerce Herbert Hoover created MacCracken's position to carry out responsibilities under the 1926 Air Commerce Act. MacCracken had helped draft the law as the lawyer for National Air Transport, a contract mail carrier he helped organize in 1925. Under MacCracken the Aeronautics Branch proceeded rapidly, leading eventually to the modern Federal Aviation Administration (FAA). MacCracken moved quickly to improve aviation efficiency and safety—especially of carrying the mail. On 7 December 1926 the Aeronautics Branch's first airway light beacon began operation, on the airmail route between Chicago and Dallas.

In February 1934, following a spate of contracting scandals, President Franklin D. Roosevelt ordered the Air Corps to fly the mail. Major General (MG) Benjamin Foulois, chief of the Air Corps, had only ten days to start the mission. Untrained, unfamiliar, ill-equipped Army pilots tried to operate in some of the worst winter weather in years. On 16 February two pilots died flying into a mountain they could not see through the snow. A few hours later another pilot flew into the ground at night. Within three months 18 Army pilots died and 15 more were hospitalized from 66 crashes.

Eddie Rickenbacker, the U.S.'s most famous ace and racing daredevil, called the first accidents 'legalized murder.' A public furor quickly had political effects. President Roosevelt gave Chief of Staff of the Army Douglas MacArthur the worst tongue-lashing MacArthur said he ever had. On 17 April an investigative board formed under former Secretary of War Newton D. Baker. On 1 June the Air Corps stopped carrying mail. On 18 July the Baker Board published its final report. As an aftershock, in December 1935, Foulois was forced to resign.

The Baker Board's report, which many Army aviators considered a whitewash, had several good effects. The board found that Air Corps pilots performed valiantly but lacked both equipment and training. The board recommended major improvements in both areas—especially, for flying at night and in bad weather. Pilots should have at least 300 hours of flying annually. The Army also adopted the Link Trainer, the first real and effective simulator. These changes, while inadequate in the eyes of many, allowed huge gains before World War II.

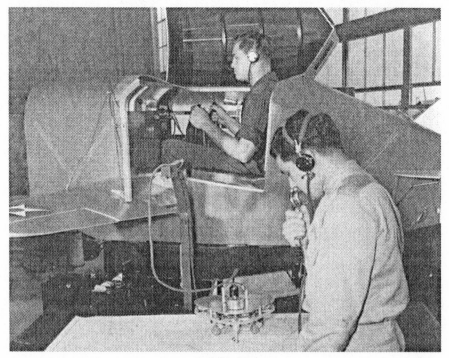

Link Trainer

Rise of General Headquarters Air Force and practical independence of the air arm

Beyond equipment and training, the Baker Board considered missions and organizations. It rejected the idea that an air force could be decisive in war. Still, the board's discussion, coinciding with Japanese and German threats appearing overseas, led to reorganizing Aviation. In March 1935 the Army created a new General Headquarters Air Force (GHQ AF).

This new organization proved unsatisfactory. GHQ AF was responsible for operations, but training and logistics remained under the Air Corps. Local commanders found themselves reporting to different chiefs, with infighting among the organizations.

Air Corps—Navy conflict driving unification of Aviation organization

The reorganization in 1939, while a vital step toward an independent Air Force after World War II, actually reflected the longstanding battle between airpower enthusiasts and the Navy. The Navy claimed bombers had no value beyond a fairly limited distance from shore. Arbitrarily the Navy picked a distance of 100 miles as the limit. Airmen were eager to invalidate that claim. In fact, this conflict triggered events leading to the consolidation in March 1939. Rather than being a triumph of airpower advocates, the reunification was meant to bring airpower renegades under control. In late 1935 the chief of the Air Corps, MG Oscar Westover, had confidentially written to CSA Malin Craig that contention between the Air Corps and GHQ AF would best be solved by putting GHQ AF under the chief of the Air Corps in peacetime.

Pursuit of technology as a driving force

Also playing into the situation was competition between the air and ground Army for scarce funds. From 1919 into the 1930s, the national policy of having only defensive forces led airpower advocates to couch their requests for bombers in terms of coastal defense. That worked tolerably in the 1920s when nothing was being funded. It let the Air Corps gain the biggest share of the Army's research and development (R&D) budget when times improved slightly. In 1936, though, the General Staff became worried about equipment for the ground forces and held back spending to develop heavy bombers. The Army's policy of trying to get the most weapons for the funds available also led to ordering the Air Corps to buy more, smaller bombers—which could support ground troops—rather than B-17s.

'Andrews' Folly'

These streams merged in a publicity stunt by a group of bomber officers in May 1938 during a joint, Army-Navy exercise. The scenario assumed aircraft carriers attacking the Atlantic Coast. Several Air Corps officers saw a chance to show what B-17s could do. They would intercept an Italian ocean liner, the Rex, several hundred miles out to sea. To make sure the world knew about the B-17's capabilities, the officers brought along correspondents from two major New York papers and a broadcast crew from NBC. On 12 May three B-17s took off to find the Rex.

Bad weather almost turned this stunt into a public-relations disaster. Dense clouds made it almost impossible to see the liner, even though superb navigation put the bombers close. Pure luck at the last minute let LT Curtis LeMay, lead navigator and later a Chief of Staff of the Air Force, succeed. The Rex was 725 miles out to sea. As the bombers flew by, they could hear the ship's band playing. Passengers were waving and taking photos.

News was broadcast immediately and made headlines around the world. Over 1800 periodicals carried a photo of B-17s passing at mast level. MG Frank M. Andrews, chief of GHQ AF, stressed to both the press and Congressmen that this was a routine flight. The Navy was furious and let the CSA know it.

Known as "Andrews' Folly," this episode had at least two unexpected effects. It ended Andrews' career and led to unified command under an even stronger advocate of airpower. Andrews had become the chief instead of Hap Arnold specifically because superiors thought Andrews was not involved in squabbles between the Air Corps and the General Staff. This incident shattered that idea. Now under suspicion, Andrews finished himself with a speech on 16 January 1939. There he described the condition of the air arm as deplorable, directly contradicting what the Secretary of War was telling President Roosevelt. Andrews was removed. In March, his compliant successor was subordinated to Hap Arnold. Thus arose a unified air command.

The fallout almost killed efforts to acquire B-17s. Army leadership prohibited any future flights beyond 100 miles. This restriction removed the one, major, acceptable justification for long-range bombers. Possibly this restriction served the interests of ground commanders concerned about the Air Corps' drift away from ground support.

B-17's approaching the Italian ocean liner Rex

Organizational aftermath through World War II

The strains between Army airmen and the Navy that underlay Andrews Folly persisted through World War II. Personal dealings between Chief of Naval Operations Ernest King and Hap Arnold were badly strained over allocation of bombers to defend convoys. As with support to ground troops, the airmen considered defending convoys a waste of scarce assets that could win the war.

Even before Andrews' firing, world events helped Hap Arnold strengthen both his personal and airpower advocates' positions. On 29 September 1938 the Munich Agreement appeasing Hitler convinced President Roosevelt that war was imminent. Roosevelt announced he would ask Congress for production of 20,000 military aircraft and facilities to build 24,000 per year. In January 1939 his state of the union speech said U.S air forces were completely inadequate. He also expanded the Air Corps' role to include hemispheric defense. That mission automatically justified a long-range, four-engine bomber.

Rapid expansion of the Air Corps, creation of four numbered air forces for regions of the Continental United States (CONUS), new coastal defense responsibilities, and residual friction among Army air organizations led to creating the Army Air Forces (AAF) on 20 June 1941. The chief of the AAF also became

Deputy Chief of Staff for Air. He directed the Air Corps, Air Force Combat Command (formerly GHQ AF), and all other air elements. This change gave the chief of the AAF de-facto membership in the Joint Chiefs of Staff (JCS) when that body arose in early 1942.

Further enhancement to Arnold's influence came on 9 March 1942, when the War Department reorganized to free CSA George C. Marshall and the General Staff of administrative burdens. Operational responsibility for CONUS passed to three autonomous, independent commands. Lieutenant General (LTG) Lesley J. McNair commanded Army Ground Forces (AGF). LTG Arnold commanded the AAF. LTG Brehon B. Somervell commanded the Army Services of Supply, soon renamed Army Service Forces. A combination of position and personal influence with President Roosevelt also gave Hap Arnold something approaching parity with the chiefs of the Navy and Army.

World War II—staggering challenges of expansion

Wartime challenges were staggering. The U.S. started its aviation build-up far short. Even with the President's urgent support in 1939, change was small and slow. In 1939 Congress increased the Army's authorization to 6000 aircraft, including several new types. When Germany invaded Poland on 1 September 1939, triggering World War II, the Army Air Corps had 26,000 officers and enlisted personnel. Of these 2000 were pilots. The Air Corps had about 400 combat aircraft. By contrast Germany's air force, or Luftwaffe, had almost 500,000 members, over 50,000 aircrews, and over 4000 combat aircraft. All Luftwaffe aircraft were more advanced than the Air Corps types. Just in training, where the Air Corps had barely graduated 300 pilots per year, the goal by mid-1941 was 30,000, with 50,000 for the following year. To meet the need, the Air Corps engaged over fifty civilian flying schools for primary training. This civilian training program was a spectacular success. From July 1939 through August 1945 a total of 317,000 students started training and 193,400 graduated. New pilots then had transition training in combat aircraft. Before Air Corps pilots went to into combat, they had about 400 hours of airtime. That compared to 150 for the Germans and less than 100 for the Japanese. To provide the other key members of aircrews, the AAF trained 50,000 navigators and 45,000 bombardiers. To do all this, the AAF eventually had 2252 training facilities on 76 installations.

Doolittle Raid—first strike against the enemy a Joint operation

After the Japanese attack on Pearl Harbor brought the U.S. officially into World War II, the AAF was the first arm to strike a blow at the enemy. On 18 April 1942 sixteen B-25s led by COL Jimmy Doolittle attacked Tokyo. To get close enough to reach the target, they launched from a Navy aircraft carrier 500 miles at sea. The military effect was negligible, but the Doolittle raid had huge morale effects. It shocked the Japanese to have the enemy hit their own homeland so quickly and easily. These same facts boosted U.S. morale, badly damaged by Pearl Harbor. The raid also foreshadowed the huge bombing campaigns the AAF would conduct through the rest of the war in both Europe and against Japan.

Indecisiveness of independent airpower

The AAF performed heroically and had tremendous effects. Just in Europe, by the end of the war, the AAF flew 1,693,565 combat sorties and dropped 1,554,463 tons of bombs. It lost 27,694 aircraft against claimed enemy losses of 29,916. Of 94,565 casualties, 30,999 airmen had died.

Still, the air campaigns of World War II fell short of advocate's vision of decisive airpower. Despite having to disperse and substitute materials, Germany increased war production up to the very end of the war. The bombing campaigns produced horrible destruction. The largest, single raid on Tokyo occurred 9 March 1945. It killed almost 84,000, destroyed a quarter of the city, and left over a million without shelter. Even the atomic bombs were not decisive by themselves. The Japanese decision to surrender resulted from a coincidence of events. Most important was Japan's inability to persuade long-time enemy, Russia, to arbitrate with the U.S. for terms of surrender. Stalin waited until after the first atomic bomb dropped to inform the Japanese he would not act on their behalf. On 8 August, two days after the first bomb and the day before the U.S. dropped the second bomb, the Soviet Union declared war on Japan. With no hope of any bargaining and faced with invasion by the hated Russians—the emperor decided to surrender.

Another air war—rise of the helicopter

Little noticed at the time, during World War II the AAF had begun a different stream of development of great importance to the future Army. That was the application of the helicopter to combat operations.

500-year wait for technology to catch up with an idea

The idea of powered, vertical flight went back almost 500 years but could not overcome the lack of critical technology until the late 1930s. As early as 1921 Army aviators had tinkered with helicopters—notably, one built by Dr. George de Bothezat. On 18 December 1922 MAJ Thurman H. Bane piloted the first public flight of this helicopter . The H-1 rose to six feet and stayed up for 1 minute 42 seconds. After testing this design through 1923, Army interest in helicopters ceased. Others had success through various workarounds, such as the autogiro—a hybrid of a conventional airplane with a rotor system that gave more or less vertical lift. A propeller gave forward motion. A free-turning, nonmotorized rotor gave lift. Among other drawbacks, autogiros were difficult to control in flight.

The key event affecting the Army was an effort by Russian immigrant, Igor Sikorsky, who had tried unsuccessfully to build a helicopter before World War I. On 14 September 1939 Sikorsky flew his VS-300, a practical helicopter. This used a single main rotor and single antitorque tail rotor—the template for all later Sikorsky models. On 6 May 1941 he set a new world helicopter endurance record—1 hour, 32 minutes, 26 seconds. Six months later the Army first acquired a Sikorsky YR-4, an adaptation of the VS-300.

Mismatch between technological need and logistical capacity

Technological hurdles aside, the physics of helicopters ill-suited the vision of warfare that airmen embraced. Total wartime procurement of helicopters was 424 in contrast to total AAF procurement of 300,000. Most were the R-4s, with small numbers of more advanced R-5s and R-6s.

Proving potentials—helicopter rescues in World War II

The key importance of the R-4s and R-6s was not numbers but what they did and the potential they suggested. The first proven values were in light transport, rescue, and lifesaving. On 3 January 1944 Coast Guard Commander Frank Olson proved the utility of the helicopter by delivering blood plasma for men badly wounded in a fire.

Air commando rescues in Burma

On 23–24 April 1944 a YR-4 performed the first heliborne combat rescues. Other rescues suggested ability to perform under very difficult conditions. Over 24–26 January 1945 a R-4 evacuated a wounded enlisted man at 4700 feet in

Burma. Hills reaching 9900 feet prevented land evacuation. The AAF air rescue unit had never used a helicopter before. Bomber reconnaissance let the R-4 pilot see the site and approaches. The distance exceeded the R-4's range and required staging. High hills used more fuel than expected, forcing a landing and refueling with gasoline dropped by a light, fixed-wing escort. Once at the site, the pilot delayed departing to receive extra gasoline and oil, as well as for cooler temperatures and wind to give enough lift. Takeoff still required a 20-foot downhill run. The R-4 got the victim to the staging point, where a fixed-wing aircraft picked him up. The mission proved the feasibility of helicopter rescue but showed the R-4's limited ability to handle high-altitude takeoffs. Rescuers concluded that the more powerful R-6 was better suited to the rugged China-Burma-India Theater.

Aviation Repair Units (Floating)—seaborne Aviation and logistical support

The most extensive uses of helicopters came from several floating aviation repair units operating under the AAF in Project Ivory Soap. In January 1944 the Air Service Command formally asked the Transportation Corps for six large vessels to create the first Aviation repair ships. On 23 May 1944, fears that flying aircraft from Army repair ships might revive Navy objections about roles and missions led to putting two helicopters aboard each ship. The ships sailed for the Pacific without informing any agencies outside the AAF about them. These helicopters were intended mainly to ferry small parts. On 29 May 1944 the Adjutant General redesignated these ships as the First through Sixth Aircraft Repair Units (Floating).

ARU(F) helicopters soon gave vital services beyond ferrying parts—notably, MEDEVAC. For example, on 2 January 1945 Lieutenant Frank Cote flew from one ship into a jungle area and brought two malaria patients out for treatment. The unit was asked to send a helicopter because no other planes could reach them. It would have taken two or three days to transport them by other means. From 16 June to 29 June 1945, First Lieutenant (1LT) James H. Brown and Second Lieutenant (2LT) John R. Noll voluntarily flew over Japanese-held territory in the Philippines and evacuated 34 serious casualties from completely isolated locations to the nearest medical facilities. Landing and takeoff characteristics of the R-4 made them excellent target for enemy fire. In 2002, former Sergeant William Garbo, one of those rescued, visited the Aviation Museum, sat in a restored R-4 helicopter, and told about his experiences. Other R-4 pilots evacuated about 70 seriously wounded Soldiers from difficult terrain east of Manila.

R-4 helicopter and flight section from ARU(F)

Other Army Ground Forces (AGF) interests—'Anything a Horse Can Do'

The AGF quickly developed an interest in helicopters for other uses. As early as December 1943 Headquarters, AGF, expressed interest in replacing light, fixed-wing aircraft with light observation helicopters as soon as they became reliable mechanically. In December 1944 the AGF established the Airborne Board in December 1944 at Camp Mackall, North Carolina, to keep abreast of air matters, including helicopter developments. This board had detachments in Europe and the Pacific, as well as liaison officers (LNO) to various AAF commands. Some airmen also saw other potentials. In 1944 COL H. Franklin Gregory, chief of AAF Rotary Wing Branch, published <u>Anything a Horse Can Do; the Story of the Helicopter</u>. Gregory foresaw helicopters as 'vehicles from which to fire rockets and medium caliber guns where it is necessary to search out the enemy.' What Gregory envisioned, when realized, later transformed the whole Army.

Birth of Organic Army Aviation—filling the gap between ground commanders' needs and air arm's support

What seemed to escape many in the Air Corps in late 1940 was that German successes on the Continent involved air forces in close coordination with ground forces. The German failure to conquer Britain came when bomber forces had to carry the load alone.

By 1940 a climate charged with both a sense of imminent threat and an ideology of decisive airpower largely obscured the tactical, combined-arms aspect of Mitchell's vision. After 20 years of hard struggle air advocates saw their day coming. They still faced acute shortages of actual material and limited production capacity. There was also suspicion, if not outright hostility, between many air and ground commanders. Under these conditions Air Corps leaders chose to throw as much into bomber and pursuit forces as they could. Maybe it would have been too much to ask more of them.

The imbalanced effort produced unsatisfactory results from many ground commanders' viewpoint. It also produced continuing conflict within the Army. In 1939 General George C. Marshall had become CSA. This former Infantryman was not disposed to see support to ground forces neglected, especially with recent events in Europe. The same year Marshall became CSA, the Spanish Civil War ended. Germany had used that as a testing ground. One obvious result was the terror value of dive bombers. The invasion of Poland used massed dive bombers to destroy troop concentrations and, replacing siege artillery, to reduce fortifications. While the Germans were demonstrating the decisive effect of coordinated air-ground operations, the Air Corps stopped buying attack aircraft for ground support.

Throughout World War II, the AAF gave short shrift to ground support. In the Tunisian Campaign in 1942, AAF support was so scarce that American Soldiers shot at any plane that came over, because they knew it was German. In February 1944 LTG Leslie J. McNair, chief of AGF, complained to Marshall about inadequate observation for artillery by the AAF. Tragic proof of McNair's complaints about tactical air came during the breakout from the Normandy beachhead. General Dwight D. Eisenhower ordered saturation bombing of enemy positions despite AAF protests that close air support (CAS) was not a feasible mission. On

25 July 1944, for the second day in a row, AAF planes dropped bombs short and killed friendly forces, including McNair.

A new generation of rebels—Artillery, Armor, and Piper Cubs

By the time Europe erupted in conflict again, the emphasis on bombing and pursuit, to the neglect of ground support, produced another split and a new rebellion among aviation advocates within the Army. Old rebels, the associates and disciples of Billy Mitchell, now ruled the Air Corps. The new rebels sprang from within the ground forces. They focused on aviation directly supporting ground forces. This split and these new rebels gave birth to modern Aviation.

Once again, the future sprang from fusing a kind of technology with a different idea. In May 1940, during a conference on mobilization plans, Air Corps representatives brushed off small, light aircraft as having no military value. Well before this meeting, though, some artillerymen had toyed with light airplanes to improve fire adjustment. This reflected their dissatisfaction with Air Corps support. Air Corps aircraft required prepared airfields and were remote from the artillery batteries. This situation could induce long delays. Speed of Air Corps observation aircraft made it hard for pilots to see smoke, and they could not loiter over the battlefield to improve or correct their reports.

Beginning in 1936, LT Joseph McCord Watson of the 61st Field Artillery Brigade had rented airplanes at his own expense to develop concepts for directing artillery. In 1938 he communicated with William Piper, a manufacturer who offered help. After the unsatisfactory meeting with the Air Corps in May 1940, Piper offered his regional sales manager, Tom Case, to participate in Army maneuvers. In August 1940 Case's success with a Cub in Army maneuvers made Piper enthusiastic. After Piper contacted Robert A. Lovett, soon to be Assistant Secretary of War for Air, BG Robert O. Whiteaker, chief of artillery for 36th Division, invited Piper to provide aircraft for more extensive testing. These tests clearly showed the value of light aircraft for artillery observation.

By early 1941 interest in light Aviation within the ground forces had taken hold. In February 1941 BG Adna R. Chaffee, chief of the Armored Forces, asked Piper to send a light airplane to Fort Knox, Kentucky. Chaffee wanted to evaluate his ideas about directing armored columns from the air. Tom Case flew to Fort Knox. At the end of the trials, Chaffee concluded that all branches of the Army needed organic aviation. In May 1941 <u>Field Artillery Journal</u> published "Wings for Santa

Barbara." This article by MAJ William W. Ford gave formal, public expression to the idea of using Piper Cubs, organic to Artillery units, to direct fire.

Aviation as life insurance—'You look just like a damn grasshopper.'

On 11 July 1941 a possibly crucial event occurred during maneuvers at Fort Bliss, Texas. MG Innis P. Swift, commanding the 1st Cavalry Division (1CD), was unimpressed by either Piper salesman Henry Wann or Wann's aircraft. Seeing Wann and the aircraft bounce around when landing in an unprepared field, Swift simply told Wann, 'You looked just like a damn grasshopper when you landed that thing out there in the boondocks.' Events took a different turn later that day. Swift's radios failed and he urgently needed some way to communicate with subordinates. Recalling Wann's ability to find him and land in the field, Swift sent a message that simply said, 'Send Grasshopper.' Wann responded, carried out this unplanned task, and proved another value to ground commanders.

This event, meeting unexpected needs and responding immediately to the ground commander, cast light aircraft in a new and more favorable light. The episode also produced a nickname and emblem for light aircraft in the ground forces—Grasshoppers.

Virtues of light aircraft technology for the ground forces

Light aircraft had several virtues as far as the ground forces were concerned, such as simplicity and ruggedness. Besides operating out of field conditions, these aircraft allowed field maintenance. Artillerymen could both operate and maintain their aircraft with little dependence on higher-echelon support. This fact fit comfortably into the Army's longstanding approach to logistical support that the operator and maintainer were the same person. Confidence in this approach showed in the fact that the Army only provided one mechanic for every two aircraft. Ruggedness and sustainability quickly proved out. During the early field tests, one pilot landed hard, broke his left landing gear, bent his struts, and destroyed his propeller. Mechanics still had the plane ready to fly the next morning.

'The Class Before One'

Once the nation went to war, events moved quickly. The Chief of Artillery solicited volunteers for both pilot-mechanics and airplane mechanics. In January 1942 the Field Artillery School organized a flight detachment—designated the Air Training Detachment—with Lieutenant Colonel (LTC) William W. Ford as director. Two officers at Fort Sill who were already pilots, 1LT Robert R.

Williams and 2LT Delbert L. Bristol, became part of this detachment. A third officer, CPT Robert M. Leich, who was a student officer, also became part of this team. Two of these three—Williams and Bristol—remained on active duty and played significant roles in Aviation. Leich left active service but remained an active promoter of Aviation for many years.

The first group of Artillery pilots, known as the Class Before One, graduated 11 officers and nine enlisted men on 28 February 1942. This number included Williams, Bristol, and Leich. Graduates split into two flights. Flight A went to Fort Bragg, North Carolina, to work with the 13th Field Artillery Brigade. Flight B went to Fort Sam Houston, Texas, to work with the 2d Infantry Division (2ID).

Both places ran simultaneous sets of tests of aerial observation using light aircraft. Locally-created boards recommended creating organic aviation for Field Artillery units. Excepting for long-range targets of corps artillery, Flight A's results strongly favored air observation posts over AAF observation squadrons. Flight B managed to bring fire on targets in an average of two minutes, while AAF pilots averaged 25 minutes for the first target and seven minutes more for each subsequent target. Sometimes AAF pilots could not find the targets at all.

A lingering concern was vulnerabilities of these light, unarmed aircraft against ground fire or pursuit planes. Conditions at Fort Bragg and Camp Blanding, Florida, let pursuit planes wreak havoc. These tests also let Bristol gain valuable tactical insights into tactics and improve survivability. Photographs showed that, to shoot down Grasshoppers, pursuit planes were often turning less than 100 feet above gun positions. This fact endangered pursuit planes as much as they threatened light aircraft.

Aviation's birth date—6 June 1942

On 6 June 1942, based on recommendations from the boards observing tests, the War Department established Organic Army Aviation. This happened despite reservations LTG McNair had about the survivability of the light aircraft and his belief that the AAF should remain responsible to perform the mission. MG Mark W. Clark, McNair's chief of staff, made the decision without McNair's knowledge. Clark saw collateral benefits in having the light aircraft, made the decision, and forwarded a recommendation while McNair was away. McNair was unhappy about both Clark's action and the recommendation but did not tell the War Department. So the War Department accepted the recommendation and issued an order creating Organic Army Aviation.

This action flew in the face of vehement opposition from LTG Hap Arnold. Arnold argued that putting light planes in the ground forces would effectively 'create a separate Air Force in the Army and that such a thing was unthinkable.' This argument failed to move Assistant Secretary of War John J. McCloy. McCloy thought that the branches ought to be more conscious of the benefits of aviation, regardless of who owned it. McCloy also felt some pressure from manufacturers of light aircraft, like Piper, who faced having to shut down their production and simply producing parts for larger planes unless the War Department bought some light aircraft. Thus, protecting the industrial base played into creating the new organization.

The directives of 6 June 1942 put two light aircraft, two pilots and one mechanic in each light and medium field artillery battalion, each division artillery headquarters and headquarters battery, and each field artillery brigade headquarters. The AAF was responsible for supply and major repairs, as well as for primary flight training. The AGF was responsible for operational training for pilots, observers and mechanics. This new organization was under direction of Field Artillery and AGF. At the same time a Department of Air Training was established at the Field Artillery School, with LTC Ford as director. The date of the memorandum creating organic Aviation became recognized as the traditional birth date of Aviation. The term applied to pilots of organic Aviation was liaison—also used for light-utility pilots in the AAF.

New challenges for AGF aviation—people, logistical support

Creating Organic Army Aviation created new challenges for the ground Army. One was acquiring pilots. The original plan of having about eighty percent of the pilots enlisted quickly proved to be unworkable. The talent required for enlisted pilots also met the standards for a rapidly expanding officer corps. Too many flight school graduates were lost to officer candidate school (OCS) once they reached troop units. There was no incentive for enlisted pilots to stay in the troop units as pilots, when they could easily get more pay and prestige. In April 1943 enlisted Soldiers ceased to be eligible for liaison pilot training. Thereafter enlisted Soldiers attended OCS before flight school.

Another situation driving the decision may have been workarounds that field units adopted to prevent losing their pilots. In 1943 reports were coming back that the enlisted pilots in the combat theaters were receiving direct commissions. This reflected combat experience that made obsolete the original thinking about crew-

ing. Originally the idea was that the pilot would just carry a qualified artillery officer on emergency missions to conduct a quick fire mission at low altitude. They
would need to get down before they were shot down. As planes proved survivable,
missions lengthened and were at higher altitudes. Experience also showed that the
pilots did more of the fire adjustment than the officer observers they carried. Also,
the missions often involved more than fire adjustment. So there was great benefit
in having two sets of qualified eyes. This lesson underlay all subsequent acquisition
of observation and attack aircraft. However, to do the job as it evolved, the pilot
needed to be a qualified artillery officer, able to serve as a staff officer in planning.
Altogether, having an enlisted pilot ceased to make sense

The changes in practice that evolved, eliminating the enlisted Artillery pilots, led
to a drastic difference in outcomes within the AGF and AAF. In Artillery the
functions the pilots performed expanded and grew in sophistication; not so, in
AAF liaison squadrons. Increased value helped account for Artillery aviation 's
survival, while AAF liaison squadrons disappeared.

Beyond getting and keeping properly trained personnel, accessing trained personnel could be hard. CPT Joseph M. Watson, nine pilots, and nine mechanics
reached England to prepare for the North African invasion. Confusion at the
reception station led to their being sent to Ireland as Infantry replacements. MG
Mark Clark and his deputy specifically looked for them but got an answer they
could not be found. Finally LT Bristol reached London and personally contacted
Clark, who got them back where they were supposed to be.

Arranging logistical support proved as difficult as manning. Common items
could be hard to obtain. CPT Robert R. Williams found the AGF supply system
impossible in standing up the new Flight Division at Fort Sill. Instructing
required blackboards, typewriters, desks, and chairs. Getting such items through
Army supply channels required a table of distribution and allowances (TDA),
which took at least six months to authorize. Training was supposed to start in two
weeks. Williams contacted an old flying companion, who was the head of
materiel at Wright Field, Ohio. When Williams related his problem, the AAF
director just laughed and shipped everything to Fort Sill. Until training left Fort
Sill in 1954, all Army flight instructors and students used furniture labeled U.S.
Army Air Corps. Others encountered similar problems elsewhere. In late
November 1942 1LT Bristol was directed to create an Air Observation Post
School in Algeria. Few artillery commanders wanted to be bothered with the air-
craft and their pilots. So the planes' shipping crates became the school's quarters.

Organizational response—placing an Army aviator in the Pentagon

Providing support for deployed aircraft led to a departure from AAF practices. The initial demands overwhelmed those assigned to distribute aircraft, as well as tending to their maintenance and supply needs. MAJ Leich, assigned to handle all this from Fort Sill, moved to the Pentagon and became the first Artillery aviator to serve on a higher staff. Leich quickly became an unofficial coordinator for all sorts of aviation-related actions. The number of people working these matters was small enough to sit at one table in the Pentagon lunchroom. That became the usual forum for resolving problems.

Informal support from the Army Air Forces

Maintenance and repair in the field caused alarm by spring of 1943. LTC Gordon J. Wolf, deputy director of the Air Training Department, found pilots and mechanics unsupported. They were not receiving kits of tools and spares. Field substitutions were wearing out engines. Desperate pilots and mechanics begged help from nearby AAF stations. Many requests for this help were denied. In some cases, as with BG Jimmy Doolittle's headquarters in North Africa, the AAF provided major overhauls and other services without any directive. Wolf feared that AGF pilots' repeated calls would wear out their welcome. Finally, in October 1943 the AGF staff fixed the situation by providing each firing battalion and divisional artillery headquarters one kit and tool set.

Organic Army Aviation's first combat—another Joint, seaborne operation

Organic Army Aviation 's entry into combat was part of the first major offensive the U.S. conducted in World War II. On 8 November 1942 successful attacks on the North African coast brought U.S. ground forces into combat. On 9 November CPT Ford E. Allcorn, CPT Brenton A. Devol, LT William H. Butler, and LT John R. Shell launched from an aircraft carrier 60 miles at sea. Operational security (OPSEC) almost ended their mission. Fearing German submarines, the USS Ranger's commander refused to break radio silence to alert other ships that friendly aircraft were in the area. Firing—first from the ships, then from the Vichy French ashore—shot down the lead aircraft. Allcorn survived but made several firsts all in the same flight: first Army artillery aviator in combat, first to fly from an aircraft carrier, first to be wounded, and first to be shot down. Butler and Shell, seeing what happened to Allcorn, tried to divert to an airport near Casablanca. Timing was bad. Arriving moments after German planes had strafed and bombed, Butler and Shell came under fire from nervous gunners. They landed near a French fort and became the first Organic Army Aviation prisoners of war (POW).

Developing doctrine on the fly—Lieutenant John R. Shell

The rest of the North Africa invasion went better and quickly reshaped doctrine. Contrary to doctrine as taught at Fort Sill, aircraft provided the primary means of artillery observation. In December 1942 LT Shell began sending out a weekly memorandum with lessons learned. Shell's practice established standard operating procedures (SOP) among pilots, mechanics, and observers of different backgrounds. Shell's memo also helped widely-dispersed aviators focus on meeting divisional priorities.

Developing improved training and 'making do'—packing crates as school

On 6 January 1943, Mark Clark was promoted to lieutenant general and took command of the newly-created Fifth Army. His interest in Artillery aviation continued. He made the locally-established school responsible for providing pilots and mechanics to all Artillery battalions in the theater. This school provided basic flight training, along with refresher training for pilots and trained mechanics. Both the AAF and AGF opposed rating the graduates. So, these pilots did not receive flight pay but raised Aviation to authorized strength in the theater. Clark also used the Artillery air subsection he created as a coordination cell for everything related to aviation. 1LT Eugene P. Gillespie, Fifth Army artillery air officer, became a critical though unofficial link and model for similar positions elsewhere.

Contributions and innovations—CPT O. Glenn Goodhand

Artillery pilots made important contributions and innovations in combat operations. For example, in March 1943 Grasshopper pilots discovered a major thrust by the 10th Panzer Division at El Guerrah in North Africa. The Grasshoppers directed artillery fire that helped stop the attack. During the Anzio invasion, an artillery pilot spotted a railway gun the Germans were operating from a tunnel to harass Allied forces on the beachhead. He coordinated fire from three battalions and destroyed the gun.

In September 1943 CPT O. Glenn Goodhand began experiments with night flying and adjusting long-range artillery fire at night in Italy. Goodhand developed methods that allowed deeper penetrations than previously possible and succeeded at night where AAF P-51s flying in daytime had failed. Goodhand's methods let any aircraft direct any battalion's fire. His efforts led to a Silver Star and his transfer to corps staff under LTG Lucian Truscott. Later, during the invasion of southern France, Goodhand developed techniques for light aircraft to direct fighter-bomber attacks beyond the range of artillery. During Patton's drive across France, liaison pilots helped control traffic by spotting broken down trucks and radioing wreckers. During operations to cross the Rhine River, LT H. E. Watson, pilot for 8th Armored Division, saw a reconnaissance patrol stalled by a blown bridge. Seeing another crossing intact, Watson dropped low enough to yell to the reconnaissance unit and led them to the usable crossing.

Some innovations in the heat of the moment did not necessarily bear repetition. CPT V. J. McGrath, a Royal Artillery officer flying briefly for Fifth Army, was the first liaison pilot to kill an enemy fighter. After a Messerschmidt chased him for several days, McGrath attracted the fighter's attention and flew into a box canyon. Turning abruptly, McGrath let the enemy fighter crash into the wall. During the Italian campaign 1LT Arley Wilson, who previously strafed Germans with his .45 pistol, mounted a one-day raid involving eight pilots who attacked a German position with bombs improvised from gasoline cans. Five other pilots dropped dynamite on German positions for lack of any artillery available. MAJ Charles Carpenter rigged six rockets on his struts and received credit for knocking out five tanks. Other pilots used rockets to attack infantry entrenchments. In the Philippines, to fly another sick pilot out through dense fog and clouds, a pilot improvised a turn-and-bank indicator by tying his pocketknife to a string and dangling it from the cockpit support.

Commitment to the ground Soldier—daring, innovation, survivability, and death

A key source of pride among organic Army aviators was their commitment to the specific welfare of the ground Soldier. This commitment led to many, small, sometimes-private acts of heroism. Sometimes these acts all but violated orders. During the Battle of the Bulge, to supply penicillin to Bastogne, LT Kenneth B. Schley defied darkness and enemy fire. To avoid an order to return, he turned off his radio.

To support pre-assault operations against Japanese forces on Okinawa, Army aviators created a device to launch and recover an aircraft from a ship that had no flight deck. The device—called the Brodie Device for its inventor, LT James S. Brodie—was like a clothesline strung between two poles hanging horizontally off the side of a ship. Landing Ship Tank (LST) #776, so equipped, became nick-named USS Brodie. One pilot who practiced with the device called it the second scariest thing he ever did.

The special concern about unarmed planes' survivability proved unfounded—mainly because the light plane was almost always part of a combined-arms team. Observation planes tried not to fly alone. So firing on one, even if successful, was likely to be observed by another. Then, these unarmed planes really had an artillery battalion's worth of firepower backing them up. Even threats from faster, armed aircraft were reduced. An enemy plane coming down to attack an unarmed obser-vation aircraft exposed itself to antiaircraft artillery that also covered the observers. The reluctance of enemy guns to fire on observation planes became so well known that U.S. fighter aircraft providing CAS would ask for an observation plane to accompany them as protection against enemy antiaircraft fire.

While not as dangerous as some predicted, observation flying did incur casualties. On 6 May 1943 LT Shell died when a 88mm gun hit his aircraft. In September 1943, during the Sicilian invasion, observation pilots first encountered fighters. German fighter pilots received two points for downing a liaison aircraft. That was the same as for an escorted bomber and twice the value of a fighter. A German fighter killed MAJ Steve E. Hatch, XIX Corps artillery air officer and graduate of the Class Before One.

No complete summary of casualties exists for organic Aviation for World War II. The closest thing covered First Army for June 1944 through April 1945. During that time 81 pilots were lost. Lost included killed, missing, or injured seriously enough to be withdrawn from flight duty. Based on an average of 270 pilots on duty per month, the casualty rate was 2.7 percent. This compared favorably. Across all services and branches for the whole war, monthly rates averaged 2.5 percent dead and 6.6 percent for all types of casualties.

Roles and missions conflicts

Cooperation between organic Army aviators and AAF counterparts was some-times very good at the worker level, but conflicts occurred at headquarters levels. Army liaison pilots simply considered themselves being responsive to their com-manders' needs. Their flexibility and innovation in adapting to momentary needs, though, led to AAF complaints. In January 1944 Hap Arnold objected that Artillery aircraft should do only fire adjustment. Based on what he saw in Sicily, Arnold singled out night flying as an example where organic Aviation exceeded the idea that justified it. Arnold recommended turning all aircraft over to the AAF. He had his complaint hand-delivered to General Marshall. As chief of the AGF, LTG McNair replied by noting the poor quality of AAF observation. Marshall agreed with McNair, and both said there was no intention to expand organic Aviation beyond Artillery. Marshall further invited Arnold to resubmit his proposal any time an expanded program was discussed.

Proven value

By the end of the war, organic Aviation had convinced a fair number of ground commanders of a continuing need for it. The 38th Infantry Division's report on operations for January through June 1945 illustrated.

> During the entire Luzon operation the need for organic liaison type aircraft, both L-5 planes and helicopter, was proved beyond question. Aircraft of this nature should be provided in addition to the organic L-4 planes of the Division Artillery. Three L-5 planes should be assigned to a division headquarters for air evacuation, reconnaissance, and courier service. When available, helicopters could be used advantageously for medical evacuation from localities not accessible by road or to L-5 landing strips.

Such assessments set the stage for retaining organic Aviation, expanding it beyond Artillery, and having a continuing battle once the AAF achieved independence in 1947.

L-4 with invasion markings in mud

BG Hamilton Howze receiving Army Aviator wings from BG Carl Hutton

Chapter 3: 1945–1961—
Toward an Air Fighting Army

The years between the end of World War II and the beginning of U.S. involvement in Vietnam produced a double set of major changes for Aviation. From 1945 to 1950 airpower advocates achieved their dream of an independent Air Force as part of a major reorganization of Defense to deal with the emerging Cold War. Three pillars of cheap defense policy, apparent decisiveness of atomic bombs, and a large but conventional military threat let the Air Force largely dominate defense discussions during this period. The Navy still strongly challenged the Air Force. This conflict largely set the terms on which the Army and Aviation within it struggled for a hearing and support. Even as airpower dominated, a competing vision gained strength. World War II experiences showed high potential in air mobility, especially using helicopters. Advocates of this vision eagerly pursued this idea, even if they lacked the means. By 1961 advocates of this vision—often fighting triumphant advocates of the older Aviation vision—had made great strides. These included adding new missions, acquiring new technologies, and creating new organizations. Most importantly, sympathetic people had risen into key leadership positions.

The Post-1945 World (1945–50): Emergence of the Cold War and a new defense structure

On 2 September 1945 AAF CPT Michael J. Novosel piloted one of several hundred B-29 bombers flying a racetrack pattern above Tokyo Bay. Below, on the battleship USS Missouri, General Douglas MacArthur and representatives of the Empire of Japan signed surrender documents. Having the B-29s make their turns beyond sight of those on the battleship created an illusion that the parade of aircraft was endless. This endless formation was designed to impress a basic point on the Japanese: The power of the United States was limitless. World War II was over. Flying back to his home base at Tinian, Novosel realized that the next day would be his twenty-third birthday. He could not imagine that another war in Asia two decades later would give him a Medal of Honor flying a helicopter.

As MacArthur concluded those ceremonies, a new world was beginning. In this new world, airpower—specifically, the combination of long-range bombers and the atomic bomb—was the dominant focus. Events would soon show that the power of this combination was an illusion, just as the endless column of B-29s. But, for the time being, American military affairs hinged on that combination. Bernard Brodie, a pioneer in the new field of operations research, expressed prevailing thought in The Absolute Weapon; Atomic Power and World Order. Ground armies had lost their usefulness. For the next twenty years the Army and its aviation evolved largely in response to the nuclear-airpower vision.

Demobilization

As after every major war, the U.S. demobilized although not as abruptly as after World War I. Within eight months the AAF shrank from 2,253,000 to 485,000. Aircrew personnel decreased by 94 percent. Maintenance personnel dropped from 350,000 to 30,000. On 15 August 1945 the AAF had 218 effective combat groups. In December 1946 it had two. Shrinkage in Organic Aviation followed the pattern but faster. Aircraft in the ground forces dropped from about 1600 aircraft to about 200 in less than four months.

New Threat and New Structures for the Armed Forces

Almost as fast as the forces shrank, the vision of a future free of military threats faded. Through 1946 and into 1947 relations with former allies, the Soviet Union and China, grew chilly. By 1948 the Cold War that lasted over forty years had begun.

In March 1947 the U.S. began a series of responses. President Harry Truman defined the "Truman Doctrine". This created a policy of global, anticommunist Containment. The National Security Act of 1947 created a National Military Establishment with a Secretary of Defense (SECDEF) as its head. This act also wrote into law the wartime organization of the JCS as a planning body. Amendments in 1949 renamed the National Military Establishment as the Department of Defense (DOD) and created a Chairman of the Joint Chiefs of Staff (CJCS). The 1949 amendments also reduced the power of service secretaries. They lost their Cabinet status. By 1958 the SECDEF was the sole spokesman for Defense matters.

The new defense organization radically changed relations between the services and the role of the service chiefs. Before 1947 the Army and Navy went directly to the President and Bureau of the Budget to ask for money. The services competed less with each other than they sought to convince Congress of the merit of their requests. This made the service chiefs salesmen to Congress. Under the new system, a unified DOD had a single budget. The services' focus shifted to competing against each other for a share of the Defense pie. After 1947 whatever let the SECDEF get the biggest budget from Congress and let a service get the biggest piece of the pie was desirable. The Army soon got the smallest piece of a smaller pie.

After 1945 what most appealed to Congress was the atomic bomb, the means to deliver it, and cheapness. Because nuclear air forces seemed relatively cheap and claimed to be decisive, they were the most attractive. Among the main services, the Army was least able to claim any of these things. The general move toward a cheaper defense especially hurt Aviation. Congress after 1945 slashed military spending. In 1947 budget cuts forced the Air Force to reduce its R&D budget by almost half. The Air Force spent this reduced budget on strategic bombers and jet fighters, not on aircraft to support seemingly obsolete ground forces.

The Army gained one small but important advantage in this new arrangement. The new way of doing business gave each service a pot of money out of the total Defense budget. Each service could decide internally what to do with its pot. This new arrangement created opportunities for lots of small projects. The Army gained both chance and reason to innovate. These conditions strongly shaped Aviation.

Independence of the U.S. Air Force

Final separation of the AAF as a co-equal member of the armed forces on 18 September 1947 was one of the steps in reshaping defense. What the Air Force celebrates as its birthday was incidental to President Harry S. Truman's signing the National Security Act on 26 July 1947. Truman insisted on signing Executive Order 9877 that generally described the functions of the Army, Navy, and Air Force. Based on this executive order, the SECDEF issued Order Number 1, which created the United States Air Force in name. This order mainly acknowledged changes going back to 1940, as discussed earlier.

Major, postwar changes came in 1946. On 21 March General "Tooey" Spaatz succeeded Hap Arnold. Spaatz created three functional commands—Strategic Air Command (SAC), Tactical Air Command (TAC), and Air Defense Command. The memorandum making this change effective also created five supporting and five regional commands overseas. This reorganization maintained a pattern of functional and regional commands already established during World War II. With slight change this defined the basic structure of the Air Force for the next fifty years.

Of special importance for future relations between the Air Force and Army, as well as for the evolution of Aviation, was War Department Circular 138. On 14 May 1946 this circular abolished the Army Service Forces. Pieces and functions were reassigned among the General Staff, the Ground Forces and the Air Forces. This circular defined the Air Forces' combat commands and added other subordinate commands. Among these was the Air Transport Command. This command gave the Air Forces primary responsibility for airlift, as well as airways communications, accident prevention, aeronautical charts, air search and rescue, and weather for the Air Forces "and for such other Government agencies as may be directed." The circular also created Air Materiel Command. This command handled R&D, testing, procurement, maintenance and repair, distribution, and technical and operating instructions for aviation material and equipment. The functions of both the Air Transport Command and the Air Materiel Command vitally affected Aviation over the next twenty years. Issues of aerial transport and logistical functions bound both the Army and Air Force together in often-uneasy relationships ever after.

On 14 December 1946 President Truman approved the Outline Command Plan, later renamed the Unified Command Plan. This ordered JCS to prepare an overall plan for all services' forces outside the Continental United States (CONUS). Under the Command Plan the services lost control of operational forces. Instead of being warfighters the services trained and equipped for regional commanders outside the U.S. Separately but related, SAC was officially recognized. Though SAC remained part of the AAF, the JCS directly controlled it.

The Army and Air Force Authorization Act of 1950 finally gave the Air Force statutory life. That became law on 10 July, two weeks after war erupted in Korea. This act merely recognized the Air Force that already existed. A final tweaking came in the Air Force Organization Act of 1951. That affirmed existing staff and command relationships but let the Secretary of the Air Force modify organization as needed.

Effects of Separation for Organic Aviation

The Air Force's independence profoundly affected the Army. The new identity that came with independence exaggerated tensions that already existed between the AAF and ground-force aviation. Also the relationship between the services was highly unequal. The Army desperately needed the support of the Air Force. The Air Force considered the Army's reason for existence all but irrelevant. Reorganizations beginning in 1947 under the unified command structure made things worse. In battles for scarce dollars, whatever the Air Force got usually came at the expense of and with little regard for what ground commanders thought they needed from the air arm.

The Air Force simply was not interested in tactical missions. As World War II ended and the AAF prepared for the postwar world, General Spaatz intended to create only two major commands—a Continental Air Force (CAF) and a strategic strike force. General (GEN) Dwight D. Eisenhower, upon becoming Chief of Staff of the Army (CSA), forced the AAF to create a Tactical Air Command (TAC). TAC's mission was to provide CAS to ground forces. The Air Force's disinterest was clear in TAC's size. In 1950—the year the Korean War started—TAC had a total of fewer than 150 officers and enlisted personnel.

This kind of neglect spurred the Army to provide its own aviation support. This neglect also set the stage for new conflicts between the Army and Air Force. Army pilots had shown repeatedly during World War II that light planes could do many things to help ground commanders. Many things, however, fell outside the scope of local taxi service and artillery observation. The Army's venturing into these other areas invited conflict with the new Air Force, to which everything beyond local transportation and artillery observation technically belonged.

Roles and Missions—Air Force and Navy conflicts, restrictions on Aviation

Much is often made of the 1948 Key West Agreements and restrictions they imposed on Aviation. A common view is that the Air Force deliberately imposed restrictions on the Army to protect the new Air Force's turf, even though the Air Force was not interested in providing the services in those realms. Another way to view the situation may be to see Aviation as a victim of its smallness at the time in both size and importance.

As before and through World War II, the main interservice conflict after the Air Force achieved independence was between the Air Force and the Navy. Ironically the final push for an independent Air Force came partly from Navy, which was trying to subvert a move to unify all the services. On 3 November 1943 General George Marshall started a unification movement with a proposal to the JCS. Rather than fight Marshall's idea head-on, the Navy proposed making a separate service out of the AAF. This approach, set out in a series of congressional hearings in 1945, was consistent with the idea of equal services that collaborated but were autonomous—in effect, a confederacy. That was an alternative to having a unified defense establishment, directed by a single commander.

The Army fought the Navy's proposal and argued that wartime, interservice cooperation would collapse in peacetime. Instead the Army favored unification for efficiency and economy. Army leaders thought that any single chain was better than a joint process. Mainly the Army was concerned about acquisition and procurement. In a joint process too many people could be involved, slowing or changing the outcome. The Navy's half-success was the Air Force's independence. Once the Air Force became independent, the Air Force and Army generally allied against the Navy.

Independence of the Air Force led to new conflict between the Air Force and the Navy. The Navy still questioned the value of long-range bombers. The Air Force claimed that large aircraft carriers could not conduct strategic air operations.

The first SECDEF, James V. Forrestal, tried to resolve the immediate conflict and establish guidelines that would prevent similar ones. First in March 1948 at Key West, Florida, then in August at Newport, Rhode Island, Forrestal convened the JCS. These conferences gave strategic air warfare to the Air Force and gave control of the seas to the Navy. Each service received secondary functions. In these areas each service was supposed to rely on whatever service had primary responsibility. More importantly, services were not supposed to develop a capability that was specifically to perform a secondary function. In the case of the Army, that ruled out such things as air transport and aerial fire support.

What is really most important about the Key West agreements for Aviation is what they did not say or do. The agreements only incidentally dealt with Aviation. In fact, the only mention occurred in the opening of Section IV, which defined the Army's functions. That simply said that the Army "includes land combat and service forces and such aviation and water transport as may be organic therein." These seemed to be throwaway lines to get to the main discussion.

In theory the Key West arrangement reduced duplicate costs and removed sources of conflict between the services by giving each service a monopoly in specific areas. For example, on 3 May 1948 the SECDEF consolidated the Air Transport Service and the Naval Air Transport Service into the Military Air Transport Service (MATS) under the Air Force. In practice, despite Forrestal's best efforts, these agreements did not settle the disputes between the Navy and Air Force.

The Key West and related agreements fed conflict between the Army and the Air Force. On 20 May 1949 Generals Omar Bradley and Hoyt S. Vandenburg, respectively chiefs of staff of the Army and Air Force, agreed on several measures to reduce conflict. Organic Aviation was set at fixed-wing aircraft weighing less than 2500 pounds and helicopters of 4000 pounds or less. These aircraft were permitted expressly to expedite and improve ground combat in forward areas. Tasks specifically mentioned were fire adjustment, route reconnaissance, and courier services. The Air Force was to maintain liaison units that could do these same things. On 29 May 1949 Joint Army and Air Force Adjustment Regulation 5–10–1 incorporated the Bradley-Vandenburg terms. Also specifically mentioned was maintaining aerial surveillance of enemy forward areas. The purpose of this surveillance was to locate targets, adjust fire, and obtain information on enemy defenses. Army aircraft could also control columns of march, inspect camouflage of ground forces areas and installations, conduct limited front line aerial photography, and lay wire in an emergency.

Aviation manpower

In the postwar period, a major problem for Aviation was acquiring and retaining qualified personnel. The Army tried at least three approaches from 1945 to 1965. One approach—accession of warrant officers (WO)—remains a mainstay of Aviation to the present. BG Hamilton H. Howze, the first Director of Aviation, made important attempts to improve accession and retention of commissioned officers. The problem Howze faced tells a lot about the status of aviation within the Army during this era. Howze's solution paved the way for great successes of aviation in Vietnam and beyond.

From the end of World War II to the Korean War, a key source of Army pilots was recruiting Air Force and Navy veterans. These veterans augmented a small flow of new aviators rated within the Army. Besides the fact that organic Aviation had so few pilots during World War II, this number all but vanished in the postwar drawdown. In 1947 MAJ O. Glenn Goodhand, who had left active duty after World War II, received a Regular Army commission and went into the National Guard Bureau. During 1948–1949 he ran a program that re-rated former Navy and Air Force pilots as Army pilots to fill vacancies in the Army National Guard.

While vital to success in Korea, this program left much to be desired. A problem was high attrition in training. This reflected attitude, not technical competency. Many of those recruited had been fighter or bomber pilots during World War II. These veterans found it hard to take direction from instructor pilots (IP) who often had far less experience than they did to fly aircraft that often weighed less than an engine on their wartime aircraft.

The Korean War, 1950–53

The Korean War was hugely important for Aviation for several reasons The very fact of the Korean War showed that nuclear deterrence could not cover all needs. Korean experience publicized the lifesaving value of helicopter MEDEVAC. Use of helicopters in Korea suggested a much larger potential for battlefield maneuver. The Korean War also showed the extreme weakness in both helicopter technology and in the helicopter industry. Korean experience showed the same neglect to ground support by the Air Force that had led to Organic Aviation in 1942. Overall, Korea led to strong support within the Army leadership to expand uses of aviation—especially helicopters. This expansion fueled conflict with the Air Force and among aviation advocates within the Army. In the end, the Army moved toward a new vision.

Impact of war on acquisition, roles and missions

By 1950, confrontation with what was presumed to be a solid, coordinated Communist bloc made the U.S. decide it needed to reverse the postwar demobilization. On 25 June 1950—just as this reversal began—North Korean forces attacked across the 38th Parallel. The Army had 668 light airplanes and 57 helicopters

The outbreak of war immediately led to adjusting the rules for Army aircraft. On 8 September 1950 General J. Lawton Collins, the CSA, asked the Air Force to remove weight restrictions in the Joint agreements. Collins said the Army did not intend to infringe the roles and missions. He just wanted to ensure short-haul transport at corps and lower levels.

It took a year to reach a formal agreement. On 2 October 1951 the secretaries of the Air Force and Army, Thomas K. Finletter and Frank Pace, replaced weight limits with a functional definition to avoid duplication. The language, from the 1947 National Security Act, allowed the Army 'such aviation…as may be organic therein.' This agreement allowed the Army aircraft that were integral part of a combat organization, limited to operations extending up to 70 miles, and improved ground combat and logistical procedures. The agreement prohibited 'close combat support, assault transport and other troop carrier airlift,' reconnaissance, and interdiction. The agreement specifically said, "Army organic aircraft will be used by the responsible Army commander as he considers necessary for the discharge of his military mission." In short, the agreement emphasized immediate responsiveness.

As the war progressed, parallel activities of the Army and Air Force brought conflict over longer-range goals. Insights coming out of Korea led the Army to seek more and larger helicopters. On 21 August 1952 the Army committed to forming twelve helicopter battalions. This prompted a second Pace-Finletter agreement on 4 November 1952. That restored weight limits. Fixed-wing aircraft could then weigh up to 5000 pounds. Range was extended to 100 miles. The Army also gained aero MEDEVAC within the combat zone, artillery and topographic survey functions. This second agreement made any future changes subject to review by the SECDEF.

Arbitrary origin of a sacred number—5000-pound limit for Army fixed-wing aircraft

The figure of 5000 pounds became a recurrent source of contention even though not intended to become a sacred standard. The way this limit evolved is a good illustration of how a momentary expedient has often had a lasting effect.

In 1952, after an incident at Fort Bragg where an Air Force and Army pilot got into a dispute about which service would fly an injured Soldier to the hospital, the SECDEF told his deputy to resolve issues of roles and missions. The Deputy SECDEF called in the two chiefs of staff and the two secretaries. The Deputy SECDEF made several decisions, including giving MEDEVAC to the Army. He also directed removing the weight limitation on Army helicopters but said nothing about fixed-wing aircraft. The Deputy then ordered the service secretaries to put the decisions into a memorandum of understanding (MOU). As an afterthought, as the service secretaries were leaving his office, the Deputy told them to include something to insure the Army did not go too far into the fixed-wing field.

Secretary of the Army Frank Pace assigned LTC Robert R. Williams as the Army action officer on the MOU. Williams was then Chief of the Aviation Branch in G-3. Williams' West Point classmate, Sid Fisher, became the Air Force action officer. Fisher and Williams could agree on almost everything for the MOU except on fixed-wing aircraft. They explored every angle they could think of and conferred with the service chiefs and secretaries as they worked. Nothing was a satisfactory dividing line. Finally all agreed the limitation had to be by weight. Meantime the 1952 Presidential election was approaching. The service secretaries wanted an agreement signed before the election. Both secretaries thought they might be leaving soon and wanted the basic issues resolved.

All concerned gathered in a final meeting on a Friday. After long discussion, Air Force Secretary Finletter finally asked LTC Williams what the heaviest Army aircraft at the time weighed. Williams told him it was the L-23, weighing 4000 pounds. Finletter said the agreement would only last a year. So why not just give the Army 5000 pounds? That was more than the weight of its heaviest fixed-wing aircraft and would let the Army do whatever it wanted with the L-23s. In another year somebody else could change the weight. Secretary of the Army Pace immediately agreed. Williams and Fisher emerged with a copy of the agreement and instructions to get the documents through the Army and Air Force staffs for signatures on Monday.

Completely contrary to the service secretaries' assumption that the criteria would be changed within a year, for better and worse, the 5000-pound figure endured for years.

Impact of Army's dependence in acquisition—contrast of Army and Marines in Korea

The Army's dependence on the Air Force to procure aircraft greatly slowed the Army's pursuit of a vision some key leaders had. This was especially true with helicopters. The impact is evident in comparing the state of maneuver between the Marines and Army during the Korean War.

Before the end of World War II the AAF and Navy had both showed that helicopters could be extremely valuable. Development, though, was an area where relationships with the Air Force were especially important to the Army. While ground commanders and a few airmen saw great promise in this emerging technology, the Air Force generally saw helicopters as having little or no military value—much as the Air Corps had dismissed light, fixed-wing aircraft before World War II. This view was so prevalent that, in 1948, the Air Force director of requirements flatly refused to obtain helicopters when the Army Airborne Panel asked for them. Since the Army had to acquire aircraft systems through the Air Force, the Air Force's resistance all but stopped the Army from developing heliborne movement.

The situation was radically different for the Marines, who got their aircraft through the Navy. In July 1946 LTG Roy S. Geiger, commanding Fleet Marine Force Pacific, observed nuclear tests on Bikini Atoll. What he saw made Geiger urge a complete review of amphibious concepts. The Marines created a special board to study how Marines could achieve surprise, speed, and dispersion to survive on a nuclear battlefield. The idea of vertical envelopment resulted, and helicopters were the key.

The Marines moved quickly to update their amphibious assault methods using helicopters. Marine Commandant Alexander A. Vandegrift created a provisional helicopter squadron, HMX-1, at Quantico, Virginia. Two colonels—one, a future Commandant of the Marine Corps—wrote the first manual of helicopter amphibious doctrine. In August 1947 HMX-1 received its first Piasecki HRP-1 helicopter. On 23 May 1948, within three months after the first Key West conference, HMX-1 conducted their first exercise helicopter assault from an escort carrier.

By the time the Marines entered the Korean War in July 1950, they had both tactical doctrine and experience in mass helicopter flying. On 21 September 1951 the Marines mounted the first helicopter-borne combat movement. Instead of conducting a nine-hour, uphill, road march, the Marines airlifted in eight minutes. By war's end, Marine helicopters had carried more than 60,000 men and 7.5 million pounds of cargo. They had also evacuated 9815 wounded.

The Army monitored the Marines' experiments and experience in Korea but had none of their own. The Army's lagging in helicopter application did not reflect lack of interest. On 14 November 1945 the AGF Board evaluated the R-6 helicopter for tactical application with the 82d Airborne Division (82AB) at Fort Bragg. The board gave highest priority to developing helicopters to replace some types of ground vehicles. The board also suggested developing larger helicopters for airborne troops. In 1946 the Army began testing the Bell YH-13 helicopter as a possible replacement for light, fixed-wing, observation aircraft. The Army Transportation Corps also saw great value in helicopters and sought them. On 17

November 1949 Board Number One concluded that the Army needed six types of rotary-wing aircraft.

In May 1950, less than two months before the Korean War started, the Army Staff approved five experimental transport helicopter companies. Intense opposition from the Air Force Staff delayed procurement until 1951. In 1952 the Army finally formed the 6th Transportation Company (Helicopter) and then the 13th Transportation Company. These units provided a basis to begin experiments like those the Marines had conducted but did not begin operations in Korea until February 1953. This was just six months before hostilities ended and 14 months after the Marines had conducted their first heliborne combat movement.

Force structure—Korean expansion of Aviation

Army experience with aviation in Korea led to organizational changes from company through Army headquarters levels.

From the beginning of hostilities, conditions in Korea led to new, informal force structures. For the first time, divisional aviation companies appeared, although not initially authorized. The number of aircraft per Army division during the Korean Conflict grew to 18, compared to 10 during World War II. Lack of suitable terrain for landing fields, growing numbers of aircraft per division, and increasing performance of aviation led many divisions to create provisional aircraft companies.

In 1952 the Secretary of the Army recognized the aviation program had become so important, expensive, and controversial that it needed a focal point on the Army Staff. He created an Aviation Branch of three officers in the G-3.

Support of ground operations, tactics, and effects

The combat experience for Army aviators in Korea did not differ drastically from World War II. Fire adjustment remained a primary mission. The differing conditions between Europe in World War II and Korea did produce different tactics, techniques, and procedures (TTP). One of the most notable was where artillery observers flew in relation to the front line. In World War II artillery observation aircraft normally flew behind friendly lines to avoid danger from enemy antiaircraft artillery. In Korea observation aircraft normally flew forward of friendly lines. The key difference was the antiaircraft threat. Initially the threat was lower in Korea. It increased especially after the Chinese came into the war and sent whole antiaircraft regiments forward. In response to this changing threat, newer aviators increased the altitude of observation flights until they were so high they had to do their spotting with field glasses. This change seemed counterproductive to some older observation pilots. At least some of the older pilots thought they could have been as safe and certainly more effective flying at about 500–1500 feet.

L-19 Bird Dog observation aircraft

During Korea observation aircraft sometimes flew within the arc of friendly shells. This practice created risk that most pilots tried to avoid. On 21 June 1952, MAJ William P. Hunt, Jr., with 1LT Marvin Stephen Murphy, was supporting a Colombian battalion assaulting a strategic hill. Realizing that heavy smoke rising from the battle area obstructed ground observation, Hunt circled the area at low altitudes under intense hostile fire, reported enemy troop locations, and adjusted artillery and mortar fire. During the mission the plane was operating within the trajectory of friendly artillery shells. Many of these shells had radio proximity fuzes that detonated upon coming within twenty yards of an object. While Hunt and Murphy were covering the Colombians' withdrawal, a projectile hit the plane. Both Hunt and Murphy received the Distinguished Flying Cross (Posthumous). A stagefield at Fort Rucker honors Hunt, while Murphy Hall is an academic building.

Poor Joint airspace coordination was another source of casualties. For example, the executive officer of the 24th Division's air section was killed when an Air Force P-51 Mustang making a ground attack pulled up through his aircraft.

In Korea, as in World War II, Air Force support to ground operations often failed to meet ground commanders' wishes. The Air Force, itself, acknowledged serious deficiencies. A study immediately after hostilities began found that many of the lessons learned during air ground operations in World War II had not been passed on. An immediate need existed to train concepts and procedures of air-ground operations. On 15 September 1950 Headquarters, TAC, ordered the Ninth Air Force to establish a school of air-ground operations. On 25 September the first class of fifteen Air Force officers began. The school later expanded to cover larger numbers from both Army and Air Force.

Lack of coordination between Air Force and Aviation in Korea had at least two causes. One was incompatible equipment. In the first several months of the war, Army and Air Force pilots effectively worked past this problem to support troops in contact. Artillery and Air Force pilots could communicate on radio frequencies both used for air traffic control (ATC). At least in the 24th Division, Army pilots overcame Air Force pilots' inability to talk to ground forces by a simple workaround. Army pilots carried a ground radio in the back seat. They put the earphone from the aviation radio on one ear and an earphone from the ground radio on the other. They taped the microphones for both radios back-to-back. Using red nail polish from nurses at a nearby hospital, they color-coded the microphone button, so they knew which microphone was which. This let Army pilots monitor and talk to both Air Force pilots and ground troops. In the first few months of the war, this brought lifesaving CAS. Air Force P-51s would loiter in the area and immediately respond to calls for help relayed via the artillery pilots.

Another cause was service rivalry. Within a few months, higher-level conflicts ended the informal workaround pilots had developed for the technical problems. Suddenly Army pilots could see P-51s in the area. When called, the P-51 pilots said they could only respond to Air Force observers. Those operated from fixed airfields miles to the rear. The Army pilots also found the Air Force observers unsatisfactory. Apparently the Air Force had cobbled together crews of an Air Force pilot with an Army or Marine observer. Given a frequent tendency of commanders to send their least able officers on details, both pilots and observers in these jointly-manned aircraft often seemed less capable than those on the ground wanted. Besides, as had been the complaint of artillerymen before World War II, this system was unresponsive to ground troops' needs. Rather than loitering in the area, the Air Force observation aircraft responded on call. When called, they would leave the airfield, fly to an area they were unfamiliar with, and then try to find and direct the P-51s that were already on station in the vicinity of the Army observation pilots. The delays and inefficiencies of this system were a bitter pill for both the troops on the ground and Artillery pilots who could only watch their comrades being overrun while everyone waited for this cumbersome system to work.

Battle over helicopter procurement during Korea

As the Army entered Korea, pressure within the Army mounted to acquire helicopters. This led to bitter exchanges between the Army and Air Force on roles and missions.

The Transportation Corps especially pressed to expand Aviation. In 1950 BG William B. Bunker, who was not a rated aviator, authored a report to the Chief of Transportation powerfully arguing that helicopters had intrinsic value in logistical roles. Bunker's report led to action at senior levels and earned him the title, 'Father of the Helicopter,' among his contemporaries. On 9 August 1950 MG Charles Bolte, the Army G-3/Operations, got five transportation helicopter companies into the Army Emergency Supplemental Budget for 1951. On 20 August Far East Command asked for four light helicopters and three cargo helicopters for each division. On 11 September 1950 the G-3 staff put forth a plan for one helicopter company per division, plus one aviation battalion per corps. This plan required 116 more H-13s and 522 cargo helicopters. The justification was better tactical mobility.

Another source of pressure was the Army Medical Department. In October 1950 the Army Surgeon General, MG Raymond W. Bliss, visited Korea. He became convinced that the Army Medical Department needed its own air ambulance helicopters. In 1951, Bliss' successor, MG George E. Armstrong, carried the argument to the Army Staff.

Army pressure for more helicopters sparked a running battle with the Air Force. On 27 October 1950 Piasecki Company informed the Army Procurement Agency that the Air Force had stopped action on all orders for H-19 and H-21 helicopters. On 4 November, the Army G-3 responded. LTG T. B. Larkins wrote: 'If we are not able to procure...the Air Force should certainly...state on the dotted line how many they will...make available to the Army for its needs.' The Air Force Assistant Deputy Chief of Staff wrote the Army Chief of Ordnance that 'close air transportation support functions could be provided most effectively by placing helicopters in assault squadrons already established by the Air Force and…aerial combat support for the Army is a primary responsibility of the Air Force.' He claimed that 100 helicopters under orders for the Air Force would cover all needs. In December 1950 MG Frank Heilman, Army Chief of Transportation, with full support of his superiors, formed an Air Transportation Service Division and further challenged the Air Force by considering the cargo helicopter a vital piece of the Army transportation system.

Besides bureaucratic barriers, the expansion of Army helicopter use hit delays caused by the immaturity of the whole helicopter industry. The lack of a commercial market in the late 1940s and the Air Force's thwarting Army acquisitions had kept the number of helicopter producers and production lines small. So the industry could not respond to a wartime surge in orders,. The Army tried to compensate by spreading orders over several companies and models. Even so, there were bottlenecks. For example Hiller and Bell could both build helicopters, but both used Franklin engines. Franklin had stopped making these engines and could not retool quickly. To ease the crunch, Bell sold Hiller available engines so the Army could have as many helicopters as both manufacturers could produce.

Finally, in July 1952 the first Army helicopter company—6th Transportation Company (Helicopter)—received H-19C Chickasaws and began training at Fort Bragg. During its operations, beginning 5 January 1953, the 6th Transportation flew more than 4000 hours, lifted 5 million pounds of supplies, 500 troops, and 1400 sick/wounded. Total flight time exceeded 8000 hours. One aircraft was lost due to an engine failure.

Aerial medical evacuation (MEDEVAC)

The most dramatic impact of helicopters in Korea was in aerial MEDEVAC, which Korea showcased partly as an accident of tactical conditions. Lacking a major air threat, Air Force helicopter units had few pilots to rescue. So, one detachment began responding to evacuation requests for Army casualties. On 3 August 1950 Army CPT Leonard A. Crosby, a former glider pilot, demonstrated helicopter MEDEVAC in Taegu. His demonstration convinced the Fifth Air Force commander to authorize using helicopters for frontline evacuations a week later. Seeing the lifesaving potential of helicopter MEDEVAC made the Army push hard to get Bell H-13 Sioux and Hiller H-12 helicopters.

On 3 January 1951 1LTs Willis G. Strawn and Joseph L. Bowler flew the first Army MEDEVAC mission. By 14 January all four pilots in the 2d Army Helicopter Detachment in Seoul had received the Distinguished Flying Cross.

Bowler went on to set a record of 824 medical evacuations in ten months. He also rigged covers for the Stokes litters mounted on each side of the helicopter. Bowler's numbers lifted were eclipsed by CPT William P. Brake, who lifted 922 casualties in 14 months. Of Brake's 567 missions, 311 were combat missions.

H-19 MEDEVAC helicopter and waiting ambulances in Korea

Even though the total number of patients evacuated by air was only about 20,000, the lifesaving effect was spectacular. During World War II 4.5 percent of patients who arrived alive at medical facilities could not be saved. In Korea that death rate dropped to 2.5 percent. This change reflected shortened delay in reaching treatment—attributable to helicopters. Aerial MEDEVAC not only saved lives but also conserved combat power. Helicopter MEDEVAC greatly reduced the burden on remaining troops, who otherwise had to carry and care for the sick or wounded.

Perhaps most remarkable is what the handful of Army MEDEVAC pilots achieved despite the limitations of their technology and the severe operating conditions. The available helicopters—especially the H-23s—were underpowered. Although designed to lift a pilot and two artillery observers, the H-23 Raven could not pick itself up to a hover on a warm day. H-23 pilots were routinely taught how to make a running takeoff—getting enough speed by skimming along the ground until the aircraft finally achieved lift. So its actual carrying capacity was often only one patient besides the pilot.

As a result of both the technical and situational limitations, helicopter MEDE-VAC became restricted to only the most serious cases. By late 1951 ground units had learned to ask for a helicopter only in narrowly-defined cases. Even then, other considerations applied—such as whether or not a ground ambulance could reach the patient, a rough ambulance ride would worsen injuries, or delay might be life threatening. The final decision was a joint judgment of the local surgeon and helicopter detachment commander.

Thus, both the number airlifted and the impact on mortality rates compared to World War II reflect remarkable achievements by the pilots involved. The success of this lifesaving led to the Army receiving a mandate to acquire a true air ambulance. The helicopter the Army acquired for that role was the UH-1 Iroquois—universally known and loved as the "Huey"—which ultimately transformed the Army.

1954–1960

From the end of the Korean War through the end of the decade, people within the Army struggled to refine and achieve a vision of greater capability through the use of aviation in the ground forces. In 1955 BG Carl I. Hutton, the first commanding general of the new U.S. Army Aviation Center (USAAVNC), used the phrase, 'air fighting Army,' to highlight the distinction between fighting units transported by air and units where aviation was an integral part of fighting ground engagements. Achieving this vision depended on adequate helicopters. The cost, complexity and availability of helicopter technology caused setbacks and led the Army to pursue larger, more capable, fixed-wing aircraft. This pursuit revived conflict with the Air Force. However, before the decade ended, availability of helicopters with turbine engines gave the Army a way to move beyond some of these obstacles. During this period, though, there was intense conflict, as well as cooperation, among Aviation advocates over the best ideas for expanding and exploiting Aviation's potential. These divergent views on what was desirable and what was possible help explain apparent inconsistencies in attitudes of some key people during this period.

Transportation Corps aviation—impact of simply increasing mobility

One result of Korea and the limited expansion of Aviation was a shift within the Army from aviation as an adjunct to Artillery to greatly-expanded transportation roles. The Transportation Corps became the major center of aviation activity and effort. In 1952 the Transportation Corps, which pushed hard to expand organic Aviation to provide mobile support to ground forces, picked up overall responsibility for Aviation. Before the end of 1953 the Army Materiel Requirements Review Panel expanded the Transportation helicopter program to twelve battalions. This time, the JCS did not question the Army's expansion of its aviation.

Following Korea, the Army acquired new helicopters that greatly increased possibilities for ground commanders. In 1953 the Army procured H-34 Choctaws and H-37 Mojaves for the new Transportation helicopter battalions. Both the H-34 and H-37 were much more powerful than any predecessors. This new technology started to reshape the battlefield. The H-34 was the first helicopter that could actually lift a squad of combat-equipped troops. Two H-34s could lift a 105mm howitzer, its ammunition, and the gun crew. The first H-34 unit deployed to Europe quickly showed the possibilities. In minutes the H-34s could put the gun crew on the ground, and then put the howitzer down with the barrel pointed the direction the crew wanted to fire. They were instantly ready to go into action. This was in sharp contrast to what had been achieved before. The Artillery School had experimented with moving 105mm howitzers by helicopter to overcome the tactical limitations that forced unarmed helicopters to stay within divisional artillery range. By March 1954 they had developed how to break the 105mm into three sling-loads. It took nine H-19s to move gun, crew, and ammunition. It also took twenty minutes at each end to break down and reassemble the gun. Suddenly the H-34s opened the possibility of airmobile artillery that greatly extended the reach of other air-supported ground operations. The effect was revolutionary. The H-37 offered even greater possibilities. The H-37 could carry 6000 pounds of cargo, a Jeep with a towed howitzer, 23 fully-equipped combat troops or 24 litters. The H-37 could even retrieve downed aircraft. That feature helped convince SECDEF Robert McNamara to approve the Airmobility concept.

Aviation logistics

Throughout its history, the logistics burden of Aviation has repeatedly challenged both aviators and the Army as a whole. This burden and alternative ways of dealing with it have repeatedly driven changes particularly in organization and technology. From the end of World War II to about 1960, Aviation saw key changes in both organization and technology related to logistics. Both changes led to major gains, both reducing the burden and increasing operational capability. Both changes reached a kind of peak or maturity during the 1954–1960 period.

Related to Transportation's push for helicopters was a reorganization of aviation logistical support. The changes reflected the trend toward consolidating aviation support functions that had characterized the rise of the Air Corps and now recurred with organic Aviation. On 8 August 1952 the Ordnance Corps transferred logistical operations for aviation to the Transportation Corps. The transfer partly reflected a breakdown in the traditional Army mindset about equipment that the operator was also the maintainer. The complexities and costs of aircraft meant that the old approach of treating an aircraft just like a truck or a jeep or generator failed to meet needs in safety and operational readiness. Korean experience also created an impetus toward ending the Army's dependence on the Air Force and Navy for acquisition, as with the H-37 Mojave utility transport helicopter and OV-1 Mohawk reconnaissance airplane. Both were acquired as a joint project with the Marines. Both had mixed results because of different considerations each service put into the design.

People outside the Army pushed for more autonomy for Aviation in these areas. In November-December 1952 Harry S. Pack, vice president of Piasecki, traveled through Korea gathering information from all the services on helicopters and their support. His report published in 1954, found that existing, dual Air Force-Army supply and acquisition channels created complexities and delays. These drastically reduced the value of helicopters and added requirements that greatly increased their cost. Pack recommended that the Army have its own acquisition and supply systems for helicopters. He also recommended that the Army train its own pilots and mechanics.

A step in these directions had already been taken in 1953, when the Transportation Corps established the Aviation Field Service Office in St. Louis. This office was the forerunner of today's U.S. Army Aviation and Missile Command (AMCOM), providing a broad spectrum of logistical support.

Helicopters the Army began procuring in 1953 drove the Army to change how it approached logistical support. In late 1953 a symposium disclosed that the Army lacked data to guide purchasing spare parts and shipping them to maintainers in the field. To meet this need, the Transportation Aircraft Test and Support Activity (TATSA) arose at Fort Rucker in 1956. The Transportation Corps also set about establishing reliable methods to predict the kinds, numbers, and intervals of parts and services these new aircraft would need. Along with TATSA and the arrival of the H-37s came a program to log 1000 hours, which equaled about three years' operational flying, in a compressed period. BG William Bunker's logic was simple. After 1000 hours, TATSA should know about what it would take to support the H-37 between major depot overhauls. Also, since the H-37 was the most complex aircraft the Army had acquired, it allowed testing methods applicable to future Army aircraft.

The Transportation Corps developed aviation facilities at Fort Eustis, Virginia. In June 1954 the Transportation School at Fort Eustis began training in aviation logistics. On 7 December 1954 Fort Eustis dedicated the Army's first airport for helicopters. This honored WO Alfred C. Felker, a graduate from the first Transportation Helicopter Pilot Course in November 1952, killed in a accident on 10 February 1953.

Advent of turbine engines—increased capability, decreased logistics burden

One of the most important changes affecting logistics was the advent of turbine engines in Army aircraft. Their collateral effects made turbines the most important technological change of the whole period after World War II. During the late 1950s the Army acquired three turbine-engine aircraft—two helicopters and the OV-1 Mohawk, which was a high-performance, fixed-wing, reconnaissance aircraft.

The Huey helicopter was the first, longest-serving, and certainly the most recognized. In 1956 the Army first obtained the YH-40. It was redesignated the HU-1 Iroquois ("Huey") in 1958, then redesignated as the UH-1as part of a change in Joint aircraft labeling. The Huey's turbine engine radically reduced the amount of maintenance required. Moreover, the Huey's 700-horsepower engine gave it a greater lift for its weight. Another advantage of the turbine-powered helicopter was its simplicity of operation. Piston-engine helicopters required continuous monitoring of the throttle to adjust engine speed to torque and lift. The turbine engine eliminated this problem by running at a constant speed, regulated by a governor. This change let the pilot concentrate more on tactics and less on mechanics of flying.

The other turbine-powered helicopter was the CH-54 Tarhe or "Flying Crane." The Army began acquisition about 1960 and received the first three in 1963. In reality the Flying Crane derived from the H-37. The two had the same transmission and gearbox. The Crane, however, had the turbine engines the Army wanted but could not get in the H-37. With upgrades the Crane soon gave the 12.5-ton lift that the 1952 Aviation Plan envisioned. Despite their small numbers, the Cranes did vital service in Vietnam, set several world's records, and continued to be used in firefighting and logging long after they left the Army. They retired from the Army as engine upgrades making the CH-47D let the Chinook lift as much weight as the Crane but without the need for a separate aircraft and its logistics support. Thus, improvements within turbine technology further reduced Aviation's logistical burden.

Move to Fort Rucker and rise of 'an Air Fighting Army'

In part Transportation's dominance of Aviation following Korea reflected disinterest within Artillery. This shifting balance led to relocating the Aviation School to its present location at Fort Rucker, Alabama. However, the beginning and consolidation of aviation-related activities at Fort Rucker also reflected something larger. This was the movement beyond aviation strictly as battlefield transportation or fire adjustment to aviation as an integral part of a combined-arms fight. The distinction was the source of tension within the Army and recurrent, heated disputes with the Air Force. The difference was partly obscured by the fact that both the Air Force and Transportation Corps seemed to represent the same thing—moving people and stuff. This similarity was central to the longstanding disputes about duplication between the Army and Air Force. In reality, these disputes largely involved people talking past each other.

Choice of location

An important step came on 16 January 1953, when the Department of Air Training at the Artillery School was abolished to create the Aviation School. This reorganization grew out of expanding aviation training and related problems with facilities. During 1953–1954 the Artillery School complained that aviation training at Fort Sill interfered with artillery training. These complaints forced moving the stagefields further out to get away from the ranges. To solve the problem the Artillery commandant proposed moving aviation training to Frederick, Oklahoma. This relocation would require building entirely new facilities. LTC Robert R. Williams, an Artillery officer then serving as chief of the Aviation Branch at Headquarters, Department of the Army (HQDA), thought this proposal made little sense. Williams argued that, if the school moved, related activities such as testing should go with it. If Aviation training was going to move a long way, it should go where adequate facilities already existed. A search led to Camp Rucker, Alabama. That post had just closed and was near Ozark Army Airfield, a former AAF facility. Local leaders eagerly supported having both the post and the airfield remain in use.

The focus on facilities hid an element in some senior leaders' thinking that permanently reshaped Aviation and the Army. MG James M. Gavin, the Army's G-3/Operations, favored Camp Rucker partly because of its isolation. Gavin saw an opportunity to create a focal point for Aviation. On 28 September 1954 Gavin told BG Carl I. Hutton, standing up school operations at Rucker, to ignore mobilization plans, even if the Department of the Army (DA) officially could not. Gavin wanted to avoid any distraction from developing aviation.

Effects of creating an Aviation Center

The larger change moved rapidly. In January 1955 DA approved a long-range plan for Aviation. This plan established Camp Rucker as the U.S. Army Aviation Center (USAAVNC), equivalent to the other combat arms centers, with collocation of schools and service test boards. As a result of these functions and consolidations, Camp Rucker became a permanent installation, redesignated Fort Rucker, on 13 October 1955. The new center quickly spawned new activities at Fort Rucker. These included TATSA, with a parallel Signal Corps Aviation Test and Support Activity (SATSA) in 1956. In August 1962 the Aviation Board, TATSA, and SATSA merged into the U.S. Aviation Test Board. In 1957 the Aviation Safety Board, which later became the U.S. Army Safety Center (USASC), stood up. On 10 September 1957 the Aviation Center dedicated Lowe Army Airfield as the first major auxiliary flight facility at Fort Rucker. In September 1958 the Aviation Board moved into its new headquarters building on Ozark Army Airfield. That later became Cairns Army Airfield (CAAF) to honor MG Bogardus S. Cairns, killed in a helicopter accident in December 1958.

The centralizing tendency evident with the move to Fort Rucker was incomplete. Training remained partly decentralized, depending mainly on type of training. Transition of flight training from the Air Force to the Army caused changes in locations. Until 1956 the Air Force had insisted on providing primary flight instruction for Army aviators. Purportedly this avoided duplication and saved money. By 1956 contractors conducted all Air Force primary pilot training. The Army argued that it could contract to train Army pilots just as well as the Air Force, and the SECDEF decided that the Army should have responsibility for all phases of training Army aviators. For this training, the Army acquired two bases the Air Force had scheduled to inactivate—Wolters and Gary, both in Texas. Gary was already training Army aviators and mechanics. In August 1956 the fixed-wing maintenance course taught at Gary began moving to Fort Rucker. Meanwhile, on 1 August 1955, the Army activated the first Aviation Unit Training Command at Fort Riley. This unit trained rated pilots to fly twin-rotor

H-21 Shawnee light tactical transport helicopters and the U-1 Otter, a fixed-wing utility plane. A similar unit for single-rotor helicopters activated at Fort Sill. In July 1958 primary fixed-wing flight training moved from Gary to Fort Rucker. Wolters AFB became Fort Wolters and trained beginning Army helicopter pilots. The first class of the U.S. Army Primary Helicopter School (USAPHS) at Fort Wolters graduated on 27 April 1957. During 1972, reflecting the Vietnam surge, Wolters graduated its 40,000[th] Army flight student. The last class at Fort Wolters graduated 15 November 1973. Then all primary helicopter training returned to Fort Rucker.

Legacies of branch interests

A major challenge to centralization at Fort Rucker came from the Transportation Corps and aviation activities already established at Fort Eustis. In early 1956 the Army started receiving H-37 Mojaves. Two were assigned to Fort Rucker for service test. Two went to the Aviation School to develop training courses. When BG Bunker recommended establishing an activity for the 1000-hour tests, MG Paul Yount, Chief of Transportation, fought to establish the unit at Fort Eustis but was overridden by the Vice Chief of Staff of the Army (VCSA), General Williston Palmer. Palmer, consistent with the vision of a centralized Aviation Center, directed basing this unit at Fort Rucker. He also expanded the mission to include providing maintenance support for Board 6 and for the H-37s assigned to the school. During 1958–1959 extensive discussion occurred about moving logistics-related aviation training from Fort Eustis to Fort Rucker, but opposition was strong. So key Aviation logistics functions remained at Fort Eustis. These included both maintenance training and the Aviation Applied Technology Directorate, an important R&D activity.

Movement toward 'an Air Fighting Army'

The idea of conducting helicopter assaults, as the Marines had in Korea, became increasingly powerful in the Army after Korea. In the mid-1950s, spontaneous experiments at the unit level occurred in several places, including both Germany and Korea. Main centers of this kind of activity were Fort Benning and especially Fort Rucker. These experiments ran on the edge of agreements with the Air Force. Even though condoned by some senior Army leaders, these experiments also sometimes caused conflict with senior leadership. However, exploiting the latitude for small projects that the Army gained under the budgeting arrangements that came with a single Defense budget in the late 1940s, advocates of these experiments laid the foundation for air assault as it developed in the early

1960s. While some names were widely recognized as prominent in this development, a number of senior Army officers were actively, if less overtly involved. As with the march toward an independent Air Force, those people less known were sometimes as critical in the outcomes as those identified with the movement.

The motivation and sales campaign—'Cavalry—And I Don't Mean Horses'

A mainspring was apparently the Army's G-3, MG James M. Gavin. As an airborne commander during World War II, Gavin personally felt the defects of parachutes and gliders as ways to deliver troops. In 1954 Gavin ordered series of staff studies to design a hypothetical cavalry organization around the potential of helicopters. COL John J. Tolson, Gavin's chief of doctrine, was in charge. Gavin also published an article in Harper's magazine "Cavalry—And I Don't Mean Horses." Gavin was behind a road show, using tactical problems used at Command and General Staff College (CGSC), to show how a few aircraft could affect outcomes. Somewhat like General Billy Mitchell, Gavin's frustration with constraints on his ideas led him to retire early. Also like Mitchell, Gavin had found and placed people who would carry his ideas forward without him.

Among Gavin's effects was elevating aviation within the Pentagon by giving it a fulltime, general officer advocate. In February 1955 Gavin appointed BG Hamilton H. Howze to head the Aviation Branch in G-3. Previously a lieutenant colonel was in charge of aviation. The Aviation Branch became a directorate under the Army Staff reorganization that combined the G-3 and Deputy Chief of Staff for Military Operations on 3 January 1956. This reorganization gave Howze the official title of Director of Army Aviation.

Others, even more senior, were pushing to integrate aviation into the fabric of the Army's capabilities. In February 1955 General Matthew B. Ridgway, the CSA, testified before Congress on the threat nuclear weapons created to the Army. Destructive effects required the Army to disperse its forces into units small enough to deter use of nuclear weapons. The Army had to be able to concentrate rapidly, destroy the enemy, and disperse again before the enemy could reply with nuclear weapons. This concept rested heavily on the 1CD's success on the Naktong River in 1950. There the commander kept most of the division concentrated in the rear and moved in response to North Korean incursions. The Army proposed to use this model, expanded to cover a battle zone 150–200 miles in depth.

When General Maxwell D. Taylor succeeded Ridgway as CSA on 30 June 1955, Taylor increased emphasis on such flexibility. He also stressed versatility. Taylor believed that nuclear forces created a stalemate in which Communist forces challenged the West through subversive movements. The United States had to abandon the idea that no response existed between doing nothing and all-out nuclear war. Instead, the nation and its allies had to be able to respond to threats at all levels. Appropriate responses ranged from diplomatic and economic actions through covert, 'special operations' to large, conventional campaigns. Taylor coined the term, flexible response, to describe this approach.

To meet all these requirements the Army envisioned a new force structure that greatly increased demands for Aviation. Exploiting the trend toward nuclear glitz, Taylor coined the term, Pentomic Division, to suggest the Army had a role in the nuclear battlefield. A Pentomic Division had five battle groups of five rifle companies each, plus one support company. These groups replaced the three regiments of the triangular division. The amount and range of maneuver envisioned for the Pentomic Division on the nuclear battlefield increased the Army commander's needs for light aircraft with improved range and lift capacity. The Pentomic Division model demanded early detection of enemy fires to let friendly forces respond. Helicopter-borne infantry—'sky cavalry'—would conduct reconnaissance, set up blocking positions, harass the enemy, and provide a quick-reaction force until reserves could assemble to destroy the enemy. These maneuver elements needed organic firepower. Such need led to statements that the Army was working on using light aircraft as tank killers. One instance came from General Paul D. Adams addressing a Congressional subcommittee in 1955. These statements were guaranteed to raise Air Force hackles.

Taylor quickly found himself at odds with political leadership so concerned about controlling the budget that it would not fund the basic needs of a ground Army. An unexpected ally and champion was Secretary of the Army Wilbur M. Brucker. Brucker, a lawyer and former Michigan governor, knew Soldiering from the ground up. He had served as National Guard corporal in the 1916 Punitive Expedition, then as an officer in World War I. Like Taylor, Brucker was frequently at odds with the SECDEF and President Eisenhower, who was personally determined to keep budgets stable.

Exercise Sagebrush—battle over air-transported or air-fighting army

A critical milestone for Aviation's development came in November-December 1955 with a Joint exercise called Sagebrush. Lasting 45 days at Fort Polk,

Louisiana, Sagebrush was the largest field exercise since World War II. It involved 110,000 Army and 30,500 Air Force personnel. Sagebrush focused on the nuclear battlefield.

Sagebrush was the debut for Gavin's aerial cavalry. On 1 June 1955 the 82AB Reconnaissance Troop (Provisional) formed—commonly called the Sky Cav. This force had three basic elements. First was a reconnaissance and surveillance element that could operate day or night by aircraft over an entire front. Second was a small, heavily armed blocking force that could be airlifted quickly to key points, such as mountaintops or crossroads. Third was a combined, artillery and antitank force. This could move quickly to contact while protected by the reconnaissance aircraft to exploit the situation the blocking force created. A fourth, Aviation Platoon, was organized and equipped like a platoon of a helicopter transportation company.

H-34s in air assault exercise at Fort Benning

The Army's plan to use its own aircraft for the Sky Cav provoked a firestorm. GEN O. P. Weyland, who commanded TAC, was the maneuver director for Sagebrush. Based on the 1952 Pace-Finletter agreement, Weyland said that the Army had to use Air Force aircraft for operations beyond enemy lines. Accepting

Weyland's decision would have grounded most of the Army's 700 light airplanes and helicopters. MG Paul D. Adams, commanding XVIII Airborne Corps (XVIII AB), disagreed on interpretation of the 1952 agreement and said the Air Force was not responding to Army needs. Adams particularly faulted the Air Force on CAS. He believed the Air Force preferred using nuclear weapons and armed aircraft accordingly. The conflict quickly escalated. GEN John E. Dahlquist, commanding Continental Army Command (CONARC), challenged the Air Force. He prohibited Army troops from using some Air Force helicopters. The Army and Air Force secretaries became involved. The dispute threatened to involve the SECDEF and possibly even the President. In late November 1955 Air Force Secretary Donald Quarles—purely for the purposes of the test—overruled Weyland. Quarles made it clear to Secretary Brucker that Weyland was correct in his understanding of the agreements. So the issue was clearly left for later resolution.

The critical difference in this dispute was how the Army and Air Force viewed organic Army aircraft. The Army claimed the helicopters were like trucks, which the Army had detailed plans to use in taking patrols and reconnaissance units behind enemy lines. The Army, however, picked up these units outside the battle zone. According to Weyland, this violated the existing understanding that provided for the Air Force to provide such airlift. The key issue was the depth of the battle zone, which the theater commander determined.

Overall, the Army regarded Sagebrush as a huge success. During the exercise, the Sky Cav made at least four leaps behind enemy lines and gathered information otherwise unavailable. Sky Cav aircraft operated from improvised landing fields. The results also pointed toward needed changes in organization. Overall, though, Army observers believed that only the equipment available limited capabilities. Moreover, the nuclear battlefield meant that commanders needed an organization capable of executing all of the basic roles of the Sky Cav.

Sky Cav in Sagebrush clearly had high-level visibility and support. On 1 December 1955 GEN Taylor arrived at Fort Polk and rode cross-country by Jeep about 20 miles to visit the Sky Cav headquarters in a mud-soaked field. He spent more than an hour walking around in heavy rain to inspect the unit and talk to its commander. The next day, Taylor and Weyland had a press conference. Taylor pronounced that the Army badly needed something like the Sky Cav—a unit that could operate behind enemy lines and be immediately responsive to the ground commander. When asked about Sky Cav's acceptability within the Army-Air Force agreements, both Taylor and Weyland just smiled.

Before Sagebrush ended it was clear that both services would push for a favorable interpretation on the whole issue of air transport. More than the exercise was at stake. Sagebrush possibly reflected a schism within Air Force leadership. Acceptance of the Army's position meant a major expansion in organic Aviation, reducing TAC's responsibilities. Weyland was fighting hard within the Air Force to increase TAC's capabilities. In 1954 the Air Force had just received the first of several hundred C-130 Hercules tactical transports. Others within the Air Force were ready to accept expanded Aviation in light of reduced overall budgets.

Hutton, Vanderpool, and experiments at Fort Rucker

Even before Sagebrush, initiatives had begun to develop the Sky Cav idea further. In July 1955 BG Carl I. Hutton, commanding the new USAAVNC, clearly defined the distinction between the concepts guiding the Air Force and advocates of Sky Cav. In his "Commandant's Column" in the U.S. Army Aviation Digest, Hutton posed the question of "An Air Fighting Army?" He noted that emerging aviation technology might be bringing within reach a major revolution in military tactics. It was time "for the Army to consider its aviation needs with a fresh eye."

> Heretofore the Army has tended to consider aircraft as a means of transporting the Soldier to battle. There has been comparatively little development in the area of using aircraft as fighting vehicles. The distinction between the two is fundamental. An airplane as a piece of transportation would logically belong to a transportation corps. An airplane as a fighting vehicle would logically belong to the tactical unit of which it is a part. In one case we would have an air transported army, and in the other case we would have an air fighting army.

Hutton's distinction between an air-transported army and an air fighting army lay at the heart of conflicts within the Army and even among Aviation advocates. Hutton was known as a radical—like Billy Mitchell and Hap Arnold, Hutton was an outspoken advocate who sometimes clashed openly with his superiors. This fact possibly led to Howze, not Hutton, becoming the first Director of Aviation. Like Frank Andrews before 1939, Howze was unassociated with squabbles about Aviation. Like Andrews, Howze could go far before arousing suspicion and opposition.

Following Sagebrush, Hutton drove efforts at Fort Rucker to create whole maneuver formations. On 27 June 1956 he wrote General W. G. Wyman, commanding CONARC, and proposed to experiment with existing types of helicopters, organized into tactical formations, to see if they could fight. Hutton said he saw nothing in regulations that prohibited such experimentation. Wyman approved with two conditions. Hutton was to coordinate his activities with the Infantry School and had to ensure that these activities did not retard the Aviation School's primary mission. On 23 August Hutton submitted his proposal for an Armed Helicopter Mobile Task Force. Three test units formed—company, battalion, and regiment.

Wyman neither authorized nor prohibited arming helicopters, but Hutton gave a mission to arm helicopters to COL Jay D. Vanderpool. Vanderpool was an extraordinary figure—not an aviator because a bad limp from a combat injury prevented him passing a flight physical. COL John J. Tolson, then at the Airborne-Aviation Department at the Infantry School and later CG of USAAVNC, considered Vanderpool the most imaginative person he had ever known. Vanderpool had conducted covert operations in both World War II and in Korea. His experience in Korea created his keen interest in helicopters. He saw how one helicopter with two pilots and a crew chief could give the mobility of a whole combat force, which remained free for other missions. Before 1955 ended Vanderpool became Project Officer and Chief of the Armed Helicopter Demonstration Team at Fort Rucker. He later became Chief of the Combat Development Office

Vanderpool's activities at Fort Rucker resembled his earlier covert operations. While his superior officers clearly condoned Vanderpool's activities, the Air Force officially viewed the arming of Army aircraft as illegal. As he had with Filipino and Korean insurgents, Vanderpool assembled volunteers, fondly called Vanderpool's Fools. During 1956 and 1957 Hutton, Vanderpool, and the volunteers worked on experimental weapons on weekdays and experimented with tactics on the weekends. Hutton was personally involved. Pilots were IPs—mostly civilians. The helicopters came from the school's training fleet. The infantrymen used to test the tactics came from the school troops. Operating unofficially, across service lines and with private industry, Vanderpool brought a wealth of interest, talent, and materiel together. The Navy consistently provided materiel. Friends within the Air Force did the same—even a B-29 gun turret, modified to mount on a H-21 Shawnee. At their own expense, General Electric and Vertol developed weapons packages.

CWO Jack Carter firing .30-caliber, skid-mounted machinegun on H-13

Vanderpool's Fools used H-13 Sioux light observation helicopters as their test vehicle. Stability of the platform was a key consideration. If the H-13 proved suitable for an armed helicopter, heavier utility types would have less difficulty in that role. Similarly the first weapon tested was the standard .50-caliber, air-cooled, aerial machinegun. Success with that heavy a gun would assure feasibility with smaller-caliber ones. Machine guns were mounted on longitudinal strips between the cross tubes of the landing skids. Weapons were bolted to the airframe. Since the guns could not move, the pilot sighted them by moving the aircraft. Vanderpool's Fools also tried Oerlikon 80 mm fixed-fin rockets because no one fully understood what rotor wash might do to rocket flight. Oerlikons had a muzzle velocity of 2300 feet per second. That was so fast that rotor wash would not affect them. The results of the armament experiments were generally better than Vanderpool and his volunteers expected, but they did find limitations. The .50 calibers tended to jam—especially when flown through trees where they picked up pine needles. Armament packages and ammunition added enough weight to the aircraft that the helicopters were always short of lift. This situation persisted until turbine engines appeared. Experiments at Fort Rucker opened windows to greater possibilities. Vanderpool's group showed the feasibility of using the helicopter as a flying weapons platform, placing heavy volumes of fire on targets during tests, rather than as a fighter bomber. This change greatly enhanced mobility.

A key concern was to develop an effective doctrine and force structure. The model used was the Duke of Wellington's from the Napoleonic era. Vanderpool and Hutton thought in terms of cavalrymen that would fight from their mounts and dragoons that would use the mounts to reach the point of battle but fight dismounted, along with their supporting artillery and trains. The Navy also heavily influenced the tactics, because helicopters allowed land forces to mimic the freedom of maneuver naval forces enjoy at sea. In 1957, MG Bogardus S. Cairns succeeded Hutton as commander at Fort Rucker. A former cavalryman, Cairns adapted the last cavalry field manual (FM) for horses, written in 1936, to incorporate the lessons coming out of Fort Rucker. The Fort Rucker crew reworked the 1936 FM, chapter by chapter, into a training text entitled <u>New Tactical Doctrine</u>. Vanderpool later lamented deficiencies in this text, which was rushed into practical application. On 5 March 1957 Fort Rucker created an undesignated Sky Cavalry Platoon (Provisional). This unit had eleven officers, sixteen enlisted, and ten helicopters. To eliminate confusion over differences in types of Sky Cavalry, the platoon was redesignated the Aerial Combat Reconnaissance Platoon, Provisional (Experimental) in November 1957. This unit went through several name changes, became Troop D (Air), 17th Cavalry, at Fort Benning in 1962, and eventually went to Vietnam as the 1st Squadron, 9th Cavalry, in 1965. To get the Armor community interested, Fort Rucker loaned its Sky Cav platoon to Fort Knox. By 1958 the Sky Cav concept also achieved a more formal name and doctrinal recognition. In June 1958 the CGSC pioneered the term 'airmobile operations' in FM 57–35, <u>Army Transport Aviation Combat Operations</u>.

Publicizing Aviation

As with the Army Air Corps in the 1920s and 1930s, publicity events during the same period suggested that the technology existed to provide the range and endurance required for Sky Cavalry operations. One example was the first helicopter to fly nonstop from coast to coast. On 23–24 August 1956 a H-21 Shawnee nicknamed, Amblin' Annie, refueling from fixed-wing escorts, completed a non-stop flight from San Diego, California, to Washington, DC. The flight took 31 hours, 40 minutes and covered 2610 miles. The chief pilot, MAJ Hubert D. Gaddis, had commanded one of the first four Army MEDEVAC units in Korea and became one of Vanderpool's successors as director of combat developments at Fort Rucker.

H-21 Shawnee 'Amblin' Annie' refueling mid-air from a U-1 Otter

The politics of Sky Cav—Maxwell Taylor, threading the needle

Through this period, advocates of Aviation as an armed, maneuver arm became bolder. By 1957 two Sky Cav platoons were active—one at Fort Rucker and one at Fort Benning. On 6 June the Fort Rucker platoon was officially unveiled for an industry symposium sponsored by the Association of the United States Army (AUSA). Present were both General Taylor and General Wyman. This demonstration emphasized only transportation aspects. Only a month later, as part of the change of command between Hutton and Cairns, Cairns decided to show the public the Sky Cav capabilities. As armed helicopters leaped into view, fired a burst, and vanished—Cairns told about five hundred West Point cadets to see themselves as pilots. In July 1958, four hundred industry leaders, along with senior Army and Air Force officers, and Secretary of the Army Brucker witnessed Operation Ammo—a demonstration of H-37s flying in Honest John rockets, much as H-34s had done with 105mm howitzers only a few years before. Cairns interrupted this demonstration to put on a show of armed helicopters' potential. These demonstrations to very important people received commensurate press coverage.

Interservice and even intraservice politics sometimes brought at least token, official condemnation. Sometime in 1956–57, while COL Robert R. Williams—the first Army Master Aviator—was president of the Aviation Board, Taylor visited

Fort Rucker over Air Force complaints. Taylor called Williams to General Hutton's office and told Williams to cease armament experiments. 'You're getting the Army into very deep trouble putting guns on helicopters.' Hutton intervened, telling Taylor that Hutton, not Williams, was doing this. Years later Williams recalled "some long, hard words" between Taylor and Hutton. The program continued.

The threat of another secretary-level agreement was always present. For example, on 26 November 1956, SECDEF Charles E. Wilson issued a policy memorandum to settle disputes arising from the Army's expanding numbers of aircraft. The immediate trigger was GEN Taylor's saying the Army would develop its own capability to move combat units by air within the combat zone. Taylor said the Army was also interested in four other areas that fell outside its defined scope—air superiority, inter-and intra-theater airlift, and aerial firepower. Wilson intervened. He again defined the combat zone as a band 100 miles either side of the contact line with enemy forces. The Army was limited to four aircraft functions—liaison and communications; observation, fire adjustment, and topographic survey; personnel and materiel airlift; and MEDEVAC. Wilson reimposed weight limits of 5000 pounds on fixed-wing aircraft and 20,000 pounds on helicopters, although he reserved the right to allow exceptions. He specifically prohibited the Army from providing aircraft for CAS, interdiction, and strategic airlift. Wilson specifically said the Air Force was providing adequate airlift for the Army. After 1956, as before World War II, the Air Force continued to push toward multi-mission fighters and strategic air operations. Close air support and other functions directly meeting ground commanders' needs languished.

This unstable situation meant that those most closely associated with these efforts had to walk a fine line. In 1957 the Ordnance Weapons Command began assigning a liaison officer at Fort Rucker. Because higher headquarters prohibited developing strictly attack helicopters, weapons development had to use existing equipment. In 1958, though, a contract was let to Townshend Company for a single, flexible machinegun system. Springfield Armory supervised this project. In April 1960 fears of provoking interservice rivalry played some part in rejecting Howze's efforts to insert thoughts about air fighting units into a basic report of the Army Aircraft Requirements Board (Rogers Board), discussed below. Howze later saw the main reason for rejecting his thoughts in the fact that the Board's mandate was limited to aviation materiel. Others said the Board considered more direct advocacy but didn't think they could 'get away with it.' Howze was allowed to add a short enclosure, "The Requirement for Air Fighting Units."

MG Herbert Powell and MAJ William Howell at Fort Benning

Fort Benning—strong command support blending air-transported with air-fighting

Another key center was Fort Benning. Developments with the Transportation Helicopter unit to support Infantry School illustrate how, within the Army, the lines between ideas about and uses of Army aircraft often blurred. It also showed how Soldiers with combat-arms backgrounds flowed across branch lines in Aviation, bringing a different perspective to problems—sometimes bringing a different result. Finally it showed how people flowed through different assignments and had unforeseeable influence.

When MAJ William A. Howell, a Transportation Corps aviator, was assigned to command the helicopter unit at Benning, his welcome was mixed. His arrival included a stern warning that he had a brief time to straighten the unit out, or the chief of staff was going to evict it from Fort Benning. In the eyes of Infantry commanders, the unit was a disgrace. It could not provide support. Aircraft were routinely down. Soldiers and officers assigned seemed to have no sense of direction. Howell's predecessor had been fired.

Howell, a World War II Infantry officer who had earned the Silver Star in the Cassino Campaign, set out to fix the problem. He quickly found two basic causes. One was a shortage of trained aviation mechanics. The other was an utter lack of esprit among the WOs who made up most of the unit. Howell found the solution to the first problem in a noncommissioned officer (NCO), Sergeant Henry Q. Dunn. Dunn said he could fix the shortfall in mechanics if Howell would let him. While there was a shortage of aviation mechanics, Fort Benning had too many motor mechanics. If Howell would let him, Dunn would recruit motor mechanics to train as aviation mechanics. Dunn would personally train them. Dunn would also promise them that, if they performed satisfactorily, he would insure they got converted into Aviation. Howell gave Dunn permission. Dunn promptly recruited and trained enough mechanics to overcome the maintenance deficiencies and meet the Infantry School's demands. Fixing the problem with the WOs was almost as easy. Howell discovered they had no understanding of their role as officers. Howell simply told them that they were officers and he expected them to act like officers.

Fixing the problems with the helicopter unit opened new avenues at Fort Benning. Most critical was to the installation commander, MG Herbert A. Powell. Powell was interested in aviation and its potential applications. As Powell's personal pilot, Howell had frequent opportunities to talk with Powell. Following a visit to Fort Rucker, Powell told Howell that he wanted Howell to teach him to fly. Howell asked why, since the general could have all the pilots he wanted to do the flying for him. Powell said he saw little future for a general officer that did not know much about aviation. Howell said he could not act as an instructor pilot without special authorization, so Powell had Howell fly him to Washington. When Powell returned to the aircraft, he had a letter authorizing Howell to teach the general to fly.

Under Powell's auspices, Howell and others at Fort Benning conducted experiments that paralleled those at Fort Rucker. In 1957 these experiments brought down the Air Force's wrath. Howell sent one H-34 to the Sikorsky plant in Connecticut for arming. Contrary to orders to return straight to Fort Benning, the pilots stopped in Washington. A reporter shot a photo that ran on the front page of the Army Times as "The World's Most Heavily Armed Helicopter." Before the crew reached Fort Benning, the CSA had heard from the Air Force chief of staff and had told MG Powell he wanted to hear nothing more about "The World's Most Heavily Armed Helicopter."

Recognizing enlisted contributions—crew chiefs, flight engineers, and the Aircraft Crewmember Badge

A sidelight of Howell's efforts to overcome maintenance problems at Fort Benning reflected the struggle to recognize enlisted Soldiers' importance in Aviation. It was much easier for officers inside Aviation to recognize the vital role than for those outside.

To assure that helicopters would achieve maximum availability, Howell wanted aircraft mechanics to fly with the aircraft. That way, if it broke down in the field, the mechanic could immediately repair it. Following a tradition that went back at least to the AAF in World War II, he called these mechanics crew chiefs. To have each crew chief invest as much pride in his aircraft as possible, Howell had each crew chief put his name on the side of his helicopter. However, he was ordered to have the names removed.

The importance of having more highly-skilled, enlisted Soldiers as a regular part of aircrews forced organizational recognition in these years. No crew chief position was authorized for Transportation companies using the H-34, organized under TOE 55–57C. That TOE was dated 12 March 1956. By the time TOE 55–57D superseded that TOE on 14 December 1959, the crew chief position appeared, listed as MOS 67310.

The advent of newer, more complex helicopters—particularly H-37 Mojaves and Chinooks with ramps, and CH-54 Cranes with heavy-lift hookups and pods—increased the range and complexity of tasks for enlisted crew members. This situation led to the designation as flight engineers.

It took several more years for the Army to give some visible recognition to enlisted aircrew members. The AAF had established an Aircrew Member wing in September 1942. This badge was awarded to several types of people, including radio operators, gunners, and photographers. The Army carried over some AAF badges. Among these was the Mechanic's Badge with Propeller. A separate bar, attached beneath the badge, identified specific qualifications, such as technical inspector (TI). This badge was issued at least during the mid-to late-1950s. However, its official status seems cloudy. In June 1962 Army Aviation announced that an Aviation Mechanic Badge would be authorized. It described this as the basic mechanic and driver's badge with "a propeller shaped bar" for attachment. A bar identifying qualification as Crew Chief and Mechanic would be suspended from the propeller bar. The article said that DA would soon announce criteria for eligibility. However, on 16 May 1962 the Army authorized the enlisted Aircraft Crewman Badge, with wings like the pilot's badge but with the coat of arms of the United States in the center of the shield. An article in <u>U.S. Army Aviation Digest</u> in May 1966 said that this badge would replace "the mechanic 'ladder' badge," awarded to crew chiefs and mechanics. At that time, eligibility was made retroactive to 1947—the year the Air Force separated. Senior and master levels paralleled those recognized for pilots. Eventually eligibility to wear this type of badge was extended to include nonflying Soldiers, including Aviation operations specialists and air traffic controllers.

Mechanic's Badge with Propeller

Aircraft Crewman Badge 1962

Non-combat Aviation—transportation and the Executive Flight Detachment (EFD)

During this era the Army's role in non-combat transportation expanded to include flying the President. On 1 December 1957 the Army first organized the EFD. Initial authorization was 17 officers and WOs, 28 enlisted Soldiers, and five civilians. The EFD, based at Fort Belvoir, shared duties with a Marine element based at Quantico. A common duty station was established at Anacostia Naval Air Station inside Washington.

Tough beginnings—MAJ William A. Howell and near-last, first flight

The beginning of the EFD was highly informal. MAJ William A. Howell was ordered to Washington and taken to the White House. The military secretary to the President asked him if he could land a helicopter on the South Lawn. Howell looked at it and said he could. Howell was then told he would become the President's pilot and should get support from Davison Army Airfield.

As with his beginning at Fort Benning, Howell's start with the EFD was rough. The commander of Davison resented having to support Howell and did as little as he could. Howell's first flight with President Eisenhower was to Baltimore with British Prime Minister Harold Macmillan onboard. The helicopter had not been properly maintained. Howell had a bad time getting it out of the landing area on the return trip. Upon returning to the White House, Howell told the military secretary he would not fly the President again. The military secretary demanded to know why. Upon hearing Howell's explanation about the flight, the military secretary told Howell that he could pick anyone he wanted to have assigned and was to make any requests on White House stationery. The Davison commander continued to be difficult but could no longer obstruct the EFD's performing its mission.

Building on earlier successes and people

The EFD built on Howell's early efforts at Fort Benning. To insure good maintenance, he called Sergeant Dunn to get him some good mechanics. Dunn said he would get the best—beginning with the best helicopter mechanic in the Army, himself. Dunn became one of the first Sergeants Major (SGM) in the Army when that grade was authorized, personally promoted by President Eisenhower.

Among the Presidential pilots, one was Chief Warrant Officer (CWO) William L. Ruf. A career Infantryman assigned as a weapons instructor at the Infantry School, Ruf desperately wanted to fly. He rode along anytime he could get someone to let him on a helicopter. One day, when Howell was going out to fly, Ruf asked to come along. Howell assumed, because Ruf was a WO, that he was also a pilot. After they got airborne, Howell handed the controls over to Ruf. Immediately Howell realized something was wrong. Shocked to learn his copilot had never flown an aircraft, Howell told Ruf that he better go to flight school and got Ruf assigned. In 1958, while flying off the coast of Lebanon, Ruf was summoned to join the EFD.

President Kennedy and SGM Henry Q. Dunn

Premium on ingenuity, adaptability

Supporting the President called for ingenuity. Members of the EFD often found ways to do things better but cheaply. Howell decided the President's helicopter should have air conditioning. When he asked Sikorsky how much it would cost to add that, the price was high. Howell decided an automobile air conditioner, costing only a couple hundred dollars, could probably do the job. That solution worked quite well. Some refinements were even simpler and cheaper. Milton S. Eisenhower, the President's older brother, had a bad back. The airline seats in the President's helicopter were soft and made him uncomfortable. The EFD solved the problem by cutting plywood to cover the seat. For aesthetics, the board was covered with kitchen-chair vinyl.

Safety, always a major concern to Howell, led to innovations. To allow emergency landing in metropolitan areas, Howell devised flotation devices. Every large city had some body of water—a reservoir or park with a lake—where a helicopter could land if it could float.

The EFD gave Aviation a number of firsts. Howell and Ruf flew Eisenhower on a goodwill trip around the world. As part of that trip, they made the first helicopter landing in Saint Peter's Square in Rome. Ruf also made the first landing on a presidential rose garden while reconnoitering a spot to land Eisenhower at Francisco Franco's presidential palace in Spain. Mrs. Franco was not pleased.

Demise of the EFD—lack of Army support?

Over almost 20 years, the EFD went through several changes. In 1976, with no more ceremony than it began, the EFD ended. Following a flight, President Gerald Ford simply asked LTC Robert G. Shain, the commander, to thank the members for their long and faithful service. Shain wrote a memorandum on White House stationery. That was it.

Reasons for disestablishment were unclear and undocumented. One possible factor was Army leadership's lack of interest. Once, during a chance meeting, a major general berated CWO George Baker, one of the EFD pilots, about the terrible waste of Army pilots in providing this service. The Marine Corps, which had shared the mission with the Army, was quite willing to take up the slack.

Providing Aviation Manpower—getting, developing, keeping talented people

In the postwar period, a major problem for Aviation was acquiring and retaining qualified personnel. The Army tried at least three approaches from 1945 to 1965. After Korea accession of WOs expanded and became a mainstay. These same years saw the start of successful accession and retention of commissioned officers. In some part, this was an achievement of BG Hamilton H. Howze as director of Aviation. The problem Howze faced tells much about the status of Aviation during this era. Howze's solution paved the way for Aviation's spectacular success in and beyond Vietnam.

Basic approaches, successes and limitations

From the end of World War II to the Korean War, a major source of Army pilots was Air Force and Navy veterans. The small number of organic Aviation pilots during World War II almost vanished in the postwar drawdown. In 1947 MAJ O. Glenn Goodhand returned to active duty in the National Guard Bureau. During 1948–1949, Goodhand ran a program that re-rated Navy and Air Force pilots as Army pilots for Army National Guard vacancies. While vital to success in Korea, this program had major shortcomings, as mentioned above.

Accession through the WO program arose from the Transportation Corps, which faced a dilemma as it sought to expand aviation. The number of pilots required exceeded the number of Transportation officers. An alternative of making NCOs into pilots had proven unsatisfactory during World War II. Artillery had started with that idea but abandoned it because of losses into commissioned ranks or through direct field commissions. Transportation was comfortable with WOs because of the Corps' experience with them in watercraft. For the purpose at hand, WOs seemed ideal. Like NCOs, WO careers focused on technical aspects of a specialty. At the same time, higher pay and privileges of WOs offered some incentive to remain. On 5 December 1951 the Army's first WO flight training class, which began its training at Fort Sill, graduated. These WOs became the nucleus for the 1st Army Helicopter Company.

The third approach was to make pilots from commissioned Army officers. In some respects, until the mid-1950s, this was the least successful. A major obstacle was the perception of aviators among career professionals. Most disdained Army aviators for what seemed to be and sometimes was a lack of ambition. Many early Army pilots simply wanted to fly. They gave little attention to those matters expected of commissioned officers. The disdain also came in part from the low status of Air Force liaison pilots. During World War II the AAF had relegated to liaison and glider duty those pilots who seemed unsuitable for bomber or fighter assignments. Career professionals also tended to view pilots, of whom many were Reserve officers, as uncommitted or unreliable. As a result, assignment officers often refused to give aviators access to advanced schooling required for promotion. In some cases, improved prospects for officer aviators within Transportation attracted able people from other branches. For example, CPT Orval H. Sheppard, who became an Army aviator after serving as an airborne artillery officer in World War II, transferred to Transportation after the assignments officer for Artillery said he would not waste an advanced course seat on someone who was both an aviator and a Reserve officer. Sheppard rose to the rank of colonel and commanded the Aviation Test Activity at Fort Rucker before his retirement.

The prevailing attitude toward aviators often led to explicit and direct discouragement of promising officers. About the end of 1951, 2LT James H. Merryman told his company commander that he had applied for flight school. The disgusted commander told Merryman that he was throwing his career away. Merryman retired as a lieutenant general and Army aviator.

The overall effect was that Aviation was barely viable. In May 1955 a study showed fewer than 2500 Army aviators. Most were low ranking. Only 4 percent held a rank above major.

Broadening assignments for WO pilots to fixed-wing

Army policies also limited the value gained from the WO pilots. Until about 1956 they could not fly fixed-wing aircraft. This situation, which reflected a personnel management policy, had at least two adverse effects. Getting the policy changed reflected the way the Director of Aviation worked under Howze.

LTC George W. Putnam, Jr., visited several installations to assess the state of Aviation for Howze. At Fort Riley Putnam found two U-1 Otter companies. Personnel people had established a policy that no one could be assigned to an Otter company without an instrument ticket and 1500 hours of fixed-wing flying time. These restrictions limited candidates for the Otter units to experienced captains. That made these officers unavailable for other aviation assignments. At the same time, Putnam found the Fourth Aviation Section in disrepair. Putnam told Howze that, with a lot of newcomers to aviation in the divisions, these sections needed the supervisory skills tied up in two Otter companies. Putnam noted that the Air Force assigned pilots to similar flying right out of school and said that WOs should be flying the Otters. Putnam called the CONARC aviation officer, who had gone through flight school with Putnam, and asked him to develop a draft table of organization and equipment (TOE) for an Otter company within a couple of weeks. This TOE should put WOs in the flying positions and officers where commissioned officers were needed. The CONARC aviation officer told Putnam that CONARC had quite a few former Marine fixed-wing pilots who had come into the Army as WOs. Putnam told Howze and asked to assign these WOs into fixed-wing jobs immediately. Howze asked if doing that created any problem. Putnam told him it did because of the Army policy that did not authorize WOs to fly fixed-wing airplanes. Very quickly, Howze directed a change in policy without the usual staffing. The supply of rated or ratable fixed-wing warrants was large enough that the Army did not need to run a qualification course until July 1959.

Dynamics of personnel and attitudes—Howze, making senior officer aviators

The disparaging attitude toward officer aviators and its adverse effects obstructed senior leaders who wanted to promote Aviation. A beginning to break those barriers came in 1954. MG James M. Gavin, the Army's G-3, convinced the CSA to let graduates of West Point go directly into aviation, rather than serving a ground tours before flight school. To make this happen, Gavin had to bypass other seniors in the Army Staff by slipping a paper on the subject to the CSA.

Later Howze substantially changed the relationship between Army careers and Aviation by arranging for highly-selected officers to become rated aviators. After himself becoming a rated Army aviator and only the third general officer at the time to wear Aviation wings, Howze set up two select classes with twelve in each class. Some earlier effort with flight training occurred at Fort Sill in 1953, but Howze allowed only officers already identified as probable general officers into these classes. Those chosen included later-Lieutenant Generals (LTG) George P. Seneff, John J. Tolson, and John (Jack) Norton, along with MG Ernest F. Easterbrook and George W. Putnam, Jr. In some cases, the officer was not even consulted. Putnam's first hint about flight school was an official invitation from MG Christopher Fry, head of the Career Management Division. When Putnam consulted his supervisor, the supervisor discouraged Putnam from applying. The next day the supervisor called Putnam and said to apply.

These classes reshaped the future of Aviation. Suddenly Aviation, which previously had almost no notable colonels, had two dozen outstanding ones. After the second class, the Army stopped these special classes but added a few senior officers to each flight class. Individual instruction was also given some general officers, like MG Powell at Fort Benning. This trend possibly underlay Powell's comment that he foresaw little future for a general officer that knew nothing about aviation. By 1959 the Army had eleven general officers that were rated Army Aviators.

Even with these front-running officers entering Aviation, old attitudes died hard. As late as 1970 seniors continued to dissuade promising officers from applying for Aviation by telling them that it held no future. That was true even when almost all of the Army's deputy chiefs of staff and many commanders of the Army's major commands wore wings. To continue an infusion of high-quality, senior-grade officers into Aviation, the Army reverted to special, selected senior-officer flight training at the end of the Vietnam period. Among the 25 selected colonels who then went through flight training was later-GEN John W. Vessey, the first Army Aviator who served as the CJCS.

Howze's changes struck veteran Army pilots as a mixed blessing. Veterans called the new, senior-officer aviators 'slick wings.' The newcomers, chosen for their rank and promise, further threatened prospects for earlier Army aviators, for whom promotion had already been slow.

Branch question—conflicting visions among Army aviators, failure of integrated approach

Even in the mid-1950s issues of pilot accession and management caused conflicts among Aviation advocates. Differences in approach led to an ugly clash over centralized personnel management in late 1954. Before the Korean War years, the idea floated of creating a centralized career program for aviators. G-1 would manage all pilots, regardless of their branch affiliation. This arrangement would allow more efficient assignment and use of pilots. The Army's G-1 and G-3 agreed, but the idea was buried in wartime workload. Some aviators and aviation advocates disliked the idea. They feared such central management would lead to a system like the Navy's, where only aviators had access to aircraft. This would recreate a miniature Air Force within the Army. In 1954 the idea revived.

A comprehensive review of Aviation that CSA Ridgway ordered on 4 September 1954 included personnel management. As part of the 1955 Aviation Plan, G-1 and G-3 agreed to establish centralized career management. With the decision already made, BG Carl Hutton wrote letters to Transportation and Artillery opposing this action. Hutton's logic was important in reflecting his broader vision for Aviation. He thought that all officers should have to become qualified aviators; so, each branch should manage its own aviators as they did all others in their branch. Transportation had the largest number of aviators, feared losing control of them, and particularly backed Hutton. MG Paul D. Adams, the deputy G-3, angrily summoned all the interested parties to sit down behind closed doors and produce a consensus. Adams was especially harsh with Hutton for embarrassing both the G-1 and G-3. Hutton still prevailed. Ridgway approved an Aviation Officer Career Program (AOCP) but in a weakened version. Thus, the question of a separate Aviation Branch, although short of that established in 1983, was an issue almost thirty years earlier.

By the time Hutton left Fort Rucker, evidence was accumulating that the approach he advocated was failing. In late 1957 Secretary of the Army Brucker announced that he supported creating separate Sky Cav units because other units were failing to use Aviation adequately. A key was the kind and amount of planning such operations demanded. Hutton addressed this problem in an article in 1958. Units had too few transport helicopters to train adequately. A prevailing trend to centralize control for economy and ease of maintenance reduced tactical availability to supported commanders. It was hard to scrounge enough lift for a division-level exercise. The aircraft shortage fostered an emphasis on safety that discouraged tactical flying.

Army Aircraft Requirements Board [Rogers Board]— standing on the threshold

From January into March 1960 LTG Gordon R. Rogers, deputy commander of CONARC, conducted the Army Aircraft Requirements Board. The Rogers Board marked important advances for Aviation, although long over shadowed by the Army Tactical Mobility Requirements Board (Howze Board) in 1962.

Rogers Board achievements—gaining attention of civilian industry and promoting airmobility

The Rogers Board made at least one major, long-term contribution. In considering the Army Aircraft Development Plan, the board reviewed proposals from the aircraft industry. Forty-five companies submitted 119 proposals to meet Army needs. For the first time, major companies really took note of a potential for

Aviation. Such support underlay the Air Force's strong political support because of the high-cost, high-glamour items it sought.

The board made key recommendations on observation, surveillance, and transport aircraft. Its recommendations moved the Army toward a simpler, modernized aircraft fleet that would reduce Aviation's logistical burden.

The Rogers Board was also important for what it failed to achieve. Most importantly, it set down the goal to replace all Army aircraft every ten years—sooner, if operational conditions or technical opportunities dictated. This approach—sound in principle—proved unduly optimistic against budgetary realities. For example, the CH-47 Chinook, which was to be replaced in the 1970s, not only survived that decade but eventually acquired a lifespan projected well into the 21st century.

Finally, the Rogers Board recommended a major study—including a unit to test feasibility—on developing air-fighting units. The Rogers Board has often been dismissed for slighting the idea of airmobility. In its recommendation the board clearly cast a vote in favor of creating something like the 11th Air Assault Division (Test) that followed the Howze Board. This recommendation was one more piece of evidence that the concept of airmobility did not spring to life with Robert McNamara and the Howze Board but had bumped along with the support of senior Army leaders for years.

The Board also showed the continuing influence of a few people behind the scenes. What LTG John Tolson called the "guiding genius" behind forming the Rogers Board was COL Robert R. Williams.

Legacies of competing technologies and interservice conflicts—Caribous and Mohawks

The Rogers Board wrestled questions about fixed-wing versus rotary-wing Aviation. The differences in these technologies, along with their presumed capabilities and uses, connected to differing visions and competing interests of the Army and Air Force. Retaining substantial fixed-wing capabilities required exceptions to Army-Air Force agreements. In 1956 the Army and Air Force secretaries concluded agreements that provided exceptions for the Army to have the CV-2 Caribou as a transport and the OV-1 Mohawk for reconnaissance. These aircraft remained sources of contention for years.

Through the 1950s fixed-wing aircraft remained central to the original role of organic Aviation—artillery observation. The L-19A Bird Dog, which first entered Army service at the beginning of the Korean War, performed many roles, as had its predecessors. In the early-1950s L-19s in Europe provided surveillance of the borders between friendly and Communist states. Fixed-wing observation aircraft had huge secondary value in artillery units through this era. Ground radios at the time were severely limited in range, especially in some types of terrain. The pilot of an observation aircraft was high enough to act as a radio relay between ground elements that could not communicate. Artillery pilots learned how to keep their aircraft in the air much longer than they were supposed to; because, when the airplane was not flying, the unit was almost blind.

Fixed-wing aircraft remained vital for other reasons. Through the 1950s the helicopter industry simply could not produce all the aircraft and spares the services wanted. Moreover, a study done in 1953 showed that, beyond forty miles, fixed-wing aircraft were more efficient and far less costly than helicopters. In 1956 an Air Force C-119 fixed-wing aircraft cost about $375,000 and could haul 28,000 pounds. An Army H-37 cost over $1 million and could haul far less. The H-37 also had to replace its main gearbox every 150 hours of flight. That gearbox cost $37,000.

The Army adopted a hybrid approach, pushing to acquire better helicopters while substituting some fixed-wing planes to fill gaps. In 1956, for example, the Army revised its Aviation Plan and substituted the U-1 Otter for helicopters in the 1.5-ton class. The Army received its first Caribous in 1959, as discussed in more detail in Chapter 4 on Vietnam.

The Army pursued common purchases with the Navy and Marines, substituting fixed-wing for helicopters, accelerating service tests, and pursuing R&D into the next generation of helicopters. Turbine engines were critical to breaking the helicopter bottleneck, but each turbine engine cost $30,000 to $40,000. This cost obstructed quick application. The Army worsened its situation by overbuying spares as a hedge against unforeseen requirements. Meantime the industry strove to improve reliability and rapidly introduced better parts, leaving the Army with an inventory that ran about one-third obsolete.

Arming Mohawk on the ramp in Vietnam

The OV-1 Mohawk was an example of the problems that came with having to rely on either the Air Force or Navy/Marine for its acquisitions. The Mohawk started as a joint acquisition with the Marines, who wanted a replacement for a light observation aircraft. The Marines needed no sophisticated sensors but did require the Mohawk to be compatible with shipboard operations. The Air Force objected to the Army getting the Mohawk from the beginning, because the Marines also required hard points to carry weapons. Some Army aviators saw the Mohawk as a way to, in fact, break barriers the Air Force imposed. These advocates pressed for more capabilities. While the Army was supposedly acquiring the Mohawk to replace the L-19 Bird Dog, the Mohawk also brought advanced capabilities, including an internal camera. Unfortunately, besides inviting conflict with the Air Force, these additions, such as sophisticated side-looking radar, increased the Mohawk's weight beyond what its engines were designed to handle. Grumman, the manufacturer, fueled the Army's conflict with the Air Force by advertising with drawings that showed the Mohawk in various attack configurations.

UH-1 Hueys in air assault exercise at Fort Benning

Chapter 4: Vietnam—the Army Transformed

'No plan survives first contact...'

Vietnam was not the war that was supposed to happen. Through the late 1950s and even into the early 1960s, the Army's focus—and Aviation's as part of that— was on a possible war of big battles in Europe. Incidental to that focus, the Army pushed toward combinations of organization, materiel, training, and doctrine that would maximize the value of its components. Aviation was a key area that many people saw as offering a great, untapped potential. So there were special efforts, building on what had already been evolving through the 1950s, to realize those potentials. Of specific, special importance were extensions of the Sky Cav idea—which, by the beginning of the 1960s, had acquired the doctrinal label of airmobility. With the establishment of the Howze Board in 1962, this thrust gained momentum. By mid-1965, it had achieved reality in the standup of the 1CD(Airmobile), with immediate commitment to battle in Vietnam.

An important part of Aviation history during the Vietnam years was working with allied forces. Most important were the South Vietnamese, to whom the burden was to shift for maintaining their own defense as the U.S. withdrew in the early 1970s. As LTG John J. Tolson noted in his 1971 study on Airmobility, a focus on Vietnamization after 1968 obscured years of previous cooperation, training, and planning. Especially in the Delta area, Vietnamese control of operations was the prevailing mode. Pursuant to the Nixon Administration's policy of Vietnamization, the Army intensified training of the South Vietnamese. This included pilot and crew instruction, joint airmobile operations, and logistics. Often collocated U. S. and Army of the Republic of Vietnam (ARVN) units worked together in these efforts. These training functions did not occur apart from ongoing combat operations. Rather, training was often integrated with actual combat.

By the end of Army Aviation 's decade-long engagement in Vietnam, the nature of the operational environment, the Army, and Aviation itself had radically changed. Numbers of Army aircraft grew from about 6000 in 1962 to over 12,000 in 1970, the peak year. The number of Army pilots and air crewmen grew proportionately. From 1962 to 1973, Fort Wolters, Texas, graduated over 40,000 Army pilots, creating the largest generation of Army aviators that ever would be, excluding the AAF in World War II. Even more important, types of aircraft shifted. Aviation entered Vietnam more than half fixed-wing. By 1970 Aviation was 80 percent helicopters.

Aviation force structure also changed. The huge increase in numbers of aircraft and demands for them led to regularly-constituted battalions, groups, and even an Aviation brigade. Units, though, did not correspond to those of similar name in the other combat arms. An Aviation company was about the size of an Infantry or Armor battalion but had a major as a commander. A lieutenant colonel commanded a comparably larger battalion. A colonel commanded an Aviation group, composed of several battalions. The 1st Aviation Brigade (1AB)—the only Aviation brigade—had more people than a combat division.

Demands on using Aviation more effectively also led to at least one major restructuring in the midst of fighting. The 101st Airborne Division (101AB) converted from airborne—parachute—to airmobile configuration. How this occurred and the success was a tribute to the imagination of people in Aviation.

The Vietnam experience and its political outcome cast a shadow over the national psyche for almost 20 years. Often lost in the brooding was recognition of Aviation Soldiers' steadfast adherence to the old Army values of "Duty, Honor, Country." Even as much of the nation and even many service members rejected the declared purpose for being in Vietnam and lost hope for the outcome— Aviation Soldiers served honorably and to the best of their ability. Especially in the last stages of the war, loyalty to comrades led to heroism that sometimes ended tragically. Out of Vietnam came a generation of leaders determined to get a return on the investments in pain and blood. These people became the backbone of a new Army and of an Aviation force that would shock the world with its capability in 1991.

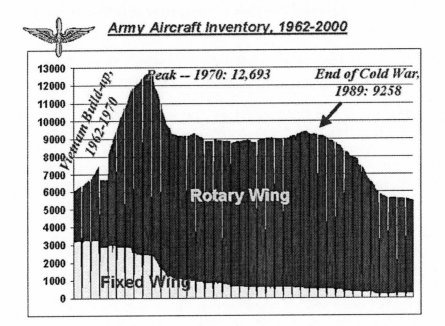

Army Aircraft Inventory, 1962-2000

The Howze Board, 1962

In hindsight it is hard not to think that the Army was focused on Vietnam in the early 1960s. The reality was far different. From the late 1940s onward, national defense focused on the threat of a major war in Europe. Emerging from emphasis on restrained federal budgets in the 1950s, the early 1960s were still bent on gaining 'the most bang for the buck.' While the credibility of nuclear deterrence had eroded, the nation was still unready to throw the DOD a blank check. In fact, the mismatch between heavy combat capabilities and perceived needs in Vietnam, along with fiscal tightness, underlay the Army's resistance to the U.S. becoming involved in Vietnam during the Eisenhower Administration.

In this context, in 1962, Aviation got a huge boost with a special study that SECDEF Robert S. McNamara ordered. Technically the U.S. Army Tactical Mobility Requirements Board, almost everyone knew this as the Howze Board, for its president, LTG Hamilton H. Howze. The study produced the mandate for the Army to develop the Sky Cav idea into a major part of the Army's way of doing business—first called Airmobility and eventually Air Assault.

Precursors—Howze's Pentagon briefings and the Rogers Board addendum

Although most commonly associated with Vietnam, the Howze Board and its results arose from concern for the big fight expected in Europe.

In early 1957 Howze as Director of Army Aviation and COL Claude Sheppard developed and presented a briefing to try to convince senior military and civilian leadership to embrace the kind of ideas and forces that BG Carl I. Hutton and others called Sky Cavalry. The briefing used the standard plan for the defense of Europe. A single, reinforced U.S. armored division would fight a withdrawal across southern Germany against three, reinforced Soviet armored divisions. Howze and Sheppard then showed the same problem using a single, heavily-reinforced, air cavalry brigade instead of the armored division.

The key to the air cavalry-enhanced division's effectiveness was its lack of dependence on ground movement. Needing no roads or bridges, tactics could shift to destroying all bridges and big culverts between friendly artillery and the onrushing Soviet forces. Because friendly forces needed no ground route to escape during disengagement, the pace of operations was much faster. Under these conditions, Soviet forces would have a hard time simply moving because of ground obstacles. Soviet forces became rich targets for airpower and artillery as they concentrated while removing obstacles. Without fratricide risks, friendly air forces could attack more violently. Artillery was more effective because scout helicopters could observe the enemy and plant forward observers on places inaccessible to ground forces. Thus, much of the air cavalry brigade's strength came from ability to bring to bear the combined effects of CAS, artillery, and engineers. Howze and Sheppard included effects of antitank helicopters, although none existed. Finally they showed heliborne riflemen, formed into tank-killer teams, ambushing enemy columns. Based on the assumptions, a much smaller air cavalry force taking fewer casualties did far more harm to the enemy than a much larger ground division.

Howze carried these ideas forward as a member of the 1960 Rogers Board. His ideas became an addendum—"The Requirement for Air Fighting Units." He argued that big gains would come from creating air cavalry units. Howze compared the current situation to that the Army had faced when horses offered the greatest potential mobility. Advances in technology would increase the advantages of air cavalry units by giving air cavalry tremendous firepower and by forcing troops to disperse, creating even better targets for air cavalry. Only last did

Howze argue that such units would work well in brushfire warfare against relatively unsophisticated opponents—the type of warfare then present in Vietnam.

McNamara's directives—Army aviators writing orders to the Army

On 19 April 1962, with no apparent warning, McNamara wrote Secretary of the Army Elvis J. Stahr two memoranda on Army aviation. The first told the Army to take a 'bold new look' at mobility. In what many within the Army considered a slap in the face, McNamara specifically told Stahr to conduct this review 'in an atmosphere divorced from traditional viewpoints and past policies.' Recommendations were to be 'protected from veto or dilution by conservative staff review.' The other memo identified six specific areas for study. McNamara ordered the Army to 'give unorthodox ideas a hearing.'

In reality events within the Army had been moving toward this climax for some time. For some time, COL Robert R. Williams had been fomenting things behind the scenes within the Pentagon. From February 1961 to February 1962, Williams was a staff officer in the Office of the Secretary of Defense (OSD). One of McNamara's key helpers, Alain Enthoven, had told Williams that Enthoven and others saw great potential in Army aviation but seemed unable to budge the Army Staff. He asked Williams for help. Williams and BG Edwin (Spec) Powell, Director of Army Aviation, sent up several draft memorandums. After Williams left the Pentagon to command USAAVNC, McNamara issued the memoranda. These named Howze and eight others, including Williams, to do the work.

Standing up the Howze Board

Once directed, events moved quickly. On 28 April HQDA sent GEN Herbert O. Powell at CONARC an implementing directive. By then, Powell had alerted Howze, along with COL John (Jack) Norton, whom Powell appointed as secretary to the board. Powell directed Howze and Norton to submit a draft plan, including units, some individual pilots, and aircraft needed. Powell set an extremely short timeline. Howze was to submit the final report to CONARC by 20 August to meet McNamara's deadline of 1 September. GEN Powell—who had earned his wings as an Army Aviator while commanding Fort Benning—went far beyond dutiful support. If the board needed anything, they were to come directly to him. If someone blocked the front door, they were to come in the back.

The timeline for the whole project led to a mad scramble. Howze asked how big the final report should be. DA said that one copy should fit into a standard Army footlocker. That guidance, along with a requirement for 300 copies, set the time for everything else. Printers needed final copy by 1 August to meet the 20 August timeline. That meant main work had to be done during June and July.

Organizing the board reflected the intense, often personal way work proceeded. Later-MG George Beatty, one of Howze's core group of colonels, recalled his first duties. Howze took the four colonels into his office and said, 'Now write a plan…My secretary will take care of you with coffee and sandwiches or whatever you need…You just sit here until you get it done.' Thereafter the board's facilities were a just-completed elementary school at Fort Bragg.

The board quickly evolved a functional hierarchy, with a steering committee that oversaw and integrated work in four functional areas—doctrine and requirements, war games/operations research, field tests, and programs, policy and budget. A separate committee designated as a group, handled major subjects under these functional areas. Excepting operations research, headed by a senior civilian, a general officer headed each group. Each group wrote a separate annex. The short timeline meant that the steering committee really only glanced at contents.

To get the whole Army to buy into the results, the board expanded to about a hundred people so that every Army agency affected had a representative. The size of the questions and the number of interests involved automatically posed problems that allowed only partial solutions. The large number of committees, each filled with capable people, created too many ideas, too many points of view, and meetings that lasted too long. Eventually Howze closed debate and forced decisions.

The board cast its net widely for information and expert advice. BG Williams led a team to visit Southeast Asia. The board also created a civilian advisory panel of civilian aircraft manufacturers and agencies. The board also surveyed about 700 officers and civilian firms for suggestions. The collected responses were overwhelming, but just asking for advice fueled interest in Aviation among leading civilian companies.

The Howze Board focused mainly on mid-intensity conflict. This reflected assumptions about how Aviation might most influence the battlefield. Mid-intensity was the worst case. In high-intensity conflict, it was easy to see a need for some kind of vehicle to go around areas where high radiation existed. In low-intensity conflict capabilities that worked in high-or mid-intensity could probably apply. Mid-intensity seemed to offer great opportunities for air assault to improve the Army's capabilities.

The board engaged several operations research organizations for analyses and wargaming. Scientifically the Board's work was weak, but that fact mattered little. Limited time seldom allowed running a scenario more than once. Howze had little confidence in the specific results but thought that including these games was essential because of their popularity in key circles. Howze believed more in the field tests. Seeing what coordinated speed, precision, maneuverability, and firepower of air and ground weapons could do convinced participants that their ideas had to be correct. That conviction inspired everyone to prove that point.

In a few cases, specific events provided useful comparisons. The board conducted some exercises first using a conventionally-equipped force and then using a force with enhanced mobility from more aircraft. Some exercises considered impracticable for conventional forces were done using experimental organizations. About 40 formally-identified tests were run, ranging from three, week-long exercises against an assumed force of irregulars to auxiliary tests of specific items of equipment. These tests were tactical experimentation of short trials to see what would work and what would not. Trials, repeating various changes as many as four times in a day, sometimes showed huge gains. For example, the time required to execute a raid on an isolated outpost shrank from 12 minutes to 90 seconds.

One example where events did provide useful comparisons was with the Air Force C-130 versus Army Caribou. To get the C-130s to land on an unpaved runway, LTG Howze had to talk at great length to a reluctant Air Force general. Then the Army had to haul bulldozers into the site. These bulldozers had to work about four hours preparing the strip. By the time about six C-130s had landed, even with bulldozers working between landings, the strip had become unusable. From that point on, delivery had to be restricted to Caribous and helicopters. Even the pilots from Lockheed, which built the C-130, said they could not compete with the Caribou under those conditions. Too much service capital was at stake for those results to appear in the Pentagon. The final report, written by the Air Force, declared that the C-130 could do everything the Caribou could.

The field trials included experiments with armed helicopters. The desire for organic, aerial firepower fueled conflict over roles and missions. The key issues were responsiveness and integration into the close fight. The Howze Board recommended putting 24 fixed-wing attack aircraft in an assault division, 20 more in a Special Forces (SF) aviation brigade, and eight in each of the other divisions.

For these aircraft the board recommended the OV-1 Mohawk. The board acknowledged that the Air Force had capabilities but argued that many missions required tight coordination with ground combat elements. The responsiveness needed could exist only if the pilots belonged to, lived with, and flew from close to the headquarters they served. To short-circuit the Howze Board's recommendations, the Air Force asked for four more squadrons for CAS. By contrast, the Navy fully supported the Howze Board. Navy technicians showed the Army how to load bombs on the Mohawk. A Navy pilot taught Army pilots how to do low-level bombing using 1000-pound bombs with delay fuzes. These delay fuzes let the Mohawk drop a bomb on one side of a hill, skid the bomb up and over the crest, and destroy a concealed enemy. The Army's demonstrating this tactic horrified an Air Force observer.

Showing the VIPs

Before the field portion ended, the board conducted a formal demonstration for McNamara and other dignitaries. These others included the CJCS, the Secretary of the Army, a general representing the Air Force Chief of Staff, the CSA, and the CONARC commander. This demonstration, involving several scenarios, almost resulted in catastrophe.

For the demonstration, the dignitaries were seated on low benches out in the woods. About 1000 yards away was a low ridge. Following a quick artillery barrage, four Mohawks skipped their bombs up and over the slope. The Mohawk's role was more impressive because, just before the show started, Howze had told McNamara that a planned, low-level Air Force strike on the objective had fallen out because of the low overcast. Right after the Mohawks' run, four Sikorsky H-34s with four machine guns and 2.75-inch rockets poured fire onto the objective. While the H-34s were still firing, about 30 Hueys rushed over the crowd, just above the treetops, and onto the objective—which was invisible because of the dust and smoke. Two infantry companies leaped out and began simulating the final seizure of the objective. Howze told the audience that the whole sequence lasted exactly 120 seconds. 'That's what we mean by air mobility.' McNamara simply asked what the dollar cost was to put each infantryman on the objective. Howze had no idea but said it would be cheaper than by conventional means.

The Caribou demonstration involved a spectacular mishap. Unmarked, waist-high weeds proved that pilots had not rehearsed there. No one realized that a localized storm the night before had soaked the ground. When the Caribou dropped onto the ground, the left wheel sank and ripped off the wing.

As bad as this was, Howze did not then know how bad things really were. Two majors—James H. Merryman and Robert M. Shoemaker—orchestrating behind the scenes did know.

During the first event, simulating the assault on a fortified objective, visibility over the objective dropped almost to zero because of all the debris in the air. As the Hueys converged to make the assault, someone on the radio yelled, 'Midair!' Two Hueys came close enough that the tips of their rotor blades hit. One Huey went down on the objective. By chance, the majors had arranged for a H-37 Mojave to be part of the field tests. A few days earlier the field test group had practiced recovering an aircraft with this Mojave. When the accident occurred during the demonstration, Shoemaker and Merryman immediately sent out the H-37 to clear the debris. The H-37 put a loop on the downed Huey and hauled it away. This accidental event turned out to be a highlight of the demonstration. McNamara, who was always interested in economy, was impressed—possibly even more so than with the planned assault. To him, the incident showed that not only could a helicopter assault take a fortified position, but also one helicopter could retrieve another from the battlefield. This meant huge cost savings. This unplanned event foreshadowed something that Army aviators did thousands of times in Vietnam. In fact, as of mid-1966, the ability to recover downed aircraft in Vietnam made the loss rate of helicopters in Vietnam negligible. For the first half of 1966 enemy fire downed one helicopter out of each 450 combat sorties, but the recovery rate made the actual loss one helicopter in 15,599 sorties.

H-37 recovering H-21 in Vietnam

In the demonstration simulating jungle, Soldiers were supposed to rappel down ropes into the trees. Soldiers thought they were closer to the ground than they were. Two dropped about 30 feet. The impact knocked them both out. A little copse of trees stood right in front, so the VIPs saw none of this. They thought the exercise was splendid.

At the end of the day Merryman and Shoemaker thought their careers were over. They had no way to know that everyone—even the Air Force—was impressed with what the Army had managed to do. The outcome was a huge success.

The final report

For the final report, the initial plan was to have the steering committee write the final version to make it a joint venture. Time prevailed. In the end, Howze personally wrote or rewrote most of the executive summary. In Howze's view, that was the only way to produce it in time.

The report presented a strong case favoring the concept of airmobility. It looked both backwards to the experience of the Korean War and forward to the kinds of combat the Army expected to face. The report discussed all aspects of tactical employment, requirements for armed helicopters, and vulnerabilities. BG Clifton von Kann and Howze formulated airmobile battlefield organizations. The main organization they proposed was an air assault division. This had three brigade headquarters, an air cavalry squadron, eight airmobile infantry battalions, and divisional artillery. The distinctive feature of the artillery was its three battalions of helicopter-transportable 105 mm howitzers, along with a battalion of rocket-firing helicopters. The latter would become known in Vietnam as aerial rocket artillery (ARA). Divisional aviation included a battalion of OV-1 Mohawks. These provided both surveillance and attack capabilities. There were also two battalions of UH-1 Iroquois (Huey) assault helicopters and a battalion of Chinook medium transport helicopters. This basic organization was the one the 11th Air Assault Division tested during its life at Fort Benning. During Vietnam this basic structure was used—minus the armed Mohawks. Howze thought this division design was good but still lacked all the aviation it really needed. It took three lifts by organic aircraft to move the whole combat echelon of the division from one place to another.

The report also advocated another organization—an air cavalry combat brigade. This brigade had enough organic lift so that everyone in the unit had a seat in an aircraft. This difference gave the unit the vital mobility to perform the cavalry mission. That never came to be.

One huge advantage of the proposed airmobile force over existing combat forces was a smaller logistical burden. The airmobile structure took four days to complete an operational plan, compared to seven days for the conventional configuration. Beyond that, the airmobile force took much less movement and support—34 percent fewer surface ships, 23 percent fewer people, and 55 percent less in supplies. An airmobile force also eliminated logistical depots and water terminals. Years later, Howze believed that no one really paid any attention to these estimates.

As the board concluded its work, longtime advocates of enhanced Army Aviation weighed in. Retired LTG Gavin, then ambassador to France, wrote:

> If there is one thing that stands out clearly in all recorded history
> of man's military endeavors, it is that innovation is essential to
> survival and is usually decisive in battle. Regardless of the system
> employed, but assuming that it is employed with reasonable
> intelligence and direction, the final criterion of effectiveness is

the product of both firepower and mobility. These may have exponential values, and in fact the mobility part usually does. It is in the thorough exploration of the field of mobility and the application of knowledge gained that we will find the greatest possibility for innovation in the future

Upon completing the report, Howze added a fifteen-page "Brief by the President of the Board" and sent it up through the chain of command. Howze's boss, GEN Powell, wrote a glowing endorsement and sent everything forward to McNamara.

Aftermath

Not everyone shared the enthusiasm for the board's findings and recommendations. Air Force Chief of Staff Curtis LeMay created a board under LTG Gabriel Disosway to disprove the Howze Board findings. Caution within Army leadership also dampened the outcome. Rather than going directly to restructuring into airmobile units, the idea floated to create a special test air assault division to validate the proposed organization.

Another key proposal was creating additional aviation structure at corps level and above. Corps aviation brigades would provide lift for troops and logistics upon request from divisions within the corps. The Board also recommended an airmobile corps artillery with lightweight 105 mm howitzers and UH-1s with upgraded engines to lift them. There would also be nine attack helicopters for ARA. At field army level the Board proposed an air transport brigade with both medium helicopters and fixed-wing transports. This brigade also had a support command with a terminal command and two Transportation movement commands. Nothing of this sort came until the early 1980s.

The Board also recognized the growing needs of special operations forces (SOF). Army SF provided some of the most enthusiastic members of the Howze Board. That fact showed in a recommendation to form a special warfare aviation brigade. This organization would help SF in their traditional missions deep behind enemy lines.

The Howze Board carefully estimated comparative costs of airmobile and conventional forces of roughly equal size over a five-year period. In start-up costs, the air assault division was half again to two and a half times as expensive as an armored or infantry division. Over five years the differences shrank but did not wash out. An air assault division would cost almost $1 billion in 1962 dollars. An armored division cost about 80 percent of that. An infantry division cost about 70 percent of that. These figures gave pause even with the numbers limited to five air assault divisions, three air cavalry combat brigades, and five air transport brigades out of an Active Component (AC) Army with 16 divisions.

These numbers obscured the operational capabilities an airmobile division could give that no number of conventional divisions could make up. The cost was relative, as when the Congressman in the early 1950s asked why the army would want to buy a helicopter when it could buy four trucks for the price of one. The reply was that no number of trucks could do what one helicopter could. The Army sacrificed capability for cost. Howze thought this was a bad trade. Like Billy Mitchell and others before, Howze fought but could not prevail against what he saw as an enormous waste. McNamara would approve forming a test division and even a large, temporary over strength to support that division.

The 11th Air Assault Division (Test), 1963–65

The immediate sequel to the Howze Board was the 11th Air Assault Division (Test), activated at Fort Benning on 15 February 1963. Over two years, the 11th validated many ideas from the Howze Board. GEN William C. Westmoreland, who commanded U.S. forces in Vietnam during 1964–1968, said that helicopter air assault was the most innovative tactical development in the Vietnam War. In part, the 11th effort was a unique piece of military history. No other army in the world then could muster the number of helicopters the 11th used in its activities.

Organization

Like the Howze Board, the standup of the 11th was quick and well supported. The commander for this effort was handpicked and received his orders directly from the CSA. GEN Earl Wheeler called in BG Harry W. O. Kinnard. Like Howze when appointed the first Director of Army Aviation, Kinnard was one of the younger, promising officers in the Army. Kinnard was the assistant division commander of the 101AB. Wheeler told Kinnard to see how far and how fast the Army could and should go with airmobility.

Kinnard was an obvious choice because of a longstanding interest in airmobility, going back to his service in World War II with the 101AB. After the war he had headed the Airborne Test Section in the Army Field Forces Board at Fort Bragg. Along the way he had become a helicopter pilot. Back with the 101AB he conducted a series of exercises using helicopters to put troops atop buildings for urban warfare. In the fall of 1962 he showed Wheeler this technique. So Wheeler naturally thought of Kinnard to stand up an organization testing the Howze Board ideas.

Wheeler promised that Kinnard could hand-pick people, including NCO, by name. Kinnard sought a particular kind of person—aggressive, mentally flexible, risk-takers. In his mind, this translated into airborne-qualified Soldiers. Such men, Kinnard believed, could easily adapt to what the Army should be doing with helicopters. For example, they could think about distances not in miles but in minutes of flight. Kinnard drew on talent the Howze Board already identified, such as COL George S. Beatty, who commanded the first brigade formed. Kinnard made LTC Robert M. Shoemaker, who had run the field demonstrations, the G-3/Operations officer. Not all chosen were airborne. Kinnard chose COL George P. Seneff to command the 11th Aviation Group. Seneff served in armor units during World War II but was among the colonels chosen for flight school in 1956. A few, like COL Delbert L. Bristol, chosen to command the 10th Air Transport Brigade, went back to the Class Before One in 1942.

Some of the Howze cadre did not become part of the 11th but occupied key positions to help. COL John (Jack) Norton was in CONARC headquarters, able to watch and pull on resources to help Kinnard. BG Robert R. Williams commanded the Test and Evaluation Control (TEC) Group that assessed the 11th.

Support for the new division extended to funding and even special help in the area of procurement. The Army created a special fund of about $1.2 million. This money let the 11th acquire, modify, or improvise equipment. Army Materiel Command (AMC) set up a liaison office right next to the 11th's headquarters to expedite actions.

On 7 January 1963 the Plan for Initial Organization, Training and Testing of Air Mobile Units was published. It designated the test division as the 11th Air Assault Division (Test) and also designated the 10th Air Transport Brigade. From its activation on 15 February onward, the 11th and the 10th Air Transport Brigade (Test) grew and changed almost continuously. The division had an unusually large number of aircraft, and the ratios of fixed-wing to helicopter forecast the future direction. Of 157 aircraft, 82 percent were helicopters.

It was easy to authorize strength but hard to get it, especially in key skills. The Army's ability to create this division was partly an accident of timing. McNamara could afford the manpower cost of the additional division partly under the guise of smoothing recruiting and retention effects of large draft call-ups in response to the Berlin crisis in 1961.While the Army as a whole had overages, even with strong support, Kinnard could not always get what he needed.

Development and test

Kinnard's charter, as he defined it, was to develop and test. His emphasis reflected a basic difference between Howze's views about the maturity of the Howze Board's results and others' estimates. Years later, LTG Kinnard wrote that, as good as the ideas of the Howze Board were, they needed much development. The 11th engaged more in repetitive trials and correcting errors than in testing prescribed organization, doctrine, tactics, and TTP. This reflected disagreement about what might be most appropriate and effective.

One requirement in this organization was to allow some basic changes in mind-sets. There were some basic differences between using aviation as adjunct to ground combat and airmobility. It was hard to convince old-line artillerymen that they would have no prime movers; rather, that a Chinook would show up at the right time and put his pieces into position. The challenges of mindset were equally great for infantrymen.

The power of the Chinook was a decisive element. That capped the weight of equipment. The slogan—'If you can't slingload it on a Hook [Chinook], you're better off without it'—was easy to say but harder to live. It led to creating light-weight organizations, such as a Signal battalion whose largest vehicle was a jeep.

Generating ideas—the Idea Center and other methods to spur innovative thinking

Finding new ways to do things better, coming up with and capturing good ideas, no matter where they might originate was vital to success for the 11th. Kinnard recognized that good ideas had no necessary relationship to rank or position. He encouraged everyone at every level to exercise what he called 'imaginuity.' Kinnard also believed that the man in the field would most likely recognize a valid change. To make sure that any potentially good idea at least got a hearing, an Idea Center officially opened on 21 January 1964. Kinnard made it known that any idea to improve the way an airmobile unit operated would be seriously considered. Nothing was out of bounds. Soldiers brought forth all sorts of ideas.

Those ideas that survived entered the division's standard operating procedure (SOP). Then all units practiced the new ways until their execution was perfect.

In this respect, Kinnard's situation was the exact opposite of Howze's. Driven by extreme time limits to produce his final report, Howze had to stifle a natural explosion of ideas that came from convening so many talented, interested people with a common goal. Moreover, Howze could try only a small number of things, usually only once. With the luxury of time, Kinnard sought to expand the flow of ideas from all quarters and then try many of them many times.

Test phases

A basic part of the whole program was a series of three, phased tests. Each phase involved a larger unit and, excepting the first, built on lessons from the preceding one. Phase I, from February to September 1963, involved one air assault infantry battalion. Phase II, from November 1963 to August 1964, started build-up in July 1963 and involved a brigade. Phase III involved the whole division. The build-up for Phase III began in January 1964, formally started in September 1964, and ended in July 1965. At that point, the division was supposed to be fully combat ready. Phase I was evaluated only internally by the Army. A Joint test involving the Air Force followed the Army's test in both Phases II and III.

Obstacles to success—internal and external

Each phase of the test required overcoming serious obstacles. For example, finding enough and the right kind of items because of the cold start and short lead times threatened success for the Phase I. Many items either did not exist in the inventory or were being manufactured in response to the 11th's requests. To bypass some of these problems, other commands suggested changing the test organization in ways that violated the recommendations of the Howze Board. Kinnard had to appeal directly to HQDA to prevent such changes. Given the timelines and scale of work to be done, even the arrival of needed items could almost be a disaster. In the first three weeks after activation, the Aviation Group alone received 15 tons of technical manuals. This huge mass of material had to be separated into proper sets and distributed. Phone calls brought a team from the Electronics Command that saved the day.

Training of Aviation for Phase I was a major concern. For example, the Army taught OV-1 Mohawk pilots only how to fly the aircraft. They knew nothing of flying in formation, aerobatics, or weapons. Moreover the Army lacked the equipment and skills needed associated with arming the Mohawks. Seneff ordered work with the Navy to get the needed equipment and skills.

For the later, Joint tests, there was sniping from the Air Force. In April 1964, while the division was ramping up for Phase II tests, Air Force Chief of Staff Curtis LeMay testified before Congress about the Army's wasteful duplication of costly resources. While Kinnard was very careful to eschew the Army's stepping into Air Force roles and missions, the division also stood up Army capabilities in areas that had been Air Force turf—for example, on 24 June 1963 the Army's first air traffic services (ATS) company stood up—the 72d Army Air Traffic Regulation and Identification Company (AATRI)—to support the air transport brigade.

Similar problems dogged the division at each stage, and it was a major tribute to those involved that things worked out overall. Readiness of aircraft suffered from shortages of spare parts and tool sets. Combined maintenance and supply problems gave Chinooks an availability rate of 15 percent and a high of 68 percent. So the Chinook battalion neither had a chance to test its tactical SOP nor worked with units it supported.

Sometimes adversity actually helped. During an early exercise, bad weather hit the Carolinas, where the division was trying to work. Conditions for flying dropped below 500 feet for a ceiling and a quarter mile for visibility. Rivers overflowed, flooding many of the tactical and surrounding areas. Umpires, used to seeing such conditions stop roadbound troops, saw heliborne troops reach and seize their objectives. Moreover, despite the severe storm, the troops arrived safely and only an hour late. This outcome severely disappointed some high-level observers eager to see the airmobility concept fail.

LTG C. W. G. Rich, director of the overall project, signed the final test report on 1 December 1964. He concluded that the Army should have the 11th or at least a division structured like it in the permanent force structure. He reached the same conclusion about the 10th Air Transport Brigade. Rich saw no need for further, large-scale tests. He also recommended that the Army should preserve intact the experience of the people involved in the buildup and tests, rather than dispersing them and their equipment, as was the normal practice. Others, including the commander of the 82AB, which had been the opposing force (OPFOR), were similarly positive.

The final report was not just uncritical praise. A key part of the 82AB commander's comments was a list of deficiencies. Most importantly, he doubted that the elements of such units could survive if exposed to ground units for extended periods. COL Bristol's comments from the 10th Air Transport Brigade highlighted the importance of ATC services in adverse weather and the severe shortcomings in the standard Army aircraft maintenance system.

Turnovers of people continued almost unabated as the 11th prepared for its major, Joint test. The quality of officer that BG Kinnard had sought in the first place made key members high-demand items elsewhere. Almost immediately after Air Assault II ended, some key officers were drafted for assignments outside the division. In February 1965 COL Seneff, the Aviation Group commander, was selected for BG and left to become the Director of Army Aviation. To compensate, units shuffled officers already onboard to take over in the key roles.

No longer (Test)—activating the 1st Cavalry Division (Airmobile) and deploying to Vietnam

By June 1965 world events overtook the test plan, which called for a final Joint test in July. In early 1965 the CSA had alerted Kinnard that, if the President decided to send a division to Vietnam, the CSA would recommend the airmobile division. Kinnard told his staff to start studying likely missions. On 16 June 1965 SECDEF McNamara announced a decision to activate an airmobile division. Everyone involved with the 11th recognized what that meant. The division was to be fully ready by 28 July. No such unit existed. Within two weeks the Army would create it. On 1 July 1965 the 1st Cavalry Division (1CD) (Airmobile) officially activated. A ceremony on 3 July marked the transition, casing the old 11th colors.

A huge amount of work went into the next four weeks. On 1 July the new division had 9489 of 15,890 Soldiers authorized. Half of those were eligible for overseas deployment. Replacements came into Fort Benning around the clock—many, with families with no place to live. An intensive training program went into high gear.

On 28 July 1965 President Lyndon B. Johnson told the American people that he had ordered the airmobile division to Vietnam. That day the first of the Chinooks had flown to the Naval Air Station at Mayport, Florida, to board a ship for Vietnam. On Friday, 10 September 1965, the USNS Boxer dropped anchor in Qui Nhon harbor in Vietnam and began offloading. Twenty more ships followed. The airmobile division was going to war.

Afterthoughts

The 11th and events related to its short lifespan reflected several key features of the way the armed forces did things in this era.

Success and survival an accident of circumstances

Among those features worth noting was the way of testing new ideas and technology. Partly because of the interservice jealousy that often tainted relations between the Army and Air Force, it was hard for the Army to devise and execute an overt, orderly, rational program to develop and test in areas involving aviation. Much depended on opportunities arising from peculiar coincidences of like-minded people in key places, such as McNamara, Williams, and Howze. Even then, successful outcomes partly depended on other, unrelated conditions, such as the residual manpower from the 1961 Berlin Crisis. Without all of these things, the Howze Board would have simply become another in a long list of interesting forays into innovation with no short-term impact on the larger institution of the Army.

The survival of the airmobile division beyond an idea also depended on an accident of history. At the end of the division's testing, advocates of airmobility did all they could to preserve the division. It had taken three years to create a working organization. Still, those handling the Army budget had not included it for the next fiscal year. So it was going away, even though Army programmers intended to reactivate an airmobile division two years later. Those involved with the 11th were horrified. To prevent this dissolution, advocates proposed deploying the unit to Vietnam. The possibility of using such a division in Vietnam had surfaced by the end of the Howze Board. The proposal in 1965 to send the airmobility division to Vietnam caused intense conflict at HQDA and climaxed in a meeting where Creighton W. Abrams, VCSA, presided. After intense discussion Abrams said he thought it 'extremely propitious' that the Army had such a division in existence at that moment and the Army would deploy it to Vietnam. Those who had advocated for the airmobile division were thrilled. They also realized that Abrams' decision was simple expediency. The Army needed something it could get to Vietnam quickly. Moreover, the Central Highlands was selected as the operational area. An airmobile unit could get back into Pleiku, whereas nothing else could. Roads had been closed for years.

Assignment to the Central Highlands had a bonus for airmobile advocates. The new division and its operational area would be separated from the rest of the buildup in Vietnam. Isolation allowed proving advantages compared to conventional organizations. GEN Westmoreland supported this decision because he clearly understood the advantages of air assault operations in contrast to what the French had done earlier. The French had consumed up to three-fourths of their strength trying to keep the roads open. By flying over, the airmobile division could both keep its lines of communication open and put its troops into combat, rather than into providing security.

The intensity of Aviation activities during and through the formation of the 11th, reflagging, and deployment to Vietnam had a human price. At least some of those involved in reorganizing the 11th, filling the 1CD, and getting things established in Vietnam had been involved almost continuously in fast-paced operations for several years. Such operational tempo (OPTEMPO) strained some families beyond the breaking point. Wives found out the 1CD was deploying before many members of the unit did. The first anyone in MAJ Bruce Crandall's unit knew about their imminent deployment was when a NCO's wife called via an amateur radio network to tell her husband she was divorcing him because his unit was going to Vietnam. In April 1966 the Director of Army Aviation announced that, for at least the next two years the Army would have to recycle aviators to Vietnam, one year in, one year out.

Combat in Vietnam—early operations and effects

While the arrival of the 1CD marked the beginning of the large expansion of Army forces in Vietnam, Aviation had already been active in Vietnam for several years. Events especially from 1961 onward set the conditions for the new airmobile division's first battle. These early, fairly-low-level involvements also set events in motion and revealed patterns that would dominate Aviation for the rest of the decade.

Rationale for early Aviation involvement in Vietnam

A key consideration in early Aviation activity in Vietnam was the Kennedy Administration's desire to support the South Vietnamese government against a growing insurgency. Conventional wisdom about counterinsurgency said that, to be successful, government forces needed about ten troops for every insurgent. Estimates of Communist guerrilla strengths made it unlikely that the Republic of Vietnam (RVN) could exceed five-to-one. The hope was that a mixture of U.S.-supplied tactical advice, firepower, and aerial mobility could make up the difference.

Aviation 's early involvement was small-scale and largely below the threshold of the public's notice. The changes were reflected in coverage in the U.S. Army Aviation Digest. In September 1962 the first article on Army Aviation in counterinsurgency appeared in the U.S. Army Aviation Digest. By January 1966 a whole issue of the U.S. Army Aviation Digest was devoted to Vietnam.

First conventional involvement—1961–1962

Not surprisingly Aviation activities in Vietnam first involved transportation. On 21 August 1961 an experimental model Caribou landed at Saigon under the auspices of the Advanced Research Project Agency (ARPA). The ARPA Caribou flew up and down the length of Vietnam. It went into airstrips normally limited to much smaller aircraft. Initially the Caribou specialized in resupplying SF outposts inaccessible by road and normally supplied by airdrop or occasional helicopters.

On 11 December 1961 the USNS Core arrived in Saigon with 32 H-21 Shawnee Army helicopters and 400 men of the 8th and 57th Transportation companies. Over the next two years, the 57th, which became the 120th Aviation Company, logged more than 17,000 flying hours, more than a million passenger miles, and more than 20,000 combat sorties. On 2 January 1962 the first airmobile combat action involving U.S. helicopters occurred—flying Vietnamese troops into a jungle clearing.

MEDEVAC—origin of Dustoff

Within a short time Aviation activities expanded to include MEDEVAC. In March 1962, a month before McNamara issued the memoranda to create the Howze Board, an air ambulance company deployed to Vietnam. This began a heroic chapter in the history of aerial MEDEVAC that eventually gave the Army a new term for that mission.

The key figure was MAJ Charles L. Kelly—callsign, Dustoff. Beginning 11 January 1964, Kelly commanded the 57th Medical Detachment (Air Ambulance) (Provisional) in Vietnam. Kelly and other MEDEVAC pilots' commitment to those on the ground was beyond question. To prove the 57th's worth and prevent medical helicopters from being converted to assault and general-purpose missions, Kelly stepped up operations and had pilots fly a circuit to check for casualties at widely dispersed bases. He personally flew almost every night—the most dangerous of times, given the limited technology at the time. Eventually his commitment cost Kelly his life. On 1 July 1964 Kelly received a request from a Vietnamese unit under heavy fire. The ground advisor warned Kelly of the danger and recommended Kelly leave. Kelly replied, 'When I have your wounded.' Fire mortally wounded Kelly, who posthumously received the Distinguished Service Cross. His callsign—Dustoff—became the universal callsign for MEDE-VAC flights. On 2 June1967 Kelly Hall was dedicated at Fort Rucker.

MEDEVAC flight in Vietnam

Development of armed helicopters—UTT, Cheyenne, Guns-a-Go-Go, AH-1 Cobra

Even before the Howze Board had finished its work, armed Army helicopters were operating in Vietnam. As Howze and others had foreseen in the mid-1950s, there was a compelling need for Army Aviation to have organic fire support. The continuing conflict with the Air Force over roles and missions, however, made efforts to meet this need tortuous and halting. For the most part, the Army's development in this area meant adapting existing systems to the armed-aircraft role. Results were often only partly satisfactory. The cost of the shortfall was often paid in blood.

Utility Tactical Transports (UTT)

Armed helicopters were operating in Vietnam at least by mid-summer of 1962. H-21 Shawnees belonging to the 8th and 57th Transportation companies were fitted with .30 caliber machineguns. To circumvent Air Force objections about armed aircraft, the Army's first unit of armed helicopters in Vietnam had a misleading name—the Utility Tactical Transport (UTT) Company. The UTT activated in Okinawa 25 July 1962 under command of LTC Robert Runkle. By October losses prompted the senior U.S. military officer in Vietnam to request armed helicopters for fire support.

The UTT helicopters were Hueys equipped with quad M-60 machinegun systems that later became standard. These systems reflected the ad-hoc, adaptive nature of Aviation armament. The M-60 was the standard ground weapon. The ground nature of the weapon persisted even in its aircraft application. The M-60 was mounted to the aircraft with a pin that allowed instant removal. Aircrew carried the standard handgrip and trigger mechanism. This way, if the aircraft went down, the crew could quickly remove the M-60s and use them for ground combat.

UH-1 gunships over Vietnam

As with much else in Aviation history, there was a direct link to the past through people. With the UTT was CWO Clarence J. (Jack) Carter. After flight school in 1959, he worked in Vanderpool's Fools' armament shop.

After its combat debut the UTT remained as an operational unit in Vietnam. One indicator of the unit's combat role was awards. For example, for actions on 3

April 1964, MAJ Patrick N. Delavan, then commanding the UTT, received the Distinguished Service Cross (DSC). He went in alone against heavy enemy fire, landed, and personally loaded a wounded adviser to avoid an unarmed MEDE-VAC having to go in. In June 1964 Delavan earned the sixth oak-leaf cluster for his Purple Heart.

Quest for more firepower—Guns-a Go-Go, and the Cobra

The gunships in the UTT were only a stopgap and were recognized as such. The need for greater firepower led to a new program that reignited conflict with the Air Force. In March 1963 a statement of requirement was issued for an Advanced Aerial Fire Support System (AAFSS). This became the AH-56 Cheyenne. At best the Cheyenne could not meet the immediate need. It would not reach the field until the early 1970s. So workarounds were sought.

A/ACH-47A 'Guns-A-Go-Go'

On 30 June 1965—the day before the 1CD officially activated—the Army ordered four armed, armored Chinooks to be delivered by the end of the year. General Frank Besson, Chief of Transportation, pushed this idea. These modified Chinooks were designated the A/ACH-47A—nicknamed 'Guns-A-Go-Go.' Like LTC William A. Howell's 'world's most heavily armed helicopter' in 1957, the Guns-A-Go-Go Chinooks looked impressive, but the Guns-a-Go-Go had limited combat success. In May 1966 three Guns-a-Go-Go went to Vietnam to form the 53d Aviation Detachment for combat evaluation. The idea was to use standard gunship tactics, which meant operating in fire teams of two. One would provide base fire while the other maneuvered for attack. Equipment malfunctions and combat damage sometimes led to single-ship missions. Single-ship missions proved unacceptably costly. On 9 July 1966 one of these aircraft took heavy damage while flying a single-ship mission at 850 feet to support a ground cavalry task force (TF). For a while, the remaining two aircraft worked with the Australians. On 5 May 1967 failure in a gun mounting caused a crash of one aircraft that killed all onboard. The two remaining aircraft continued to work in ARA raids, reconnaissance and convoy escort, and preparation of landing zones (LZ). During February 1968 one of these Chinooks was shot down and destroyed. Without the ability to operate in two-ship teams, the remaining aircraft returned to normal use.

'Easy Money'—CH-47 of Guns-a-Go-Go

The Cobra—buying an off-the-shelf (OTS) solution

Even as the Guns-a-Go-Go ships were readied, the Army sought another interim gunship. In this case, though, the Army sought a system specifically designed for the mission. On 18 July 1965 the Commander of the U.S. Military Advisory Command Vietnam (COMUSMACV) stated a requirement for an improved design of an armed helicopter to provide armed escort of troop-carrying helicopters. This became the basis for the Army's buying the AH-1G Cobra gunship from Bell Helicopter.

The Cobra was a case study in the relationship between the helicopter industry in the U.S. and the military, as well as of the kind of resistance the Army could sometimes mount against itself. During 1964 managers in Bell Helicopter became "acutely aware" of needs to improve on the performance of the UH-1B Huey as an aerial weapons platform. Concerns were speed, endurance, maneuverability, range, and protection for the aircraft and crew. Bell had also discovered some technological potential for higher speeds than previously thought. An improved rotor system, combined with a more powerful engine and more streamlined fuselage, looked feasible as a low-risk project. Based on that, Bell undertook to produce a prototype that first flew on 7 September 1965.

Bell emphasized, at least for public consumption, that this prototype was not a new aircraft but only a design change. This claim let both Bell and the Army bypass obstacles of delays inherent in getting any new development going. It also bypassed Air Force objections to the Army developing an armed aircraft. That was already a sore subject with the AH-56 Cheyenne.

The next step involved internal Army wrangling. In response to the COMUS-MACV requirement, the CSA directed AMC to evaluate helicopters then available within industry. There was opposition to buying OTS. Opponents within the Army advocated waiting for the Cheyenne or modifying another older, slower aircraft—basically, Guns-a-Go-Go. BG Seneff, the new Director of Aviation, advocated for the Cobra with the CSA, who overrode opponents. On 13 April 1966 Bell received a contract for additional UH-1Bs and UH-1Ds—including 110 Cobras.

The Cobra's origin as a derivative of the Huey was a key feature. That eliminated delays in creating and filling the logistical pipeline. It also eliminated needs for a separate training pipeline for either maintenance personnel or pilots. Another key gain in the Cobra was redesign of the cockpit. All previous gunships had the pilot and copilot sitting side-by-side. This design had at least three disadvantages. One was the width of the fuselage—which meant air resistance, slower speed, and less maneuverability for the same power and lift. Second was visibility. In side-by-side seating, neither the pilot nor copilot could fully see nor aim at some possible targets. The Cobra copilot seated in the front had an unrestricted view of 230 degrees. He could fire weapons throughout this arc. Fore-and-aft seating became a key characteristics for all future attack helicopters, although its rationale took occasional reminding when people proposed adapting utility aircraft to an attack role to save costs. The narrower profile of the Cobra let it fly at 170 knots and 190 knots in a shallow dive. The Huey's maximum cruising speed was 138 knots, and it began to tear itself apart at 165 knots. Over a 50-mile mission, the Cobra could reach the objective in half the time, had twice the firepower, and could stay on station three times as long. Other changes increased survivability—self-sealing fuel tanks, armoring of key areas, and the Cobra's narrower profile.

Cobra acquisition as response to proven combat necessity—losses to unescorted lift ships

Acquisition of the Cobra was a clear case of combat urgency driving decision-making. Needs in Vietnam dictated acquiring something. Dangers to unescorted lift ships became one of the most pronounced lessons of Vietnam, even though this lesson was relearned and reproved in later operations, such as in Grenada in 1983.

Because of the extra weight and drag, improvised UH-1B gunships could not keep up with lift ships. The burden fell on individual air crewmen to complete their missions and stay alive. Often they could not do both. Several place names at Fort Rucker memorialize people who died in such situations. Stagefields honor CWO Joseph A. Goldberg and his crew chief, Specialist 5 (SP5) Harold Lee Guthrie who died flying a H-21 Shawnee on a combat support mission in 1962. Classroom buildings remember Specialist (SP4) Donald Leon Braman, gunner on a Shawnee in 1963, and CWO 3 Manford Kleiv, a pilot shot down during a support mission in 1964. Kleiv, a World War II Ranger, was one of the pilots in the original 1000-hour tests for the H-37s at Fort Rucker. To send a distress call for his downed crew he repeatedly braved enemy fire to return to the aircraft and was mortally wounded. His actions let the rest of his crew be rescued. Posthumously he received a Silver Star.

Another role for armed helicopters—aerial rocket artillery (ARA)

Another role of armed helicopters that evolved as part of the 11th was their use to provide direct-fire support beyond the range of ground artillery. This function, called ARA, consisted of helicopters equipped with pods of rockets. ARA units could provide a heavy volume of fire. In their basic configuration, each ARA helicopter carried two pods, each with 24 rockets. All 48 could be fired in four seconds. While originally designed to provide fire support for airmobile troops beyond the range of conventional artillery, ARA became a method of choice for many troops on the ground. There were major advantages to ARA over conventional tube artillery. The fire was direct and directly-observed. This let ARA provide a lethal barrage within 50 meters of engaged troops—much closer than conventional, indirect fire support or CAS.

The first ARA unit in Vietnam was the 2d Battalion, 20th Artillery, which was part of the 11th. This unit, with the mythical Griffin as its emblem, immediately established itself as a superb counterbattery weapon.

The helicopter gunship was possibly the most-feared aerial weapon on the battle-field. Such, to the dismay of some superiors, were the findings of an Air Force team sent to Vietnam to interview POWs. The POWs did not really worry about fixed-wing, fighter aircraft. An observation aircraft circled around beforehand. So the enemy knew there was going to be a strike. Then the observation aircraft told the enemy exactly where the strike would be by marking it with a rocket. All the enemy had to do was move. By contrast, helicopters were relentless. These gun-ships would fly with a fire team of three. When one was pulling around and could not fire at the enemy, another was in position to fire. So the enemy always had to keep his head down or risk getting caught.

Over the years, ARA did not gain strong support within the Artillery Branch. In the eyes of at least some ARA veterans, this fact reflected an undue fixation on conventional gun technology, to the exclusion of more innovative and possibly effective approaches.

AH-1 Cobra in Vietnam

A shifting concept from escort to direct fire support

The kind of role the ARA performed corresponded to a shift in the way Army aviators talked about armed helicopters. In November 1966 BG Robert R. Williams, the Director of Army Aviation, signaled this shift. In discussing tactical airmobile operations, Williams said that it was time to clarify a point in discussing the firepower Army helicopters could deliver.

Previously 'suppressive fire' had been used. This put the main emphasis on escort missions. According to Williams, Vietnam showed that equally important was 'direct fire support.' The key distinction between that and what the Air Force delivered in CAS was the degree of integration with maneuver. The degree desired was possible only through the crew's participating throughout the planning and execution. Gunship pilots often had already served as lift pilots—experience that gave them personal, as well as technical knowledge of the commanders and units they supported with fires. Williams answered the recurrent charge that the Army was duplicating capabilities by reference to a "spectrum of firepower," which ran from the pistol through bombers and missiles. "Each means of firepower has its degree of responsiveness and killing power. None are truly duplicative; they overlap and each has its role to play in the battle."

Establishing key places—Pleiku, Camp Holloway, the A Shau Valley

Early Aviation activities in Vietnam established operations in places that became central to future events. As the Howze Board was finishing its work in August 1962, the 81st Transportation Company opened Camp Holloway near the town of Pleiku in the Central Highlands. Camp Holloway claimed to be the highest permanent helicopter base in Vietnam. A strategic point, it became a focus of repeated military efforts by both friends and foes. Viet Cong (VC) attacks on Camp Holloway and the airfield at Pleiku on 7 February 1965 clearly showed the need for U.S. combat units in Vietnam to protect bases there. The JCS believed that strong U.S. forces in Vietnam would discourage North Vietnam from continuing the war. On 11 February the JCS alerted the 173d Airborne Brigade on Okinawa for Vietnam duty. This lit the fuze that brought the new airmobile division a few months later.

Escalation in the Highlands—regular forces in direct combat

Even before the 11th conducted its final test, combat against well-organized but still irregular forces changed into combat against a mix of irregular and regular forces. About 0230 on 9 June 1965 VC attacked the SF camp at Dong Xoai. Fighting over the next several days was intense, with Army helicopters transporting troops of the ARVN in the thick of it. On 10 June Hueys landed at Dong Xoia and rescued all survivors. For their actions two pilots, MAJ Harvey Stewart and CPT William N. Fraker, each received the Distinguished Service Cross. By autumn of 1965 combat increasingly involved regular, main forces on both sides. Such combat took rising tolls on helicopters. On 18 September 1965 initial lift helicopters came under heavy fire and all 26 reinforcement helicopters were damaged beyond repair.

Growth of Aviation force structure—Aviation battalions and Aviation groups

The buildup of operations in Vietnam drove a major expansion of and change in Aviation force structure. Up to that time, only a few Aviation battalions existed. These were almost all designated as Transportation units. For the most part, Aviation organizations, even at division level, were designated as companies.

As the size of these organizations grew for Vietnam, these companies were reflagged as battalions. For example, in February 1957 the 25th Aviation Company, assigned to the 25th Infantry Division (25ID), activated in Hawaii. This later became the 25th Aviation Battalion. The first next-larger echelon was the 11th Aviation Group, constituted on 1 February 1963 as part of the 11th Air Assault Division. By the end of 1964 Army Aviation in Vietnam consisted of several major organizations.

Transition into major combat, 1965–66—1CD in the Pleiku Campaign

By the time the 1CD reached Vietnam, the situation there was regarded as serious. Meeting with the CSA, MG Kinnard received a mission type order. He recalled it as, 'Harry, your job with your division is to prevent the enemy from cutting Vietnam in two through the Vietnamese highlands.'

Preparations for major combat

As with standing up the 11th, Kinnard approached the task methodically and incrementally. As soon as he knew that the division would deploy, Kinnard got permission to send two types of advanced party. One was to get some people into units that were already in Vietnam to learn the peculiarities of operations there. The other was to start developing the base for the division.

The importance of a crawl-walk-run approach was vital because of decisions at the national level. President Johnson had chosen not to declare an emergency. So the new division lost many experienced Soldiers and had to absorb an even larger number of new ones. Kinnard told his commanders to use any periods they could in transit—which was by ship—to train their units. Besides learning to fire their new M-16 rifles at apple crates thrown off the fantails, Soldiers got to know each other, their leaders, and their capabilities. The incremental approach continued beyond arrival into first combat operations. Most of the troops were green. Nervous Soldiers fired many rounds at ghost targets. One casualty was Maggie, the mule mascot of the 1st Squadron, 9th Cavalry Regiment (1–9 Cav).

The tactical responsibility given the 1CD would surely test the concept of airmobility. On 28 September the division took responsibility for almost 16,000 square miles in central Vietnam. This was the largest tactical area ever given a single division. This area covered three Vietnamese provinces. So Kinnard gave each of his brigade commanders main responsibility for one province. LTC John B. Stockton's 9th Cavalry was responsible for reconnaissance over the whole area. The 9th would also supply troops to support each of the brigades in operations. Kinnard intended to fight with two brigades outside the base area. One augmented brigade would be responsible for the base area.

On 10 October the division began its first real offensive. Most of the enemy that the operation was to capture had escaped beforehand. One VC battalion chose to dig in and fight. This fight lost two MEDEVAC helicopters and changed the practices for evacuating the wounded from what the division had done before. Suddenly lift ships were told to extract wounded on their way out, as well as delivering troops and supplies on the way in. The new practice especially applied when LZs were under fire.

Protecting the division's aircraft was a key concern for the whole division and shaped base operations. The biggest threats were mortar and rocket attacks. The infantry battalion responsible for base security aggressively patrolled outside the perimeter to a distance beyond the range of these weapons. Also, as darkness approached each day, the Cavalry flew the area to check trails for anyone approaching the zone where mortars could reach the base. Preplanned artillery fires through the night pinpointed known or likely locations for attackers. Thus, from the outset, protecting Aviation, which gave the division both mobility and combat power, also consumed a large amount of attention and combat power.

Crew Chief Jimmie Sanders, 1st Cavalry Division, with his OH-6

Battle of the Ia Drang Valley—October-November 1965

The first real combat test for the division came in late October 1965. Intelligence revealed that two, fresh North Vietnamese Army (NVA) regiments had come down from the north and linked with a VC regiment to form a division. Clearly these forces threatened Pleiku as a first step to cutting Vietnam in half. The location and nature of this situation blended with the need to prove the new type of division. Coincidentally, for the Communists, this battle was meant to be a shakedown of the NVA to operate with divisions under a higher command. So both sides had high stakes. What followed marked a major shift in Vietnam from SF to conventional operations.

The battles began on 19 October. That night NVA infantry attacked the SF Camp at Plei Me. The NVA quickly overran the southern outpost. Air strikes began by 0345 on 20 October. Two armed helicopters and a flare ship of the 119th Aviation Company (Air Mobile Light) gave illumination and air cover until Air Force flare ships and fighters arrived. Later in the morning two armed UH-1Bs of the 119th took intense automatic weapons fire from all quadrants while escorting MEDE-VAC helicopters from Plei Me. One of the gunships went down with no survivors. Lack of helicopter lift kept SF from responding from Pleiku until 21 October. An ARVN ground column ran into a major ambush enroute and did not reach the camp until 25 October. Only 1CD's airmobile artillery allowed the relief column to reach Plei Me at all. This artillery leapfrogged along the flanks, harassed the attacking enemy, and escaped before the enemy could overrun the guns. About 0900 on 26 October COL Elvy B. Roberts, commanding 1st Cavalry's 1st Brigade (Airborne), arrived for a full briefing.

Beginning on 27 October Roberts' brigade spread out across western Pleiku province to find, fix and ideally destroy the 32d and 33d NVA Regiments. These units were withdrawing toward the Cambodian border after their abortive ambush of the relief column. The regiments had planted caches of supplies for their return, but the constant activity of the air cavalry often prevented reaching their supplies. On 30–31 October teams from the 1–9 Cav started to find and attack the enemy in small actions. On 1 November the 1–9 Cav found and engaged a battalion that had stayed behind to cover part of the movement. Cavalrymen from four battalions converged. In the fight that followed, the enemy lost 99 killed. Eleven Cavalrymen died. On 3 November, along the Cambodian border, the cavalrymen ambushed a supply column and killed 73 Soldiers of a newly-arrived 66th NVA regiment. This battle lasted into the night and occasioned two firsts—the first night combat assault landing and the first night use of aerial artillery. On 9 November Kinnard pulled the 1st Brigade back to rest.

Landing Zone (LZ) X-Ray—desperate times, conspicuous heroism

The Pleiku Campaign reached its dramatic climax on 14–17 November. The 32d NVA struck eastward again. The 66th Regiment, along with survivors of the 33d, remained behind at the base of the Chu Pong Mountains. Intelligence had correctly identified a training area there. On 14 November LTC Harold G. (Hal) Moore's 1st Battalion, 7th Cavalry, assaulted into the midst of the 66th's base camp. Thus began an epic fight, retold in the book and later film, <u>We Were Soldiers Once…and Young</u>.

Events over the next few days showed the tight knitting of air and ground Soldiers in the airmobile units. On 14 November 1965 MAJ Bruce Crandall, who commanded Company A, 229th Assault Helicopter Battalion, picked up Moore, and flew a reconnaissance. They picked spots they designated LZ X-ray and Firebase Falcon. In preparation for the assault, Chinooks lifted artillery into Falcon.

Aircraft on first assault into X-ray took no fire, but then things changed. The fourth lift took fire. On the fifth lift fire was intense. Six people were shot off of the assaulting aircraft. Four of eight aircraft had to be grounded. Intense, direct enemy fire prompted Moore to close the LZ. Crandall knew that Moore's unit was in trouble and asked for volunteers to go back. Neither Crandall nor Moore knew that things were about to get much worse. The NVA front commander, alerted by radio, had ordered the 32d Regiment to return and join the fight.

Casualties mounted quickly. The need for MEDEVAC was urgent, but the recent experience of losing these helicopters came into play. The unit called for MEDE-VAC, but the new division policy for MEDEVAC required a cold LZ for five minutes. That was impossible. This left the lift unit to carry out wounded.

The remaining fight for LZ X-ray demanded extreme commitment of the Army aviators involved, and two eventually received special recognition—Crandall, who received the Distinguished Service Cross, and CPT Ed Freeman, who belatedly received the Medal of Honor. When Crandall first called for volunteers to help the besieged cavalrymen, Freeman was the only one who came forward. After he did, the rest of the unit followed. Crandall and Freeman flew 14 separate missions, delivering critically needed ammunition, water, and medical supplies. On the return trips Freeman evacuated about 30 seriously wounded Soldiers. Some would not have survived had he not acted. Each trip, both ways, meant taking his unarmed helicopter through a gauntlet of enemy fire.

By the time the fight at X-ray ended, 79 cavalrymen had died. Enemy dead numbered 643. Three days later, a meeting engagement became an intensely personal fight that left 151 more cavalrymen and 403 more enemy dead. A follow-up operation beginning 20 November caught and destroyed one battalion of the 32d Regiment that was trying to escape.

Pleiku Campaign in hindsight—glass half full and half empty

The Pleiku Campaign was a defining moment for the course events would take in Vietnam. To most observers on the U.S. side, it was a resounding success. In the first combat test of an airmobile division, the 1CD had achieved its objective. It forced the enemy to abandon an offensive that was planned to conquer the Central Highlands. The major encounters also showed the flexibility of the air-mobile organization in several situations. The actions also allowed Kinnard to let each of his brigades try their tactics and gain experience. The pressure of contin-uous contact not only wore down the enemy but also produced a continuous flow of valuable intelligence to refine operations as they went. Finally the operations and results answered several key questions. Among these were whether or not the logistical pipeline could hold up and whether or not enough coordination to allow success could almost literally be done on the fly. In both cases, the answer was yes. All of these results encouraged Army and national leadership that further, similar military operations could lead to strategic success.

At the same time, these battles and their outcome had an alarming undertone. While the U.S. had won a major victory, the NVA set the terms of the fight in time, place, and length. Possibly more worrisome, the battle confirmed intelli-gence reports that infiltration into South Vietnam was greater than previously believed—by a factor of three. That increase came despite intensive U.S. bomb-ing. In response to this news, Westmoreland notified Washington that U.S. forces must more than double his estimate made less than six months earlier. That shift brought both the SECDEF and CSA to Saigon for a face-to-face meeting. Following that meeting, McNamara told a press conference that the Ia Drang fight allowed only one conclusion: 'It will be a long war.'

At least one of those involved with these operations also saw another flaw in the unfolding pattern. When interviewed in 1978, COL Delbert Bristol thought the Army had relied too much on airmobility, to the exclusion of taking and holding ground. The emphasis on search-and-destroy failed to establish reliable lines of communication.

Among the impressive features of the campaign was the scale of the effort mounted. Between 23 October and 28 November helicopters moved whole infantry companies 193 times. Supplies and ammunition delivered to the troops exceeded 13,000 tons. The division flew 27,000 hours and lost only four helicop-ters shot down. From 23 October to 26 November 1965 just the 229th Assault Helicopter Battalion flew 10,480 sorties in direct support.

The operations also highlighted a number of flaws in existing arrangements. Both levels and amounts of combat exceeded expectations. The 1CD lacked enough resources to reinforce in critical situations as at LZ X-ray. Besides manpower, there was a supply shortage—notably including aviation fuel. That reached crisis in October. Aerial firepower also proved inadequate to stop enemy assaults. Distances involved outreached initial capabilities of communications, although using a Caribou as an aerial relay station partly compensated. Leaders down to the individual unit took away lessons to be used later. For example, Crandall concluded that they had made a planning error in relying on refueling 14 miles away. They could have moved that to within four miles of LZ X-ray. The difference seemed small but translated into minutes. Minutes sometimes meant life or death.

One lingering effect of the high profile of these battles was a misperception that the Ia Drang and within that the events of 14–17 November was the 1CD's one and only big fight while Kinnard commanded the division. In reality, the 1CD conducted another, longer, equally difficult, and equally successful campaign. This was often called Bong Son after a SF camp in the area. This campaign came in Binh Dinh province, which was vastly different from the Ia Drang. Binh Dinh was heavily built-up, with many clusters of hamlets and about 800,000 people— four times that in the Highlands. Much more than the Ia Drang, Binh Dinh resembled the situation Kinnard had shown the CSA at Fort Campbell and that led to Kinnard's heading the 11th. In the Binh Dinh operation, every brigade in the 1CD participated and the division maintained continuous contact with the enemy for about 60 days. In Vietnam, where maintaining contact to wear down the enemy was the objective and the enemy generally avoided that, it was extremely hard to achieve contact for anything like that long. The battles in Binh Dinh were also significant in another way. Operations in this case started off with bad weather, reminiscent of the adverse conditions in the Carolinas during Air Assault II. In this case, although the enemy sought to disperse, the air assault units achieved surprise. Air cavalry repeatedly trapped enemy forces between attackers and blockers. In 41 consecutive days of combat the combined U.S. and ARVN forces largely destroyed three regular NVA regiments. Those elements that survived were scattered, disorganized, and isolated. The ARVN took control of large areas that the NVA and VC had long dominated.

By the time he left command of the 1CD in 1966, Kinnard was highly impressed by an air assault division's ability to strike over great distances. Even more impressive was the ability to do that repetitively. He was also impressed at air assault's capability to mass. Even when the enemy initially had more forces and achieved surprise, this ability to mass made a critical difference. The division also developed new TTP during combat. Among these was the idea of seizing an area that could be used briefly for artillery to support an assault. This tactic was distinct from what later became institutionalized as the firebase, of which Kinnard thought less highly.

In all this, Aviation was the linchpin—the key combination of technology, ideas, and people who made it all possible.

Build-up, 1966–1967

Even before the Pleiku Campaign ended, it was clear that Army involvement in Vietnam would grow dramatically. By the end of November 1965, estimated numbers of required U.S. troop strengths that were less than six months old more than doubled to almost 500,000. This escalation had several effects on Aviation. The most obvious was creation of the new, 1AB, which stood up in Vietnam. Through 1966 and 1967, Army forces in Vietnam continued to expand, as did Aviation 's engagement. These expansions created huge strains across the board. A few examples will illustrate.

Increasing operational tempo (OPTEMPO)—tripling or more

By mid-1966 the OPTEMPO of Army Aviation in Vietnam was astonishing. As just one measure, by April 1966, Army helicopters flew 12 times as many combat sorties as the U.S. Air Force and Vietnamese Air Force (VNAF) combined. In December 1966 the CSA noted that, comparing July 1965 to July 1966, Aviation had flown four times as many sorties, four times as many passengers, three times as many hours, and more than three times as much cargo. Despite the huge buildup, the number of Aviation Soldiers killed by hostile action remained about the same. Fort Wolters had tripled its monthly output of new pilots to 300. Among the most pleasing achievements was that helicopter evacuation of the wounded had cut deaths from wounds from about ten to one in prior wars to about one in a hundred. By late 1966 confidence in Aviation as a core part of future warfare was running high, as reflected in GEN (ret.) Howze's conclusion from a visit to Vietnam. Without the helicopter the U.S. would be subject to defeat just as the French earlier. The French had succumbed to "the tactic of ambush." The helicopter let U.S. forces travel without being subject to such ambush and allowed quick reinforcement when ambushes did happen. This fact greatly reduced the effectiveness of guerrilla tactics. More importantly, Howze saw the characteristics that made

Aviation important in Vietnam largely applicable in operations against more sophisticated enemies—the large, European battlefield.

Howze especially praised the door gunners, who he noted were highly regarded for their skill and courage. The door gunner was every bit as much a fighting man as was an infantryman. Aviation Soldiers shared that view of their roles. In July 1966 articles in the U.S. Army Aviation Digest proposed creating a Combat Aviation Badge or, copying the practice of the other services, designating Air Aces to recognize those who had served in combat. Authors argued that the Aviation badge only reflected a skill and was inadequate.

Door gunner with the 1st Cavalry Division

Adapting to meet immediate needs—Lightning Bugs and Chinook 'bombers'

As Aviation participation in Vietnam expanded, the creativity of Aviation Soldiers appeared in many adaptations of existing systems to meet practical needs. One example was the Lightning Bug mission, using C-123 landing lights mounted on a helicopter. Lightships operated in a team with an armed helicopter particularly to locate and destroy hostile boats operating on large rivers and canals. This innovation quickly spread to other units, where more ideas improved effectiveness. As in World War II, Army Aviators adapted normal aircraft to offensive missions. To help two companies of the 173d Airborne Brigade pinned down where vegetation was too thick for the companies' mortars, aviators rigged a wooden trough in the doorway of a Chinook and dropped mortar rounds. This technique killed or wounded about 200 VC.

Advent of the OH-6 Cayuse light observation helicopter (LOH)—Loach

In 1967 inadequacies of the venerable OH-13 Sioux for operations in Vietnam led to choosing a new light observation helicopter. As the HU-1 became the Huey, the OH-6 Cayuse LOH soon became the Loach.

Early recognition that losses of scout aircraft were high helped determine the characteristics of this new helicopter. Life expectancy of a scout aircraft was short. Many Loaches did not survive long enough to require its first 300-hour scheduled maintenance. So the new aircraft had to be cheap. This requirement led to both the rise and rapid demise of the Loach. When the Army returned to the manufacturer to buy replacements, Hughes raised the price. Rather than pay the new price, the Army reopened the competition for LOHs. After an ugly fight that involved Congress, the Army adopted the Bell OH-58 Kiowa—off-the-shelf, based on the civilian Jet Ranger.

To reduce the logistics burden, the Army insisted that Bell use the same engine in the OH-58 as was in the OH-6. This change degraded performance of the OH-58, which weighed 600 pounds more than the OH-6. This difference quickly gave the OH-58 a bad reputation within the air cavalry. A common belief was that the selection was a political sell-out.

The Loach first reached Vietnam in October 1967 in the 7th Squadron, 17th Cavalry Regiment (7/17 Cav). Its pilots and troops that worked with it in the field generally loved the Loach. It was extremely maneuverable at low altitudes and low speeds. The aircraft had the shape and structural virtues of an egg—extremely crashworthy. It could stay aloft for about two and a half hours. It had enough power to hover and inspect enemy areas while still carrying an extra door gunner with an M-60 machinegun. Loaches literally flew down trails under the jungle canopy and tracked NVA, then burst up through the canopy when the enemy sprang out at the aircraft.

The Loach's capabilities changed tactics. Previously, the reconnaissance squadron of the 1–9th Cavalry used its gunships and scout helicopters in pairs—two of each type of aircraft. The OH-13s would fly close to the ground, doing the scouting. Two gunships would fly above them and provide cover. With Cobra and Loach, organization changed to independent pairs of a gunship and a scout. This became known as a Pink Team—from the former White Team designating the scouts and Red Team designating the guns. By 1969 the Pink Team had proven so successful in the air cavalry that the rest of the Army adopted it. This new tactic maximized the effectiveness of the Cobra but greatly increased the danger for the scout crew.

The Loach pilot and his crew chief/gunner lived precariously. Flying almost at ground level, the Loach crew was within range of any weapon. The enemy also had a big incentive to hit the Loach. The enemy knew well that, if the Loach discovered him, he was almost as good as dead. So, Loaches faced a wide range of countermeasures, including wires strung between hillsides and specially-rigged booby traps. One type was a VC flag flying on a pole and attached to a large shell. If a Loach pilot or gunner grabbed the flag for a war trophy, he detonated the round.

OH-6 on a scouting mission

Ethical challenges—firing on noncombatants and Soldiers not resisting

By the Bong Son campaign in February 1966, an aspect of the Vietnam War that would become one of its hallmarks appeared. That was the dilemma for Soldiers to decide whether or not to kill people that rules of warfare and a basic sense of humanity normally protected. Every war challenges each combat Soldier on basic values, but Vietnam became notorious in this aspect. One scout pilot's experiences illustrated such challenges.

In February 1966 David Bray flew a H-13 Sioux scout helicopter in Operation Masher. He and fellow scout pilots quickly found that their usual tactics of finding the enemy and then firing on them to fix them in place until infantry, artillery, or air strikes could come in were unnecessary. The enemy was so thick in the area that no spot reports were needed. All the scouts could do was draw fire and try to stay alive. At one point in this melee, Bray and his fellow scout helicopter found themselves crossing a large rice paddy with about eight small villages around it. Like spokes of a wheel, paths ran from the center of the paddy to each village. Enemy machineguns were all around the paddy. Several Hueys had already been shot down and were burning in the paddy. At the altitude the scouts were flying—about ten feet—the enemy held fire with their heavier weapons to avoid hitting neighboring villages. Mostly the scouts took sniper fire as they crisscrossed the paddy. Suddenly Bray realized that an old woman was right in the middle of the paddy. She seemed to be paying no attention—just planting rice. After they flew past her the first time, Bray realized that the woman must be acting as a pointer for the gunners. She could see above the treetops all around the paddy. Whichever way the helicopters approached, she would face. That alerted the gunners and let them concentrate their fire. Bray told his gunner to shoot the woman. Before he could turn for another pass, the other scout had shot her.

Bray had more trouble killing some NVA Soldiers he encountered a few days later. After some very heavy fighting with the 1CD, the NVA regiments simply started to evaporate. Groups of three or four NVA split off, dispersed in the midst of the fighting, hid, and would rejoin their units later to resume fighting. Bray was among scout pilots assigned to locate the fleeing enemy and call for an infantry platoon to come pick them up for questioning. Once the scouts found the enemy, they called in for the infantry but were asked if the enemy was showing signs of surrender. Bray said no. The order came to kill them, because no one could come take them prisoner. Bray found this task hard, because he seemed to be killing in cold blood. He had to accept the idea that this was the only way to counter the enemy's tactic of dissolving into such small groups that they could not be handled conventionally.

Restraint on killing was not unusual. Roger Paulmeno, a Loach door gunner, said, "I didn't hate the Vietnamese. I didn't even dislike them…I only killed in self-defense or when our lives were in immediate jeopardy. I always allowed the other fellow the dignity of firing first."

Creation of the 1st Aviation Brigade (1AB)

The signal organizational event for Aviation during the Vietnam period was creation of the 1AB, officially constituted on 25 April 1966 as Headquarters and Headquarters Company, 1AB. This was the first time Aviation had a unit at this echelon.

The organization was born on the run. BG Seneff, the brigade's first commander, was already the Aviation Officer in Headquarters, U.S. Army Vietnam (USARV). Between 1966 and 1973, the 1AB played vital roles in supporting operations in Vietnam. In June 1970 the 1AB reached its greatest strength. It had four combat aviation groups, 16 combat aviation battalions, 83 companies with more than 4000 aircraft and 27,000 Soldiers. On 24 March 1973 the unit redeployed from Vietnam to Fort Rucker and deactivated on 6 April. Its legacy continued. On 18 February 1977 the 1AB reactivated at Fort Rucker as a school brigade. In 1982 an exception to Army policy let the 1AB as a TDA organization wear the insignia of the old, field 1AB.

Worldwide drain of Army aviators and expansion of WO aviator program

The rapid expansion of operations in Vietnam created a worldwide crisis for Aviation in manpower. This had several effects—both immediate and long-term.

The Army Staff level clearly saw a gap between numbers of aviators and planned deployment of aviation units. In January 1966 HQDA told Military Assistance Command, Vietnam (MACV) that the Army had only 9700 pilots against a requirement of 14,300 for June.

Several alternatives were used to meet requirements. One was to underman companies in Vietnam—to the point units could not fly aircraft they maintained. Pilots flight time rose to 140–160 hours per month. That OPTEMPO began to take a toll. The Army also drained aviators from other parts of the world. These shifts often disrupted families. The Army also assigned relatively senior officers to lower-grade duties. Some companies that went over in the initial build-up had 15 to 20 majors in them, just filling cockpit seats. For many, assignment to Aviation duties in Vietnam became repetitive, damaging careers tied to ground tours.

Another effect was to expand numbers and importance of WO aviators. This expansion created some misgivings. This new WO would only have about 220 hours of flying experience. Often he was only 19 years old. Those who doubted, including BG Seneff, changed their minds after the first WOs had been in Vietnam for about two months. The new WO pilots were superb for two reasons. These youngsters had been carefully selected. The Army could be very selective, because the WO pilot program was very popular.

Support to special operations forces (SOF)

During Vietnam Aviation played an active part in supporting SOF—particularly insertion and extraction of covert forces, as well as fire support. This support involved both regular units, which responded as needed, and separate detachments assigned directly to SOF. Much of this work involved the Military Assistance Command Vietnam—Studies and Observation Group (MACV-SOG). This was a Joint, covert unit created to run covert operations that the military had taken over from the Central Intelligence Agency (CIA) in January 1964. SOG missions were truly Joint/Combined operations. Usually they involved both rotary-wing and fixed-wing assets of at least the U.S. Air Force and VNAF, as well as Army helicopters. Often the missions also included Marine aviation.

Innovations—extraction devices and techniques

Supporting SOG involved a variety of unorthodox techniques and innovations. Among these were two special extraction devices. First Sergeant Norman Doney developed one device from aluminum cable ladders from Chinooks, also adapted for Hueys. This device reduced the need for perilous entry into a restrictive LZ. Anyplace a Huey could hover 28 feet above the ground allowed insertion or extraction.

SGM Charles McGuire developed a device for emergency extractions that was simply a 100-foot length of rope with a loop in the end. Within that loop was a padded seat. The McGuire rig let the passenger sit just as if on a playground swing. This rig was much faster than a winch and allowed much quicker escape. It also posed hazards of snagging in trees that forced cutting the line and meant hovering vulnerable to fire. Exposure could be fatal for riders flown through bad weather.

Bad experiences with the McGuire rig, even after a wrist loop was added, led to devising the STABO rig—an acronym made from the first letter of the five inventors' last names. This rig allowed a man to attach a special yoke to a web harness. The STABO rig also let the man rescued fire a weapon.

Increasing risk in SOG operations—including layered air defense (AD)

SOG operations became riskier as the war progressed. By mid-1967 the NVA had developed techniques to alert them to the approach of helicopters. One method was to dig a four-foot-wide hole into a hillside. That let an observer hear vibrations long before he could hear the helicopter. He signaled nearby forces that relayed the signal. The NVA also regularly watched possible LZs and trail crossings. The NVA even used radio direction finding, pinpointing locations to within 200 yards for precise fire. The NVA also learned to attack teams after they had entered areas where terrain masked radio calls for help. By late 1967 SOG teams also became the targets of elite, North Vietnamese counter-reconnaissance units.

By late 1967 there were signs of far worse to come for Aviation. One was increasing density and sophistication of air defenses inside Cambodia and Laos using mobile, 12.7mm antiaircraft guns. Another was a shift in priorities. In Cambodia SOG operatives became bait for NVA gunners hunting helicopters.

Special importance of gunships—role of Cobra and ARA

In 1967 helicopter gunships acquired a new, vital role for SOG in Project Daniel Boone. This involved SOG teams operating inside supposedly-neutral Cambodia. Everything was under conditions of strict deniability. U.S. operatives in Cambodia had no identification, used foreign weapons, and would be denied as having any connection with the U.S. if captured or killed.

The only support for these teams was helicopter gunships. These could fire only in self-defense or to help an endangered team escape. Weekly reports for Project Daniel Boone from July through December 1967 showed about two gunship missions for every three missions.

Aerial rocket artillery (ARA) units, with their high volume of direct fire, were especially valuable for SOG.

The Cobra, when it arrived, proved ideal for SOG. The Cobra could turn tightly at treetop level. It carried a huge store of ordnance. Above all, for teams in contact, the Cobra could fire its minigun to within 20 meters of friendly troops.

Special satisfaction of working with SOG

While support for SOG teams was the most dangerous kind of mission, aircrews considered it the most desirable. These operations often included being part of peak events. For example, in 1970 Army Hueys from the 57th Assault Helicopter Company and Cobras from the 361st Attack Helicopter Company carried out a daring operation to snatch a truck driver on the Ho Chi Minh Trail in Laos in an area saturated with NVA. Not one prisoner had come out of the area in over a year.

Suitability of the young, WO Aviator

Army WO pilots were superb for SOG operations. Some seemed too young for the dangers to faze. WO Mike Taylor of the 57th Assault Helicopter Company told a Marine colonel who said that the tactics Taylor described were suicidal that 'the tactics are sound—the mission is suicidal.'

Logistical demands and responses

In large measure, success in creating the airmobile division and especially in expanding combat operations in Vietnam depended on the logistical tail for Aviation. The logistical structure that existed before 1962 was inadequate in several aspects to meet the new challenges. Over the next several years, several key changes occurred. Besides a vast expansion in scale, these changes included different ways to organize supply and maintenance. The section above about the 11th has already touched on some aspects. Some of those carried over to other parts of the Army. However, there were also changes in ideas, organizations, and technology that emerged directly in response to the battlefield, as well as in anticipation of the way events in Southeast Asia seemed likely to go. Some of the ideas that emerged and became practice during Vietnam reemerged a generation later. Among these was the idea of some kind of Aviation logistical facility afloat. As always, behind all of these changes were people who came up with the ideas and made things happen.

Meeting the demands for aircraft—making war in peacetime

The vast expansion of Aviation with Vietnam strained industry to produce helicopters. Partly the strain reflected the still-small, highly-specialized nature of the rotary-wing industry. The difficulty in responding to a surge demand, though, also reflected some basic changes in the nation in the 20 years from the end of World War II to the ramp-up in Vietnam. In that time, American commerce and industry had grown profitable in a consumer-oriented economy. There was relatively little interest in shifting away from those sources of income to meet military needs.

The initial production order for the UH-1A Iroquois (Huey) called for 173 aircraft. That run was finished in March 1961. Production of the UH-1B began in March 1961 and went into 1965, with slightly more than 1000 produced for the Army. As the Army's use of the Huey increased in Vietnam, the other services also wanted Hueys, as did more than a dozen other nations. Production of the UH-1D, which began in 1963, delivered more than 2000 to the Army by the end of production in 1967. The Army acquired more than 3500 UH-1Hs. These were identical to the D except for a more powerful engine. Another 1300 of the UH-1Hs went to other nations.

As demand rapidly grew after 1965, Bell, the manufacturer of the Huey, had increasing trouble keeping pace with the Army's delivery dates. At one point, when Bell was producing about 75 new aircraft each month, an Army official visited Bell and asked how long it would take to double production. Bell was already producing as many transmissions as it could and had already subcontracted with every other maker of the transmissions for all they could produce. The only way to increase production was to build another transmission factory. The official said, on the spot, that if Bell would build the factory, the government would provide the equipment for it. Subsequently at the peak, Bell could produce about 150 Hueys each month.

Aviation repair and the USNS Corpus Christi Bay— Aviation repair afloat

Even at the beginning of unit-size Aviation operations in Vietnam, concerns surfaced about supplies, maintenance and repair. At the same time, senior leaders saw the need to expand in-theater support to Aviation. One spin-off was work toward establishing something similar to the Aircraft Repair Unit-Floating (ARU(F)) of World War II. This emerged as the USNS Corpus Christi Bay, which played a small but valuable role over several years and occasionally reemerged in later years as the touchstone for a concept to provide forward-deployed, depot-level support.

Rising demands and creative solutions for Aviation maintenance in Vietnam

Throughout 1962 Army aircraft in Vietnam consistently exceeded programmed flying hours and exceeded availability norms. Availability ran about 75 percent. This level, though, defied inadequacies in the supply and support systems. People overcame these inadequacies by continuous, maximum use of people and facilities. Success also required innovative techniques. Among these techniques was extensive cannibalizing.

An early response to shorten the turnaround time for growing numbers of repairs to a growing number of aircraft was to pull depot-level work back from civilian contractors and put it within government facilities. The Army terminated its contract in the CONUS for overhauling helicopter engines. The work shifted to the Army Aeronautical Depot Maintenance Center (ARADMAC) at Corpus Christi, Texas. The Army established a regular flow of broken aircraft from and repaired aircraft to Vietnam using Air Force cargo aircraft.

Intratheater support—idea of a floating aircraft maintenance facility (FAMF) revived

At the same time, senior leaders saw the need to expand in-theater support to Aviation. One spin-off was work toward establishing a floating aircraft maintenance facility, similar to the Aircraft Repair Unit-Floating (ARU(F)) of World War II. On 9 November 1962 LTG Frank S. Besson, commanding AMC, assigned LTC John F. Sullivan as project officer for Operation Flat Top. Sullivan's mission was to create a floating aircraft maintenance facility. LTC Sullivan was a direct, personal tie between the World War II ARU(F), code named Ivory Soap, and the new program. Sullivan had served in the AAF and was directly involved in the ARU(F) project.

Choosing a specific ship, planning and designing the changes for its new use, and then converting it proved to be a complex, lengthy, frustrating, and expensive task. A special team, including several enlisted men like Marcellus Karrigan, who had started as aircraft mechanics trained by the Air Force in the mid-1950s, crawled through all sorts of ships. They finally chose a decommissioned, World War II seaplane tender. The team then designed shops. This was a cumbersome process because of the technology at the time. For each design, craftsmen would build a three-dimensional model, used to estimate funding required. The project slowed down for almost a year and threatened to stall altogether over a host of issues, including legal issues about a civilian crew under the Geneva Convention, costs of conversion, and interservice concerns. Eventually Sullivan got Congressman Mendel Rivers of South Carolina to help. Rivers, chairman of the House Armed Services Committee, wanted work in his district and talked the SECDEF into supporting the project.

The project ran up costs. Initial cost estimated at less than $5 million became $25 million with design changes. The ship also required standing up two, new Transportation battalions. These would alternate manning the ship and augmenting the depot at Corpus Christi, Texas, when not deployed.

On 18 February 1966 the ship, renamed the USNS Corpus Christi Bay (CCB), finally sailed for Vietnam. After transit of six weeks, on 2 April 1966, the ship began seven years of service. Production increased slowly and stayed below planned through mid-1967 but was still highly valuable. Its work avoided costs and, more importantly, returned aircraft to use more quickly. The ship returned deadlined aircraft in an average of six days compared to 18 days for aircraft returned to CONUS. By mid-1974 a host of factors converged and led HQDA to reject continuing the project. Among considerations were direct costs of maintaining the ship during a time of fiscal constraint in the Vietnam drawdown, along with the increasing promise of having air-transportable temporary repair facilities and eliminating the two battalions. On 8 January 1975 the CCB left Corpus Christi, Texas, for stripping and further disposal.

The overall value of the CCB and its contribution were debated. Combinations of resistance both within the Army and between the services prevented the original idea of having a fleet of five ships becoming reality. The predominant argument at the time was over the cost-effectiveness of the ship and its operations. In part, issues of costs and benefits were a byproduct of the arcane way the federal government compartmentalizes funds—what is often called different colors of money. The value of work done on the CCB depended on who was counting. Production fell under two types of accounts. One type the Army in Vietnam directly paid for; the other, it did not. Favorable appearances in the ways costs were accounted by command weighed more heavily than the utility or even the comparative repair/replacement costs of items the ship the turned around.

Assessments of the value of a floating aircraft maintenance facility varied. LTC Joseph P. Cribbins, who retired from active duty while working on this project and became a civilian special assistant to the Deputy Chief of Staff for Logistics (DCSLOG), did not see the CCB making a substantial difference. He did believe that the ship provided immediate, stopgap support at the tactical level. This included the ability to make spare parts that were in short supply and difficult to obtain through supply channels outside the theater. This kind of service was the main purpose and achievement of the ARU(F) during World War II. LTG Seneff expressed very similar views in 1978. The one value Seneff particularly saw was the basic quality that has justified Aviation through its life—responsiveness to the ground commander's needs. Usually the ship had the part someone needed; if not, the ship could usually make it. The idea of some similar capability reemerged over the years. In 2004 AMC again considered the basic idea.

Basic organization of maintenance in Vietnam

During the years of Vietnam, the organization of Aviation logistics—particularly maintenance and supply—changed.

Echelons of maintenance—from five to three

When the Army acquired the responsibility for aircraft maintenance from the Air Force, the Army retained the basic ideas of organization. These provided for three categories of maintenance. At the lowest level was organizational maintenance. The using unit performed this type on its own equipment. It involved inspecting, cleaning, adjusting and replacing minor parts. The next higher level was field maintenance, done by units providing direct support (DS) to the users. This involved repairing or replacing broken or worn-out parts and subassemblies. Above this was the depot level. This was mainly major overhauls or complete rebuilding, requiring extensive and expensive tools and skilled people.

Where the Air Force had defined three echelons for this maintenance, the Army broke these functions into five. First and second echelons were organizational. Third and fourth were field. Fifth was the depot level.

Over the years in Vietnam, the Army compressed this arrangement. It first went to four levels. By 1973 the Army had only three levels. These were defined as Aviation Unit Maintenance (AVUM), performed within the using unit and incorporating some of the work previously done by the DS unit. AVUM included all preventive and some corrective maintenance. Intermediate Support

(IS) combined DS and general support (GS) maintenance. IS included repairs that required some special tools, test equipment, and skilled procedures. IS also included trouble-shooting and assistance teams. Later IS was redefined as Aviation intermediate maintenance (AVIM). Depot maintenance remained what it had been. The differences rested on the cost and sophistication of the tools and skills of people at each level.

Providing responsiveness in the field—KD teams to Aviation Unit Maintenance (AVUM)

Among the more important organizations in the aviation maintenance scheme were DS maintenance detachments structured to support specific aviation units. The most well known were the detachments that supported each Assault Helicopter Company equipped with Hueys. These were called KD teams. KD was not an acronym but a composite designation, referring to an exhibit in a specific publication, TOE 55–500. That TOE laid out the units, their missions, where they fit in the overall organization, their capabilities, and their basis of allocation. A similar DS maintenance team existed for each Transportation helicopter company that required field maintenance but did not have other such support. A KD team accompanied each of the first helicopter companies that deployed to Vietnam. For these first helicopter units, mostly operating in local areas, there was no formal network of support. The units relied heavily on help from civilian contractors, CIA support personnel, and the KD teams. Units heavily cannibalized damaged aircraft for parts. That practice, along with lots of improvising, kept aircraft flying far beyond the official intervals for hours between repair and replacement.

Subsequent to the deployment of the 1CD in 1965 as additional non-divisional aviation companies were activated in CONUS for deployment to Vietnam, a 55–500 DS Detachment was activated, equipped and trained to deploy with it and support it in country. In Vietnam, these units were normally co-located with the aviation company they supported, but their chain of command was through DS maintenance rather than aviation channels.

Within the first few months of aviation operations in Vietnam, USARV determined that it would be advantageous to integrate these detachments with the aviation units they supported. Essentially, they became an organic element of the aviation unit under a unified operational chain of command. The result was more responsive and effective maintenance operations at unit level. Maintenance crews took great pride in the increased aircraft availability that resulted from pooling the resources of organizational and DS maintenance into a cohesive team that performed more disciplined scheduled and unscheduled maintenance in a command supported environment. Because aviation unit commanders were now fully responsible for both organizational and DS maintenance, they exercised greater discipline in the commitment of aircraft for daily operations. This change ultimately achieved a prudent balance between operations and maintenance that gave consistently high availability rates. USARV found that under this maintenance arrangement, aviation unit commanders were less likely to 'fly their units into the ground' as had happened in some units in the early stages of the build-up. This integrated maintenance approach was what became commonly referred to as the decentralized maintenance concept.

In 1967 USARV recommended to HQDA that the decentralized maintenance concept be adopted across the board and institutionalized in the TOEs of all aviation units. In spring, 1968, CSA Harold K. Johnson advised LTG Bruce Palmer, USARV deputy commander, that Johnson had approved the decentralized maintenance concept for all non-divisional aviation units. Johnson hesitated to approve the concept for divisions until it could be tested. He directed Palmer to test it in an infantry division. Palmer and MG Robert R. Williams arranged with MG Julian Ewell to test the concept in the 9th Infantry Division. The USARV Aviation Plans Office worked with the 9th's division support command (DIS-COM) to structure and implement the decentralized maintenance system. It worked reasonably well but did not achieve the significant improvement in availability rates found in the 1AB and later in the airmobile divisions. The difference reflected the paucity of aviation in an infantry division as then structured.

The move to decentralized maintenance in the 1CD followed that in the 1AB but was slower. The delay reflected the unavailability of small, compact tool sets such as later fashioned for the 101AB. Originally units were limited to unit-level maintenance. Experience with the 1CD, though, proved that this constraint did not let the unit achieve an operational readiness (OR) rate high enough to support combat requirements. That led to adding DS detachments to handle about 60–70 percent of this type of work. By 1969 that approach had proven unsatisfactory. So, in 1969, two of four DS companies were broken up. Their assets went into 19 helicopter units in the 1CD. This change, along with adding 175 more maintenance technicians at the division level, raised overall monthly availability from 63 hours to 88.

At least one more major change occurred. Bottlenecks occurred at the depot level because critical parts were unavailable to restore aircraft to flying condition. This situation was called Not Operationally Ready—Supply (NORS). A particular problem became T-53 engines for the Cobras after Tet in 1968. In part, this situation reflected how workload was assigned at different echelons. Too much maintenance had been pushed down to the DS level. There simply were not enough skilled technicians, parts, and facilities to keep up the pace. So Vietnam held a backlog of unserviceable engines. At the same time, those broken engines were not getting back to CONUS depots to be fixed and become available there. To fix this situation, logisticians established a routine shuttle of Air Force C-141s. Three C-141s ferried unserviceable engines out of Vietnam and carried serviceable engines back. This system worked superbly. Thereafter, even though flying hours and combat increased, NORS for engines disappeared. A byproduct of this change was a decrease in the total numbers for many costly parts in the logistical pipeline.

By 1971 it was clear that the distribution of workloads at the different echelons of maintenance was out of balance with the structure. About 70 percent of the DS maintenance was at unit level, and about 75–80 percent of GS maintenance had migrated back to depots in CONUS. On that basis, the decision came to realign structures from four to three levels. During 1971 three-level maintenance was implemented, but in Korea, rather than Vietnam. Success of that trial led to revising doctrine to have only three echelons, which became the post-Vietnam standard.

Reducing frequency and intrusiveness of maintenance—TIMS

One way to improve the availability of aircraft was to reduce the number of times and amount of time per event that an aircraft was down for some kind of scheduled maintenance. Even before the Vietnam buildup, Army logisticians realized that the Army was artificially lowering availability by over-maintaining aircraft. Too frequent and intrusive inspection resulted in damaged parts. Parts that were fine got broken when someone tried to remove or install them during inspection.

Events overcame plans to remedy this situation. With operations ramping up in Vietnam, the Army leadership decided not to tinker with scheduled maintenance. By 1966, though, the impact of scheduled maintenance on aircraft availability drew enough attention to force a change. This was especially true for the training fleet at Fort Rucker.

In 1966 the Army adopted what it called the Tailored Inspection Maintenance System (TIMS) at USAAVNC. TIMS phased scheduled maintenance to minimize longer periods of downtime. With this change, the man-hours required to maintain aircraft dropped by about two-thirds while availability at Fort Rucker jumped from about 55 percent to 80–85 percent. TIMS proved so successful in the training fleet that the intention was to field test it in Vietnam. That plan fell victim to disruptions from the Tet Offensive in 1968. Nonetheless the success led to a study begun in 1971 and Project INSPECT. This sought to cut down the number and frequency of inspections only to specific components meeting certain conditions. These were where the inspector could detect deterioration or where potential failure could be seen or forecast. This shifted the basic concept to what was called On Condition Maintenance (OCM).

Dealing with the aftermath and a shift in concept

As combat ended in Vietnam and aircraft began to return to CONUS, logisticians discovered that units had kept their best aircraft and turned in their worst for overhaul. This put an unexpected strain on the depot system. However, since what the units had done made perfectly good sense from an operational viewpoint, logisticians simply changed the way to handle the situation. They established Project EXTEND. Under this concept, all aircraft returning from Vietnam went through a modified depot overhaul. This returned aircraft to the units at about one-third the cost of a depot overhaul. This approach also led to abandoning the idea of having a complete overhaul of Army aircraft every five years in peacetime. Instead, the Army opted for OCM. Under this system a team performed an aircraft condition evaluation (ACE) every year and assigned a numerical rating. Individual aircraft were then inducted for depot maintenance based on a priority of Worst First. By 1975 this approach cut the number of aircraft undergoing programmed overhaul by about 20 percent and avoided costs of about $14 million.

Lessons in hindsight—emergency responses become the norm

One of the larger observations that came out of experience with Aviation logistics in Vietnam was that changes that were almost always the response to an emergency often became the norm after the emergency ended. Sometimes structures that developed to meet emergencies proved so useful that they carried over long after the emergency ended. One example of that was the creation of intensive management for support, maintenance, and retrograde of key pieces of equipment. Initially this focused on major pieces of ground equipment—tanks and armored personnel carriers (APC). Special problems with helicopter engines led HQDA, to extend this approach to those Aviation items in 1967. In November 1967 U.S. Army Pacific (USARPAC) hosted the first conference for this purpose. This two-week conference in Hawaii evolved into an annual conference at Aviation Systems Command (AVSCOM) headquarters in St. Louis. The scope of concerns addressed also expanded to all aspects of Aviation. Eventually this conference became the annual Worldwide Aviation Logistics Conference (WALC) that still continues.

Aviation as key part of logistical support in Vietnam

One of Aviation 's key roles in Vietnam was logistical support. Providing this support took Aviation in several directions. Among these was the acquisition of new aircraft. Another was innovations in TTP using existing aircraft.

Development of the CH-54 Tarhe (Flying Crane)

Expectations of requirements for high-volume, sea-based logistics led the Army to acquire the CH-54 Tarhe (Flying Crane). The first Cranes arrived in the 10th Air Transport Brigade in 1963 while the 11th was undergoing its trials. Expecting that a lot more would come by sea than air, the CH-54s would allow direct offload from ships offshore, eliminate the need for port facilities, and allow faster offloading. In practice the Cranes did little of this work but found heavy use ashore.

The Flying Crane reflected the way technology adapted in response to immediate needs. The CH-54 evolved from the H-37 Mohave, after the German government asked Sikorsky for a helicopter that could lift more than the H-37. Sikorsky modified the H-37 by removing most of the fuselage. The first Cranes were limited in their lift because they used H-37 transmissions and engines. Later conversions to twin gas turbines engines and an upgraded transmission let the Crane lift 12.5 tons. Lessons from the H-37 led to innovations on the Cranes. The retracting landing gear on the H-37 led to a jack-and-kneel system, which let the Crane stoop closer to a load, attach more snugly, and eliminate sway. Experience with the H-37 also led to letting the flight engineer handle the load from a jump seat in the cockpit That feature eliminated the need for a third pilot.

During the 11th Air Assault Division tests the Cranes performed well. In September 1965 the 478th Flying Crane Unit deployed to Vietnam as part of the 1CD. Cranes proved invaluable in lifting heavy construction equipment to mountaintops to create firebases, then emplacing heavy pieces of artillery into these often-isolated positions. As early as July 1966 Cranes had recovered aircraft worth $37 million—more than four times the cost of the four CH-54s. The Cranes also hauled a detachable pod that could be configured as a surgical operating room, with seats for up to 67 combat-loaded troops, or as a tactical operations center. The 'people pod' initially caused some misgivings among its passengers, who feared that it might detach in flight. This concern was overcome by installing positive-locking bolts. The imaginuity that Kinnard had fostered led to a way to create an instant LZ using a Crane with a 10,000-pound bomb. Only marginally useful for its basic purpose because of chest-high tree stumps it left, the technique effectively cleared hostile forces from the LZ.

CH-54 at Kontum firebase, 1969

The evolution of the Cranes in Vietnam reflected the kinds of adaptations that operations in new conditions often demand. To combat major problems with corrosive effects of dust in the engines, in 1967 Sikorsky applied engine air particle separators from earthmovers. Because the Crane's engines had so much more power than the transmission could take, these separators did not affect the Crane's performance.

Before the Vietnam era ended, the Crane, flown by Army pilots, gained international fame. During October–November 1971, Army aviators flying the CH-54 set a series of world records. The Crane beat the record for time-to-climb to 9000 meters previously held by the F-4 Phantom jet.

The Cranes eventually left the Army as a casualty of advancing technology. In the early 1980s the Chinook upgraded to the D model with improved engines. The CH-47Ds had the lifting capability of the Cranes. Other features of the Chinooks gave it more flexibility. Retiring the Cranes eliminated all the separate logistical pipelines associated with another aircraft type.

Transfer of the Caribous to the U.S. Air Force

One very controversial decision during the Vietnam years was the Army's decision to give up the Caribou to the Air Force. During the early years the Caribous had provided unequalled service to units in the field. The Air Force's takeover was strictly based on issues of roles and missions. It was well known that the Air Force had no aircraft with equivalent capability. Even so, after long and bitter wrangling at senior staff levels, on 6 April 1966, the Army and Air Force chiefs of staff agreed to the transfer of all Caribous. To no one's surprise, use of the Caribou in Vietnam became much more restricted, leaving many places previously served beyond that kind of support. Soon the Air Force dropped the Caribou from its fleet. Two lingering questions have been why the Army gave up the Caribou and what the relative costs and gains from this decision were.

Background of the Caribou

The Army received its first Caribous in 1959 under an exception to the weight limits imposed by the 1956 Army-Air Force agreement. Army planners saw the Caribou filling a gap between the C-130 and other Army aircraft. The Caribou was a companion to the Chinook to move Pershing missiles. Despite the 1956 agreement, the Air Force hated the Caribou, which could carry 32 passengers and had superior short-field characteristics. It easily went where the Air Force generally would not.

Troops ready to load Caribou in Operation Masher, 1966

The Caribou went to Vietnam because it was available and the Army wanted to support the troops in the field with a short take off and landing (STOL) aircraft in places that did not require a helicopter. When the first Caribou deployed to Vietnam in 1961 for field testing, Army aviators discovered the aircraft could operate out of all 130 military airstrips in country. Air Force C-47s and C-119s could use only 30. To improve its capabilities, the Army stood down the whole fleet and installed reversible propellers on them. That allowed the Caribou to pull up much more sharply without brakes.

Troops in the field loved the Caribou. In early 1963 the Caribous underwent six months of formal testing in Vietnam. Availability was consistently high. The Caribous supported Green Berets in inaccessible places. Later all sorts of cargoes were lifted into all kinds of fields. Whole villages of Montagnard tribesmen were resettled—complete with their families, chickens and cattle. Fuel was delivered to stranded helicopters. Casualties, when they occurred in large numbers, were quickly lifted to hospitals. The Caribous also lifted spare engines and parts, fresh water, food and other vital cargo. Its availability was a key asset. There were no long lead-times needed for processing requests; no tortuous channels to go through. If a commander felt he needed logistical help he just called his support-ing Caribou detachment commander. Seldom was a request denied. Almost never was a commander disappointed with the performance.

Reasons for the transfer—cargo versus gunship support

The transfer of the Caribou to the Air Force—Operation Maple Leaf—was almost as unpopular within the Air Force as within the Army. The Air Force really did not want the Caribou. Even some senior Air Force officers were unhappy about it. Limits on size and weight for aircraft were largely irrelevant, because the Army had already exceeded those.

In the end the driving force for the transfer was what the two service chiefs of staff saw as a distracter from the real business of supporting rising OPTEMPO in Vietnam. The issue was settled between the two, personally, one Saturday morn-ing. The two chiefs met in a closed-door conference. They hammered out the agreement and handed it out the door to CPT Carl J. McNair, the action officer for the Caribou and Buffalo in Office of the Chief of Research and Development.

Those around the CSA knew the rationale for the decision. Immediately upon taking over as Director of Army Aviation, BG Robert R. Williams was told the CSA would want to see him about the Caribou agreement. When they met GEN Johnson told Williams, 'We have had a long fight with the Air Force over arming helicopters. I believe the attack helicopter is vital to the Army. I am willing to give away the Caribou for the Air Force promise to stop its opposition to the Cheyenne.'

The decision to abandon the Caribou to the Air Force posed an ethical problem for some officers loyal to Aviation and the good of the Soldiers on the ground. COL Delbert L. Bristol, who had had the Caribous in the 10th Air Transport Brigade and was interim Director of Army Aviation, fought a rearguard action to try to get the decision reversed. When appeals within the Army failed, Bristol wrote directly to the SECDEF, who called in the CSA to explain. The CSA gave Bristol the options of finding a job elsewhere or retiring. Bristol immediately received several job offers and went to the Army Transportation Materiel

Command, but the Caribou episode probably kept him from becoming a general officer.

Larger impact

At least as seen from the headquarters level, the interservice agreement to transfer the Caribou to the Air Force in 1966 had relatively little impact in the short term. At the field level, the picture was different.

MAJ Dick Teipel, a Caribou pilot from the 11th and then with the 1CD in Vietnam, noted vast differences between Army and Air Force pilots making deliveries. Army pilots tried to make offloading and handling as easy as reasonably possible for the ground Soldiers who had to handle the cargo. He was disgusted to see Air Force crews dump cargo off ramps in ways that either broke bundles or forced the Soldiers to go into mud or other bad areas to retrieve their supplies and equipment.

BG Seneff, commanding the 1AB, saw a severe drop in service in the months following the transfer. The Army had operated the Caribou on the basis of responsiveness to needs in the field. If an isolated Aviation company needed one engine, the Army would send a Caribou with just one engine. The Air Force did not consider that cost-effective and would wait until a whole load built up. The difference translated into lots of Army aircraft sitting on the ground waiting for critical parts. Where it could, the Army started using Chinooks to support outlying areas the Caribous had served. A Chinook cost five times as much per hour to fly as a Caribou. Cost-effectiveness depended on who was paying the bill.

Sometimes the difference translated into endangering the lives of Soldiers. Years later, LTG (ret.) Seneff recalled such an incident. The 1st Infantry Division (1ID) had to be airlifted to rescue a brigade that was caught in the middle of the jungle and getting chopped up. Troops started flying out in mid-morning. An Air Force officer stopped operations mid afternoon because temperatures rose above 100 degrees. The 1ID had to truck its troops to the Air Force's main airfield, delaying half the brigade's arrival until next morning. The delay meant a lot of people getting killed. Seneff was furious.

Part of the difference in operations reflected the Army and Air Force pilots flying the Caribou. Army Caribou pilots were usually very senior, experienced WOs—among the best fixed-wing aviators to be found. They were also highly motivated to get their aircraft onto a thousand-foot strip and make the delivery without damaging the aircraft. In the Air Force pecking order, flying a Caribou was about as low as a pilot could go. So Air Force pilots often lacked the skills to do what the Army pilots had done and had no incentive to take risks Army pilots had taken.

In one sense, the horse trade between the two service chiefs was a windfall for the Army. Basically the Army relinquished totally to the Air Force both fixed-wing transport aircraft and the related mission. More importantly from the Army's standpoint, the Air Force recognized the Army's need for an armed helicopter. The major development at the time was the AH-56 Cheyenne. However, the high losses of aircrews in Vietnam had led the CSA to order buying Cobras to replace UH-1B gunships rather than wait for AH-56 Cheyenne. In March 1966, the month before the deal was struck on the Caribou, program approval was given for the AH-1G Cobra. The movement to acquire the Cobra had worsened the disputes between the Army and Air Force. Moreover, preparation was all but complete for deploying armed Chinooks. In giving up the Caribou and the Buffalo, the Army won acceptance of the idea that the Army had a mission of aerial fire support. The Air Force won an airplane they did not need and that was incompatible with their view of what an airlift airplane should be.

Training for Vietnam

Training for combat in Vietnam involved a huge expansion and took several forms. Prior to the build-up, only a hundred or so pilots graduated from Fort Rucker each month. Requirements grew to 700 a month. A key part of this expansion was increased use of simulations, which involved both air and ground Soldiers.

Simulations—Combined Arms Training System (CATS) at Fort Benning

A key part of preparing leaders for combat was capturing, building, and passing on the experience of Army aviators who had already been in combat. This occurred through sometimes relatively crude but effective use of simulations. At the Infantry School, an Aerial Employment Committee taught airborne and air assault operations. Members of that committee also wrote many of the new programs of instruction (POI) and were primary authors of some aviation manuals, including FM 57–35, Army Transport Aviation Combat Operations. A project called Combined Arms Training System (CATS) tried to simulate command and control of air assault operations from a helicopter. The team used what was then state-of-the-art technology—tape recorders, television sets, four salvaged airframes mounted on platforms with terrain boards, and mock-up consoles. Infantry officers going to Vietnam received about two days' training with the CATS. This included working through scenarios and staff who played the role of the ground commander and Soldiers doing battle on the ground, then a scenario where they had to fight a simulated battle against controllers. This simulation, though very basic, trained people to deal with battle from the third dimension. Battalion and brigade commanders that went to Vietnam wrote back and said that it really put them in good shape. Eventually CATS became a full-blown, computer-based family of simulations at Fort Leavenworth under BG Benjamin L. Harrison, an Army aviator.

Expansion of Aviation training during Vietnam

In response to the wartime expansion of the Army, Aviation expanded beyond most expectations of a few years earlier. The nucleus for this growth of Army aviation was USAAVNC, which had to respond in several ways.

Changes in length, content, and end-results of training

In 1964 USAAVNC developed and submitted a POI for an advanced flight training course to qualify new graduate helicopter pilots for assignment directly into operational Army aviation units in Vietnam. Rotation policies and ever-increasing commitments in Vietnam would soon require all new graduates to go directly to Vietnam. The challenge was unique because no other service sent newly rated pilots directly into combat. Also, a new course would take more critical resources in aircraft, instructor pilots and dollars, much in demand elsewhere.

In July 1965 Fort Wolters, Texas initiated the resulting POI—the 16/16 concept that replaced the previous 12/20 concept POI—12 weeks at Fort Wolters and 20 weeks at Fort Rucker. A concurrent change occurred with course content to ensure compatibility with the mission of training aviators for Vietnam. If training, such as cold weather operations, could not be utilized during the tour in Vietnam, it would be forgotten and was dropped. In terms of attrition, the results were highly favorable. Attrition that averaged 25 to 35 percent in the mid-1950s dropped under the 16/16 program. Many entering had flight training in Reserve Officer Training Corps (ROTC). Those who could not or preferred not to fly avoided flight training. Motivation levels increased with eager high-school graduates going into Warrant Officer Candidate (WOC) training and with fewer long-term NCOs entering. Many NCOs had applied only to get a transfer. Reducing the harsh regimen in WO orientation also reduced self-initiated losses. Dropping an arbitrary standard of soloing within 10 hours and adjusting training to the individual helped.

By contrast, low attrition in helicopter training at Fort Rucker had been and remained constant. From 1962 through 1966, losses never exceeded 2.5 percent or fell below 0.6 percent of input. It appeared that quality actually improved because of more demanding requirements and higher standards for completion. Feedback from Vietnam indicated graduates were successful. Ideally a new aviator would be qualified to be a copilot in Vietnam for his first six months, but new graduates were becoming aircraft commanders within 2–3 months after arriving. Safety data was also highly favorable:

Expansion in facilities, resources

Growth of the school during January 1966-June 1967 greatly exceeded any other period. The flying hour program at Fort Rucker more than doubled, from 31,000 hours per month in January 1966 to 70,000 in June 1967. In 1968 the yearly total was about a million flying hours. In late 1967 USAAVNC and satellites started building up to graduate as many as 7500 students annually. That exceeded all aviators in the Army before this buildup.

This growth meant acquiring and activating satellite training sites for initial entry primary fixed-wing training at Fort Stewart in July 1966. Hunter Air Force Base became Hunter Army Airfield, training Cobras. During 1966 USAAVNC installed three tactical ground control approach (GCA) radars and five tactical radio beacons. Total traffic count was 2,072,342 under visual flight rules (VFR) and 54,530 under instrument flight rules (IFR).

Changes in November 1972 signaled the beginning of the Vietnam drawdown. On 3 November Fort Wolters graduated its 40,000th student. On 11 November the Fixed Wing Qualification Course at Fort Stewart ended after six years.

Over only a few years Aviation had expanded its training base enough to produce the largest generation of aviators and Aviation Soldiers that would ever be, excluding the AAF in World War II. Responding to the demands of combat flying conditions, it had produced more capable aviators. The number of aircraft had more than doubled, while Aviation also transformed from half fixed-wing and half helicopters to 80 percent helicopters. It was a remarkable set of achievements.

Unit training—the finishing school

The training each pilot and air crewman received in school was only initial training. Much of what new pilots learned in the field units was at odds with what they had learned in flight school, and each unit had its own methods of completing preparations for actual tasks.

For pilots this ordinarily meant flying with more experienced pilots, even if these were more junior in grade. Many times the command pilot who taught a new lieutenant how to stay alive in Vietnam was a WO 1. Many times this command pilot had only a few months' experience. Any doubts about a newly-graduated pilot's status were erased by common terms of reference, like sandbag, implying that his ignorance made him dead weight in the cockpit.

Units expected new pilots to achieve basic proficiency quickly. An initial check ride was often the first flight on a mission. A new lieutenant would be assigned as a section leader but flew with each of the aircraft commanders in the section before being considered qualified. He had a final check ride with the platoon leader. Only then did a pilot get his callsign—usually composed of the unit's nickname, the platoon, and his position within the platoon. So, callsign of the second platoon leader in the 17th Assault Helicopter Company—Kingsmen— was Kingsman 26, with the number 6 always identifying the commander.

Units and even individual leaders at different levels had their own methods to evaluate new pilots. A particular concern was reaction under stress. Sometimes a practical joke tested these reactions, such as faking an attack on a group in an LZ when a new pilot was onboard.

1968—watershed and bloodiest year

For U.S. forces 1968 was the bloodiest in the war. From January through July 1968, the rate for killed in action (KIA) exceeded not only the Korean War but also both the Mediterranean and Pacific theaters during World War II. These rates led to reducing the OPTEMPO to hold down U.S. losses. A huge event, both militarily and psychologically, was the Communists' Tet Offensive, which began on the night of 30 January 1968—the lunar New Year. Although Communist forces suffered a crushing military defeat, people at home were shocked to see the television news showing U.S. forces trying to retake the U.S. embassy in Saigon. The tide of public opinion throughout the Free World shifted to a pessimism about the final outcomes. SECDEF McNamara resigned, and President Johnson announced that he would leave the Presidency at the end of his term. The course of events shifted to withdrawal from Vietnam, culminating in President Nixon's 'Peace with Honor" address to the nation on 23 January 1973.

The year 1968 opened with a high OPTEMPO for Aviation and occasioned many examples of heroism among Aviation Soldiers. January opened with demands for heroism. Within three days, MAJ Patrick H. Brady, a MEDEVAC pilot, and Private First Class (PFC) Gary G. Wetzel, a door gunner, distinguished themselves enough to receive the Medal of Honor. For actions on 31 January 1968 CWO Frederick Edgar Ferguson received the Medal of Honor. From the earliest hours of the Communist Tet offensive, Aviation was in the thick of things. Army helicopters brought help to the besieged Marines at the embassy. Throughout the fighting in Saigon, helicopter gunships engaged in house-to-house fighting. The gunships' miniguns and rockets were invaluable against structures the VC used as cover. Beyond Saigon, Aviation played its usual, vital roles as it airlifted assaults under fire into key places.

Both the power and limitations of air assault were reproved. In the bitter, months-long siege of the Marines at Khe Sanh, the 1CD was crucial to success. On 1 April, the entire 3d Brigade air-assaulted directly into key terrain. On 3 April the 2d Brigade air-assaulted into position southeast of Khe Sanh. The next morning the Marines began their own attacks. Over the next week, Joint operations broke the back of the besieging NVA. On 12 April, for the first time since the previous September, the 42 miles of road from Dong Ha to Khe Sanh was open. In the public's mind, Khe Sanh symbolized what was wrong with the whole war—an objective immediately abandoned after huge expenditures of men and materiel. Operation Delaware into the A Shau Valley drew less public notice but foreshadowed things to come. Intense AD shot down ten helicopters and damaged another 13 just in the first assaults.

Personal Courage—CWO Hugh Thompson and the massacre at My Lai

Sometimes great demands on courage come outside direct combat. Such a situation befell CWO Hugh Thompson, a Loach pilot, during the aftermath of the Tet Offensive. On 16 March 1968 Thompson and crew were enroute to support an operation called TF Barker, sweeping an area where VC guerrillas had been killing U.S. Soldiers by ones and twos with booby traps, mines, and sniper fire. As Thompson and his crew approached a village called Song My, which included a hamlet called My Lai, they saw large numbers of dead or wounded. When they discovered that a massacre of civilians was in progress, Thompson and his crew intervened—ultimately involving an armed confrontation. Their efforts allowed them to save several Vietnamese villagers. Eventually Thompson's action, along with those of some others aware of the events, led to an investigation and criminal charges against key figures involved in the massacre. Thompson meantime was interrogated by the House Armed Services Committee and defense attorneys, and was shunned by some fellow Soldiers. Finally, on 6 March 1998, at the Vietnam Memorial, an Army representative presented the Soldier's Medal to Thompson and his door gunner Lawrence Colburn—and posthumously to crew chief Glenn Andreotta, killed in action Vietnam. In 2004 Thompson was inducted into the Army Aviation Hall of Fame.

Conversion of the 101AB to Airmobile

Among the major events during 1968 was the creation of a second airmobile division with the 101AB converting from airborne to air-assault configuration. This transformation of a unit in the midst of wartime showed not only the flexibility of the Army as an institution but the impact of creative individuals.

Conversion almost did not happen because it threatened to reduce combat power following Tet. The initial plan provided for in-country conversion using non-divisional aviation units. These units were being activated in CONUS and were scheduled to deploy. After Tet the plan was revisited for a way to proceed without disrupting combat power. LTC Orlando E. Gonzales, the USARV Aviation Plans Officer, found that, to get DA approval for the conversion, USARV had said that the conversion could be done in-country using USARV manpower spaces and equipment. The spaces and equipment would come from non-divisional aviation units scheduled to arrive through the summer and fall. Upon arrival, these units would deactivate and restructure into airmobile units. Gonzales proposed simply activating the new aviation units in their airmobile configuration. That way, when they arrived, units would be combat-ready and increase combat power. This relatively simple solution overcame a major obstacle to the conversion.

Even then, Aviation shortages of tools and equipment almost stopped conversion. The 101st hoped to profit from the experience of the 1CD and the 1AB. This meant a decentralized structure. The key to this structure was making tool sets available. Supply catalogs listed only large, van-mounted sets originally designed for large DS maintenance companies. USARV Plans maintained that those tool sets were too large and cumbersome for airmobile operations. Smaller, lighter, more compact and tailored tool sets were needed for DS detachments in the decentralized concept. MG Williams, commanding 1AB, and MG Jack Norton at AVSCOM found a workable arrangement. Williams offered airmobile tool sets being procured for the 1AB to activate detachments on a schedule matching units they were to support. Within a week AVSCOM designed the smaller sets and sent a team to Vietnam that briefed the structure. The result was an organization that tied a maintenance cell with each company-sized aviation unit. This cell provided both DS and avionics maintenance. With these adjustments, the 101st had its Aviation group headquarters and most of its aviation units in place by August 1968.

1969—Beyond Tet, increasing and continuing dangers

Aviation operations in Vietnam did not slacken greatly after Tet. That was partly because Aviation remained central to the ability to conduct operations under prevailing conditions, even as those changed. In April 1969 U.S. troops reached their greatest number at 543,400. These factors made 1969 a peak year for Aviation. Annual output of pilots peaked at more than 7300. The 1969 Army flying-hour program was about 6.5 million hours.

The nature of the war had changed. Indigenous VC forces were destroyed during the Tet offensive. To fill VC ranks, Hanoi infused large numbers of regular Soldiers. By mid-1969 North Vietnam also adopted a strategy that used many, highly-trained, well-equipped sapper teams throughout South Vietnam. These teams would strike, night after night, and eventually bleed the South into submission. So the level of combat remained high and almost constant—especially at night.

MEDEVAC as a measure of the war—Medal of Honor, CWO Michael J. Novosel

One measure of the enemy's initiative was the demand for MEDEVAC: 1969 was the busiest time. For example, from March 1969 to March 1970, every pilot in the 82d Medical Detachment logged more than 1000 combat hours. The number of air ambulances at the end of 1969 was 140, compared to ten at the end of 1965.

The kind of dangers pilots in the 82d faced was reflected in events on 2 October 1969. That day, with no gunships or other cover available, CWO Michael J. Novosel flew 15 trips into intense enemy fire to save 29 ARVN Soldiers. For these actions, Novosel received the Medal of Honor. As a sidelight, Novosel's Medal of Honor was a byproduct of his efforts to look after his troops. In light of their extraordinary support, Novosel initiated Silver Stars for them. His write-ups caught GEN Creighton Abrams' attention, and Abrams recommended Novosel for the Medal of Honor.

Danger of aircraft fire—Sergeant First Class (SFC) Rodney J. T. Yano, Medal of Honor

1969 also produced a Medal of Honor for SFC Rodney J. T. Yano, a crew chief on an air cavalry command-and-control helicopter. During action against enemy forces in dense jungle, a grenade exploded prematurely. Yano was covered with burning white phosphorous and severely wounded. Flaming fragments caused ammunition to start detonating. Dense smoke filled the aircraft. The pilot could not see and lost control. Partly blinded and with only one arm usable, Yano began hurling blazing ammunition from the helicopter. Yano's actions saved the aircraft and crew, but his wounds were fatal. Yano's death reflected the need for fire retardant flight gear that the Army had just begun fielding in 1969. A maintenance training facility named Yano Hall stands at Fort Rucker

Aviation ground combat

Not all Aviation heroism involved aerial action. A recurrent event throughout the period was sapper attacks. On 11 May 1969, after a mortar barrage, about 100 sappers attacked a firebase where SP5 Orville W. Sergent was with the 366th Aviation Detachment (Provisional). He moved through the barrage to a position on the perimeter. When the barrage stopped and the sappers stormed the berm, Sergent fired on them with a rifle. As the sappers broke through the defense line, Sergent left the shelter of a bunker and engaged in hand-to-hand combat. He shot one sniper who had wounded a Soldier and killed two more of the enemy while fighting his way to two other wounded men, whom he removed to safety. A sniper killed the detachments sergeant, who was trying to get ammunition from a container. Sergent killed that sniper and began carrying ammunition to various firing points. For over two hours he remained in the open, fighting the enemy. His actions were key to preventing another penetration of the firebase. Sergent received the Distinguished Service Cross.

1970—the beginning of the end

By 1970 the war entered a different phase. Public support for the war, shaken in 1968, had eroded badly. A coup in Cambodia led the Nixon Administration to go after Communist sanctuaries there. Widespread campus protests followed. Congress repealed the Tonkin Gulf Resolution that had opened the door for expanded U.S. participation in Vietnam. By December 1970 U.S. troop levels had dropped to 280,000—about half the peak. U.S. losses fell dramatically. During the last week of October, 24 U.S. troops were KIA—fewest since the same week in 1965.

For Aviation 1970 was more like business as usual. During a typical month the 1AB carried more than 605,000 passengers and 60,000 tons of cargo. Each month 1AB aircraft logged more than 155,000 flight hours. In 1970 the number of Army aircraft peaked, and 82 percent were helicopters.

Changing force structure—inactivation of groups and battalions

One symptom of the overall drawdown was inactivation of Aviation units. For example, on 15 May 1970 the 10th Aviation Group inactivated at Fort Benning and the 20th Aviation Battalion inactivated at Fort Carson. Thus began a cascade of inactivations that paralleled the rapid expansion a few years earlier. At the same time, MEDEVAC OPTEMPO continued high. In 1970 for the first time, Medical Service Corps officers commanded battalion-size ambulance units.

Cambodia

In April 1970 a major ground offensive into Cambodia turned Vietnam into a true, Second Indochina War. The motive was the Communists' longstanding use of Cambodia as a sanctuary. When the enemy broke contact, it was easy to slip back across the border and become immune from pursuit but within easy striking distance any time they chose to attack again.

The change in MACV commanders represented different strategies. Time described GEN Westmoreland as 'a search-and-destroy and count-the-bodies man.' His successor, Creighton W. Abrams, was 'an interdict and weigh-the-rice man.' Abrams wanted to destroy the enemy's infrastructure. By 1970 trends in Laos increased interest in doing something about Cambodia. A military coup on 18 March 1970 gave the U.S. and Republic of Vietnam (RVN) an opportunity.

From 14 April until 30 June U.S. and ARVN forces ranged into Cambodia. By the end of the incursion, the allies had captured huge stockpiles of weapons and supplies. The allies also claimed to have killed 11,349 enemy Soldiers.

Aviation was essential to successes in Cambodia. U.S. forces had already begun drawdowns. The 4th Infantry Division (4ID) had lost a brigade and removed its headquarters east. Aviation had moved two of the 4ID's brigades from the eastern third of Vietnam to Cambodia without any forward operating bases.

The operational environment created special concerns for Aviation. The area was mountainous, with thick, triple-canopy jungle. LZs were scarce, could seldom handle four helicopters at once, and were well watched. Flying into Cambodia was unpredictable—sometimes without resistance and sometimes facing lethal AD, mainly from light weapons. Under prevailing conditions, dependency on Aviation caused problems. Over-extended supply lines haunted the whole operation. A lack of aviation fuel forward specifically hampered operations. Inadequate logistics cost lives. Shortage of spray oil to suppress dust in landing sites led to at least one fatal Aviation accident. Billowing dust disoriented a Chinook pilot, who landed atop a truck full of Soldiers.

Firebase Ripcord—'Thanks for saving our asses' and Medal of Honor of LTC Andre C. Lucas

Another event in 1970 that showed the value of Aviation to the ground Soldier was the bitter battle for Firebase Ripcord under COL Benjamin L. Harrison, an Army aviator. Ripcord, the last major battle that Army Infantry fought in Vietnam, ended only when Aviation extracted the 3d Brigade on 23 July.

Soldiers knew the importance of Aviation to them. On 23 July, amid intense mortar and small arms fire, a helicopter picked up six Soldiers. One handed the crew chief a note scrawled while waiting under fire. The one line said everything: 'Thanks for saving our asses.'

In the fight at Ripcord, Aviation's role in command and control occasioned another Medal of Honor. LTC Andre C. Lucas, commanding the 2d Battalion, 506th Infantry, constantly directed the defense from a helicopter. He flew at tree-top level for three hours above an entrenched enemy, dropped grenades to his troops, and tried to rescue a crewman trapped in a burning helicopter. On 23 July he was mortally wounded during the withdrawal. At Fort Rucker a stagefield, for many years officially designated 10C, was called Lucas Stagefield. That name was finally, officially adopted.

1971—Lam Son 719 and near-mid-intensity conflict

January-March 1971—close encounters with a new air defense environment

In 1971 efforts to replicate successes in Cambodia led to a desperately heroic time for Aviation and started to reshape doctrine, training and Aviation systems.

After Cambodia the North Vietnamese redoubled efforts to bring supplies and reinforcements through Laos. By late 1970 intelligence indicated preparations for a large offensive into South Vietnam. President Nixon did not believe that the South Vietnamese forces could stop the build up and decided to preempt the North's offensive. In December 1970 GEN Abrams conceived synchronized operations of U.S. forces inside South Vietnam to adhere to Congressional restrictions imposed after Cambodia incursion, along with incursion into Laos by Soldiers and Marines of the Republic of Vietnam. This part was called Lam Son 719.

Lam Son 719 depended on Aviation. On 8 February about 650 U.S. Army helicopters transported RVN troops into Laos. Until operations ended in early April, Aviation provided covering fire and evacuated casualties. RVN forces air-assaulted into Laos.

The operation began with several handicaps. The timeline from initial idea through execution was extremely short. To preserve surprise, information was tightly restricted. Among those briefed in the planning phase, intelligence estimates of enemy troop strength drew disbelief.

Army aviators had encountered nothing like the AD in Laos. From the very first day, conditions called for intense commitment, sometimes including deliberate self-sacrifice. A tiny number balked. A very few became combat-ineffective. The rest carried on. They realized that, if they failed to take their turn, everyone else would have to make more trips. Pilots went into some LZs having already made peace with themselves that they would not survive.

Under these conditions leadership depended solely on deeds. MAJ William R. (Bob) Bunting, commanding the 48th Assault Helicopter Company, was shot down the first day. Despite injuries, he flew back every time, leading the Blue Stars from the front.

Loyalty to each other and the mission led many to risk injury and death. On 18 February 1971 CWO Gary Green saved two crewmen when their gunship was shot down. Green landed his Cobra in heavy ground fire, ran to the downed helicopter, and pulled out the two wounded Soldiers. After placing them on his Cobra's rocket pods, Green opened fire at NVA Soldiers who were within 15 meters of his helicopter. Green received the Distinguished Service Cross.

This impulse to help fellow air crewmen on the ground became an obstacle to completing missions with minimum casualties. MAJ John A. G. Klose, operations officer of the 223d Aviation Battalion, realized that pilots diverting their aircraft to aid downed comrades exposed more aircraft to dangers that had brought at least one down. Also, the more aircraft diverted, the more trips to finish the mission—and the more crews lost. Orders went out to leave rescues to the aircrews specifically designated. Klose's wisdom showed when the Air Force concentrated all efforts to rescue a downed pilot, aborted dozens of CAS missions, and lost hundreds of RVN lives.

Lam Son 719 led to conspicuous heroism among enlisted Aviation Soldiers. Among these was SP5 Dennis Fujii, crew chief aboard a Huey sent for an emergency MEDEVAC. A mortar brought the Huey down. Fujii, who had shrapnel wounds, was left behind in the rescue. He found a radio, warned all aviators to stay clear, and became a hero over the next four days. He called coordinates of any NVA fire to Air Force forward air controllers and voluntarily stayed behind when others were rescued at another LZ. Rescued and recovered, he returned to Vietnam to complete his tour. Fujii received the Distinguished Service Cross, was the Army Aviation Association of America (AAAA) Soldier of the Year for 1971, and entered the Army Aviation Hall of Fame in 2004.

Some paid the ultimate price. A lingering wound was that many never knew others' names—only callsigns. On 18 March "Music 16" led an attack helicopter section covering extraction of ARVN Soldiers about to be overrun in a bomb crater. Dust and debris completely obscured the site from the air. To let rescue Hueys, led by CPT Richard M. Johnson, find the survivor, Music 16 called Johnson to follow him. At the time the Cobra had no ammunition or rockets left. Intense fire knocked down the Cobra and killed the crew. Only years later did Johnson and MAJ Klose learn the names of CPT Keith Brandt and 1LT Alan Boffman. Their actions got Johnson into the crater. There, 24 survivors scrambled into or clung onto the Huey. The overloaded Huey reached several hundred feet before beginning to fall. Johnson faced the choices of some or everyone dying. He ordered the crew chief and door gunner to throw three ARVN Soldiers off. The Huey landed back in Vietnam with 25 people onboard.

Similar efforts ended less happily. on 20 March, MAJ Jack L. Barker died trying to rescue ARVN Soldiers at LZ Brown. Of 40 aircraft that went into Brown, 30 were hit and several destroyed. Barker posthumously received the Distinguished Service Cross.

Officially 197 helicopters were irrecoverably lost in 54 days. This experience reshaped Aviation. Tactical innovations occurred spontaneously, amid combat. For example, Klose, contrived a trick to counter preregistered fires on LZs. Pilots approaching a designated LZ would turn away and try an alternate site if they drew heavy fire. Pilots called this tactic "Klose's Musical Mortars" because it resembled the game of musical chairs. Klose also advocated a twisting maneuver for landing and takeoff, because the enemy's 23mm gun could not track simultaneously on three axes. Terrain-hugging flight also minimized the time an enemy had to engage an aircraft.

People began analyzing lessons even before the operation ended,. On 20 March 1971 BG Sidney B. Berry wrote a long memorandum for record with his observations. Berry noted that the kind and sizes of NVA forces defined the environment as 'mid-intensity conflict'—much like Central Europe if the Soviets attacked. Lam Son 719 confirmed the ability to insert, support, and extract air assault forces under such conditions. As some pioneers of Aviation had said following World War II, the helicopter meant there would never again be 'a bridge too far'—referring to the disastrous experience of airborne forces parachuted behind German lines in 1944, only to be trapped and almost crushed when the relieving ground forces failed to break through.

Lam Son 719 also held ominous portents for the future. Loss rates among helicopters—about one per 500 sorties—caused immediate realization that Aviation had to change. An emphasis arose on low-level flying to use the terrain for cover and concealment. Specialized night vision devices and new, more survivable aircraft—AH-64 Apache and UH-60 Black Hawk—started development. Training also changed.

Cambodia in 1971—CPT Jon E. Swanson, much-delayed Medal of Honor

Continued operations in Cambodia in 1971 led to the only Medal of Honor given to an Army aviator in Vietnam for primarily an aggressive action. On 26 February 1971 Loach pilot CPT Jon E. Swanson had a mission to pinpoint the enemy's positions for a TF of ARVN Soldiers. He successfully destroyed five bunkers and took on several machinegun positions. Despite being critically low on ammunition and his aircraft being badly crippled, Swanson continued his mission until his aircraft was hit and exploded. Nomination for the Medal of Honor was lost in rapid turnovers of people and reorganizations. Almost 30 years later, action was completed. On 2 May 2002 the President presented the Medal of Honor to Swanson's widow and daughters.

1972—turning out the lights, almost

Aviation structure in Vietnam shrank rapidly. In July 1971 the 1AB had about 24,000 people and 3200 aircraft. By July 1972 personnel fell to 5000 with 984 aircraft. On 26 October 1972 Secretary of State Henry Kissinger declared that 'Peace is at hand,' and South Vietnamese President Thieu demanded all NVA troops leave South Vietnam. Communists responded by seizing as many hamlets as possible. Aviation activity remained disproportionately high to the very end. The last major loss of life among U.S. service members in Vietnam came on 31 October 1972 when a Chinook was shot down, killing 22.

The 1972 Easter Offensive

On 30 March 1972 the NVA opened a major offensive. Even more than LS 719, this battle brought Aviation full circle to the kind of mid-intensity conflict the Howze Board believed was the test case for airmobility.

The size of forces, along with their tactics, clearly showed a major shift in the NVA's approach to conquering the South. Lam Son 719 convinced the NVA that tanks and heavy artillery could win—and that only conventional warfare could win. So, North Vietnam threw in all but one of its divisions.

The Easter Offensive made heavy calls on Aviation Soldiers. The antiaircraft environment was lethal. Even veterans of Lam San 719 responding to initial calls on 5 April were amazed at the antiaircraft fire. The first Cobra lost was making a rocket run at almost 4,000 feet when hit. Events produced several awards of the Distinguished Service Cross.

An Loc

The NVA's culminating point came in the battle and siege of the city of An Loc, which the NVA planned to turn into the capital of a Provisional Revolutionary Government (PRG). By 9 April, the NVA had isolated An Loc. On 13 April the NVA launched a major tank attack into the city. This battle and siege lasted for four months but finally blocked the path to Saigon.

Antiaircraft fire seriously challenged efforts to resupply defenders of An Loc. By 26 April antiaircraft fire had severely damaged every transport aircraft over An Loc and shot down five. On 11 May, the NVA added heat-seeking SA-7 Strella missiles. The SA-7s specifically went after Cobras, which more effectively than tactical aircraft attacked infantry hugging NVA tanks.

The siege of An Loc was a milestone for Aviation history. On 13 April 1972 CW2 Barry McIntyre killed the first tank using a Cobra. A U.S. adviser on the ground especially praised the Cobras that hit NVA tanks within the city. At one point, as a tank column approached the 8th ARVN Regiment command post, the Cobras stopped the attack literally in its tracks.

One key to success at An Loc was effective, Joint/Combined aerial fires. Those fires created successive, lethal, layers of defense. Navy, Air Force, and VNAF attack aircraft bombed NVA forces as they massed. These attacks reduced the NVA forces able to enter the city. NVA entering An Loc then suffered from Cobras working with Air Force AC-130 and AC-119K gunships. The situation became so desperate that B-52 strikes were ordered on staging areas very close to An Loc. Skilled, coordinated, direct, aerial fires were vital as NVA forces closed within 20 meters of friendly troops. These were the kinds of danger-close situations that those who had argued for organic gunships had in mind in squabbling with the Air Force over roles and missions. Chinooks were vital, airlifting in 105mm howitzers that chewed away NVA attackers.

The Nixon Administration declared the NVA defeat at An Loc proof that Vietnamization had worked. Those close to the fight warned that An Loc was more the avoidance of defeat—attributable to U.S. advisers and heavy air support. COL William Miller, senior U.S. adviser to one ARVN division, especially noted the vital role of Cobra gunships. Cobra crews were willing to provide close support to ground forces despite the heavy antiaircraft fires.

Distinguished Service Crosses (DSC) during An Loc

An Loc produced several Distinguished Service Crosses for Aviation Soldiers. Two went to Loach pilot CPT John B. Whitehead and door gunner Sergeant (SGT) Raymond F. Waite, who flew through tear-and-vomiting chemicals and rescued nine people who got in or hung on to the Loach, Another DSC went to CWO 2 Ronald Tusi, a Cobra pilot who flew through intense antiaircraft fire to single-handedly kill four tanks, damage a fifth, and force other tanks attacking a division headquarters to withdraw. Among the recipients was a black Loach pilot, CPT Ronald A. Radcliffe

Tactical innovations, surface-to-air missiles (SAM), mid-intensity conflict, Cobra gunships, and Joint operations

Tusi's success came from innovating tactics on the spot. Gunship tactics were diving fire, but reports said that tanks were hiding in buildings. So standard tactics could not reach them. Tusi got an oversize load of rockets and flew down streets until he found the tanks. He then got behind the tanks and unloaded his whole load from a hover position.

An Loc was important to future thinking about the nature of war to come. An official study by Headquarters, U.S. Pacific Air Force, opened saying that "The battle for An Loc may well prove to be a classic study in the use of tactical airpower in the years to come." The study emphasized the AD threat—especially, the introduction of the SA-7 missile, its impact on aerial resupply, and changes in the use of gunships. AC-119 gunships were ineffective in their primary role as CAS for troops in contact and shifted to interdiction. AC-130s, which had mainly been for night interdiction and armed reconnaissance, shifted more to CAS. B-52s, designed as a strategic bomber, became highly-valued CAS, dropping to within 800 meters to friendly troops.

Hawks Claw—emergency stopgap leads to longer-term solution, XM-26 to AH-1S

Helicopters specifically equipped for tank-killing made their combat debut during the Easter Offensive, of which the siege of An Loc was a part. On 2 May 1972 the 1st Combat Aerial TOW Team (Hawks Claw) used the XM-26 armament subsystem in combat for the first time. This system allowed the helicopters to use the Tube-Launched, Optically Tracked, Wire Guided (TOW) missile. MG John G. Hill, the ground commander, later credited two air cavalry troops, operating in conjunction with the 1st Aerial TOW team, with saving the city of Kontum. In its only combat use in Vietnam, the attack helicopter as an antitank system decisively showed its value.

Precision, direct fire in close combat

While the TOW gunships made a useful demonstration, the overwhelming value of Army gunships came from the Cobras firing their smaller, lighter ordnance supporting troops in close combat. Sometimes this was within 10 meters of friendly troops engaged in house-to-house fighting. The Cobras never received a call for check fire or ceasefire

Continuing need for flexibility and adaptability in tactics

The gunship experience at An Loc also showed the continuing need for flexibility and adaptability in the realm of tactics. Whereas a key lesson of Lam Son 719 the year before had been the need to fly low to stay alive, gunships in the Easter Offensive found the reverse. They first tried to operate at low level but found that untenable because of the 12.7mm guns. Army gunship pilots, though, found that the enemy seemed to reserve the larger weapons—23mm and 27mm—for larger aircraft, such as the AC-130 Spectre gunships and C-123 cargo planes trying to deliver resupply. So Cobra pilots returned to higher altitudes and conducted most of their work at angles of 30–35 degrees.

1973—going home

Officially, for the U.S., fighting in Vietnam ended in January 1973. On 15 January President Nixon ordered a halt to all offensive military action in Vietnam. That included air strikes, shelling, and mining operations. On 27 January the final peace agreement to end the Vietnam War was signed in Paris.

What was left of Aviation in Vietnam began to wither away quickly. In March 1973 the 1AB completed its redeployment from Vietnam to Fort Rucker. It was the last major combat unit to leave Vietnam. By then, according to one source, the 1AB had flown 30 million sorties. The 1AB also lost 1703 KIA and 5163 wounded in action. The number of sorties may have been right as a general measure of orders of magnitude of the Aviation effort. The reported numbers for KIA and WIA were low. Names in the Vietnam Memorial Room of the Army Aviation

Museum, based on lists compiled by the Army's Adjutant General (AG), run over 4000. Those lists were known to be incomplete because of the lack of an Aviation Branch and consequent lack of a good way to identify many Soldiers as having been part of Army Aviation.

On 11 March 1973 the 57th Medical Detachment (Medical Evacuation) flew its last mission. The 57th, the first air ambulance unit deployed to Vietnam, was the last unit to depart Vietnam. There was still residual Aviation and there was still residual combat. On 29 March 1973, a SA-7 missile hit CPT Joseph Bowen's Huey flying at 3200 feet.

By then, Army leadership was already looking ahead toward other enemies. One battleground involved discussions about the relative merits of fixed-wing versus rotary-wing aviation. In March 1973 BG William Maddox, Director of Army Aviation, testified before the Senate on Vietnam's implications. Maddox said the helicopter made a difference the French lacked earlier: While the loss rate for attack helicopters was higher than for others, that loss rate was below the Air Force's. The Army needed more capable, armed helicopters. Europe had stated an urgent requirement for them.

Crew Chief pulling AH-1 turret maintenance in snow at Fort Drum, 1975

Chapter 5: 1970s Through Operation Desert Storm (ODS)—the New Generation

The post-Vietnam operational context

Vietnam was a watershed. By 1972 most people outside the Air Force no longer believed Airpower, which had largely dominated the Defense discussion from 1945 well down into the 1960s, could be decisive except under very restricted conditions. Airmobility had proven itself in combat that ranged from mixed forces of regulars and guerrilla to large, well-equipped conventional ones supported by strong air defenses. In October 1973 the Mideast War between Israel and its Arab neighbors gave a stark view of the mid-intensity battlefield. Neither side used helicopters extensively, but that war showed the kind of environment Army Aviation systems might have to operate in. That environment was much more lethal than Vietnam. Arab combatants used sophisticated Soviet equipment on a large scale. There was heavy emphasis on antiaircraft and antiarmor weapons. The Arabs were equipped for extensive nighttime operations. Electronic warfare (EW) capabilities were prevalent. Finally well-trained Soldiers and combined arms tactics made the decisive difference. From then until 1989, rising regional concerns vied for attention with the possibility of a major war in Europe. The changing conditions forced continual reassessment of U.S. national military objectives. The collapse of the Soviet Union and Warsaw Pact in 1989 relieved the threat of the major war on the Central Front but added to uncertainty. Uncertainty, coupled with dramatic advances in materials and technology, led to constant debates but favored greater sophistication of and demands on Army Aviation. As the development of airmobility had dominated the period from the end of World War II through the Vietnam years, the development of deep attack and a movement toward Aviation as part of a Joint fight characterized the two decades following Vietnam.

The world of Aviation as viewed in the mid-1970s

By the end of Vietnam, Army Aviation was a force composed of 90 percent helicopters, most serving as true combat vehicles. Aviation in Vietnam proved the concept of airmobility as the Howze Board envisioned it. However, in the years immediately following Vietnam, the situation Army Aviation faced changed decisively. While action in Vietnam was often intense, Aviation faced a major air defense threat only near the end. By then, relatively few aviators remained to have and share this experience. At the end of the Vietnam War, Aviation showed the capability of the aerial TOW missile against tanks. The overwhelming conclusion drawn was that Aviation faced a much more hazardous operating environment. A series of articles in the U.S. Army Aviation Digest captured and reflected these views.

By late 1974 the commanding general (CG) of USAAVNC was focused on a wide range of changes in response to this emerging environment. In two articles in November and December, MG William J. Maddox said, "It is my conviction that no aviation unit in the Army today could have avoided unacceptable losses if committed in that environment. In fact the best units in Vietnam…would have been cut up badly in the Middle East because they were neither trained, equipped nor mentally prepared for the type of combat encountered." Maddox described deficiencies in three key areas—doctrine, training, and staying power.

In doctrine Aviation needed to revise its concept of fighting to include operating against armor supported by sophisticated air defense weapons. Maddox saw a void, with nothing coming along to provide a concept for the new battlefield as the Howze Board had provided for airmobility. Tactical units would receive the new Cobra/TOW [AH-IQJ] in 1975, but Maddox questioned how it would be used against tanks and on a battlefield with heat-seeking missiles and radar-controlled antiaircraft guns. People were thinking of attack helicopters in terms of air cavalry—light combat, avoiding decisive engagement, teams of two attack helicopters possibly with aerial scouts going against an enemy target. Instead, Maddox believed it was time to think of employing attack helicopters the same way as tanks—in mass, by platoon, company and battalion. Moreover attack helicopters had to be integrated with other ground elements, with suppressive fire from artillery and tactical air. With the Cobra/TOW, the air cavalry combat brigade (ACCB) was a heavy combat unit, capable of decisive engagement. Army Aviation also needed to operate around the clock. The October 1973 war had shown Soviet intentions to maintain an offensive at night and in icing conditions. So Army Aviation needed to be able to do likewise.

As Maddox saw it, there were grievous deficiencies in training. Aviation needed realistic training for both the AC and Reserve Components (RC) on tactics, nap-of-the-earth (NOE) skills, night and instrument operations, and electronic warfare (EW) conditions. USAAVC had tripled use of synthetic flight trainers, dramatically improving quality of the graduate while reducing time in training. Beyond the schoolhouse, Maddox saw four conditions preventing effective tactical training. These were a lack of threat awareness, a lack of standardization, a misplaced emphasis on safety, and inadequate readiness standards. One installation prohibited any aerial gunnery flight below 100 feet and any night flight below 500 feet. The 1974 Aviation Systems Program Review (ASPR) had noted these things, and Maddox declared it was time to act

Staying power involved several things. The post-Vietnam force structure included only one airmobile division—101AB. The 1CD was reverting to an Armor configuration. A skeleton ACCB existed at Fort Hood. Aviation was decentralized to the tactical level to meet ground commanders' immediate needs. The new environment suggested many deficiencies in equipment. These included systems to give Aviation more survivability and effectiveness. In aircraft the overwhelming need was the Advanced Attack Helicopter (AAH)—which ultimately became the Apache. Maddox also saw an urgent need for an advanced scout helicopter (ASH) with greater capabilities than the OH-6 Cayuse LOH. This need sprang from the need to conduct 24-hour operations. However, this acquisition depended on progress in night vision technology, which did not seem to offer immediate fulfillment. Maddox foresaw a need to modernize a fleet composed mainly of 20- and 30-year-old aircraft, such as the U-6 and even C-47s. The Army also needed tactical navigation aids and communications. Maddox saw some bright spots in steps for integrating Army and Air Force training on air support and firepower. The services had established joint working committees. TAC and U.S. Army Training and Doctrine Command (TRADOC) had jointly published a draft manual on airspace management. Excepting in attack helicopters and utility fixed-wing transportation, the RC had first-line aircraft. The Army was at or near its authorized acquisition objectives except in those two areas. The Army's combat readiness flying program had been updated. That included orders for the Army as a whole to conduct NOE training. In light of new legislation on flight pay, Aviators were coming under an Officer Personnel Management System (OPMS).

Others shared some of Maddox's views but also saw the Army facing a severe squeeze for a decade or more. LTG John R. Deane, the Army's chief of R&D, saw a conflict between increasing possibilities to pursue through emerging technologies and a lack of funds that forced the Army to be selective in what it pursued. Deane saw this becoming even more acute after the Army completed funding its Big Five projects. These included a new tank, two new helicopters, a mechanized infantry combat vehicle, and an air defense system. The cost of these programs meant that Deane could not foresee any further Aviation programs until at least the mid-1980s. At the same time, a desire at the national level to retain a strong U.S. defense technology base meant a much wider use of improvements to existing systems.

Complexity of Army flying after Vietnam—impact of ground air defense threat

The need for more and better simulators partly reflected the increased complexity of Army flying that came with more capable aircraft systems and the new threat environment. Pilots could anticipate facing radar-controlled antiaircraft guns and shoulder-fired, infrared (IR)-seeking missiles. To defeat these threats, pilots would employ NOE flight, taking advantage of masking terrain, as well as chaff against radar and smoke as visual and IR obscurants. Night flight and NOE relying on tactical instruments could allow pilots to operate below and out of the visibility of enemy gunners. With this complexity came increased demands for training time to attain and retain proficiency.

An illustration of the problem was a series of seven articles on the topic of tactical instruments in the <u>U.S. Army Aviation Digest</u> during 1975–1976. The fourth of the series dealt with tactics pilots would use in a high-threat environment to survive. The article described flight profiles that a pilot would use simply to move from one point to another from a corps rear to a forward unit in a brigade. Each profile included combinations of maneuvers with several changes of altitudes and directions. The article emphasized that each mission would have to be planned individually with proper altitude profiles to avoid both enemy and terrain obstacles. A single movement could involve several changes between VFR and IFR, as well as handoffs between a flight operations center (FOC)/Air Force control and reporting center (CRC) and division flight coordination center (FCC). The threat environment also could require pilots to fly under tactical instrument conditions at the same time they had to deal with an EW environment or conditions demanding radio silence. By 1976, reflecting the new conditions, FM 1–60, <u>Army Air Traffic Operations</u>, issued in 1968, was superseded by FM 1–60, <u>Army Air Traffic Management in the Combat Zone</u>.

At the same time, there was an increasing emphasis on skill in instrument flying to allow Aviation operations around the clock and in bad weather. Demands for round-the-clock Aviation operations increased aircrews' exposure to hazardous weather conditions. Among these was icing, which previously had not been a special concern for helicopter pilots. For the most part, helicopter pilots had avoided flying in conditions that might cause aircraft icing. The new operational environments took away that luxury. Even for pilots with extensive fixed-wing experience, icing brought unfamiliar situations in helicopters. For example, until 1974 no one had noticed the effects of icing on autorotation. Icing tests then showed that a modest accumulation of ice on inboard parts of particular rotor blades created a condition where safe autorotation was impossible. Even the shedding of ice in flight could cause catastrophic situations. Ice coming loose from a rotor blade could imbalance the rotor system to the extent of causing it to crash. Different rotor systems with different numbers and types of blades had different characteristics when it came to these problems. Even for the same rotor systems, behavior varied widely according to temperatures around the aircraft. So the amount of knowledge pilots needed rapidly expanded.

Demands for round-the-clock operations on a high-threat battlefield also affected maintenance. During Vietnam, crew chiefs achieved availability far above the programmed—averaging 140–150 hours per month with OR at 75 percent—by pulling night maintenance. However, through most of the Vietnam period, basing was more or less fixed, and the threat was low enough that maintainers could work in lighted conditions. The conditions expected by the mid-1970s and beyond allowed neither fixed locations nor working under highly-lighted conditions. The result was exercises at Fort Hood in November-December 1974. These exercises looked at various approaches to lighting in a tactical environment for an integrated direct support maintenance (IDSM) element. Meanwhile the Transportation School conducted a study called Concept of Night Aircraft Maintenance (CONAM). By 1976 the conclusion was that training offered the greatest potential to improve night maintenance in the shortest time, but night maintenance was also highly inadequate. Night maintenance was not part of the school experience, and field exercises seldom lasted long enough to require units to perform night maintenance under field conditions.

Looking toward European scenarios, Aviators also had to confront the possibility of conducting flight operations on a nuclear, biological, or chemical battlefield. By 1976 a new FM 90–1, <u>Employment of Army Aviation Units in a High Threat Environment</u>, appeared. The implications of these possible conditions were not warmly received. In 1980 the VCSA held a systems program review (SPR) on nuclear operations. After the SPR, GEN Donn Starry, CG, TRADOC, sent a broadcast message to senior leaders. He said to stop treating these complexities as oddities: "What I prefer to see is…to drop the word integrated and automatically understand the battlefield as including nuclear and chemical. If there is to be a study or analytical excursion, the excursion should be…conventional."

The shift to mid-/high-intensity threats demanded more complex and intensive crew training. The changing view was apparent in an article in the 1976 U.S. Army Aviation Digest that reviewed the progress of Army Aviation from the beginning of Vietnam to the present. "The days of unlimited taxi service are gone. The aviation commander can no longer depend upon 'services rendered' to the ground arms as all-inclusive success criteria." Nap-of-the-earth (NOE) and formation flying at night were complex operations that required adequate training. Safety guidelines had to be reviewed; a 'punitive' safety policy could not be allowed to prevent adequate training for the probable conditions of the next war. Employment of attack helicopters en masse required deliberate, thorough planning that involved every crewmember. Flying 30 minutes in the new environment could be expected to be more exhausting than the 10-and 12-hour days in the cockpit in Vietnam.

The new conditions of flying—especially night NOE and the use of Aviation in an antiarmor role—also demanded advanced knowledge of mission planning. By September 1976 Aviation leaders had to factor physiological and psychological effects of differing lengths of and intervals between NOE flights into mission planning.

Evolution of night flying in the 1970s-1980s

One of the most important developments to come out of the years following Vietnam was night flying to allow around-the-clock operations. Achieving this capability required substantial changes in technology, as well as doctrine and training. It even involved changes in the personal lifestyles and habits of Army aircrew members. The development of this capability was costly in human terms. From the mid-1980s onward this improved capability paid off handsomely. By 1991 the Army had achieved a spectacularly superior capability in this realm and in operations that depended on it.

The changing nature of the operational environment after Vietnam dictated Army Aviation expanding their ability to operate at night. Enemies now had much greater air defense capabilities. Even to operate near the forward edge of the battle area (FEBA) could require night flying to avoid being detected by sophisticated weapons. Combined with NOE, night capability reduced the enemy's ability to detect friendly aircraft by electronic as well as visual means. Night operations also increased the shock value on the enemy of ordinary operations. The preface to Training Circular (TC) 1–28, <u>Rotary Wing Night Flight</u>, which the Army issued in 1976, noted that "a new horizon" confronted Army aviators and had to be explored. TC 1–28 provided basic information to use for training.

Early development

As with many things in Aviation, the idea was not new. In 1910 Charles K. Hamilton made the first documented night flight. In October 1917 the memorandum on 'the "Air War"' that the Italians Caproni and Douhet wrote to the Air Service advocated using masses of long-range bombers in night raids to destroy industries in Germany and Austria. By September 1918 the technology had already started to evolve. Ninety-one night bombers were part of General William (Billy) Mitchell's first thousand-aircraft raid. By the end of World War I, night reconnaissance was considered an integral part of military operations. Specific techniques evolved, such as flying with the moon behind the aircraft to reduce glare. Pilots found that different natural lighting conditions required different techniques and produced different results. A bright moon allowed detection of movements along open road up to about ten miles away from altitudes of 1500–2000 feet. A half moon required a pilot to drop to 1000–1500 feet. Even then such periods produced the most inaccurate observations. Night flying aids included maps that had only the most visible features on them. Even so, night flying remained difficult and often dangerous. In February 1934, when President Roosevelt gave the Air Corps the mission to fly the U.S. Mail, one of three pilots killed within a few hours on 16 February simply flew into the ground at night.

Army Air Corps—U.S. Air Force approaches, 1930s-1980s

The real and perceived difficulties of night fighting led the Army Air Corps to give relatively small emphasis to this capability. The prevailing tendency was to see night fighting as 'a specialized form of aerial fighting requiring specialized equipment and training.' Because the Army Air Corps anticipated night bombardment, some embedded, night-fighting capability was viewed as necessary. The suggested way to solve the need for specialization was to put a night fighter squadron in each group, rather than have a separate night fighter group. Even so, proficiency would remain something that was the realm of specialized people, organizations, and equipment, rather than something spread widely across the air forces. As a result, the AAF formed the 422nd Night Fighter Squadron in the European theater during World War II. This unit's training emphasized air-to-air interception, not ground support.

During World War II night fighters did attack ground targets—notably, enemy airfields, lines of communication, and targets of opportunity. Tactics, however, emphasized working under conditions of artificial illumination, rather than actually conducting operations in a darkened environment. Initially formations first dropped flares and then flew underneath the flares seeking enemy troop concentrations. Tactics did become slightly refined. One aircraft dropped flares while the others in the flight strafed. Because of the simplicity and lack of technical improvements in night air-to-ground fighter employment, the Air Force used these same tactics in Vietnam and Operation Desert Storm (ODS). These tactics, however, leant themselves largely to use against stationary targets.

During Vietnam the Air Force did develop at least two systems that gave a much higher, more flexible air-to-ground capability against moving targets at night. AC-130s and AC-119Ks had extensive night sensor equipment that could address moving vehicles. This equipment included IR detectors that could pick up the heat of engines and exhausts and low-light television. These aircraft also carried a system called Black Crow that detected vehicles by registering electrical emanations from operating internal combustion engines. AC-130s and AC-199Ks existed in very limited number. F-111s also had round-the-clock, all-weather capabilities. No night fighter had these capabilities until the F-15E came along in the late 1980s. So, none of these aircraft represented a widespread asset, readily available to support the ground commander.

Ground Force Aviation approaches

The importance of night operations to ground commanders fostered greater efforts to improve night capabilities among Ground Forces aviators. During World War II Army aviators tried various ways to conduct night operations. An example was CPT O. Glenn Goodhand's experiments in Italy, discussed in Chapter 2.

The path that led to modern night vision systems began with the Germans in the 1940s. They experimented with image intensification systems. In the 1950s the Army was experimenting with derivatives of this technology. The results were mixed. In May 1957 a helicopter in a night-flying demonstration at West Point hit power lines and exploded in flight. An investigation of the accident revealed an inability to discriminate among light sources. That ended a 6-month series of trials with infrared. It also stalled efforts to develop night-vision devices for flying.

Setbacks with advanced technologies did not stop spontaneous efforts to develop other techniques. During early 1958 MAJ Vernon L. Poynter, an Armor officer serving as the Aviation Officer in the 1CD in Korea, began conducting unusual training missions with the utility helicopter section. These included night flying, making approaches to flashlights in the mountains. These activities were related to a demonstration of air assault that Poynter developed using the 13th Transportation Company. Division commanders who saw the demonstration responded favorably to it. During the early stages of Army involvement in Vietnam, night flying increased as part of efforts to support ground troops. Notable in this aspect were MEDEVAC activities of MAJ Charles L. (Dustoff) Kelly.

For the most part in Vietnam, the night was more enemy than friend for the Army and Army aviators. The limited ability to operate at night made it a favorite time for the enemy to attack. A recurrent pattern was for the Viet Cong to attack a base camp at night, with an air assault pursuing the attackers the following day.

By 1969 some Army aviators began to regard the night as their friend. Lessons from combat showed that nap-of-earth (NOE) or high flight, dummy LZ, inclement weather, night operations, and different routings all reduced vulnerability of helicopters. Army aviators tried various ways to offset the limitations in night-fighting ability. Some resorted to simple but sometimes-effective tricks. During 1969, A Company, 25th Aviation ("Little Bears"), improvised what they called their Nighthawk gunship. The Nighthawk was a Huey that had a Xenon searchlight mounted along with a machine gun. By June-July 1969 they had a Nighthawk with an IR capability and a 4000-rounds-per-minute minigun. After the enemy figured out that that thing was murderous, they would not shoot at a Nighthawk. Nighthawk pilots would turn on all lights to look like a resupply ship. They would hover at about 200–300 feet to draw fire, and then use the minigun to devastate the area. Night Aviation operations also played especially important parts in SOF missions, such as the famous Son Tay Raid on the night of 20–21 November 1970 to rescue 75 or more Americans. Although the raid failed in its immediate goal, the raid was a spectacular achievement that showed the kind of possibilities night operations offered. In 1971, during Lam Son 719, friendly units often had to move by night to break contact with the NVA.

Night flying and nap-of-the-earth (NOE) as response to the air defense threat

The lethal air defense environment appearing by the end of the Vietnam War increased interest in night flying. Nap-of-earth (NOE) tactics that gave protection from radar-aimed air defense systems could not be used at night without search-lights or other means that were unacceptable in a combat situation. In July 1972 the U.S. Army Combat Developments Experimentation Command (USACDEC) also conducted a series of Attack Helicopter Clear Night Defense Experiments to determine training requirements and abilities of aviators to perform without night vision aids.

By 1975 there was an urgency about developing night-flying skills. In February 1975 a classified briefing, "The Implications of the Middle East War on U.S. Army Tactics, Doctrine and Systems" identified major lessons from the October 1973 Arab-Israeli War: Among the key points was increased needs for night oper-ations and new tactics for aircraft to avoid unacceptable losses. Operation Nighthawk at USAAVNC tried to determine what kind and how much training should be added to Initial Entry Rotary Wing (IERW) and selected advanced courses. In April 1975 a random class of students drawn from the Officer Rotary Wing Aviator Course (ORWAC) and Warrant Officer Rotary Wing Aviator Course (WORWAC) flew a 40-hour series of night contact maneuvers. In May 1975 the final phase of USAAVNC night vision flight training was completed when 16 IERW students received a special course in low-level night flight with-out night vision aids.

Before 1976 little doctrine had been developed for using helicopters in a night NOE role. In February 1976 Training Circular (TC) 1–28, Rotary Wing Night Flight, was published. In September 1976 USAAVNC produced FM 90–1, Employment of Army Aviation in a High Threat Environment. This FM reflected newer concepts of survivability through NOE and night flying. FM 90–1 also reflected the shift in focus from the Vietnam experience toward Europe. In 1977 the 101AB developed 100 units of an in-house, low-cost night landing "T." The 101AB tested these units during Return of Force to Germany (REFORGER).

Development of aided night flying—night vision goggles (NVG) and safety

While the emphasis into the mid-1970s was on flying without night vision devices, people were also experimenting with NVG. In 1969 the Army demon-strated the use of a type of NVG for aviators. The existing goggles, though, designed for ground uses such as truck driving, had serious limitations when adapted for aviation use. The goggles could be adjusted within a narrow range for pilots who needed minor corrections, such as for simple myopia. When that was done, near vision might be compromised. The stress of NVG flight usually brought on severe sweating, causing lenses to fog—a very dangerous condition. To reduce this effect, surgical hoses were added as vents to draw the moisture away from the lenses. Resolution with the early goggles was marginal at best. In fog the pilot quickly became blind and might not even know it.

People at the Night Vision Lab at Fort Belvoir made important strides. They produced a good bit of scientific literature. By 1972 the lab also developed a set of NVG that allowed relatively good acuity and range. Tests using second-generation NVG in Cobras, OH-58 Kiowas, and Hueys showed advantages over unaided flight at 90 knots and 50 feet altitude. Flight using NVG also proved to be superior to flight without any aids. So Project Modern Army Selected Systems Technical Evaluation and Review Program (MASSTER) recommended adopting these improved NVG for both air and ground use, and the Army type classified the Army-Navy Portable Vision System 5 (AN/PVS-5) in 1972. In 1973 the decision followed to provide AN/PVS-5 NVG to Aviation units.

Part of the problems with NVG was incompatibilities with existing equipment. By about 1980, a pink light filter was developed to provide a landing light or searchlight compatible with an aviator's night vision goggles. In 1980 lighting compatible with NVG was installed in OH-58 Kiowas and Huey aircraft.

While materiel development was ongoing, the Army developed institutional training for pilots to use NVG. Night NOE flying remained especially dangerous and drove efforts to develop standardized techniques and training. In November 1974 a flight of standardization instructor pilots (SIP) from USAAVNC completed an initial NVG training course. In January 1976 a NVG IP qualification program began at USAAVNC. In 1977 the first resident training using NVG flight began at Fort Rucker. This involved 4.5 hrs of familiarization training for IERW students—mostly traffic pattern work. Students were not considered qualified. Before the decade ended, Aviator's Night Vision Imaging System (AN/AVS-6) entered advanced development. In June 1983 USAAVNC increased IERW flight training with NVG to 10.5 hours. The type of flying also shifted from simple traffic patterns at the airfield to tactical flight along established NOE routes. This training went beyond familiarization to providing qualification.

Entry into night flying produced new requirements for pilots that few probably anticipated. Experiments with night vision showed that common practices degraded a pilot's ability to see at night. For example, smoking from two to thirty cigarettes per day effectively cost an individual 20 percent of his night vision at sea level because of effects on the blood's oxygen-carrying capacity. Alcohol had even greater effects. Fatigue, illness, poor nutrition, and poor physical conditioning compounded night vision problems. In effect, night flying could call for major changes in lifestyle. As a result, Training Circular (TC) 1–28, <u>Rotary Wing Night Flight</u>, issued in 1976, had a whole chapter on night vision.

At the same time people recognized a clear need and were striving to develop ways to respond, knowledgeable people were also expressing grave concern about the adequacy of existing systems, techniques, and training. On 6 August 1974 CWO Tusi, who had received the DSC in Vietnam, was killed flying a Cobra in "Night Owl" tests. In 1976, Edward Firth, who had conducted experiments with aided flight in 1956, expressed concerns to the director of the night vision lab about the safety of using NVG designed for infantry to fly. The lab's director passed Firth's concerns on to HQDA. Efforts to increase the safety of night flying continued.

Fears had some foundation. After the Army Aviation Training Brigade began flying regularly with NVG designed for infantry use, the practice quickly spread worldwide. In April 1978 the first fatal crash involving flying with NVG occurred in a Huey at Fort Rucker. The cause was sudden fog, cutting out enough moonlight required for goggles to work. In July a second fatal crash occurred for the same reasons.

Part of the problem was a real, unmet need in the field. Pilots increasingly had to operate at night, and they needed something better than they had. In April 1980, use of infantry NVG contributed to the failure of the Iran hostage rescue mission that brought down the Carter Administration. The aborted Iran hostage rescue gave an added push to developing night-flying capability, and that push was very strong within the Army. Improved night-flying capability was tightly bound up in a simultaneous effort to develop Special Operations Aviation (SOA)—code named Project Honey Badger. Among the work done as part of this project was a 10-hour NVG syllabus, followed by long-range navigation training that included flights lasting up to 7.5 hours wearing AN/PVS-5s.

The ability to conduct night operations with existing technology became an emotional and controversial matter through the 1980s, with continuing efforts to overcome the sources of problems. By summer 1981, deficiencies in night operations were one among several key areas affecting Aviation that senior Army leadership identified. In August 1981 General William R. Richardson, CG, TRADOC, wrote on airmobility in the 1980s. He identified key "doctrinal voids" to get Army aviation thinking for an Army Aviation Mission Area Analysis (AAMAA). Among several was night operations. In 1982 the Army contracted with ITT Electro-Optical Products Division and Varian Associates for initial production of AN/AVS-6 NVG, but production problems delayed initial deliveries until 1985. In June 1983 U.S. Army Aeromedical Research Laboratory (USAARL) and USAAVNC completed evaluating versions of modified AN/PVS-5 faceplates. Based on this evaluation, DA approved a standard modified faceplate for NVG. The standard instructed Army aviators to cut away the facemask on NVG. The Army and Air Force also banned flying with full-face NVG. The night vision lab director obtained a promise that the Army would restrict aviation usage of NVG to takeoffs and landings. In February 1984 the first Night Vision Goggle Safety Workshop was held at the U.S. Army Safety Center, Fort Rucker. That workshop produced the <u>Night Vision Goggle (NVG) Aircrew Training Manual</u>. This aircrew training manual standardized training tasks. It also established a range of stringent training policies and requirements. Among these, it prohibited NVG operations by a single pilot and limited flight airspeed at specific altitudes. In September 1985 known advantages of 3d-generation AN/AVS-6 NVG over modified AN/PVS-5s led the Secretary of the Army to direct accelerated procurement. Also, application of Phase II lighting modification began to make all helicopter lighting compatible with NVG.

Continuing crashes and concern about the safety of night flying led to additional measures. In December 1986 the Second Night Vision Goggle Safety Conference produced the Night Vision Flying Accident Prevention Kit, briefed to aviation units worldwide. In 1987 the CSA reviewed the safety of NVG, night tactics, and training polices. This review caused a revision of flight formation and multi-aircraft training procedures. New policies included updated preflight briefing procedures and a consolidated revision of publications. In May 1988 two NVG training tapes were jointly produced and distributed to all Aviation units by the USASC and USAAVNC. On 27 December 1988 Training Circular 1–204, <u>Night Flight Techniques and Procedures</u> superseded its predecessor, published 11 October 1983. By March 1989 the Army had fielded about 8700 AN/PVS-5 night vision goggles for Aviation use but already had 4068 of the far better AN/AVS-6 goggles against an initial quantity of 12,928.

Despite these efforts, accidents continued. On 3 March 1988 two Black Hawks cruising at 90 mph collided killing 17 at Fort Campbell when overcast blocked moonlight during flight with NVG. On 25 October 1988 a Marine Huey and CH-46 Sea Knight from Camp Pendleton collided while flying in clear weather and full moon. Pilots were using NVG. Ten were killed. These crashes inspired a series of articles entitled "Death in the Dark" that sparked national attention. On 4 December 1988 Edward Humes, a reporter for the <u>Orange County Register</u> in California, published the first of the series. Humes focused public attention on deficiencies of infantry NVG for aviation use. He reported that budget cuts delayed completed fielding of NVG designed for aviation use from 1991–92 to 1995–96.

Aircraft-mounted night vision systems—TADS/PNVS

While development of head-mounted NVG progressed, a whole separate stream of development was underway for systems imbedded in aircraft. The initial contract award for the target acquisition and designation system (TADS)/pilot night vision sensor (PNVS) for the AAH was planned for March 1977. The initial flyoff was set for 1979. On 1 February 1979 the Development Test Training Detachment activated to train selected people to use the TADS/PNVS. In April 1980 HQDA, announced that Martin Marietta won the flyoff with Northrop for the TADS/PNVS for the AAH.

'We own the night.'

For Army Aviation, there were some ironies about the timing and thrust of Humes' articles in 1988 and Congressional hearings that flowed from them. For one, 1988 was Army Aviation's safest year to that point. There were 1.84 Class A accidents per 100,000 flying hours. Also, the Army had undertaken intensive training to try to reduce dangers. In fact, by 1988, night aviation training averaged about 30–38 percent of all training for the preceding 10 years. Finally, the Army's efforts improving equipment, training and doctrine were paying off handsomely. In 1987 night flying capabilities of SOA were vital in stopping Iranian mine laying in the Persian Gulf. In December 1989 night flying capabilities were vital in Operation Just Cause in Panama—an operation that was planned around the Army's superior night vision capabilities. Results of Just Cause led the CSA Carl E. Vuono to proclaim, 'We own the night.' Thirteen months later, in ODS, the Army made the point again much more dramatically on a much larger stage with the whole world watching.

Personnel changes in the 1970–80s—creation of the Aviation Branch

As following World War II, the end of the huge buildup in Army Aviation for Vietnam had huge manpower effects in the years after the war ended. The immediate effect of the end of Vietnam was a huge reduction in the number of aviators the Army needed. The Vietnam surge had created a huge population of Army pilots that peaked in 1972 at 26,000—up almost fourfold from 1962. The length of the war and the timing of the expansion also meant that, for future and near-term Army requirements, the Army had a huge excess of commissioned officers in more senior grades where they were not needed and mostly could not be used. At the same time a need existed to refresh the entry-level population to fill future middle- and senior-grade requirements. The combination of all these things was a major force driving the decision to create the Aviation Branch.

Officer Personnel Management System (OPMS)—the Dual Track System and Aviation

A key step toward addressing these imbalances was a change to officer personnel management. In 1972 the new OPMS concept required dual-track development. This system recognized that the increasing sophistication of systems and operations across the Army made the traditional view of the officer generalist at least partly obsolete. All officers were supposed to develop a secondary skill in addition to their branch qualification.

A critical event for the course of future Aviation came when Congress passed the Aviation Career Incentive Pay (ACIP) Act of 1974. This act restructured development and policies for managing commissioned and WO aviators. At the 12- and 18-year points in their careers—referred to as "gates"—the law required pilots to have at least 50 percent of their years in operational flying positions. If they failed to achieve these minimums, they lost continuation of flight pay. The rationale for imposing these gates was that aviators were too expensive to train and then use for something else. Failure to meet the gates did not exclude an officer from consideration for command. Rather, Congress would use overall success in meeting these gates as a measure of how well or poorly the Army was using its personnel.

This ACIP forced the Army toward the decision in 1982 to create an Army Aviation Branch. Under the system that had applied from 1942 onward, being an aviator was treated as a skill, like Air Assault. Army aviators competed for retention and promotion in their basic branches, based on performance in their non-aviation functions. The Army had tried to compensate for time spent in aviation duties by rotating pilots between aviation and ground assignments. The ACIP Act effectively killed the Army's ground rotation policy, because the threshold amount of time flying could not be met if the Army continued to assign officer pilots to ground duties. That meant that future aviators officers would spend most of their careers up through the rank of major in flying assignments—further reducing their chances to remain competitive in their basic branches.

By 1975 the Army was looking at different ways to approach managing aviator officers. One affected WOs and involved centralized management. On 1 May 1975, HQDA revised the Military Occupational Specialty (MOS) for Aviation WOs. In July 1975 Warrant Officer Division (WOD) was formed in U.S. Army Military Personnel Center (MILPERCEN). This centralized management of WOs.

The other approach affected commissioned officers and retained decentralized management. On 12 September 1975, following recommendations of a detailed study, MILPERCEN also approved adding Aviation to the list of specialties under the OPMS. For commissioned officers, two main Aviation specialties were recognized. The first, Specialty 15, was simply designated as Aviation and involved operational aspects of Aviation missions. Positions under this specialty included airfield commanders, aviation advisers, experimental test pilots, and safety officers. The other specialty was 71, Aviation Materiel Management. This encompassed lifecycle management, procurement, maintenance, supply, test and evaluation, and transportation. Specialty 71 was a primary specialty for Transportation Corps officers but could be an alternate specialty for aviators of other branches. Excluded from Aviation (15) within the OPMS were Army Medical Department—Dustoff, MEDEVAC—aviators (67J). Also excluded were research, development, test and evaluation test pilots (51C).

By October 1976 the guidance for implementing Aviation as a specialty was beginning to push a clear separation of those who were designated and those not. Local commands were charged closely to monitor the flying status of aviators assigned. The guidance specified priorities in assignment to flying positions. There were also movements within OPMS to manage Aviators the same as other specialists. Among the guidelines related to this was an assumption that an Aviator would normally serve a minimum 3-year operational flying assignment upon graduation from flight school. Aviation-qualified officers having completed their initial utilization were to be assigned duties that would increase their expertise in their basic entry specialty—such as Infantry, Armor, or Artillery—or an advanced specialty. For those aviators not designated 15 or 71, efforts were supposed to be made to assign them to non-Aviation duties as soon as possible. Those affected would receive continuous flight pay as long as they remained eligible under the ACIP and met other requirements, such as passing annual written examinations and flight physicals. However, they were explicitly warned not to expect future assignments to flying duties.

For the short term, creating the OPMS Aviation specialty could not fix imbalances of commissioned officer aviators and positions allowing such an officer to serve in an operational flying assignment as the ACIP required. The imbalance especially affected officers in the grade of MAJ and above. The vast expansion for Vietnam put most field-grade aviators past mid-career. The Army did not initially limit the number of officers redesignated into the Aviation specialty to the Army's requirement for aviators in the senior grades. That produced an excess that made it impossible to give each Aviation-designated officer recurrent assignments in Aviation. Many of the existing pool of majors and lieutenant colonels could not meet the ACIP minimums even if they were assigned continuously to flying positions. Moreover, as a result of the post-Vietnam build-down, by 1977 there were only 44 Aviation battalions in the Army against about 950 lieutenant colonels in flying status. So a gross mismatch existed between opportunities for command in Aviation at lieutenant colonel and the number seeking such positions. At the same time, aviators' prospects looked poor for command in their basic branches. In 1977 only 14 aviators were selected for non-aviation commands at the battalion level. For colonel, there were only seven OPMS aviator commands, and overall about 100 requirements for colonels existed against over 400 colonels in flight status. The Army did have eleven general officer positions designated as operational flying, and ten other positions allowed the incumbent to perform flying duties if rated.

The situation for officers who went into the OPMS Specialty 71, Aviation Materiel Management, was not much different. The one bright spot was that there were only 20 designated colonels for 22 positions. This picture was misleading, because positions were double-listed as opportunities for Specialty 15 officers and for those in Specialty 71. At the same time, though, advancements in aviation technology substantially increased the challenges for those in Aviation logistics roles.

By late 1977 the future looked the same or worse. While seriously over strength in Aviators in Year Groups up through 1970, the Army was seriously under strength in aviators beginning with Year Group 1971. These officers could expect heavy utilization in Aviation to meet the Army's needs. The Army could not allow all individuals opportunities at each grade to develop both their required specialties. So there would be gaps in their qualifications for assignment in at least one area.

Steps toward an Aviation Branch

The increasingly discouraging implications of OPMS for Aviators created alarm, if not anger, among some senior officers who had worked long and hard to make Aviation successful. One was MG George W. Putnam, one of the colonels effectively drafted for flight school under Howze's program. As early as 1971, when he became the Army's Director of Military Personnel Policy, Putnam had tried to deal directly with the issues that OPMS was about. Putnam had inherited an OPMS study that the CSA had thrown out after being unable to get any of the major commands to agree with the results. The CSA directed Putnam start a new study that lasted three and a half years and recommended forming an Aviation Branch. GEN William E. DePuy, commanding TRADOC, disapproved a branch but did approve making Aviation a basic entry specialty.

Putnam retired in early 1977 but was recalled to head the Secretary of the Army Council of Review Boards and the Army Disability Agency. These positions occasioned his continuing to sit in the Deputy Chief of Staff for Personnel (DCSPER) meetings. Upon reading an article by MAJ James Gass that essentially said there was no future for aviator officers in the combat-arms branches, Putnam decided he had to do something. He initially discussed his concerns with BG Charles Canedy, the Aviation Officer in Deputy Chief of Staff for Operations (DCSOPS). With a representative of the DCSPER, Canedy co-chaired an Aviation TF to look at the effects of the ACIP. With no action evident, Putnam took his concerns directly to the DCSPER. In February 1978, MG James F. Hamlet, another Army aviator then the Army's Inspector General, called MG Putnam for his thoughts on a paper that Canedy had staffed for comment.

At that point MG Putnam decided to "rattle the cage" by writing directly to the CSA, Bernard Rogers. In his letter of 9 February 1978, Putnam cut through what he saw as a false problem. He enclosed a marked-up copy of Gass's article and a copy of a letter from BG Sweet, the DCSPER co-chair of the Aviation TF. As MG Putnam interpreted it for the CSA, Sweet's position was that law tied the Army's hands. MG Putnam said he had reviewed the law and its legislative history. In his view, the Army's hands were not tied by the law. The problem was that the Army was giving measures to insure continuous flight pay after 12 years of aviation service a higher priority than adequate career development of combat arms aviators. Rogers asked Putnam to meet with the TF and also with another group of personnel officers to discuss aviator management.

1979 decision not to create an Aviation Branch

On 23 January 1979 the TF briefed Rogers, but the CSA was not ready to make a final decision. At least two factors weighed in his mind. One was a close-hand understanding of the effects the Aviation Specialty would have on younger aviators. Roger's son was an Infantry captain and also an Army Aviator. CPT Rogers faced the same dilemmas that Gass' <u>Aviation Digest</u> article had indicated. The other factor was the view of the senior Army leadership. GEN Rogers held a meeting with all the four-stars about creating a separate branch. During that meeting he directly asked each for his opinion and not one favored a separate branch.

On 13 April 1979 GEN Rogers sent a message that declared Aviation an entry specialty. Each officer going into that specialty still had to select a basic branch—called a "carrier branch." The CSA emphasized that aviators had to be developed professionally without the requirement for branch qualification through ground assignments: "…they must be experts first in Aviation." The CSA defined three areas where additional technical qualifications existed—maintenance, intelligence, and medical. The message said that the impact would be to require aviators to develop only two, rather than three specialties. The CSA stressed that, as the Army implemented training at an annual rate to overcome shortages in company-level officers, the Army had to develop both stability and confidence in a career pattern for its aviators.

From a larger Army viewpoint, the policies in Rogers' 13 April 1979 message partly addressed career progression but failed on other concerns. Among these was where and how commissioned officer aviators would learn the basics of the Army. The experience level of those entering Aviation plummeted. In 1980 eighty percent of those commissioned officers entering Aviation had prior experience in a ground assignment; a year later, that dropped to 20 percent.

1982 Galvin panel on training

Issues came to a head again in the Army Aviation Systems Program Review (AASPR). That convened in March 1982 to look at the results of the first Army Aviation Mission Area Analysis (MAA). GEN John W. Vessey, the VCSA, was an Army aviator who later became the first Army Aviator to become the CJCS. The MAA had identified 134 doctrinal items that needed corrective action. The AASPR boiled those down to 27 doctrinal and concept issues. Among those, the AASPR chose ten to take to the CSA. General officers chaired the panels looking at different issues.

MG John Galvin, commander of the 24th Infantry Division (24ID), chaired the Training Panel. Galvin's panel found a direct connection between the deficiencies in training and absence of an institutional base within Aviation where a cadre of subject matter experts who wrote training materials also taught and contributed to doctrine and materiel development. Creating the system that would let this all happen was the basis for the basic and advanced courses at the branch schools. In the absence of such an institutional base, it was impossible to train and to create the training publications required for Aviation. Galvin's panel further concluded that the basis for any combat arm is the main tactical system. In the case of Aviation, this was the helicopter. Just as the tank required specialized skills and tactics, each type of helicopter—scouts, attack and assault—had unique characteristics that demanded special skills. In fact, unlike the tank, the helicopter demanded a three-dimensional approach to both fire and maneuver. Galvin concluded that it made no sense to fragment a tactical area that, by its very nature, should be a consolidated arm. The end result of the existing situation, MG Galvin reported, was that doctrine was in such disarray that the only sensible solution was to create an Aviation Branch with a branch school responsible for all matters of doctrine, training, and developing materiel.

Galvin struck at the root of objections by noting the distinction between strategic and tactical aviation—the same that Billy Mitchell had defined in World War I. Galvin noted that the Air Force was created because it had a strategic as well as a tactical requirement. Army Aviation, however, was entirely tactical, although the capabilities it brought to the ground force had strategic values. The increasing technological challenges of Aviation made it increasingly difficult for officers to master their professional requirements in two or three branch areas. Galvin noted a critical flaw in the existing system for developing leaders. Specialty Code 15 officers coming through a carrier branch school, going to flight school, then going to a first assignment in a specific type of aircraft lacked any occasion to learn how to lead and fight in Aviation units.

During the discussion of the panel reports, MG John W. Woodmansee finally put things in terms that made sense to everyone. He stated that no professional football team would hire players, train them as linebackers, and then expect them to play the wide receiver position. That, Woodmansee said, is exactly what the Army was doing with its commissioned officer aviators.

Following this discussion, Vessey directed GEN Glenn K. Otis, commander of TRADOC, to 'wrestle this branch question to the ground.'

TRADOC Review of Army Aviation (TROAA) and Branch decision

A follow-on to the AASPR, beginning in May 1982, was a study group called the TROAA. The head of this group was LTG (Retired) Richard West, a former Comptroller of the Army and non-aviator. The other members were MG (Retired) Benjamin L. Harrison, COL Frank Estes, and CWO 4 John Valaer. Harrison had a highly distinguished military career as both an Infantry officer and an Army aviator. Both Estes and Valaer had worked for MG John Galvin's Training Panel. Estes was the Director of Training Developments at USAAVNC and had a highly distinguished career in both the Field Artillery and aviation. MG Carl McNair, CG, USAAVNC, appointed Estes because McNair believed that Estes would be impartial and was not outspokenly committed to forming a separate Aviation branch. CW4 Valaer headed the Warrant Officer Career College.

Over the next few months, the TROAA group visited 12 installations, interviewed 38 general officers, and surveyed over 600 commissioned and warrant officers. Of the commissioned officers surveyed, almost half were not aviators. Several core findings emerged—none, new or startling. The core findings were two: Aviation was inadequately supported at the main branch schools and had no prospects of that being fixed short of creating a separate branch. Also, Aviation was inherently expensive and complex, safety of operations was a central concern, and skilled and experienced aviators were essential to manage Aviation. On these bases, TROAA recommended centralizing Army Aviation proponency at USAAVNC and establishing Aviation as a basic branch of the Army. TROAA recommended a 12- to 24-month detail to a ground arm upon initial entry into Aviation. This reflected the bedrock concern that Army aviators have an intimate knowledge of the combined arms.

In October 1982 GEN Otis briefed the Army's four-star conference. There was strong opposition to the branch proposal. Among those speaking against it were two icons among Aviation general officers—Hamilton H. Howze and Robert M. Shoemaker. They, along with some others, believed that qualification in both Aviation and the ground arms was vital.

On 9 March 1983, despite this opposition, CSA General E. C. Meyer sent Secretary of the Army John O. Marsh a memorandum recommending Aviation as a basic branch of the Army. On 12 April 1983 Secretary Marsh, approved Meyer's recommendation. The date of Marsh's approval became the official birth date of the Aviation Branch.

Personal fallout

Creating the Aviation Branch was professionally painful for some. Strong emotions were involved and quite often openly expressed both in support of a separate Aviation Branch and against the need for a separate branch. In some cases this led to real, as well as perceived unfair treatment of individuals. An example was COL Frank Estes' experience. Along with the other TROAA Group members, Estes traveled to various installations. At one post, a major general who was fiercely opposed to a separate Aviation Branch pointed at Estes and growled, 'putting him on this Study Group is like putting the fox in the hen house!' After completing his assignment with the study group Estes returned to his duties as the Director of Training Developments. His directorate was tasked to finalize and distribute the TROAA Report, and then to develop and field the Aviation Branch Implementation Plan (ABIP). Estes was also tasked to travel to and brief all the major commands on these matters.

Even though the Army decided to form the Aviation Branch, Estes experienced many emotional outbursts during his travels—both for and against the Aviation Branch. For four years as a colonel, Estes was passed over for brigade-level command, despite a highly successful career that included early promotion and an early selection to battalion command. He decided that his involvement in the TROAA and ABIP efforts had somehow damaged his career. On that basis, he prepared to retire and took an assignment at a post in an area where he and his wife wanted to live. After Estes had served a few months at the new post, a general officer called him with congratulations on Estes' selection to brigade-level command. Estes told the general there must be some mistake; almost no one got selected in their fifth year of eligibility for brigade command. He later learned that two major generals on the brigade command selection board noticed that Estes had not been selected previously for brigade command. Both generals were aviators whose successful careers resulted from their remaining closely tied to their basic branches. These officers championed Estes' cause with the selection board and led to his belated selection. Estes' case was but one of many where an officer's career suffered from involvement in forming the Aviation Branch or even expressing an opinion favoring creation of such a branch.

The Branch insignia

An interesting sidelight of creating the branch was the choice of design for the new Aviation Branch insignia. On 22 June 1983 the Directorate of Training and Doctrine (DTD) forwarded three selections for insignia of the new Aviation Branch. First preference at USAAVNC was vertical rotor blades on aviator wings.

This design specifically emphasized the role of helicopters in having squared tips and straight blades. The second choice was an updated Army Air Corps insignia. Third choice was crossed rifle and saber behind aviator wings. Fourth was crossed rotor blades behind aviator wings.

On 7 August 1983 the CSA approved the DCSPER recommendation of the winged propeller—the updated Army Air Corps insignia. The CSA also approved the branch colors. These included the branch insignia on an ultramarine blue background with a golden orange fringe. These colors were those used by the Army Air Corps during its existence.

Impact of changes on WO aviators

The drawdown in Vietnam heavily affected WO aviators. They dropped from more than 14,000 at the peak to less than 5500 by 1977. As with commissioned officer aviators, the drawdown created imbalances that created special problems of professional development. For example, to try to deal with imbalances and provide equity in opportunities for professional development, the Army limited Aviation warrant officers (AWO) to a single aircraft and a single career track. If a WO was already qualified in the Cobra, he would not be considered for qualification in another aircraft. A WO trained in Aviation Safety would not be considered for training in Aviation maintenance.

There were a variety of proposals to adjust the structure of the WO programs. Some of these blurred, if they did not erase, the differences between commissioned and warrant officers. In 1971 the AAAA proposed to the Secretary of the Army to redesignate the Aviation Warrant Officers (AWO) as Army Flight Officers, along with expanding the grade structure for these officers to include CW5 and CW6. In 1972, a tri-level education system was established providing formal training at the basic or entry level for WOs in 59 occupational specialties. The educational system further provided intermediate level formal training in 53 specialties and formal training for 27 specialties at the advanced level. This educational structure began to more closely parallel the tiered system for commissioned officers.

Management of assignments paralleled changes for commissioned officers. In 1972 the Warrant Officer Study called for centralized management of WOs. The study claimed that such centralization would produce greater cross-utilization and flexibility between MOSs where there were overages and shortages. Centralization would also simplify administration by providing a single point of contact. Advocates also foresaw greater identity for the WO Corps as a separate, distinct category of personnel. It would provide more uniformity in applying policies and selection for schools, retention and promotion. Finally it would allow closer coordination over development and implementation of the program. Disadvantages foreseen were loss of functional branch identity, less use of collective expertise in established career branches, reduced effectiveness of the WO Aviation Branch as a focus for Aviation matters, and possibly reduced morale.

Another effect of the drawdown was a shuffling of some Army aviators between commissioned officer and WO status. Some commissioned officer aviators at the end of the Vietnam buildup had once been WOs. Faced with reduction in force (RIF) in the commissioned ranks, some of these people reverted to WO grades. Some of these same individuals later reconverted to commissioned officer ranks. In some cases these changes led to morale and even discipline problems.

The creation of OPMS Specialty 15 for commissioned officers anticipated changes for WOs. OPMS policy assumed that any position calling for a commissioned officer but simply identified as Pilot or Aviator would go away or become a position for a WO. Any commissioned officer position was supposed to involve specific supervisory or staff duties.

One area of special concern was the differences in flight incentive pay between commissioned officers and Army Flight Officers. In 1972 the AAAA proposed changes to equalize flight pay. By the late 1970s Aviation experienced a retention problem with WOs. In June 1979 projections of training rates forecast that losses would exceed gains and the Army would face three alternatives: train more, recall more, or retain more. In light of this information MILPERCEN and Army Research Institute (ARI) conducted a survey. The survey found seven major irritants affecting AWO retention, and unequal flight pay topped the list.

Rather than fixing WOs' concerns, creation of the Aviation Branch increased misgivings for some. In developing the implementation plan for the Branch, USAAVNC proposed that WO aviators would wear Aviation Branch insignia, rather than the WO Corps device. Related to this was the question of who would manage WO assignments. Some feared that the change would destroy the WO Corps. The change would put WO assignments under commissioned officers that understood little and cared little. The idea of WO aviators coming under the Aviation Branch drew an impassioned objection from the Warrant Officer Association. In the end, the idea of including WOs within the Aviation Branch was simply dropped.

Officer personnel management through the late 1980s

Creation of the Aviation Branch, combined with the expanded Aviation force structure that came with the Army of Excellence (AOE) in 1983, set a course to fix some of the problems that had haunted Army aviation for years. The same changes that fixed some problems also had doubtful if not undesirable effects.

Creating Aviation brigades, with their subordinate units and with their grade structure aligned with similar formations across the rest of the Army, greatly helped relieve the imbalance of qualified Aviation officers with no command opportunities. Still, the Vietnam expansion left a huge bulge of qualified middle- and senior-grade officers in a narrow band of year groups. When the new brigade and battalion commands opened for fill, this bulge created a pool of highly-qualified candidates. However, the drawdown and diminishing developmental opportunities for more junior aviators created an opposite situation when the first group of Aviation brigade and battalion commanders completed their tours. Suddenly there were fewer highly-qualified candidates than commands to fill. This created a period of uncertainty about the wisdom of creating a Branch. The situation also gave ammunition to those who had opposed creating the Branch. It took several years for the flow of the new generation of initial-entry Aviation officers to grow up through the new Aviation units to completely fill the pipe.

The immediate effect of forming the branch depended on who a person was, how well the person had done up to that point, and where in the progression through a career a person was. For those who were mid-career or beyond, as were most in 1983 and who had been highly successful, the choice of whether to stay with their basic branch or convert to Aviation was hard. Many who had been most successful stayed with their basic branches. This caused a brain drain for Aviation. For those mid-career and beyond who had been only moderately successful, the choices were often simpler. Most who were early in their careers enthusiastically embraced the Branch. Perhaps most important for the long run, creating the Branch provided a magnet for the best and brightest to enter Aviation—something that they really found exciting that now provided a reasonable expectation of a fully successful career.

Basic problems with WO accession and retention continued into the mid-1980s. In 1986 WO force structure requirements for 1992 exceeded budgeted end strength (BES) by more than 3000 spaces. This shortage briefly led to reconsidering an Enlisted Aviator Program (EAP), an idea resurfaced occasionally.

The experience with post-Vietnam personnel management fostered efforts to find some method to avoid the boom and bust cycle. The result, on 2 October 1988, was the Army Aviation Personnel Plan (A2P2). This plan outlined a methodology to standardize accessions, eliminating needs for large reductions in force, and to prevent improper utilization of aviation officers.

Efforts to smooth accessions and losses closely tied to other efforts. A critical area was training throughputs. A key element in managing those was matching accessions and assignments of aviators into different airframes to meet Armywide requirements. There were efforts to improve this matching. During 1988 USAAVNC prepared to implement the Multitrack approach to IERW. Preparations included anticipating how many aviators would be needed in each track each year and developing a method to test students for aptitudes for the different tracks. The U.S. Army Research Institute Aviation Research and Development Activity (ARIARDA), a tenant at Fort Rucker, focused efforts on optimizing methods for selecting and assigning aviators. ARIARDA validated a new battery of Flight Aptitude Selection Tests (FAST).

Enlisted/noncommissioned officer (NCO) issues

The same increases in complexity of systems and operations that ultimately drove creation of the Aviation Branch also affected enlisted Soldiers and Aviation NCOs.

As with officers before 1972, the Army tried to retain a generalist approach to Aviation NCOs, but complexity of systems forced change by the mid-1970s. An example of affected areas was quality control for Aviation maintenance. For several years commanders, Aviation safety officers, and others complained that the types of inspectors available were unequal to the tasks at hand. Inspectors were of two types. There was a MOS 67F, Airplane Technical Inspector, responsible for all fixed-wing aircraft. The other type was MOS 67W, Helicopter Technical Inspector. The 67W, as the MOS title suggested, took care of all rotary-wing aircraft. As the number and complexity of systems increased, the general-purpose TI simply could not keep pace. Not all inspectors were trained on all the aircraft they had to inspect. Moreover, someone not trained on an aircraft could learn only by a lengthy period of on-the-job training (OJT). That created an additional workload for other inspectors and possible risk to flight crews.

By February 1977 the decision was made under the Enlisted Personnel Management System (EPMS) to create a Narrow Range Technical Inspection

Program. Under this program, fixed-wing maintenance personnel through grade of E-6 would become MOS 67Gs. Helicopter maintenance personnel through grade E-6 would have different MOSs, depending on the specific type of helicopter they worked on—scout/observation, utility, attack, medium lift or heavy lift. Airplane and helicopter TIs would merge under 67W and become quality control supervisors. This change would let commanders pick their most highly qualified E6 in a specific MOS to perform as an inspector. By rotating NCOs from TI to maintenance supervisor, commanders could also develop NCO leaders as well as technicians.

Force restructuring for heavy combat

The In October 1973 the Yom Kippur War jarred the Army into a series of efforts to improve major force structures. Proposals to change Aviation organizations came along with these, particularly in response to the air defense threat. To accommodate new profiles of flying came a more extensive system of airspace management and navigational aids (NAVAID) throughout a corps area. To respond to the growing needs and complexity in these areas, the U.S. Army Air Traffic Control Activity (USAATCA) was established at Fort Huachuca, Arizona, in 1973.

From airmobile back to heavy divisions

The Mideast War drove reorganizations designed to handle heavy, sustained combat. The 1CD reorganized from airmobile to an armored division on the old Reorganization Objectives Army Division (ROAD) model. Instead of an ACCB as part of the division, a separate 6th Air Cavalry Brigade formed. However, in mid-1975 TRADOC began reassessing the ROAD's suitability to meet the Warsaw Pact challenge. On 4 May 1976, GEN William E. DePuy formed a special Division Restructuring Study (DRS) Group. DePuy's special concern was to have a force that could fully use a new generation of improved equipment coming in the early 1980s. The ROAD inefficiently used 1970s weaponry and probably could not keep pace with tactical changes emerging from advances like antitank missiles.

Even before this study ended, the DRS had shown serious deficiencies. The new TRADOC CG, GEN Donn A. Starry, began another initiative, called Division 86. Unlike DePuy, who had sought to build organizations around weapon systems, Starry sought to build organizations around battlefield functions. In July

1979 the DA formally absorbed the Division Restructuring Study (DRS) into Division 86. In 1983 a blending of concepts began fielding as the AOE division.

Army of Excellence (AOE) and Aviation Brigades at division and corps levels

The new AOE design radically increased Aviation force structure. By November 1983 HQDA decisions were pending on the new Aviation force designs for divisions, regiments, and corps. Inclusion of Aviation at the corps level was important because of a basic structural change the Army had made in 1973. In 1973 the Army eliminated the field army as a force structure element. The corps became a logistical as well as operational headquarters. This made the division the major operational echelon to concentrate maneuver combat power. The AOE restructuring called for 10 AC and six Reserve Component (RC) combat aviation brigades (CAB) for light divisions, one brigade for the air assault division, six corps aviation brigades, and three regimental aviation brigades. On 23 November 1983 General John A. Wickham, Jr., CSA, issued directions to implement the AOE.

The creation of the Aviation brigades in the AOE design had huge effects for Aviation. These brigades brought unprecedented opportunities for Aviation colonels to command at the brigade level. Unlike in Vietnam, where there was one nominal Aviation brigade, ordinarily commanded by a major general and a number of Aviation groups as force providers, the new structure made Aviation brigade commanders part of the maneuver command structure. Prior to that there were only five or six positions for aviator colonels in the entire Army. Having both the grades and numbers of positions was a prerequisite to creating a viable Aviation Branch, as well as to creating a corporate expertise that could fully employ the capabilities emerging in the new Aviation systems of the mid-1980s and beyond.

The question of Aviation force structure in the division had been a key element in considerations of whether or not to create a separate Aviation Branch. For example, in November 1979, MG James H. Merryman, CG, USAAVNC, wrote on the Air Cavalry Attack Brigade (ACAB) in the Division 86 Aviation organization. The ACAB was "designed to maximize the capabilities of aviation within the division." It would also "provide a future for the commissioned aviator by giving him a career pattern similar to the other combat arms and aviation organizations of the other military services." He noted that, in the absence of such structure, the Aviation commissioned officer would no longer have access to command organizations of the other combat arms. Also, over the preceding 25 years, the number of aircraft a major commanded had almost doubled. At the same time the sophistication and complexity of aircraft and missions had increased.

At the same time the new AOE brought great gains for Aviation, it also created a problem that the Army never completely overcame. The number of people required to fill all of these positions in this expanded force structure exceeded what the Army had or could obtain. Manpower within the AOE organizations was insufficient to do the mission. That overall shortage of manpower applied to those brigades created a whole series of what became known as the AOE deficiencies. Shortages ran the spectrum from lacking support battalions to not having door gunners or assistant crew chiefs. There were not even second pilots for scout aircraft. The maintenance structure was well below the officially-recognized minimums.

The AOE deficiencies for Aviation came to a head during the summer of 1990 in an ASPR at Fort Rucker. A briefing to the VCSA and the other four-stars resulted in a formal list of AOE deficiencies. That list only highlighted the problem of the bill that went with that. The Army needed about 8300 spaces to fix the deficiencies. By 1990, the beginning of the drawdown following the end of the Cold War meant that there was no way to pay that bill when balanced in the Total Army Analysis (TAA) process across all the Army's needs. The solution to the AOE deficiencies carried over into the mid-1990s, eventually to be addressed by the Aviation Restructure Initiative (ARI).

One area that made gains was Aviation logistics. On 4 May 1987 the CSA approved creating the Aviation Unit Maintenance Companies (AUMC) in Aviation Battalions and Squadrons that currently had AVUM Platoons within Headquarters and Headquarters Company. AVUM Platoons would be consolidated into Companies with no increase in total personnel. The AUMC would remain organic to the Aviation Brigade or Group. About 87 AC and 37 Reserve Component (RC) AVUM platoons would become companies. That change created 124 new command positions for Aviation captains holding Specialty Code 15T Aviation Logistician. This marked the first time that 15T Aviation Logisticians had an opportunity to command in their specialty area at the captain level.

Increasing Aviation force structure, role of key people—GEN Herbert Powell

In retrospect, the transition from the ROAD to the AOE continued a trend that had been evident beginning with the ROAD. While the major focus for the

1960s had been the spectacular rise of the airmobile division and proof of that concept, the Army's use of Aviation had also been expanding in the heavier forces. The ROAD TOE had at least two or three times as much aviation in it as the predecessor Pentomic and earlier force designs.

These increases showed the continuing influence of key people. In the case of the ROAD the key figure was GEN Herbert A. Powell. In 1961 Powell, commanding CONARC, made private, separate deals with the chiefs of several branches, including Infantry, Armor, and Artillery, to transfer some spaces from their branches to create aviation units serving their parochial interests. Only after the branch chiefs had separately agreed on their respective pieces did he bring them all together and lay out the whole design. The overall reaction, when the branch chiefs saw the total size of increase in aviation, was shock. However, each branch chief saw enough in the changes of advantage from his own viewpoint not to object. The net result was a major increase in Aviation across the Army.

Aviation training in the 1970–80s

Through the 1970s and 1980s Aviation training showed two trends. One was a movement toward functions becaming more centralized, with Fort Rucker becoming a worldwide hub. The other was an important expansion in the use of simulations, which not only served training but played increasingly important roles in other areas.

Consolidation of flight training

Even before Vietnam ended, there were efforts to consolidate flight training to achieve efficiencies. Among the results was the beginning of Joint training at Fort Rucker. On 3 March 1971 Fort Rucker received the first class of Air Force initial entry rotary-wing (IERW) students. In May 1974, the Government Accounting Office (GAO) recommended consolidating all undergraduate helicopter pilot training (UHPT) at Fort Rucker. In August 1974 the Interservice Training Review Organization (ITRO) established a Flying Training Committee (FTC) to study the feasibility of that recommendation. This began a prolonged effort that, despite Congressional pushes at various points in time, never reached completion.

The end of Vietnam brought a rapid reduction of activities at other training sites. The last class began at Fort Wolters on 15 July and graduated on 15 November 1973. The last school commandant departed for another assignment immediately after that graduation ceremony. Subsequent IERW training was consolidated at

USAAVNC, Fort Rucker. Before 1973 ended, AH-1F Cobra training moved from Savannah, Georgia, to Fort Rucker. On 21 August 1974, with the graduation of Aviation Qualification Course (AQC) Class 74–2, the U.S. Army Aviation School Element at Fort Stewart, Georgia, deactivated.

In August 1988 practically all leadership training for warrant officer candidates (WOC) became consolidated at Fort Rucker with creation of the Warrant Officer Candidate School. A Company, 1st Battalion, 145th Aviation Regiment (1–145), provided administration and operational control. WOC programs at Fort Sill discontinued in April and at Aberdeen Proving Ground, Maryland, in July. A small RC program continued at Fort McCoy, Wisconsin.

In October 1988 command of the U.S. Army Aviation Logistics School (USAALS) transferred to USAAVNC. Both Fort Rucker and Fort Eustis had provided maintenance training. Several studies over more than 20 years tried to determine the advantages of consolidation at one place or the other. Conflicting interests and anticipated costs of expanding facilities at either location prevented any change.

Closely related to the goal of giving coherence to doctrine were steps to give coherence to organization. One of the key areas for making Aviation work was ATC. During the Vietnam years, training of Army air traffic controllers had migrated from the Air Force at Keesler AFB to Fort Rucker. In mid-1968 the ATC School started at Fort Rucker. The course was 16 weeks long. There were only a handful of people in the class. Most had another MOS and were asked if they would want to go to ATC School. Facilities were part of the sprawling, World War II-era hospital complex. On 20 September the first ATC Familiarization Course graduated. Efforts immediately began to improve facilities and resources. In late November USAAVNC allocated funds to the Naval Training Devices Center at Orlando, FL, to begin procuring radar simulators needed for the Advanced ATC Training Course.

Despite the movement of training, ATC remained one of those areas where the responsibility for doctrine remained fragmented. On 1 July 1973 the Air Traffic Control Office (ATCO) was established under the U.S. Army Communications Command (USACC). In 1973 USAATCA was established at Fort Huachuca, Arizona. Finally, in 1986, Army ATC transferred to Aviation Branch. With that, USAATCA moved to Fort Rucker. This continued the consolidation of key Aviation-related functions recognized in the decision to form the Branch. At the same time, though, Information Systems Command (ISC) transferred ATC to the Army major commands. This created a division of responsibilities that persisted and led to further reorganizations beyond 2000.

In 1988, as part of the general plan to consolidate Aviation training under the Aviation Branch, the USAAVNC Noncommissioned Officers Academy (NCOA) arranged to absorb the advanced noncommissioned officer courses (ANCOC) for two MOSs—Avionic Equipment Maintenance Supervisor (35P) and Air Traffic Control (ATC) Systems/Subsystems and Equipment Supervisor (93D). The U.S. Army Signal Center at Fort Gordon, Georgia, previously taught these courses. First classes were scheduled for January 1989.

In 1991 the detachment of the School of the Americas evolved into the Spanish Helicopter School Battalion (HSB), a part of the Aviation Training Brigade (ATB) within USAAVNC. It reflected and extended the worldwide influence of Aviation.

While Aviation training tended to become more centralized at Fort Rucker, other Aviation-related functions gravitated elsewhere. Of special importance were matters related to Aviation maintenance and logistics. These generally flowed to Fort Eustis, Virginia, reflecting the longstanding tie between the Transportation Corps and Aviation maintenance. On 19 June 1974 TRADOC assigned proponency for logistics materiel, as well as responsibility to plan for Aviation ground support equipment (GSE), to the U.S. Army Transportation School (USATCFE) at Fort Eustis.

RC—particularly National Guard Aviation—also assumed vital training roles at other sites. On 15 May 1982 the first two Army National Guard (ARNG) Army aviators graduated from the Eastern ARNG Training Site (EATS) at Annville [Fort Indiantown Gap], Pennsylvania. In 1985 the Colorado National Guard established the High Altitude Army Aviation Training Site (HAATS). Initially to teach Colorado Guardsmen how to fly in the mountainous terrain, the HAATS quickly expanded its training to other aviators. In 1978 the National Guard Bureau (NGB) developed a concept plan for a Western Army National Guard Aviation Training Site (WAATS) to meet a critical need for basic and advanced aviation training for the ARNG. WAATS was organized on 1 October 1986 and began a phased introduction of training to become fully operational in Fiscal Year 1990. WAATS conducted NGB attack helicopter, aerial gunnery and aeroscout training for National Guard IPs, aviators, and enlisted Soldiers where this training was beyond a State's or unit's capability or authority to perform. Training was done using aircraft, aerial gunnery ranges, and full motion flight simulators.

Simulators after Vietnam

One of the most important changes to emerge in the early 1970s was a great expansion and improvement in simulators. Even before the Army had completely withdrawn from Vietnam, increasing demands on Army aviators to operate regardless of weather, terrain, or enemy conditions drove the advent of more sophisticated flight simulators and an increasing emphasis on their use. The threat environments emerging clearly indicated that attaining proficiency needed to survive in the new conditions could be expensive in time, materiel and lives. Improved simulators were a way to reduce all these costs.

The first prototype of a Huey simulator was completed in 1972. That simulator trained emergency procedures and instruments. Minicomputers drove the system through a narrow range of motion. By 1973 that simulator, known as the Synthetic Flight Training System (SFTS), was installed and operating at Fort Rucker. On 21 March 1974 USAAVNC officially accepted the first SFTS. It was a huge installation, with cockpits, consoles, ladders, lines and lights. Hydraulic power drove individual cockpits through motion in five axes, producing the sensations a pilot had in actual flight.

The SFTS gave some huge advantages. An hour in the simulator cost $65, compared to about $250 per hour in the actual aircraft. No time was lost in refueling or due to extended downtimes for maintenance. The simulator gave a degree of dependability well beyond that of the actual aircraft, and it was unaffected by bad weather. By 1976 use of the SFTS reduced the number of actual Hueys in the fleet at Fort Rucker by 50, making those aircraft available to operational units. Use of simulators, requiring fewer aircraft, also had a huge effect in reducing other requirements, including ground support equipment (GSE), airfield space, and airspace. In a mobilization emergency, the amount of training could be doubled in the SFTS.

By 1977 the combination of increased demands for combat skills in flying and availability of simulators led to revamping the IERW course. Until 13 June 1977, students had 180 hours of actual flight time and 20 hours in a simulator. The new POI had only 175 flight hours but had 40 hours in the simulator. The new, six-phase sequence also included 20 hours of night qualification and 60 hours of combat skills. The last part of the night qualification included low-level autorotation, dealing with NVG failure, operations in confined areas, reconnaissance, and operations on pinnacles and ridgelines. In the combat skills phase, most exercises required coordination with ground units, tactical air (TACAIR) and artillery. The highlight of the course was actually conducting a troop lift. This was done in conjunction with Ranger training at Eglin AFB, Florida.

The SFTS also had an enormous value beyond acquiring basic flying skills. It began to allow units to experiment in an unprecedented way for actual combat operations. Beginning in 1975, the SFTS began arriving at other installations—eventually, around the world. These devices were especially important to units that faced the possibility of having to go rapidly into actual combat. The SFTS replicated a 256-square-mile area that could be adapted for any geographical location. This fact allowed units to test contingency plans requiring IFR flight and allowed commanders to insure that their pilots would be able to react effectively if they had to execute a contingency plan. The SFTS also allowed units to conduct command post exercises (CPX) that integrated the efforts of different members of the combined-arms team.

Based on the success with the Huey simulator, other SFTS trainers were built for several other aircraft, including the Chinook and AH-1 Cobra. Though based in part on the Huey SFTS, the simulator for the Chinook took a different approach. The Huey SFTS was an instruments-only trainer. The Chinook simulator also had a visual representation. A gantry moved a tiny camera over a large terrain board, producing what the pilot saw. The Chinook flight simulator gave the pilot and copilot views both forward and through the chin bubble. The Cobra simulator not only simulated most visual flight maneuvers but integrated weapons, to the extent of simulating tracer fire and impact detonation.

Simulators and simulation became more important with more advanced aircraft and related capabilities. An example came with the fielding of the Apache and its PNVS. During the early fielding too few Apaches existed both to fill operational units and provide training aircraft. Under these circumstances the Army generally opted to push the new combat systems to the field, leaving the schoolhouses without current systems to train operators on. To close the gap on the Apache night navigation systems, USAAVNC adapted an AH-1S Cobra by installing a PNVS. This surrogate trainer allowed pilots to qualify with the PNVS system but also differed from the actual aircraft in ways that required a pilot to unlearn a certain amount before starting to acquire real tactical proficiency.

Antiarmor role of Aviation, evolution of Deep Attack, and advent of the Apache

By the time Vietnam ended, the need for a more capable attack helicopter was apparent. The most telling confrontations came during 1972, fighting tanks at An Loc and Kontum. While rocket-firing helicopters were credited with saving the day, costs were considerable. In a key fight at An Loc, F Battery, 79th Artillery (Aerial Rocket Artillery) destroyed 20 NVA T-54 tanks; but lost eight of the 32 Cobra crewmen engaged in this action. In May 1972 the ground commander credited two air cavalry troops, operating in conjunction with the 1st Aerial TOW team, with saving Kontum. As the focus shifted back to Europe and, especially with insights from the 1973 October Mideast War and possibilities of a major conflict in Korea—senior leaders saw an urgent need for a more capable attack helicopter that could help offset disadvantages the U.S. might face in numbers of tanks on the battlefield. Moreover, in conjunction with new armored systems the Army would field in the mid-1980s, the new generation of attack helicopters would have to be able to conduct missions well into hostile territory.

Studies of the attack helicopters as antitank weapons—Ansbach Trials

The insights gained from Southeast Asia led to serious studies of attack helicopters for an antitank role in Europe. At the same time the battles were underway at An Loc and Kontum, the North Atlantic Treaty Organization (NATO) Armaments Group was conducting a series of trials at Ansbach in Germany. The final report, issued in December 1972, concluded that 'antiarmor helicopters employing hovering fire at standoff ranges are extremely effective in destroying attacking enemy armor.' In some situations, kills per attack helicopter lost exceeded 30 to one. When committed in a European environment to counter a breakthrough during delaying or defensive operations, antiarmor helicopters might kill 15 enemy tracked vehicles per helicopter lost. Also during 1972 an analyst in the U.S. Army Combat Developments Command claimed that the attack helicopter offered the best available force to block a massive Communist armor attack in Europe. Similar conclusions were coming out of tests at Fort Hood of an ACCB with the Triple Capability (TRICAP) Division.

The results of the Ansbach trials and increased concern about armored forces in Europe promoted a continuing interest in attack helicopters. However, within the Army there was disagreement on how to organize these, and some approaches were seen as too costly in the post-Vietnam climate. On 30 June 1973 a report by the U.S. Army Combined Arms Center provided the TRADOC concept for organizing and employing attack helicopters on the post-Vietnam battlefield. The study evaluated three branch proposals: Infantry, aerial artillery, and Armor's integrated fire and maneuver. Infantry assigned attack helicopters at all levels from battalion to division but was impractical because of the large numbers required. Aerial artillery created several ARA battalions centralized at corps, using artillery fire direction nets for control. This option was rejected because it did not respond to ground commanders and lacked scout helicopters. The approved concept envisioned an attack helicopter company of 21 attack and 12 scout helicopters in each division. In addition, each division would have an air cavalry troop or squadron. Attack helicopters were assigned roles in antiarmor, reconnaissance and security, and fire support. Aerial escort, the original role, was considered a part of fire support.

When the 1973 Mideast War jarred the Army into adding more heavy divisions to the force structure and the 1CD reorganized as an armored division. The 6th Cavalry Brigade (Air Combat), a unique combat unit, activated at Fort Hood instead of an ACCB as part of the division.

Adapting existing technology—the TOW Cobra

From a technological standpoint, the first step toward a more capable system was to adapt the Cobra with a more capable missile. On 3 March 1972 the Army awarded a contract to modify 290 AH-1G Cobras by adding the TOW missile system, which gave Aviation a first-shot, armor-killing capability. With the TOW missile the primary mission became antitank, but the Cobra could still provide fire support, escort, and reconnaissance. The AH-1Q carried eight TOWs in two-round pods on the outboard pylons and could still carry 2.75-inch rockets on its inboard pylons. In June 1975 AVSCOM accepted the first AH-1Qs, and U.S. Army Europe (USAREUR) received its first AH-1Q on 25 January 1976. The AH-1S series began with modifications to existing Cobras in 1976. The AH-1S had a Telescopic Sight Unit for the TOW system, and some AH-1S's received a C-NITE upgrade. This let the gunner acquire and designate targets at night or under bad operating conditions. Through 1981 the Army made a series of additional upgrades to the AH-1S. These improvements included such things as a Helmet Sight Subsystem, laser rangefinder and tracker, and IR jammer.

Quest for a long-term, objective system—Cheyenne to Apache

While a major step forward in antiarmor capabilities, the TOW Cobra was a stopgap. The cancellation of the AH-56A Cheyenne on 9 August 1972 created a delay. Research and development (R&D) for the superseding AAH, which became the Apache, was scheduled through 1978.

Controversy and proof of requirement and capabilities

The question of the Army acquiring such an aircraft like the Apache was contentious, despite the 1966 agreement struck between the Army and Air Force over the Caribou. Contention over use of attack helicopters grew so intense that the Senate formed a special subcommittee to investigate. That committee issued its report in 1972. Before 1972 ended the Air Force began developing the A-10 ground attack aircraft to show Air Force commitment to the Army.

The issue remained that of responsiveness to the ground commander and integration as part of the ground fight. In April 1973 GEN Creighton Abrams, CSA, defended the attack helicopter before Congress. GEN Abrams described the AAH as one of the Army's Big Five procurement initiatives. Its main role would be antiarmor. Questioned about duplication with Air Force tactical aircraft, Abrams said the ground commander had a full-time need: The helicopter gave a unique capability to give precise, close fires to engaged infantry.

The Advanced Attack Helicopter (AAH)—differing approaches to a technological solution

On 22 June 1973 the Secretary of the Army announced that Bell Helicopter Company and Hughes Tool Company's Aircraft Division won the five-company competition to develop an Advanced Attack Helicopter (AAH). Bell and Hughes took radically different approaches to the challenges of survivability that were part of the required operational capability (ROC). The aircraft had to be able to continue operating despite direct hits by a .50 caliber round to the rotor mast. Bell approached this problem by beefing up components. The Bell Model 409, which the Army designated the YAH-63, was based on the Model 309 KingCobra and was a massive aircraft. Hughes addressed the same problem by creating redundant systems, at the cost of greater complexity. While superior in many respects, the complexity that came with the Hughes approach became one of the chronic sources of criticism of the resulting Apache—that it would not work in the field because it was too complex and would be impossible to maintain.

Emerging requirements and responses—ground systems outrunning their support, Aviation as key enabler

The importance of the attack helicopter to the Army was only one facet of a larger relationship between Aviation and the Army's overall capabilities. Through the late 1970s those trying to address the imminent battlefield in Europe and other likely points of conflict, such as the Korean Peninsula, increasingly focused on several key requirements. One was the prospect of fighting an enemy that had overwhelming superiority in numbers of armored systems. Second was the fact the enemy's basic doctrine was to use these larger numbers in continuous attacks—eventually expecting a breakthrough somewhere. To achieve this, heavy armored forces would be arrayed in echelons, going many miles back from the line of contact. Forces held in reserve would move rapidly to exploit a break-through wherever it came. Another key factor was that none of the places U.S. forces had to defend allowed enough maneuver room to fight a classic defense-in-depth. Falling back on the Korean Peninsula could mean getting pushed into the sea before there would ever be enough attrition to stop attacking forces. In addition, the political goals of fighting required more than just reestablishing conditions before fighting began; combat had to win to the extent of creating a whole new situation for negotiating from a position of advantage. The last consideration was systems the Army would acquire by the mid-1980s. This new generation of weapons included the M-1 Tank, AAH, and the Multiple Launch Rocket System (MLRS). Other systems coming along at the same time would not only allow commanders to kill deep targets but also would let them identify targets and shift attacks quickly enough to take advantage of this deep-kill capability.

One benefit of the changing battlefield was reduced interservice squabbling. By 1976 the Army and Air Force service chiefs agreed on the Army's need for its own antiarmor capability. On 7 April 1976 the Air Force and Army chiefs of staff jointly wrote the chairman of the House Armed Services Committee (HASC). They said that the attack helicopter was organic to the Army ground maneuver unit. It did not perform CAS but complemented Air Force CAS. They noted that Air Force CAS capabilities were centrally controlled, while attack helicopters belonged directly to Army combined-arms teams.

Deep attack doctrine—AirLand Battle (ALB)

By 1981 these factors had created a new way of thinking. Operations attacking deep into the enemy's ranks were no longer a luxury; they were essential. The new battlefield would necessarily be a combined-arms fight. Doctrine thinkers had trouble even finding terms to properly describe the new environment. They thrashed about with various terms, including 'integrated' and 'extended.' On 29 January 1981 GEN Donn A. Starry, TRADOC commander, sent out a message that declared AirLand Battle to be the official term that best tied together all the concepts. In March 1981 he formally published the new operational concept, which went hand-in-hand with the new force structure to be fielded by 1986.

By March 1982 when the VCSA held the Army Aviation Systems Program Review (AASPR) at Fort Rucker, the nature of the operational environment clearly dictated a new role for the attack helicopter. The AASPR took account of the fact that U.S. forces would fight significantly outnumbered in main battle tanks.

A key insight emerging during the AASPR was the centrality of Aviation in the new fight. That was inherent in the nature of the emerging technology. Units with the new M1 Tank might outrun their combat support and combat service support elements. Under these conditions, Aviation forces could be the only means to provide armor units with security, fire support, and resupply needed in thrusts for deep objectives. Aviation thus became a key catalyst to executing ALB. Ironically tanks now faced the same problem of outrunning their fire support that had driven the development of the tank as fire support for infantry in World War I. Attack helicopters now assumed a role like that the tank had originally emerged to fulfill.

The environment also created urgency about completely integrating Aviation into a Joint/combined-arms fight. Survival on the emerging battlefield required a combination of being able to fly NOE, shoot at standoff distances, minimize exposure to enemy air defense systems, and neutralize enemy forward air defenses whether ground-based or aerial. The last particularly required support from the Air Force or, depending on the situation, Navy or Marine systems.

Fielding the Apache

On 30 September 1983, two months ahead of schedule, the first of 535 programmed Apaches rolled out at the Hughes Aircraft Assembly and Flight Test Center at Mesa, Arizona. In January 1984 the first 315 Apaches were delivered to the Army. In May Apache instructor and key personnel training (IKPT) began at Yuma, Arizona. On 16 January 1985 the first Apache arrived at Fort Rucker.

As with most new systems, the Apaches had teething problems. An early incident involving inadvertent activation of the backup control system (BUCS) fed aviators' mistrust of the BUCS and led the Army to suspend use of the BUCS. On 21 August 1987 a fatal crash involving an Apache occurred at Fort Rucker. A fleet-wide grounding and adverse publicity followed.

Demands for Apache crews were high from the outset. In 1987 the Apache Aircraft Qualification Course (AQC) was restructured from 14 to 10 weeks in order to increase student output.

Technology creating new ideas and collateral effects—deep, deep attack operations

As the Army felt its way through fielding the Apache, the capabilities latent in the new technology began to drive new ideas about how to use it. An example occurred in 1986 with the First Unit Equipped (FUE) at Fort Hood, Texas. Previously attack helicopters did not generally operate beyond the forward line of own troops (FLOT). Pilots of the fielding unit—7/17 Cav—carried the thinking that went with their flying Cobras over into the cockpits of the new Apaches. LTG Crosbie E. Saint, III Corps commander, ran an exercise that forced them into thinking how to exploit the Apaches' unprecedented survivability, night-fighting, antiarmor capabilities as that related to the shift in thinking about how to fight the ALB.

LTG Saint contrived a scenario that involved Apaches striking simulated armored forces beyond the limits of the military reservation in a night operation. The most important attribute of the Apache was its forward looking infrared (FLIR), which could find armored vehicles on the move at night. The only other systems that had that capability at the time were FB-111 Air Force bombers and the Navy/Marine A-6 Intruders. The A-6s would not ordinarily be part of an Army fight, and the FB-111s would be committed beyond the corps commander's area. The Apache, which was available to the corps commander in the new Aviation brigade, had this kind of capability. The Apache was ideal to take advantage of the battlefield conditions that would apply to moving armor. While the Apache could not survive against integrated air defense systems, such systems could not operate on the move. Those AD systems moved to protect the armored forma-tions. Moreover, if the AD systems turned their radars on to detect the Apaches, the Apaches automatically knew where to look for their prime targets.

For this exercise, III Corps set up plywood silhouettes of enemy vehicles. Heater blankets on the silhouettes let the FLIR find the targets. The III Corps exercise went off splendidly. The Apache pilots were thrilled at their ability to find and destroy the simulated armored vehicles at night, 20–30 kilometers beyond the supposed FLOT.

During the after-action review (AAR), which LTG Saint personally conducted, he walked up to the large map and posed a new question. If the Apaches could destroy enemy armored forces moving into contact with his divisions, what prevented them from going much deeper—and he deliberately pointed to a position well off the map—and destroying the forces that would be moving at night to come into contact the next day or later? Saint then explained. If those large, reserve, armored formations just sat in place, that was fine. Then they posed him no threat and were ideal targets for other assets, like B-52 bombers or other Air Force strike aircraft. As the corps commander, Saint's real concern was armored formations moving from reserve at night that would enter the battle later. So, instead of talking in terms of Apaches going 20–30 kilometers, LTG Saint was talking about 100–150 kilometers. That was far beyond the range of previous attack helicopter operations but still completely outside the ability of the Air Force to support and an essential piece of the ground commander's fight. Instantly the Apache pilots' whole vision changed. They were no longer talking about a raid but about a deliberate, deep-attack operation as a routine part of the ground fight. Moreover, the new problem became how much fuel they could haul.

AH64 Apache with auxiliary fuel tank on the flight line in Afghanistan

Ripple effects of a new idea—maps and logistics burdens

The shift to a deep attack as a part of the corps commander's fight had all sorts of consequences for attack Aviation. Some were mundane but still problematic. For example, until then, planning and execution was done using 1:50,000-scale maps. When the Operations Officer (S-3) only had to worry about a division's area of operational responsibility (AOR), he had only a limited number of these maps to acquire and maintain. Suddenly, if he was going to have to support the corps, he had an area that was many times as large to cover. That multiplied his demand for the number of different maps he needed, as well as the volume and weight he had to maintain and move around. The solution was changing the scale of maps Aviation used. The squadron went to using the 1:100,000 and even 1:250,000-scale maps that the corps planners used.

Apaches and Joint suppression of enemy air defenses (SEAD)

The deep fight also required basic changes in the way Aviation dealt with the air defense threat and forced aviators' changing their vision of their own place in the larger scheme of things. When deep meant less than 30 kilometers, SEAD included support from ground-based artillery. To provide this support used the assets of all the division artillery in a corps. When deep meant 100–150 kilometers, ground-based artillery was irrelevant. SEAD required Aviation either to go on its own or required coordination for Joint air support. Now Aviation, even though still an integral piece of the ground commander's fight, had to work as part of a Joint air team. The responsiveness and flexibility that had been Aviation's hallmarks from the beginning became slightly constrained by the sheer nature and complexity of the new battlefield.

Natural progression into Joint/Combined operations

Even before the Apaches were fielded, Army aviators, especially in Korea, were becoming increasingly involved in Joint and Combined operations. In 1977 CPT Daniel J. Petrosky was leaving the 101AB for an assignment with the Aviation group in Korea. His mentor shared some insights with him: Petrosky would learn a huge amount about Aviation for the future, which was in Joint and Combined operations. At that time the Joint command had not even formed in Korea. Although he did not entirely grasp all of what he was told, Petrosky quickly learned that Korea was a place to learn a lot. The nature of the missions often involved providing planning and lift for Republic of Korea (ROK) forces. Terrain was the dominant factor. Missions often involved long-distance insertions. Legs of 70 kilometers or more were common. Landings occurred in difficult terrain with treacherous winds. Occasions to go into the field came frequently. The Aviation group frequently worked with naval forces in river crossings. There were major annual exercises—Team Spirit—that involved all forces. Operations required knowing the air tasking order (ATO) and identification friend or foe (IFF) codes—things that many Army aviators did not worry about. Everything about the prospective battlefield was fluid. The fact that North Korea had huge numbers of standing forces and that the South Korean capital of Seoul was easily within the range of North Korean guns created a severely challenging situation. At the time, there was no place an officer could go to study these things in such depth.

Impact of creating Aviation Branch on Joint capabilities

The creation of the Aviation Branch enhanced the ability of Aviation to play increasing roles in the Joint arena. One effect was that it created an expanded cadre of senior leaders that could help develop true experts in Aviation operations. A key part of this professional development was the restructuring of Aviation units to align them in size and grade structure with other units in the Army. Previously the company commander was a major, compared to a captain in other branches. The size and complexity of unit he had often resembled a battalion in other branches. The same problems of span of control went on to battalion and, where present, group command. This force structure gave little opportunity for sequential, progressive development of Aviation leaders. Moreover, with time and attention split with their basic branches' requirements, there was little incentive or time to develop real aviation proficiency. The creation of the Aviation Branch, along with brigades and realignment to create their component battalions and companies, created both a framework and incentives to grow professional Aviation leadership. The expertise and attention that accrued to the officer corps carried over into the NCOs, which now had more proficient leaders who could both coach NCOs and hold them accountable.

The advent of new technology and particularly the advent of the ALB concept both demanded and exploited this higher level of proficiency and sophistication. Operations like deep attacks were very tough, compared to earlier type of missions. By the late 1980s, Aviation had grown a generation of battalion commanders who knew how to do the complex, hard things involved—like establishing drive-through forward area refuel/rearm points (FARP) that minimized the amount of time that aircraft were on the ground—both out of the action and more vulnerable to attack.

Through the late 1980s large exercises, such as Return of Forces to Germany (REFORGER) and Team Spirit, gave Aviation leaders the occasion to practice the skills required on a highly fluid battlefield, unlike the more static situations in Vietnam. When the Cold War ended in 1989, the emphasis on being able to move far and often increased. The key points in the Cold War battle area were well known and had been studied for years. After 1989 USAREUR no longer could know where the fight would be. The focus changed to training to make lots of moves. This set the stage for a capability that proved invaluable in ODS and beyond.

Jointness drives new requirements—solutions by accident: Apache Have Quick radios

With the new demand for coordinating for Joint air to support came a new need for communications that could talk across service lines. Here luck entered the picture.

The Apache was equipped with an ultra high frequency (UHF) radio, but the specifications did not call for a secure or antijam mode. While the first Apaches were being built, the manufacturer of the radio that met the Army's specifications ceased to make that radio. Rather, the manufacturer shifted all production over to a more sophisticated, frequency-hopping system, called Have Quick, developed by the Air Force. Because the less-capable radio was no longer available, the Apaches just got the Have Quick radios by default. However, nothing about the extra capability made its way into the training materials as the Apache was fielded.

Only by chance did the Apache pilots learn they had this Joint capability built into their aircraft. Pilots in the FUE had begun to experiment with manually changing frequency as a way to improve their ability to operate in the kind of EW environment they could expect. Early on, some of the first Apaches from Fort Hood went to Nellis AFB. While there, an Air Force officer asked to sit in and look around the cockpit. He commented that the radio was Have Quick. The Apache pilots had noticed extra positions on the radio switch but could find nothing about what these positions did. The Air Force officer explained. Immediately the Apache crews became interoperable with the Air Force.

The only obstacle was that the Army, having not procured the system, had none of the equipment necessary to synchronize the Apache radios with other aircraft. Nor did the Army receive the document that contained the daily codes. So, to use the system in its advanced mode, Apache crews had to get a timing signal and the proper codes from Air Force aircraft. The Air Force helped the Army by sending an Air Force instructor for 30 days to teach the Army pilots on the system. The use of the radio was written into the manual for Joint air attack teams (JAAT). By the fall of 1986 USAAVNC was teaching the Have Quick system and its use as a normal part of Apache instruction.

Natural evolution of Joint air attack teams (JAAT)

Experience of the first Apache unit working with Air Force aircrews quickly developed additional, Joint capabilities that airmen of both services embraced. One area was target designation. The Apache came equipped with an ALQ-136 radio frequency (RF) jammer. This system created interoperability with the Air Force because of tactics the services jointly developed. The Apaches could jam ground-based air defense radar for Air Force A-10 and F-16 CAS pilots. The Apaches could also use their TADS to put a laser on a target that the Air Force CAS pilots could then follow up with a precision guided munition (PGM). Air Force CAS pilots quickly decided that they wanted to fight in teams with the Apaches. These and related procedures became part of the JAAT manuals. Similar practices developed with the Marines. The early Apaches worked extensively with the Marines' Harrier jets. With the Apache acting as the target designator and the Harrier providing the air-to-ground munition, the Apache crew could save their HELLFIRE missiles and still kill enemy targets quite effectively.

Importance of right leadership

Much of this burst of new ideas and TTP reflected a happy coincidence of leadership. Both LTG Saint at III Corps and his Air Force counterpart were determined to find ways to fight jointly. LTG Saint, who had started out as a tanker, made several trips to Nellis AFB. He brought fixed-wing aviation into the night fight with the Apaches. Saint also not only flew missions in the Apaches so he knew what the gunner saw but also insisted that any very important visitor spend at least a day with the Apache units. That included time to fly a complete mission with the aircrews, from preparations through the entire mission, to the after-action report (AAR). He encouraged bringing Air Force and Marine pilots in to similarly fly missions in the Apache, so they knew what happened and how their actions would affect outcomes with the Apaches. The result was a huge amount of learning all around.

New conditions driving greater mutual awareness and appreciation among Army aviators

The evolution of Apaches in the deep attack also forced Army aviators to become more conscious of each other and work more closely together. For the Apaches to conduct their deep attacks, they needed the protection that only good, current battlefield intelligence could give. As a result, Apache pilots became much more aware and appreciative of their fixed-wing, Military Intelligence (MI) counterparts.

Importance of fielding location

The fact that the FUE was located at Fort Hood had big benefits. Because of III Corps being there, all the warfighting elements that the Apache crews needed to get to know, understand, and work with were collocated. It was not hard for an Apache crew to go visit these other units and vice versa. As a result, through contact and casual exchange, as well as through formal processes, mutual understanding and respect developed. New ideas with novel combinations of new and old technologies developed and grew into effectiveness.

The air defense threat and air-to-air combat role of Aviation

The relationships between Army attack Aviation and the air defense threat changed following Vietnam as part of Aviation's becoming part of a deep, Joint fight. By the mid-1980s Aviation was no longer just concerned about how to avoid air defense but had become an integral part of those assets, along with Joint air and artillery, that had a defined role in the SEAD. Along with this change also came an increased awareness of helicopters in a possible air-to-air combat role.

Gunship-to-gunship threat

The early 1970s saw a new threat evolve that enhanced the emphasis on developing advanced gunships within Aviation. As early as 1972 the West became aware of a new Soviet assault helicopter, which became known within NATO as the Mi-24 Hind. The Hind carried a squad of eight combat-loaded troops but also had auxiliary wings to carry ordnance to clear a path to the LZ. By early 1974 at least two units with these helicopters were fielded, and experience with them changed tactics. The Hind proved capable of acting as an airborne tank in its own right. Moreover the Hind could also destroy helicopters in air-to-air combat.

As a result of this growing, recognized threat, the Army explored the idea of attack helicopters in a dual, air-defense and air-to-air combat role. FM 1–107,

Air-to-Air Combat, was published 12 October 1984. Also in April 1986 JCS Publication 26, Joint Doctrine for Theater Counterair Operations, gave ground commanders at corps levels and below the responsibility for their own counterair operations. Aviation, as part of that ground maneuver force, would be part of the counterair campaign.

To some, the use of Aviation in such roles seemed revolutionary. However, the difference was more apparent than real. Use of Aviation in operations against air targets beyond the FLOT were similar to deep strikes of Apaches against tanks. Only the targets differed. The main difference lay in the formal recognition of these roles. By 1988 USAAVNC was writing doctrine that directly tied offensive counterair (OCA) to deep attacks. The main assets involved would be corps-level Apaches, OH-58Cs, and OH-58D Kiowa Warrior. These armed helicopters would use sophisticated aircraft survivability equipment (ASE) and night vision devices, along with NOE flying, to increase their survivability. They would work in concert with EW and ground fires for SEAD.

Increasing demands for coordination—the battlefield control element (BCE)

The uses of Aviation envisioned by the mid-1980s created an additional requirement for coordination between ground commanders at corps level and below and with Joint force commanders. Doctrine defined the battlefield control element (BCE) at the tactical air control center as the mechanism for this coordination. These changes implied minimum levels of manpower and expertise among the individuals filling these roles.

Importance of planners and commanders recognizing deep attacks as high-risk with scarce assets

Use of attack helicopters in these new roles—particularly in OCA—implied increased risks of losing scarce assets. Decisions regarding this use, therefore, implied a weight of judgment balancing the risks and potential benefits to be gained. Such judgment presupposed an increasing depth and breadth of knowledge not only about Aviation but also about the whole combat force, doctrine, and the dynamics of the battlefield.

Producing commanders and staff officers with the knowledge to make these decisions highlighted concerns about having enough time and other resources to develop leaders who were both technically proficient in matters related to Aviation and knowledgeable in the other aspects of the combined arms. Disagreements about the best way to achieve a workable balance were fundamental to the debates over whether or not to have a separate Aviation Branch before 1983. Those who opposed a Branch often did so at least partly on the grounds that someone raised in an Aviation pipeline would not acquire enough knowledge of the ground aspects to become competent beyond the technical aspects of flying. Some who opposed a Branch also thought that having a Branch would deprive non-aviators of the opportunity to learn enough about Aviation to employ it properly as combined-arms leaders. Those who argued for a Branch believed that not having a Branch deprived the Army of officers sufficiently well versed in the Aviation to realize the potentials within its capabilities.

Whichever way the decision went, the future held a serious challenge of how to develop decision makers with the breadth and depth of knowledge to use full capabilities of Army ground and Aviation assets—challenges that were increasing greatly as the battlefield became increasingly a Joint fight.

Implications of the new conditions for Army Airspace Command and Control (A2C2)

The increased presence of Soviet attack helicopters on the projected battlefield increased the likelihood that U.S. Army attack helicopters would find themselves in a counterair role merely in proximity to their own forces. The likelihood of both friendly and hostile attack helicopters intermingled in a limited maneuver space near ground forces put an increased premium on command and control (C2) of airspace. Thus, the battlefield envisioned by the mid-1980s created a kind and amount of complexity in airspace management that exceeded anything encountered before.

Dual, air-to-air (ATA) and air-to-ground (ATG) capability

Another effect of the presumed presence of Soviet attack helicopters was a need for U.S. attack helicopters to have a dual capability. They would need an ATA capability for self-defense simply to be able to conduct their air-to-ground missions. Even utility and observation helicopters might need to be armed with ATA missiles to protect themselves. The possibility also existed of armed helicopters having to protect areas where the enemy had destroyed friendly ground AD assets or where terrain prevented establishing ground AD.

One means to meet this need was the Light Helicopter Experimental (LHX)—a combined scout/attack aircraft. The LHX would have an ATA combat capability. It would also be equipped with a worldwide navigation system, secure and hardened avionics, and capacity to self-deploy to Europe. LHX could conduct deep attacks under cover of darkness and would replace part of the existing fleet.

By March 1988 MG Ellis D. Parker, CG, USAAVNC, declared that "Air combat operations are no longer fiction and words; they are now a reality." USAAVNC had begun worldwide staffing of a revised FM 1–107, <u>Air Combat Operations</u>. That FM synchronized ATA TTP with the combined-arms team, with the Forward Area Air Defense System (FAADS), and with ALB doctrine. MG Parker credited this new doctrine to lessons from Phase I of the ATA Combat Test (ATAC I), as well as cooperative studies by other NATO countries. He projected that ATAC II, the second phase of these tests, to occur in 1989, would be as significant for air combat as the Ansbach Trials had been for antitank operations. He also warned that realistic training would be essential for success. Aviation had asked the Army leadership to allow forming several OPFOR helicopter detachments, so that the Combat Training Centers (CTC) could create an awareness of and skills needed for these operations.

Proof—operations through ODS

During the years following Vietnam, Aviation engaged in a wide variety of non-combat operations. Aviation also was involved in key combat operations that showed both the strengths and weaknesses of people, organizations, doctrine and training, and materiel. Most important of these were Operation Urgent Fury in 1983, Operation Earnest Will in 1987–88, Operation Just Cause in 1989, and ODS in 1991.

Noncombat operations—HART and MAST as examples

As throughout its history, Aviation responded to needs that often fell outside its obvious realms. Through the years following Vietnam, Aviation expanded its roles to meet special needs of the nation. Each reflected the unique capabilities that the Army had.

High Altitude Rescue Team (HART)

A small but important expansion of this kind of the Army's noncombat role came in 1973. In that year the Army formed the High Altitude Rescue Team (HART) after a military aircraft crashed at 14,000' in the Wrangell Mountains of Alaska. A Chinook performed this rescue. In subsequent years, the HART would perform a number of spectacular lifesaving missions under the most difficult conditions. On 27 May 1988 CW4 Myron Babcock and Randy Mullen, flying a Chinook, conducted an 80-foot hoist rescue at 18,200' feet on Mount McKinley. On 9 June 1995 CW4 William Barker and CPT Jason Turner landed twice at 19,600 feet—the highest-altitude MEDEVAC ever performed to that time.

Military Assistance to Safety and Traffic (MAST)

As it had in prior decades, Aviation participated in a wide array of humanitarian assistance and disaster relief operations both domestic and abroad. In 1969 the SECDEF suggested the possibility of using military assets to respond to highway accidents. On 15 July 1970 a pilot project began. Military helicopters augmented local emergency medical services but were not intended to replace them. Service was limited to serious, civilian, medical emergencies, such as evacuating accident victims, transferring patents between hospitals, transporting key medical personnel or organs. On 1 July 1974 Congress created the MAST Program.

A key figure in establishing MAST was MG Spurgeon Neel. Neel was a pioneer in MEDEVAC, a driving force in selecting the Huey as an air ambulance, and the first commander of the Army Health Services Command, which became the U.S. Army Medical Command. Neel had commanded the hospital at Fort Rucker. He died in 2003, and on 2 April 2004 the USAARL was renamed the Neel Aeromedical Science Center to honor him.

Scientific research support—Army astronauts

Aviation also performed or supported scientific research missions in various ways. For example, the Army conducted high-altitude flights in 1974 to let National Aeronautics and Space Administration (NASA) astronomers observe the Hakoutek comet. Army aviators also became part of NASA astronaut program. On 3 February 1984 LTC Robert L. Stewart, the first Army astronaut, went into space as a Mission Specialist on the space shuttle Challenger.

Foreign military sales (FMS) and training

Aviation played an important role in support to allies of the U.S. Especially important was training. In 1983, at the request of the U.S. State Department, a detachment of the School of the Americas was formed to help El Salvador train pilots. In 1991, out of the need to provide Spanish-language instruction for helicopter pilots grew the Spanish Helicopter School Battalion (HSB).

Public relations and passive deterrence—winning the World Helicopter Championships

During this period Aviation also participated in international competition that showed the extremely high quality of Army aviators. In August 1981 the U.S. Helicopter Team won the 4th World Helicopter Championship, held in Poland. CWO 3 George Chrest was named the World Champion Helicopter Pilot. The U.S. Army team won the championship by a wide margin, despite rule changes made during the competition to try to keep the U.S. from winning.

Combat Operations

Operation Urgent Fury—debut of Special Operations Aviation (SOA)

Operations repeatedly proved Aviation's value, along with the overall strength and durability of its people and systems. In October 1983, barely six months after the Aviation Branch formed, members of the new Branch saw combat during Operation Urgent Fury in Grenada. Urgent Fury also was the debut for the SOA organization that had grown out of the Desert One fiasco. Urgent Fury also provided an unintended but very real combat test of the newly-fielded Black Hawk's survivability. This aircraft, designed to take much more punishment than the UH-1 Iroquois ["Huey"], proved itself under unexpectedly harsh conditions. For Aviation, Urgent Fury meant relearning some basic lessons from Vietnam about employing helicopters under fire—notably, that air assaults should never operate without gunship escort and cover. Urgent Fury successfully evacuated U.S. citizens but not without cost. Despite highly visible disconnects among the services, Urgent Fury foreshadowed adaptive, Joint approaches that led to success elsewhere.

Urgent Fury showed the increasing, if not dominant role of military aircraft in key political-military situations. From the outset success depended entirely on the ability of U.S. military aircraft to transport, supply and protect landed forces despite initially-intense antiaircraft fire, inadequate facilities and almost continual operations.

One of the most notable aspects of Urgent Fury was the short time between the decision to mount an operation and the actual beginning of operations on the ground. Discussion of contingency planning for a noncombatant evacuation operation (NEO) began after a coup in Grenada on 12 October 1983. Much more radical Marxists removed Grenada's Marxist leader, Maurice Bishop, who had already alarmed Washington by his drift since 1979 toward the Soviets, Cubans and Libyans. Anxieties left from the Iranian hostage crisis and Desert

One drove the extremely short timeline. Policymakers wanted to avoid a similar hostage crisis and so hastily contrived Operation Urgent Fury to remove American medical students on Grenada. Early in the morning of 25 October 1983, assaults began on airstrips at Point Salines and Pearls on Grenada. Over the next nine days US troops would rescue American citizens, restore a popular native government, and eliminate a perceived threat to the stability of the Caribbean and American strategic interests there. The combat phase of Urgent Fury ended on 2 November 1983.

The extraordinarily short timeline from decision to execution, combined with OPSEC and C2 structures for Joint operations, made Urgent Fury a case study in worst-case planning and execution. At 1654 Saturday, 22 October, the JCS issued their execute order to Admiral (ADM) Wesley McDonald, Commander-in-Chief of U.S. Atlantic Command (CINCLANT). Despite McDonald wearing NATO as well as Joint hats, his staff was mainly Navy officers. Although they had put together a NEO package, they were unprepared and unequipped to handle a large-scale, land-combat operation. Moreover, no standing forces were already organized that could simply execute the mission. So a Joint Task Force (JTF) had to be formed. That task fell to Vice Admiral Joseph Metcalf, who had been in command for three months and was similarly ill-equipped to organize and execute a land operation. Complicating the situation was the requirement, for diplomatic purposes, to include forces from small, Caribbean nations in the forces. Their role was to create the appearance of a coalition, rather than a U.S.-only mission. Finally the plan had to include participation by both State Department and CIA.

The hastiness and location of planning increased chances for key gaps. A hasty, high-level planning conference on 22 October happened so quickly that the representative of Military Airlift Command, which would have to provide all transport aircraft, could not even reach the meeting in time. Similarly, no senior Marine or SOF representative made the meeting. So the only real participants were Navy staff, unfamiliar with key aspects of the forces involved and the requirements for their success. A contingency plan in the Pentagon gave overall command of a Grenada intervention to U.S. Forces Caribbean, with the CG of XVIII AB on-scene commander. CINCLANT staff had discussed this plan and included it in assumptions for the NEO but omitted even discussion of it for the actual invasion. ADM McDonald, concerned about the uncertainty of opposing forces, called the CJCS. The CJCS approved using the 82AB but stressed the need for OPSEC. So participants from the 82AB and SOF would not be informed of the nature of the mission or other details. They would simply be told it was an exercise. On that basis, the normal lead-time for a deploying of 18 hours was reduced. By Sunday, 23 October, the staff presented McDonald a plan. That night the President approved and JTF 120 activated.

Overall, to succeed without considerable risk, the plan depended on surprise, which depended on information. That was absent, and there was no time to fill gaps. The ripple effects were catastrophic. Some, believing they were only conducting an exercise, left items like flak vests at home. Units arrived with no clear objectives, no detailed plans, and no mission rehearsal. The hour to launch the attacks slipped. Surprise was lost. The result was confusion and casualties. The operation still succeeded.

The 82d Airborne Division (82AB) Experience

Because of extreme security requirements, the 82nd Combat Aviation Battalion was not informed or brought into the planning until Sunday, 23 October. Then only five battalion planners knew about Grenada. That same day a terrorist bomb in Beirut, Lebanon, killed 240 Marines.

Not only was the timeline short but the plan changed as it evolved. As late as 1700 on Sunday, the plan was to self-deploy one company of Black Hawks to Grenada. All day Sunday the Black Hawk company commanders worked with the battalion staff on overwater routes and fuel availability. They concluded that a self-deployment would take two days enroute. So, late Sunday evening, planning shifted to deploying via C-5A transport to Barbados, 130 ocean-miles from Grenada. Still OPSEC prohibited any loading until the operation was underway.

Morning of 24 October began routinely for everyone in the battalion but the planners. Planning continued until 2000. At 2100 the battalion began its alert. At 2300 there was a division briefing. A tourist map with military grids overlaid was distributed. At that point, those present learned they were going into Grenada. They also learned that a coordinated assault by Army Rangers and Marines would precede entry of the 2nd Brigade of the 82AB onto the island.

The division briefing showed that intelligence was badly deficient. The G-2 said that resistance was expected to be light. As a result, attack helicopters were specially left behind. Only one Black Hawk company was requested for mobility.

Preparing for air assault into Grenada

Uncertainties about actual conditions led to continuing to prepare contingency options, which became layers of contingency options. For example, too many unknowns existed to plan airflow only into Point Salines. So the brigade might airland by C-141 at Grenada or at Barbados as the intermediate staging base. Which happened would depend on the enemy situation and the condition of the runway at Point Salines. If the landing were at Barbados, the brigade would download into C-130s. Again depending on the conditions, they would either conduct a parachute assault or airland at Grenada. On Tuesday, 25 October, shortly after the Ranger parachute assault began, communications were established between U.S. Forces on Grenada and the 82AB. Resistance was much stiffer than expected. The Division decided to issue parachutes to both the 2nd Brigade and troops in the assault command post (CP) in case an immediate parachute assault was necessary. As it turned out, the Division was able to land its C-141s at Point Salines, but there was only enough ramp space for one C-130. All C-141s had to offload at the end of the active runway.

LTC Robert N. Seigle, who commanded the Battalion, was also the division Aviation Officer. He chose to go into Grenada with the division assault CP so he could assess needs and help prepare for the one, known company's arrival. By the time he reached Point Salines, more elements of the Aviation Battalion were preparing to deploy, including another Black Hawk company and a company of fully-modernized Cobras. Other assets included a company C2 section, a forward support platoon, a headquarters operations, supply and pathfinder element. Eventually almost the whole battalion was on or around Point Salines.

Contrary to the initial plan, the DISCOM bypassed Barbados and went directly into Grenada. This left the transiting units at Barbados on their own to stage, reconfigure, and move onward as needed. The unexpectedly heavy, early ground fighting immediately required more helicopters. Seigle flew to Barbados to help with offloading the first Black Hawk company. He arrived amidst mass confusion. Black Hawks, deployment kits, parts and C-130s were intermixed all over the ramp. About every 30 minutes someone would tell a crew chief trying to complete a rebuild that all Black Hawks had to move so a C-130 could leave for Grenada. Just prior to dusk B Company had reassembled their aircraft and prepared to fly into Grenada. By then all pilots and crews were exhausted from three non-stop days. A decision was made to allow them six hours' rest.

By 0300 on Thursday, 27 October, B Company was enroute to Grenada. Once there they learned that fuel had not reached Point Salines although the DISCOM's petroleum, oil and lubricants platoon had been ready for two days. Facing these conditions, the Black Hawks improvised their own hot refuel point. They took 500-gallon bladders to the USS Guam, filled them there, and returned to Point Salines.

Early on the afternoon of the 27th, the Black Hawks received orders to take the 1/75th Ranger into Calivigny Point Military Barracks as soon as they could be ready. MAJ Bill Elder, B Company commander, and the Ranger commander studied available aerial photographs to plan the assault. The only landing zones were inside the barracks compound. Conditions could be bad. Because of preparatory artillery and Naval air bombardment, the assaulting force could expect a lot of debris as well as fire. Within 30–40 minutes after initial briefing, they were conducting the assault. They planned for flights of four into the center of the compound.

It took three turns to bring the whole Ranger Battalion onto the objective. The first flight of four aircraft had a catastrophe. The third aircraft going in was hit while about six feet off the ground and spun into the second. The fourth aircraft dove to avoid flying debris and crashed into the center of the compound. The second flight of four had more time to avoid the downed aircraft. It landed into the southern end of the camp. The Rangers rapidly secured the compound and held it through the night. The following day, Friday, 28 October, the helicopters were recovered and the Rangers extracted.

Separate from the assault on Calivigny Point Military Barracks, CPT Francis B. Kaufman as platoon leader, planned a troop insertion with the commander of the 2d Battalion, 505th Airborne Infantry. That action led to capturing the head of the short-lived government and showed the value of the helicopter as an intimidating presence. The command-and-control Huey hovered around the house where the Grenadian general and his bodyguards had holed up. The Huey flying around, peering into windows, and creating a continuing presence disheartened the general enough to make him surrender rather than fight.

Old lessons relearned—gunship escort

For the 82AB and its Aviation, Urgent Fury gave some new lessons and refreshed some old ones. The 82d Aviation Battalion learned valuable lessons about aircraft performance in a hot climate: The fully modernized Cobra proved able to carry more armament with a full fuel load than expected. Urgent Fury was also the first battle test of the Black Hawk. The Black Hawk clearly proved itself in both inserting troops under harsh conditions and in establishing its own hot refuel operations. Urgent Fury also showed that Aviation maintenance was healthy. None of the aircraft experienced any significant maintenance problems, despite austere, dusty conditions.

Some lessons were relearned. As in Vietnam, Aviation proved its value in a quick reaction force (QRF). The 82d Aviation Battalion gave the airborne infantryman range and speed that extended his combat power, supplied his needs, got him to medical facilities when needed, and extracted him at the end. Urgent Fury also revalidated the role of the command-and-control Huey.

Grenada reconfirmed the lesson, already bought in blood in Vietnam, that gunship escort was vital to protect troopships in air assaults. In Vietnam it was almost doctrine not to commit assault helicopters without covering fire support, whether that was artillery, TACAIR, or gunships. As the focus in the 1970s had shifted to the attack helicopter's role as a tank killer, the escort role receded. Combined with flawed intelligence, this lack of emphasis cut the gunships out of the initial force package. By the time they arrived, the fighting was over.

To those who had seen the evolution of the air assault concept from the Howze Board through Vietnam, it was distressing to see the gunships omitted. MG Carl

H. McNair had just become the Deputy Chief of Staff for Combat Development (DCSCD) at TRADOC. He was close to Urgent Fury, because three good friends were key commanders. As the DCSCD, McNair was in constant contact with Army leadership. The questions began to flow, as to how and why Army doctrine and concepts were so outdated as related to low-and mid-intensity conflict. To MG McNair the point was simple: "Conflict is conflict wherever, and you need to train as you will fight." In the heat of battle and with a sense of urgency, the commander committed his troops and assault helicopters before the gunships arrived. Soldiers paid the price.

Perhaps the importance of the gunships to the commander on the ground was best shown in a comment that MG Edwin L. Trobaugh, 82AB commander, made about AC-130 Spectre gunships from an Air Force Special Operations Wing (SOW). These aircraft supported the 82AB on Grenada as a secondary mission. When the AC-130 requested to redeploy, Trobaugh asked to delay until all enemy Soldiers were accounted for. He told the JTF that he would give up his offshore naval gunfire, ground-based artillery, and helicopters before he would give up the AC-130s. These gunships provided a combination of instant surveillance and instant, accurate firepower. Trobaugh described exactly the kind of on-station presence and responsiveness to the needs of the ground commander that was Aviation's bread and butter. In this case, the Air Force, not the Army, provided it.

Special Operations Aviation (SOA)

Urgent Fury was the debut for Army SOA. That had grown out of the April 1980 failure of Operation EAGLE CLAW to rescue U.S. hostages in Iran. Desert One led President Carter, in May 1980, to create a study commission of six senior military officers. Findings included the fact that the military lacked aircraft and crews trained and prepared to perform these types of missions. The bitter experience of Delta Force with Desert One determined members of that unit never again to depend on another service for helicopter support. The Army turned to the 101AB in what was called Project Honey Badger. 101AB had the most and greatest variety of helicopters in the Army. It showed the greatest potential rapidly to develop a rotary-wing special operations capability. Honey Badger centered on the 158th Aviation Battalion, which had the new Black Hawk helicopter. 229th Attack Helicopter Battalion provided pilots and later manned the light attack component, using OH-6A scout helicopters (Little Birds). Both Black Hawks and Little Birds were chosen because of their size and ease of transport. Little Birds could land in very restrictive spots.

Tactical conditions on Grenada leant themselves to using SOF. Rough terrain and hazardous beaches restricted conventional units' landings to two airstrips—Pearl in the northeast and Salines in the southwest. Intelligence indicated that the bulk of the population, including the American students, several enemy battalions and the seat of government were all in southern Grenada. Many key points were not immediately accessible from Salines. Reconnaissance showed that enemy forces were too heavily armed and numerous for small special units to handle by themselves. Intelligence before the mission located only a third of the American students. It would be important to engage and destroy the enemy forces before they could harm or take hostage the rest of the U.S. residents. Capture of the two airfields would fully engage the enemy, keeping them too busy to go after U.S. citizens. Because of the nature of conditions and forces, the JTF divided the island into two zones, with the Marines taking the north in a conventional operation. The southern zone was given to the Joint Special Operations Command (JSOC)—an organization formed after Desert One. This force included the Rangers. If the JSOC failed, the 82AB was to take on the SOF missions.

Altogether SOF attempted 13 missions—10 special and three conventional. Of those conventional missions, two were successful. The third was the Calivigny raid, hastily thrown together using the Rangers against the only enemy battalion still thought to be holding out. In reality, this was an air assault, more suitable for line Infantry with substantial supporting fires. Because the LZ was tiny, any helicopter attack into the narrow streets was extremely high risk. When briefed to the Ranger battalion that carried it out, it was assessed as 'a suicide mission.' The result was three helicopters lost, three killed, and 15 wounded. Casualties would have been higher if the supposed enemy battalion had, in fact, existed. In hindsight it was assessed as a classic misuse of special warfare units. Excessive haste led to not having onsite intelligence. Where such intelligence existed, SOF produced success in Grenada.

A worse intelligence failure came in the effort to rescue political prisoners at Richmond Hill Prison on 25 October. In that instance, the 160th Aviation Battalion flew Delta Force Soldiers. The pilots were unaware of the well-organized air defense network surrounding the capital city of St. George. One helicopter was shot down and others were damaged. One pilot, CPT Keith J. Lucas, died and several Soldiers were wounded. The captives in the prison escaped without armed aid because the U.S. attacks elsewhere made the prison guards panic and flee.

The action in which CPT Lucas died showed the heroism of Soldiers combined with effects of poor planning and execution. Lucas was part of C Company, assigned to take a mix of Rangers and Delta Soldiers into Richmond Hill Prison. During the brief, it was clear that little was known about the objective or the conditions there. The brief said nothing about obstacles or enemy resistance. Lucas was told that they would have the element of surprise. It should be a 'walkover.' All they had to do was set their passengers off in a field. AC-130 gunships would provide supporting fire if any was needed.

As Lucas and his crew flew in daylight from Barbados to Grenada, it became clear at least some of what they were told was untrue. Tuning to the frequency of Radio Free Grenada, which the SEALs already should have seized and silenced, they caught a broadcast that the invasion had started. By the time Lucas reached the northeastern part of the island, the sun was up, they were already over an hour late for the time to arrive at their objective, and one of the M-60 door guns had jammed on test firing. As the Black Hawks approached their objective, they met a hail of antiaircraft fire. Moreover, they could find no open space as described. The prison sat atop a ridge that would have allowed assault only by the helicopters hovering overhead, providing a stationary target. Moreover, another ridge, 300 meters away and 150 feet higher, dominated that ridge. Atop the adjacent ridge sat Fort Frederick with its antiaircraft guns. As the Black Hawks flew low, looking for some way to get close to their objective, Fort Frederick's firing guns were at the same level or above the helicopters. Moreover, the promised AC-130 backups were fully engaged at Salines and unable to help. Navy attack aircraft from the USS Independence could have helped, but no one had briefed Navy pilots on the Ranger/SOF operations. Beyond that, all Navy aircraft had been forbidden to fly south of the northern sector until after midday.

As Lucas' helicopter turned, banked and twisted with bullets coming through, men in the back began to be hit. Under the conditions, aimed fire was impossible for the door gunners. Within moments, Lucas was hit in his right arm. One of the crew chiefs, SP4 Loren Richards, was hit in the leg. All five Black Hawks pulled away out to sea to regroup. All had taken repeated hits but were flying.

About 0630 the Black Hawks received orders to go in again. As they went in, five rounds through the windscreen hit Lucas in the chest. He died instantly. The copilot, CWO 2 Paul Price, was hit in the head but controlled the aircraft, which was trailing smoke. Price tried to keep altitude long enough to land near friendly forces and to avoid crash-landing in the water with wounded aboard. The crippled helicopter passed almost directly over one of the People's Revolutionary Army (PRA) bases. Firing from there locked the aircraft controls. The Black Hawk crashed into a hill, broke in half, and burst into flame. Several were able to escape or were thrown free in the crash. Three were already dead. Two more were trapped inside as the aircraft turned over and burned. The wounded waited three and a half hours for help. Contributing to this delay was apparently a lack of qualification among Army pilots to land on Navy ships and a lack of arrangements for Navy ships to be reimbursed for refueling Army aircraft. During this wait, nine men from one of the Black Hawks rappelled down to the crash site to provide security and aid the survivors. Troops from the People's Revolutionary Army (PRA) approached but, after a short firefight, retreated when an AC-130 arrived and engaged. About 1000 a Navy helicopter arrived and took everyone out.

Of 19 U.S. service members killed in Grenada, 16 were engaged in SOF missions, as were 36 of the 115 wounded.

The Importance of Operation Urgent Fury—Congressional mandate toward Jointness

From Urgent Fury came the most sweeping reassessment of the Defense establishment since the 1947 National Security Act. Despite the success in achieving its specified goals, Urgent Fury, on top of Desert One, convinced Congress that the armed forces and DOD would not take the steps needed to get past service parochialism. It seemed increasingly clear that military success demanded those steps. A Congressional investigation of Urgent Fury revealed the critical need for Joint doctrine, since the services had failed to integrate their efforts adequately during the operation.

On 1 October 1986 Congress passed the Goldwater-Nichols Defense Reorganization Act of 1986. This act radically changed the way the services operated within the Joint Staff. It centralized operational authority through the chairman, as opposed to the service chiefs. It streamlined the command authority from the SECDEF to the unified commanders worldwide. It also reshaped future service leadership by encouraging Joint assignments for officers. Much as the 1947 reorganization had taken away the power of the service chiefs by creating a single Defense budget that led to the infighting among the services for their individual share of a single pie, Goldwater-Nichols forced the services' interests to be subordinated in large measure to the priorities of the Joint warfighting commanders, who had to see things from a perspective of what worked operationally.

Further action addressed the deficiencies in SOF that had shown up in both the Iran hostage rescue attempt and in Grenada. The Cohen-Nunn Amendment to the 1986 Defense Authorization Act created the United States Special Operations Command (USSOCOM) to unify all SOF under one command. This included the Joint Special Operations Command (JSOC) headquartered at Fort Bragg, the parent headquarters for the 160th Special Operations Aviation Regiment (160 SOAR).

160th Special Operations Aviation Regiment (Airborne) (160 SOAR) after Urgent Fury

The experience of Urgent Fury directly affected the 160 SOAR beyond the lost aircraft and loss of one life.

Urgent Fury forced recognition that the 160th needed more resources, including helicopters. The Army activated the 129th Combat Aviation Company under direct control of the 160th although located at Hunter Army Airfield near Fort Stewart, Georgia. The location gave the unit ready access to one of the key force-projection bases in Continental United States (CONUS). Hunter AAF had the Army's longest runway east of the Mississippi River and could handle the Air Force's C-5 Galaxy transport. Hunter was also near Savannah's deep-water port facility and excellent rail and road networks. Thus, Hunter positioned 160th assets for rapid deployment almost anywhere in the world by any mode of transportation. Eventually assets at Hunter expanded to become the 3d Battalion of the 160th, with the 1st and 2d Battalion located at Fort Campbell, collocated with the 101AB. The 160th also had other units assigned to it. The 245th Aviation Battalion of the Oklahoma National Guard gave the 160th more Cobras and Hueys.

Goldwater-Nichols led to further reorganization. On 16 October 1986 the 160th was redesignated as an Aviation Group. That moved toward creating a separate, unifying headquarters that included all Army SOA. Discussions began about forming a SOF Aviation brigade at Hunter. TRADOC began developing a concept plan, and USAAVNC proposed designating the 160th as the 7th Aviation Regiment. Discussions with 1st Special Operations Command (SOCOM) through November 1987 led to designating the unit as the 160th Aviation Regiment, based on its prior combat citations and placement under the Army's Regimental System.

Operation Earnest Will

With ink barely dry on Goldwater-Nichols, a new challenge emerged to the nation that specifically drew in SOA. In 1987–1988, during Operation Earnest

Will—the so-called Tanker War—the 160th Special Operations Aviation Group decisively proved Aviation's versatility and value in Joint operations. Events during Earnest Will also showed the extremely high quality of Army aviators—especially, senior WO aviators, independently able to make critical judgments and act decisively in ambiguous tactical situations.

A bitter, bloody war erupted between Iran and Iraq in September 1980. As it suffered reverses, Iraq resorted to economic warfare and in 1981 began attacks on oil tanker ships trading with Iran. President Ronald Reagan restated the longstanding U.S. position supporting freedom of navigation and commerce. The Carter Administration had created the Rapid Deployment Joint Task Force (RDJTF) to respond to military contingencies anywhere in the world but especially in the Persian Gulf. On 1 January 1983, President Reagan replaced the RDJTF with a new United States Central Command (USCENTCOM). CENTCOM's AOR included Southwest Asia (SWA) and northeast Africa. This reorganization reaffirmed that freedom of access to Persian Gulf oil resources was a vital strategic interest of the U.S.

In March 1984 Iraq began to attack Iran's oil shipping terminals. Iran retaliated in May 1984 when it also began to attack oil tankers. This began a so-called Tanker War. Ships bound for Kuwait had to steam about 450 nautical miles up the Persian Gulf. The Gulf's shallow depth restricted tankers to a narrow corridor along Iran's exclusion zone. Iran equipped its Revolutionary Guards Corps (Pasdaran) with coastal patrol craft that were small, cheap and easy to crew, but that had serious firepower. The Pasdaran stationed their patrol craft at mainland and island ports, and at gas and oil separation platforms. At these points they could easily watch ship traffic and make attacks. In 1986 Iran began using naval mines and Silkworm missiles as cheap, effective ways to menace ships. By late 1986 the situation became critical for Kuwait, the U.S., and many other nations. Ships belonging to key oil-carrying nations refused to call on Kuwait, and Kuwait asked to register eleven of its national oil company's tankers under the U.S. flag. Reflagging would make these ships eligible for U.S. Navy protection. On 10 March 1987 President Reagan agreed to allow the Kuwaiti reflagging.

After reflagging, CENTCOM developed an escort mission, designated Operation EARNEST WILL, between the Strait of Hormuz and Kuwait's oil terminals. A five-ship naval force, designated the Middle East Force (MEF), provided naval escort. On 24 July 1987, during the first convoy, an oil tanker Bridgeton, struck a mine. Iran had directly challenged the U.S. To maintain its credibility and counter Iran's threats, the U.S. had to expand its forces rapidly.

The threats from mines and small boats required capabilities beyond minesweeping. To deter mining and small boat attacks on convoys, MEF needed to conduct surveillance and patrol missions in the northern Persian Gulf. For these missions, CENTCOM needed SOF. Within two weeks the U.S. Army's 160th Special Operations Aviation Group (Airborne) (TF-160), along with Navy SEALs, received orders to deploy.

The 160th was brought into this operation for specific reasons, reminiscent of problems leading to Desert One. A night mission was hazardous for the Navy. Navy SH-60B Seahawk (LAMPS) helicopters had no night vision systems, armament, or training for the type of engagement.

On 25 July 1987 Marine GEN George B. Crist, CENTCOM's commander, laid down some very severe constraints for the 160th detachment commander The detachment would be under the operational control (OPCON) of Commander, Middle East Forces (COMMIDEASTFOR). The detachment would have no shore-based maintenance. It would have no separate Army communications links. There would be no separate Army resupply flights. Moreover, Crist limited Army personnel to 44, including staff, flight crews, and mechanics.

On 4 August 1987 TF 160 departed CONUS for Bahrain. Ready cooperation of others let TF 160 be fully operational by 6 August. The basic concept of operations (CONOPS) was for Navy's LAMPS to acquire, track, and vector the armed MH/AH-6 Little Bird helicopters to suspicious targets.

Years of training, high-quality people, and commitment to succeed paid off on the night of 21 September 1987. CWO 4 Robert Fladry spotted what he suspected was an Iranian crew placing mines in the water. Under the rules of engagement (ROE) U.S. aircraft could fire only if fired upon or if they made a positive identification of forces engaged in hostile actions. CW4 Fladry judged the situation correctly and fired. Follow-up response seized the ship, confirmed that the Iranians were laying mines, and revealed documents outlining the Iranian mining campaign. As a result of Fladry's judgment and prompt action, the US had definitive proof of Iran's terrorism in international waters. This proof gave vital international support for US operations.

More opportunities for the 160th to prove their worth followed. On 8 October 1987, a short but intense firefight destroyed three Iranian gunboats and ended Iranian attacks for several months. In July 1988 TF 118 from the 18th Aviation Brigade replaced TF 160.

SOA participation in Operation Earnest Will was a smashing success. It had decisively proven Aviation's versatility and value in Joint operations. The 160th's success in Earnest Will was important not only for the Army but for the Joint community. The 160th's deployment was the combat debut for the 160th's brand new parent command, U.S. Special Operations Command (USSOCOM).

Two "Little Birds" of the 160 SOAR make shipboard landing

ODS—Culmination of the Post-Vietnam experience and effort

In January-February 1991, all the trends coming out of Vietnam and running through the 1980s spectacularly merged in Operation Desert Storm (ODS). During very short operations, the Army conducted the largest, longest air assault in history to that time; proved the extraordinary capability to operate as part of a Joint team conducting a vital attack under difficult conditions in TF Normandy; and showed the exceptional capability of the new Apache and HELLFIRE missiles as a devastating combat force.

Context

On 2 August 1990, after a prolonged dispute with other Arab states about oil production and pricing, Iraq invaded its neighbor, Kuwait. Iraq's 120,000 troops and 2000 tanks seized control in less than four hours. Within a week Iraqi dictator Saddam Hussein proclaimed Kuwait as Iraq's nineteenth province. Iraqi troops began massing along the Saudi border and breached it in places. The unexpected invasion raised grave fears about the security of Saudi Arabia and worldwide access to vital oil supplies. With his seizure of Kuwait Saddam Hussein controlled almost one-fourth of the world's oil. On 6 August Saudi Arabia invited U.S. and other forces to enter and defend it and to protect other Gulf states from further Iraqi aggression. President George H. W. Bush ordered U.S. forces to Saudi Arabia. He also began a concerted effort to mobilize American public opinion and form a worldwide coalition to oust Iraq. Over the next several months, the international coalition assembled massive forces to attack Iraq if it did not withdraw from Kuwait otherwise. The U.S. military deployment rapidly grew into the largest since Vietnam.

To his detriment, Saddam Hussein timed his invasion to catch U.S. forces at a historic peak in numbers, readiness, capability, and potential flexibility caused by the end of the Cold War and collapse of the Warsaw Pact. Initiatives beginning in 1986 between NATO and the Warsaw Pact to reduce the mutual nuclear threats had greatly enhanced U.S. conventional capabilities in Europe. Conscious of Vietnam-era problems, GEN Crosbie E. Saint, who commanded USAREUR, maintained high training levels, even as unit strengths fell. He also created a much more agile, capable VII Corps. By August 1990 the economic collapse of the Soviet bloc also created a huge, global excess of shipping capacity. Thus, contracted vessels were readily available to haul military equipment to SWA. Finally, through the 1980s the U.S. had developed the Maritime Prepositioning Force (MPF). That provided everything a Marine brigade would need to fight for 30 days. At the same time Saudi Arabia's prior investments in modern, high-capacity seaports and airports allowed extraordinary throughput.

In November 1990 United Nations Resolution 678 authorized force to expel Iraq from Kuwait if Iraq did not leave by 15 January 1991.On 12 January 1991 Congress voted support of the UN resolution. On the deadline of 15 January Saddam Hussein showed no signs of leaving Kuwait. President Bush authorized military action. As 0300 Baghdad time, 17 January 1991, the largest air campaign since World War II began. On 27 February 1991, the fourth day of the ground campaign, Kuwait City was liberated.

Aviation in Desert Shield

The first phase of the response to Iraq's invasion of Kuwait was creating a deterrent to his going on into Saudi Arabia and building up forces, preferably to pressure him to withdraw from Kuwait but to mount a major offensive if he did not. The name given to this phase was Operation Desert Shield.

Aviation played a key part in Desert Shield, from the very beginning. Some Kiowa Warriors were already operating in the theater as a legacy of the Tanker War. These detachments, sometimes headed by a CWO, were completely used to working in a Joint environment—especially with Navy Light Airborne Multi-Purpose System (LAMPS) helicopters that gave the OH-58Ds contact range and bearing. On 18–19 January, these OH-58Ds may have taken the first Iraqi prisoners of war from armed oil platforms in the Persian Gulf. A week later, 26 January, other OH-58Ds took control of an Iraqi-held island—claimed to be the first Kuwaiti territory liberated.

Immediately after President Bush announced that U.S. forces would deploy to the Arabian Peninsula, Aviation units in Europe were committed to this effort. Six of Black Hawks of the 45th Medical Company self-deployed through Italy beginning on 21 August. The largest early deployment from USAREUR was the 12th Aviation Brigade from V Corps. On 14 August the unit received its alert.

As in many other key times and places, C2 and logistics became major obstacles to achieving desired ends. CENTCOM badly wanted the 12th Aviation Brigade to reinforce the thin forces already in SWA, but plans rapidly fell apart. Lack of deployment experience, despite REFORGERs, caused frustrating, time-consuming missteps. Simple matters, like updating immunizations and wills, in processing people for overseas movement became complicated. One problem after another arose with rail transportation, then at the seaports. Among the major results of the Aviation Brigade's deployment were checklists and procedures to smooth deployments of the rest of the USAREUR assets.

Logistics in ODS

As with every major campaign, logistics played a key role in success for ODS. The sheer volume of people and materiel moved drew worldwide attention. LTG William G. (Gus) Pagonis, who headed 22d Support Command, captured the essence of what the world saw in the title of his book about logistics in the Gulf War—Moving Mountains. More than 1.2 million tons of materiel arrived in theater in the first 90 days. Even more remarkable were the pace of and constraints on execution. In less than one-fourth of the year required during Vietnam, Desert Shield built the forces in theater up to 184,000 and with a logistical structure less than one-third of the projected requirement.

Wholesale to retail—Aviation providing logistical support

To do the troops any good, though, the mountains had to get down to the Soldier. Aviation provided a key part of the logistical backbone of the theater. The tonnage moved was small compared to that moved by ground vehicles. As from Korea forward, what Aviation moved, when it got to its destination, and how that fit into the larger scheme of operations were sometimes far more important than how much. Air movement in ODS was often especially important because of the long distances from point to point, the road and other environmental conditions, and urgent demands for speed. The climate was among the most severe on earth. Temperatures climbed so high that asphalt pavement literally melted, making ground transport dangerous and sometimes impossible. Throughout operations in SWA, Black Hawks performed invaluable MEDEVAC. Once fighting started, Black Hawk helicopters working as part of attack units performed vital work in extracting POWs. As in every conflict, U.S. Soldiers engaged in impromptu humanitarian relief. After the ground war in ODS, this even extended to wounded, starving, and demoralized Iraqi Soldiers. Aircrews often saw them while flying. Crews often dropped their MREs, as well as bottled water, to them.

Supporting Aviation in the fight

The Aviation component of ODS was on a scale with the rest of the operation. Initial plans anticipated about 900 Army aircraft in theater. That number increased to about 1600 and eventually exceeded 1900. The size and complexity of this fleet, as well as its deployed nature and urgency of the needs, created huge challenges. Moreover, unlike during Vietnam, where about the same size of forces had been deployed at the peak, funding remained more tightly controlled. The result was conducting operations of similar scale as at the peak of Vietnam with less than half the aircraft and severe restrictions on flying hours. Through some "daring funding procedures," by diverting people and available parts, by improvising, and by starving Aviation units not in the theater—AVSCOM successfully maintained the deployed fleet above the standard for the 100-hour war. Even so, some aircraft were at the ragged edge.

Supporting a huge number of aircraft halfway around the world strained Aviation logistics in several ways. At the beginning, without enough strategic airlift to do the whole job at once, Aviation units and their support deployed by different means. Most aviation units deployed by air. Supporting units deployed by sea. The resulting lag sometimes put units in position to fight without the critical support to let them fight.

Even after the surge phase of deployment, distribution of parts remained a major problem. During ODS Aviation logistics used both push and pull systems: The push system moved the bulk of supplies. The pull system shared many features with the commercial, overnight-delivery services found in the United States. This pull system used intra-theater delivery, called Desert Express, which the Air Force created, for low-volume repair parts that small fleets of high-technology systems needed.

To meet Aviation logistical support needs in the theater, AVSCOM created the Theater Aviation Maintenance Program—Saudi Arabia (TAMP-SA). This was under operational control (OPCON) of the Aviation maintenance battalion within the 1st Corps Support Command (COSCOM) in XVIII AB. TAMP-SA Forward at Dhahran—the main airhead into Saudi Arabia and a few miles from the main seaport at Dammam—provided rapid repair, modifications, and return to user units. The other element in Abu Dhabi provided overhauls and acted as a depot. Inability to predict requirements led AVSCOM to put most of its skilled people as far forward as possible. Most were under the OPCON of the AVIM battalions of the first three divisions ashore. TAMP-SA coordinated. Even this structure could not service all systems vital for combat—notably, the Apache's TADS/PNVS and the Kiowa Warrior's mast mounted sight.

A large part of the Aviation logistical support structure was composed of contractors, who generally seemed to perform quite well. One apparent logistical lesson from ODS dealt with contractors' future roles in Aviation maintenance.

For logisticians, as well as operators, some deficiencies that popped up were frustrating because they seemed like things that should have been fixed long beforehand. Reductions in Defense spending, combined with continuing inflation through the 1980s, meant that Aviation was not logistically ready to support a long, big war. The drawdown coming at the end of the Cold War worsened the problem. Much of the existing fleet was old, making aircraft both difficult and expensive to maintain. Because of stringent budgets, for some years, an aircraft had sometimes sat for months awaiting a part. As a result, much of what needed to be done on an emergency basis for ODS was covering well-known, documented deficiencies. An example was the absence of antimissile systems on Black Hawks. The Black Hawks were supposed to have them, but the systems were unfunded.

Shortage of maps posed a major problem throughout ODS but specially concerned some Aviation units that had to cover huge areas and had no other reliable means of navigating. Logistical agencies recognized the deficiencies in Army aircraft navigational systems, and accurate navigation was an ASE issue. So it was treated with urgency. Even so, last-minute efforts could not compensate. AVS-COM looked at several expedients, including GPS. None were both suitable and available. GPS was highly preferred as, by far, the most accurate, but the Army had about 800 sets to cover both Aviation and ground units. Procurement started for 8700 more, but these would not arrive until after the ground war. Logisticians heard rumors of "significant" local purchases. For example, 4th Battalion, 159th Aviation Regiment (4–159), had only two GPS in the whole unit, and one belonged to a Soldier who had just bought it

Shortages had ripple effects on operations. Lack of navigational aids (NAVAIDS), for example, degraded the overall synchronization of fires as envisioned in ALB.

Sometimes even where procurement could respond, the solution posed new challenges. The promise of additional navigation systems for some aircraft raised questions about where and how to install them. At least one logistician mused, "Where are we putting this equipment in an already packed cockpit?"

The austere structure of Aviation units created problems in getting materiel from the wholesale level to the user. Companies and battalions needed more cargo carrying vehicles than they had to maneuver with their required rations and spare parts. Units at these levels had trouble moving their basic ammunition load. Sections double- and triple-handled stuff to use the same vehicle for something else.

Shortages in supported ground units posed problems. Supported units were supposed to have the items and knowledge needed to rig external loads for aircraft. That was often not true.

Pilots themselves quickly learned they could avoid some key problems with the technology in this environment just by changing their ideas about flying. For example, a huge potential logistical problem was availability of Apache rotor blades. Pilots in the first Apache battalions deployed quickly figured out that they could stretch the life of their blades by taping their blades and changing their landings. Rather than hovering, they did roll-on landings that kept the dust back. This change not only reduced erosion on parts but also increased safety in landings by reducing the dangers of brownout—losing visibility and orientation as the cloud swirled up around the aircraft. In preparing to fire, they also learned to do running fire and to fly racecar track patterns to keep out of the dust.

All sorts of challenges popped up as operations began—sometimes leading to imaginative applications of things already present for other reasons. For example, types of lighting to guide aircraft into a location outside an established airfield were compatible with either NVG or FLIR but not both. Workarounds emerged. One was to procure chemical lights that were also compatible with NVG. Another approach was to use a type of chemical heating pad found in MEDE-VAC units. These pads were much larger than some of the chemical sticks, needed only two teaspoons of water to activate, and were reusable. The reuse potential quickly made the heating pads more cost-effective. A box of five, 15-inch chemical sticks cost $73. The heating pads cost $3.19 apiece.

Sometimes logistics problems resulted from poor flows of information. Sometimes this resulted from overzealous OPSEC. Especially after the ground war started, the intelligence officer (S-2) of the 4th Battalion, 159th Aviation Regiment (4–159), could not get release of information from corps on locations of air defense artillery—enemy or friendly. This lack of knowledge it made risky to fly some missions. Timely flow of information also affected FARP operations. FARPs moved without battalion S-3s knowing. Crews flew to locations where nothing was available. That could be create a dangerous situation in an area the size of that covered by ODS. Remoteness of some units or lack of equipment to pass or receive information created critical bottlenecks. AVIM companies complained of only sporadically receiving Aviation safety action messages (ASAM) and other messages giving specific procedures, inspection criteria, and other vital information.

The same kinds of problems arose with manpower. Existing levels of unit manning could not sustain the OPTEMPO in ODS. Outside taskings for guards and door gunners further reduced availabilities. Maintainers successfully peaked efforts, but aircraft readiness began to decline after the first day of operations. The surge in flying hours and resulting maintenance work also demanded full-time maintenance test pilots (MTP). These were unavailable.

Slim manning of units became especially troublesome when plans changed mid-stream. For example, on 27 February plans for establishing a forward operations base (FOB) had to change in response to the unexpectedly rapid movement into Iraq. Lift aircraft had to fly enough longer distances to need refueling. A FARP already existed to refuel attack aircraft but lacked enough people to support the Chinooks and Black Hawks. Those, unlike the attack aircraft, had to set down loads before they could refuel.

Attack Aviation

From the very first, attack Aviation played vital roles in SWA. One of attack Aviation's first roles in Operation Desert Shield was providing C2 for hasty defense. Attack helicopters, working in concert with other services' CAS assets, gave substance to the shield in Operation Desert Shield. For example, intelligence sources indicated that the Iraqis might try to seize the northeastern oil fields of Saudi Arabia on the night of 5 September. On 5 September 2nd Battalion, 229th Attack Helicopter Regiment, conducted a reconnaissance of what was becoming FOB Bastogne for the 101AB sector along Tapline Road. On 7 September 2–229th deployed a C2 element, FARP package, and an attack company to Bastogne. From then into October the only fire support beyond 10 kilometers north of Bastogne was CAS. The Joint force air component commander (JFACC) established a 40-kilometer kill zone southward from Kuwait's border. This let Apaches control CAS as they would conduct numerous hasty attacks in sector. CAS, attack Aviation, and extensive, preplanned fires were configured to whittle away potential enemy forces around Bastogne. As the Marines established boundaries and more Army units arrived, two Apache battalions from the 101AB gradually moved north and west, extending this preliminary type of defense.

Importance of the Chinook

Although attack Aviation received the most public attention, ODS proved the vital role of lift. The Army's 163 Chinooks alone flew a total of 16,955 hours. Without this massive effort, the long reaches of GEN Norman Schwarzkopf's "Hail Mary" plan would have been impossible. During Operation Desert Storm, the Chinooks also inserted and extracted SOF and conducted combat search and rescue (CSAR) missions, recovering downed pilots. The Chinook was often the only mode of transportation that could shift large numbers of personnel, equipment, and supplies rapidly over the distances required. The Chinooks' combination of cargo capacity and speed gave Coalition commanders an unequalled capability.

During ODS, as during Vietnam, Chinooks played a key role in fire support. Chinooks sling-loaded Air Assault Artillery into position so that these ground elements could provide close, continuous fire for division operations.

Complexity of Aviation operations in ODS—TF Stalker

One characteristic of Aviation operations in ODS was their increasing complexity, requiring extensive coordination both vertically and horizontally, as well as Joint involvement. This was true even for very small-scale operations.

An illustration of this situation was TF Stalker, created to conduct long range surveillance (LRS) for XVIII AB during the ground war. TF Stalker's mission was to insert and later extract three LRS teams about 150 miles behind Iraqi lines. Each LRS team had five or six members. Aviation conducted aerial insertion of these teams using teams of Black Hawks with Apache escorts. Three Black Hawks took the teams to the objective with three Apache aircraft providing security escort. One Black Hawk and one Apache remained on standby in the assembly area to conduct internal CSAR if needed. Each aircraft had a GPS for navigation. The Apaches provided security—which, in this case, meant using the Apache FLIR to steer the flight away from observed enemy positions and, if necessary, provide suppressive fires.

Besides the lift and attack assets, this mission required other Army and Joint assets. Coordination involved sending two LNOs to the 3d Armored Cavalry Regiment (3ACR) for crossing the line of departure. These LNOs were OH-58 Kiowa pilots with their aircraft. An EF-111 from the Air Force jammed Iraqi radio waves for non-lethal SEAD. An Army Military Intelligence (MI) Guardrail aircraft allowed long-distance communications via radio retransmission. Guardrail/Common Sensor (GR/CS) was a fixed-wing-borne system for collecting signals intelligence and locating targets. One Black Hawk also had an upper antenna for UHF transmissions to Military Intelligence (MI). Route planning was detailed and involved several echelons, from flight companies through the corps deep operations cell. The route was also checked using a computerized mission planning system from 160 SOAR. A full dress rehearsal was done.

On 23 February 1991 the Black Hawk and Apache teams successfully inserted three LRS teams 150 miles behind enemy lines in Iraq. The operation went off with no enemy forces observed during the flight. About 0115 on 24 February, one of the LRS teams called and asked for extraction, because they had been compromised. The CSAR team launched about an hour later, after extensive coordination with XVIII AB and the 3ACR. The CSAR team safely returned the LRS team about three hours later.

Instrument and night flying—two of "the "Big Three" bear fruit

In March 1973 BG William J. Maddox, Jr., CG at USAAVNC, defined Aviation's "Big Three" training objectives for the post-Vietnam period—instrument qualification, night proficiency, and NOE capability. During ODS, all three but most especially instrument and night flying capabilities proved invaluable. They let Aviation succeed where the other services could not. That was sometimes true even in tasks that were within the other services' primary sphere.

A clear example came on 16 February 1991. Kiowa Warriors had been operating from Navy ships to provide security since departure of TF 160 in the Tanker War. The Kiowa Warriors had a mast mounted sight (MMS) that contained an IR imager, low-light television, and laser range-finder/designator. This package gave the Kiowa Warrior great capability in over-water scouting. Contacts could be identified at 10 miles or more, depending on conditions. The MMS was so good that it was even installed on ships operating in the Persian Gulf. As part of the naval buildup for ODS, on 15 January 1991, what had just been TF-118 officially became 4th Squadron, 17th Cavalry Regiment (4/17 Cav). On 16 February two Kiowa Warriors launched from the USS JARRETT for coastal reconnaissance. JARRETT redirected the OH-58D Kiowa Warriors about 40 miles north to assess bomb damage on an Iraqi Silkworm antiship missile site that had been the target of Navy A-6 Intruders—all-weather, day/night, fixed-wing, attack aircraft. Flying conditions were terrible. The Kiowas flew on instruments through heavy rain and found the Silkworm site intact. The Kiowas were ordered away to clear the area for another strike by carrier-based jets. The Kiowas returned to the JARRETT and refueled, and relaunched but with HELLFIRE missiles and more complete target information. An unmanned air vehicle (UAV) from the battleship USS Missouri found the Silkworm site had survived the second Navy attack. So the Kiowa Warriors were ordered in. They again flew on instruments and fired a HELLFIRE. That missile lost the target. On the next pass, a HELLFIRE destroyed the Silkworm launcher. Reinspection by UAV confirmed that the second HELLFIRE destroyed the primary target but the first had also destroyed an ammunition dump. Destruction of this Silkworm site removed a threat to an amphibious feint to tie down Iraqi forces. The feint was a spectacular success, enabled in a small but key part by Aviation.

The Apaches' superior FLIR let it adapt to meet special needs in the extreme conditions. Apaches of 1st Battalion, 101st Aviation Brigade, did not participate in tank-killing sprees but provided invaluable reconnaissance and other special roles. The FLIR cut through the haze and dust and gave Apache pilots much better visibility than the scout helicopters had. The 1/101 Apaches occupied forward locations before the ground war to support JAATs and artillery. Once the ground war began, they started cross-border reconnaissance operations because of Apache's gun camera capability. Eventually they were reconnoitering for the next FOB. OH-58C Kiowa scout helicopters had neither the survivability nor video recording capacity needed for conditions. So Apaches moved into the scout role. Once the ground war began Apaches also became seeing eyes for Black Hawks carrying Pathfinders to plant beacons for Chinooks.

Aviation compiled an impressive record during ODS. The part that received the greatest public attention was the performance of the Apaches. Apaches reportedly destroyed more than 500 tanks plus hundreds of other vehicles. Although it is always risky to accept any particular figures as being wholly reliable, this rough number clearly showed an impressive contribution to the overall fight. On 27 February 1991 CENTCOM briefed the results of the campaign to that point. The official estimate of Iraqi equipment destroyed stood at almost 2400 tanks, more than 1400 armored vehicles, and more than 1600 artillery pieces. If that figure was accurate, Apaches accounted for about 20 percent of all tanks destroyed. The Apaches' lethality owed partly to the suddenness with which Apaches could arrive and destroy. Apaches repeatedly caught Iraqi air defenses totally by surprise, with their weapons oriented upwards for high fliers and helpless against the Apaches. Significantly, of 35 aircraft lost in combat, not one was an Apache. As a bonus, Apaches' OR rate exceeded 85 percent.

Even with the high visibility of the Apaches' success, few people took any note of another, highly important aspect of their performance. As for Operation Just Cause in 1989, Apaches had shown that they could self-deploy over long distances. This ability reduced both time and amount of strategic lift to put them into action.

TF Normandy—opening the air campaign

One of the smallest yet most successful and important Aviation operations in ODS was TF Normandy. This consisted of eight Army Apaches working with four Air Force MH-53J Pave Low helicopters. The purpose was to blind Iraqi air defense in the opening minutes of the air campaign. This created an unobstructed pathway for fast-moving Navy and Air Force bombers to go directly into the heart of Iraq and attack key facilities.

Technology and timing of its arrival played a key role in TF Normandy. Through the 1980s a worldwide network of GPS satellites stood up. In the few months just before ODS, this network allowed accuracy to within 100 meters around the clock in SWA. For properly-equipped aircraft or vehicles, an unprecedented precision of navigation was possible over long distances, even at night and in bad weather.

Within two weeks after Iraq invaded Kuwait, C-5A transports delivered the first MH-53J Pave Lows helicopters of the Air Force 20th Special Operations Squadron (20 SOS) to Saudi Arabia. As immediate threat from the Iraqi forces declined, a cell including officers from the 20 SOS formed to plan an air campaign. Part of this was an operation to puncture Iraq's air defenses and let Allied aircraft go deep into Iraq at minimum risk. Using mostly French and Soviet equipment, the Iraqis had built a fairly dense, integrated air defense system. This included both medium-and long-range SAMs along with antiaircraft artillery. The combination gave overlapping coverage against both high- and low-altitude aircraft. The Iraqis also had powerful early warning (EW) radars that could identify and track aircraft hundreds of miles away. These EW radars could pass critical information on the size and axis of an attacking force to a sector operations control (SOC). The SOC decided how to maximize the value of the AD assets. Knocking out a SOC could cripple an integrated AD system, but the SOCs were usually deep inside hostile territory and well protected. To minimize casualties in the air campaign, something had to be done to take out the eyes and ears of the AD system.

Planners focused on two EW radar sites that sat right in the path of the planned air attack. Total, simultaneous, instantaneous destruction of these sites was vital. If attacked, they needed only seconds to pick up the telephone and alert the hub. That would activate the entire Iraqi AD system, with the knowledge that the attack was coming from a specific direction. It was also vital to take out two adjacent sites, because all sites had overlapping coverage. Taking out any single site would still leave enough capability to threaten attacking air forces.

Options leading to a mixed Apache-Pave Low mission

Planners considered several options: inserting SOF on the ground, having Air Force Pave Low helicopters attack using their .50 caliber machine guns, and using cruise missiles. All involved high risk that something might survive or be missed. Helicopters offered the best options, because their pilots could loiter on station, assess damage, and reengage targets until they were sure nothing was left.

The best idea overall seemed to be using Apaches, because they carried a mix of weapons that could assure destruction of both hard and soft targets. Apaches, though, could not do the job alone because their navigation systems were not good enough. Also the featureless terrain made NOE flight treacherous. Attacking both sites at the same instant required two aircraft teams to maintain an absolutely consistent average speed across their entire route. The combined requirements seemed beyond the Apaches' capability.

The result was a hybrid option using Air Force Pave Lows with Apaches. The Pave Lows' onboard GPS assured precise navigation, while their terrain-following radar could provide the safety for the Apaches to maintain precise speed along the route.

Even teamed with the Pave Lows, using the Apaches posed challenges. With a full weapons load, the Apache could barely fly the mission on internal fuel. They had little margin for avoiding unexpected threats or bad weather. The idea of establishing a FARP inside Iraq was abandoned because of its complexities and fears from Desert One. Eventually an external fuel tank replaced one 2.75-inch rocket pod.

On 25 September 1990 COL Jessie Johnson, chief of special operations for CENTCOM, called in LTC Richard A. Cody, commanding the 1st Battalion, 101st Aviation Brigade. Cody's Apache battalion had reached Saudi Arabia on 17 August 1990 as the lead element for the division. Cody, who started in the Transportation Corps, was emphatic about maintenance. His battalion stood out in its OR. Johnson told Cody the nature of the mission and asked if Cody could guarantee completing it with 100 percent success. Cody said yes.

Preparations and overcoming skepticism

In early October crews selected for the mission came together to start rehearsals. 1/101st had 24 Apache crews. Cody picked eight but later said that any of the 24 could have done the job. Members of the chosen crews averaged about 26 years in age but included at least three WOs fresh out of flight school. This resulted from the normal method of rostering crews. The least experienced pilot became the front-seat, or gunner, paired with the more experienced pilot in the unit. One pilot had just graduated from flight school in August and reached the unit in the desert. He was paired with the senior IP in his company, CWO 3 Shawn Hoban. This new graduate went through his Readiness Level progression in the desert while training for the mission.

OPSEC was a major concern. To preserve the covert nature of the training and avoid suspicions, Cody continued commanding the rest of his battalion during preparations. Crews did not know their mission or target until the last minute. The same concerns of long-range surveillance that had changed routing practices in Europe existed. All training occurred 700 miles away from the attack area. The crews never practiced the actual route. Even the movements to the actual operational base were masked. The Air Force and Army crews flew separately. By the time they moved into position, at time, King Khalid Military City had so much air traffic that they attracted no attention when they stopped to refuel.

Despite the rehearsals, the choice to use the Apaches had to overcome skepticism. During the fall, the Apaches crews received orders to fly a specified route of about 100 miles at night, sneak up on a gunnery range, and blow up some targets at a precise time—down to the second. They did, unaware they were being tested. The battalion S-3 was in the range tower with the CENTCOM staff. With 15 seconds to go, nothing was visible, although the Apaches were passing the tower. A staff observer asked the S-3 where the Apaches were. With three seconds to go the observer said, 'I guess they're not going to make it.' The area around the tower lit up as all four Apaches fired at the designated time. That clinched the decision. If the Apaches could sneak that close to people who knew they were coming and were looking for them, the Apaches had the stealth for the real mission.

As late as the week before Christmas, there was a final review. Both the CJCS and the SECDEF flew to Riyadh to review the war plans personally. When General H. Norman Schwarzkopf, commanding CENTCOM, came to the Apache-Pave Low mission, he called in COL Johnson and his superior, who commanded the 1st Special Operations Wing. Schwarzkopf pointedly asked if they could guarantee 100-percent success. Both answered yes.

Preparations for TF Normandy reflected some of the longstanding challenges in integrated Joint operations. The Apache and Pave Low crews had never worked with each other before. The different types of units, coming from different services, had different TTP. Each group was unfamiliar with the others. There was a natural, mutual mistrust. Differences in equipment required workarounds. For example, Apaches operated at night using infrared and needed no ambient light. Pave Lows lacked FLIR capability and used NVG, which depended on ambient light. The teams had to find ways to accommodate these differences.

Both Cody and his Air Force counterpart, LTC Richard Comer, knew that success lay in developing a high level of cohesion and mutual confidence. They took a phased approach to training. For example, crews first practiced basic formation skills to learn each other's capabilities and limitations. The actual mission called for flying at night at an altitude of 100 feet, so crews started flying in daytime at 200 feet. They gradually worked to nighttime flying at 100 feet. Training continued regardless of how many crews or aircraft were available, because the real mission had to go so long as one Pave Low and one Apache could execute it.

By December, the crews formed two teams, Red and White. Comer's Red would attack the western radar site. Cody had White. On 10 January the final training flight involved actual timing and distances to identify and fix any problems.

The mission

On 14 January, Air Force and Army helicopters deployed separately to Al Jouf. This was a barren, Joint airfield 500 miles away from the 101AB's home base and about 130 miles south of the Iraqi border. On the afternoon of 16 January the final decision was made on timing the raid. That night, crews for the first time were briefed on the mission. They received maps and photos. One crewmember remarked that it looked like everything they had been practicing. Crews were told to get some rest and write a letter home, just in case. At 2330 crews began pre-flight checklists. At midnight they started engines.

Because their target required a longer flight, White Team left first. The first White Pave Low lifted at 0113. The Red team flight lead left seven minutes later. The two flights wove past any ground lighting they saw to preserve OPSEC. Red Team encountered an unexpected observation post that was extremely brightly lit. The team diverted slightly but noticed small-arms fire. Near the border the White Team drew a missile. Apparently an Iraqi fired in response to the sound of the helicopters. At 0212—right on time—the first Pave Low crossed the Iraqi border.

About 20 miles inside Iraq the Pave Lows reached the initial point and dropped chemical lights so the Apaches could update their inertial navigation systems. With those updates, the Apaches' TADS automatically slewed to the azimuth of their primary targets. Targets appeared, exactly where they should have been. The Pave Lows turned and went to their holding point, ready to provide refueling, CSAR, or extra firepower if needed.

From the initial point, the Apaches flew in at about 45 knots. They achieved complete surprise. All radar systems were tuned high, not looking for helicopters. At precisely 0238 hours the Apaches opened fire with HELLFIREs beyond the range of antiaircraft guns. Intelligence monitoring the sites noted that the radar signals immediately ceased. Each aircraft had a primary target, along with another Apache's primary as a secondary target. That arrangement assured that every piece of the site had redundant hits. The intent was to assure not only that the site could not operate but also that it could not easily be repaired. At four kilometers the Apaches started firing Multipurpose Submunition (MPSM) rockets and then the 30mm cannons. After that they fired flechettes to tear up wires and cables connecting parts of the site. Nothing would be repairable. The whole attack, from first to last shot, took only a few minutes.

After making a final check to be sure that nothing remained intact, the Apaches turned and rejoined the Pave Lows for the return trip. As the TF Normandy helicopters flew out of Iraq, strike aircraft roared by toward Baghdad. At the Saudi border, the Pave Lows disappeared to resume CSAR duties. The Apaches returned to their original base.

Assessing TF Normandy

TF Normandy succeeded beyond any expectations. Both radar sites were completely destroyed. Two days later, an AC-130 gunship went to the sites to destroy anything left. The AC-130 found nothing left to shoot at. Casualty results of the first night of the air campaign were the real measure of success. Planners expected high losses among the aircraft attacking the heart of Iraq on the first night. The losses did not occur.

TF Normandy represented the supreme expression of several streams that had flowed from the latter days of Vietnam forward. The success of TF Normandy was a testimonial to Aviation's continuing ability to attract and retain extremely high-quality people, to train them well in the basics, and to let them adapt to urgent but unusual demands. The mission was a testimonial to those people, their dedication and their stamina. This was a long mission, lasting from lift off at about 0130 until arrival home about 1400. Almost six hours of the mission was on night systems. Cody said that any of the crews in his battalion could have done the job. More significant is that the state of people in Aviation by 1990 was that, quite likely, crews in any Apache battalion in the Army could have done the job. There is little reason to doubt that U.S. Army attack aviation was the dominant force of its kind in the world at that time.

The success also showed the gains made in key technology since the end of Vietnam and the ideas that lay behind it. Most obvious was the leap in capability that came with the Apache, the HELLFIRE missile, and night-vision devices. For those who doubted the performance of the Apache, TF Normandy should have been enough proof. To prepare for and execute this mission, aircraft had to operate at high levels of readiness for long periods under horrible environmental conditions. The Apaches in 1/101st proved they could do this. There was also the huge leap in precision navigation that came with the GPS. Only a year or two earlier, this mission would have been impossible. Worries about air defense threats that had arisen in the early 1970s were not idle. Besides the missile fired at the Apaches on the way in, one Pave Low had a close encounter with a SA-7 missile while returning to the border. The infrared countermeasures system located on top of the external fuel tanks apparently worked, decoying the missile enough to miss.

Finally TF Normandy showed the effects of dramatic changes in thinking about the battlefield and how to organize it. In many respects, TF Normandy fulfilled ideas about deep attack and Aviation as part of SEAD that had evolved into ALB. It also showed the decisive movement toward integrated, Joint operations that was fundamental in the thinking behind ALB. Above all, it reflected the imaginative ideas of people like GEN Crosbie E. Saint, who in 1986 asked the III Corps Apache pilots what kept them from going "Up there"—pointing way off the map. TF Normandy was way off the map in many respects and a huge success all around.

FLIR imagery from Apache gun camera in Task Force Normandy

100 Hours

After 38 days of continuous air attacks, major ground operations began at 0100 on 24 February 1991. At that time, coalition ground forces spanned about 300 miles from the Persian Gulf westward. The XVIII AB had the western flank. VII

Corps occupied the middle of the line. The eastern third of the line was held by a composite of formations from Egypt, Syria, and Saudi Arabia along with the I Marine Expeditionary Force. In the far west the 101AB and French started a massive envelopment. A ground assault sought to secure the allied left flank while an air assault established forward support bases deep in Iraqi territory. In the center 1CD attacked north into a concentration of Iraqi divisions. The eastern forces attacked north into Kuwait. Faced with major attacks from three widely separated points, the Iraqi command had to begin its ground defense of Kuwait and the homeland by dispersing its combat power and logistical capability Within 100 hours Iraqi forces had been crushed.

The first day of ground operations showed the way that Aviation had become an integral part of the Joint/Combined fight. The French 6th Light Armored Division was first across the line of departure, surprising outposts of an Iraqi division. Gazelle antitank helicopters were the first of the French division into the fight, immediately attacking dug-in tanks and bunkers. Kiowa Warriors directly supported the Gazelles. In no time the French had 2500 POWs and controlled the area. The French raced forward and took their objective without opposition. An expected Iraqi counterattack never came. The allied left was secure.

Even before the ground offensive started, Aviation had been working closely with French and Joint assets in preparation of the battlefield. For example, the 3d Battalion, 227th Attack Helicopter Regiment (3–227), conducted two deep attacks at night against moving targets detected by French and U.S. intelligence on 20 February. Sensors included the Air Force Joint Services Targeting and Reconnaissance System (JSTARS) and the French side-looking airborne radar (SLAR) called Horizon. This was the first use in ODS of direct data downlink to support attack helicopter operations. Moving target information went directly to the aviation brigade's tactical command post via frequency modulation (FM) communications from Army Quick Look Special Electronics Mission Aircraft (SEMA), as well as from the French Horizon downlink station. This same mission showed the increasing complexity of Aviation operations. Army RC-12 Guardrail aircraft provided precise location. Also involved were Air Force EF-111 Raven and EC-130 Compass Call aircraft providing non-lethal SEAD. Plans also had three artillery battalions on call to provide lethal SEAD, if needed.

This speed, success, and Aviation's role in the French advance reflected the larger pattern. The 82AB followed the French attack and cleared a two-lane highway into southern Iraq. Fog over the objective caused a two-hour delay before the 101AB started the XVIII AB 's main attack with Apaches and AH-1 Cobras screening. Black Hawks and Chinooks from the 18th Aviation Brigade began lifting the 1st Brigade of the 101AB to seize the initial objective. That was FOB COBRA, 110 miles inside Iraq. It took 300 helicopters to get all the troops and equipment into the objective area. This event was one of the largest heliborne operations ever, if not the largest. Chinooks carried all sorts of things into COBRA, which quickly became a major base, 20 miles across. While 700 high-speed support vehicles dashed northward toward the Euphrates River, 101AB began to leapfrog from COBRA using its helicopters. By nightfall, the 101AB had cut Highway 8—170 miles inside Iraq. This closed the first of several escape routes for Iraqi forces in Kuwait.

The basic operational plan called for the XVIII Corps blocking Iraqi forces to be crushed by the VII Corps and other forces further east. The main focus was the elite, armor-heavy Republican Guard. In XVIII Corps' envelopment, the 24ID had the central role. The 24ID came to this mission with extensive desert training and extraordinary firepower. The 24ID's brigades raced forward, finally stopping on a line about 75 miles inside Iraq after little opposition. Meanwhile, VII Corps, which had the main mission of destroying the Republican Guard, used 11th Aviation Brigade assets to move infantry units into trouble spots and to help armor kill tanks. For this work, the VII Corps had 223 attack helicopters.

The lightning-fast advance threatened to unhinge overall operations. Tanks moving up to 50 miles per hour quickly outran artillery batteries that could move only 25–30 miles per hour . This situation was exactly the kind the 1982 ASPR had foreseen and that initially led to emphasizing Aviation's role in deep attack. To compensate, LTG Gary Luck, XVIII AB commander, leapfrogged his artillery and supply elements. This cut ground-based fire support in half but worked against weak Iraqi resistance.

The effects of synchronized, Joint air-ground operations were devastating to the Iraqis. An example was the 1st Armored Division (1AD) first contact with outpost units of the Iraqi 26th Infantry Division on 25 February. With the 1AD still 35–40 miles from its objective, CAS strikes began. Attack helicopter strikes followed these. At 0200, 2d Battalion, 1st Aviation Regiment (2–1 Aviation), went 30 kilometers across the FLOT to destroy targets consisting of rockets, tube artillery, and tanks. VII Corps had received intermittent fires from these positions. The Iraqis were dug in and in fortified positions. Weather was a factor. There was no illumination. Ground fog and haze created a zero visibility at times. Otherwise visibility was limited to about three kilometers. Ceilings varied. Attack helicopters devastated the targets. As 1AD came within 10–15 miles, artillery, including MLRS and Army Tactical Missile System (ATACMS), unleashed barrages. As division lead elements came into visual range, psychological operations teams broadcast surrender appeals. If Iraqis fired on the approaching forces, 1AD repeated artillery, rocket, and missile strikes. Only once did the Iraqis mount an attack after a broadcast. Then, 1AD destroyed 40–50 armored vehicles in 10 minutes.

Operations on 25 February showed several aspects of Aviation as it had developed during the post-Vietnam years. One aspect was the effects of some investment strategies for Aviation systems. The Army did not develop Aviation systems to a common baseline for maneuver under varying conditions as it had with the post-Vietnam generation of ground vehicles—the M1 Abrams tank, the High Mobility Multipurpose Wheeled Vehicle (HMMWV), and the Bradley Fighting Vehicle. The effects of this lack of a baseline showed on 25 February. Command and control (C2) was difficult when 2–1 Aviation went 30 kilometers across the FLOT to destroy part of the Iraqi 26th Infantry Division. The air tactical command post (ATAC) controlling this mission operated in a Black Hawk. For night navigation, Black Hawks depended on NVG, which were not nearly as capable under bad conditions as the Apaches' FLIR. As a result, during the fast advance, the ATAC could not keep up with the Apaches. This situation created a dependence on long-haul communications that the Apaches lacked. So, to maintain contact with the ATAC, OH-58 Kiowas were used as a relay to minimize communication lag. This all but replicated the condition that artillery pilots had found in Europe 40 years earlier: without an observation aircraft aloft as a relay, forces that were supposed to provide fires were blind and largely ineffective. So, attack helicopters formed parts of ad-hoc, air-ground killing teams.

On 25 February, a battle that drew three Iraqi battalions southward, letting coalition forces swing behind the Iraqis, showed the survivability built into the Apache. Pilots of Company C, 1–227th Aviation Regiment, expected a low-threat mission. It turned into one of the fiercest fights the 1CD had during the 100-hour war. During this fight a ground-launched missile brought down the only Apache lost in combat. It was a frightening moment for CWO 4 Michael Butler and CPT Michael Klingele. As they were searching for targets, Butler saw a flash just to the left of his nose. He had turned the Apache about 10 degrees when the missile hit. Butler fought to maintain control but saw the ground rolling. Klingele recalled seeing the crash in slow motion. The aircraft hit hard and knocked the wind out of both pilots. The pilots scrambled out of the Apache and asked each other if they were okay. Behind them, they heard machineguns. Their wingmen, CWO 2 Edward Sanderlin and 1LT Robert Johnston, had already landed, while the rest of C Company created a perimeter of fire for the rescue. Butler and Klingele ran to the waiting Apache, hooked onto the wing, and signaled to go. Klingele recalled that hooking on went just as planned. They were let down in a safer area and transferred to Kiowas for evacuation. Both were quickly back in the fight.

On 26 February the XVIII AB entered the Euphrates River Valley. 24ID hit the heaviest resistance of the war. Two regular Iraqi divisions, plus one division of the elite Republican Guard, and a commando brigade took heavy fire but stood and fought. For the first time the terrain gave the enemy a clear advantage. Firefinder radars, though, let U.S. forces return up to six rounds for every round incoming. Six Iraqi artillery battalions were destroyed. Weather became a major factor. A shamal in the objective area, along with darkness, favored the U.S. Superior technology—notably, thermal-imaging systems in tanks, Bradleys, and attack helicopters—let U.S. crews hit Iraqi tanks 2.5 miles away, well before the Iraqis even saw anything. The overwhelming, violent combination of superior weaponry and technique brought surrendering Iraqi troops out of bunkers and vehicles. Similar effects appeared in the VII Corps sector. Events moved so well and so rapidly that U.S. Army, Central Command (ARCENT), released the theater reserve.

By 26 February, much of attack aviation's role had devolved to exploitation and pursuit. Some units never received a formal order—only a verbal warning and graphics. There was a measure of juggling and confusion as FARPs began to run low on fuel and aircraft getting fuel or ammunition at one FARP had to go to another to leave fully loaded. There were occasional problems integrating attack helicopters with artillery, as well as Air Force A-10s. In some cases Apaches did not get into the fight at all because ground commanders would not shut down their artillery long enough to get the Apaches in.

Morale among the attack crews was high, and they were eager to get into the fight. Events did not always work as expected. Sometimes units had to actively scour to find forces to engage.

By the end of operations on 26 February, 24 Iraqi divisions were gone. Iraqi Soldiers surrendered faster than CENTCOM could count them, but military police estimated POWs exceeding 30,000. 24ID had outrun its fuel trucks. Junior officers took the initiative to lead refueling convoys across the desert at night. They searched out and refueled vehicles, restoring the 24ID's mobility by midnight.

The fourth day, 27 February 1991, flowed into the morning of the fifth and simply saw remaining Iraqi forces implode. On 27 February coalition forces continued to close the vise on the Iraqis. The Iraqis had no intelligence that let them avoid U.S forces. After securing two airfields, 24ID began to run down a highway and devastated hundreds of Iraqi vehicles trying to redeploy or simply to escape. Unsuspecting Iraqi drivers fled in every direction, abandoning military vehicles and sometimes seizing civilian ones, only to run off highways, jump out and surrender. The Republican Guard's Hammurabi Division crossed the front of the 24ID. That let MG Barry McCaffrey concentrate fire of nine artillery battalions and an Apache battalion on the once-elite force. Hundreds of destroyed vehicles littered Highway 8 and the desert. XVIII AB Corps casualties were negligible. Meanwhile VII Corps bore into the remaining Iraqis with the largest array of armored and mechanized power fielded since World War II. The only setback for VII Corps was a fratricide incident, when an A-10 supporting the British fired on two British infantry fighting vehicles, killing nine Soldiers. On the eastern flank, Marine Central Command (MARCENT), along with the Tiger Brigade of 2d Armored Division (2AD) and the Joint Forces Command North, produced similar results. On the morning of 28 February, VII Corps artillery units fired an enormous preparation involving all its long-range weapons, including tube artillery, rocket launchers, and tactical missiles. Attack helicopters followed.

Cease-fire and Conclusions

President Bush ordered a ceasefire, which went into effect at 0800 on 28 February. By then, coalition forces had nearly destroyed the Iraqi ground forces. The Iraqis lost 3847 of their 4280 tanks, over half of 2880 armored personnel carriers, and nearly all of their 3100 artillery pieces. Five to seven of 43 combat divisions remained capable of offensive operations. There were about 60,000 Iraqi POWs. The U.S. forces had lost 147 KIA. ODS had been the fastest and most complete victory in American military history.

ODS clearly confirmed the concept of ALB. It also confirmed the national investment in advanced military technology—particularly, night vision, location and navigation. Among weapon systems, none was more spectacularly successful than the Apache attack helicopter with the HELLFIRE missile. A single Apache company—B Company, 4th Battalion, 229th Aviation Regiment (4–229), commanded by CPT Ben H. Williams—conducted two classic deep attacks and received credit for defeating an entire armored brigade of the Iraqi 10th Armor Division. Together 4–229 destroyed a whole division ahead of advancing friendly forces. ODS also showed the triumph of Army training in the post-Vietnam years—particularly, the development of junior officers and NCOs. Experiences in logistics repeatedly proved the wisdom of those senior leaders at the 1982 ASPR, who had foreseen Aviation as essential not only to extend the reach of the ground commander's fires but also to push resupply forward fast enough to keep agile ground forces moving. As short as the 100-hour war was, it lasted long enough to provoke criticism of supply. The fuel consumption of helicopters in closing the gap between advancing forces and supplies of fuel and ammunition meant that the war would have had to pause, had it not ended so quickly with a ceasefire.

The 100 hours of the ground war showed some of the inherent advantages attack helicopters gave over fixed-wing attack aircraft. During the so-called Battle of the Causeway on the afternoon of 27 February, attack helicopters operated decisively against Republican Guard forces that had escaped destruction during their flight from Kuwait along the "Highway of Death" the day before. Air Force aircraft could not operate because of huge clouds of smoke from burning vehicles and oil fires. Fleeing Iraqi forces were so far ahead of advancing ground forces that no other types of fires were available to bring to bear. When the shooting was over, the attack helicopters alone had destroyed something between one and two divisions' worth of vehicles. Had they not done so, most of this equipment would have escaped, because the 24ID did not reach this location until 2 March. Again, as the 1982 ASPR had foreseen, the only forces that could prosecute the ground fight were those of Aviation—providing both the tooth and essential tail.

In this series of events, the independence and flexibility of action characteristic of Aviation also proved vital. There was no time to conduct nor information to support detailed planning. Attack pilots from the 229th Aviation Regiment received the barest instructions: Fly due north, pick up the Euphrates river, fly due east along the Euphrates about 50 kilometers to a causeway that led towards Baghdad, and intercept the Republican Guard forces that were trying to escape. All the information the pilots had on the enemy was that he was on the causeway. The only graphic measure was that friendly forces were south of that highway.

The biggest problem the 229th encountered was logistical support. The attack helicopters were so far beyond ground forces that, since the afternoon before, the helicopters depended entirely on an air-supported FARP. For these same reasons, the other major problem the attack pilots had was shepherding their ammunition so that they would have something they could use effectively against a target array of unknown kinds and amounts.

The main hazards to the helicopters were unusual. Several times Iraqis fired SAMs, but none actually hit. The large number of fires and dense smoke from burning vehicles and oil wells apparently confused the guidance systems. At least once a SAM flew toward an Apache, then veered skyward, only to turn and plunge down past the nose into the ground right in front of the Apache. The greatest practical dangers seemed to be natural—inhabitants of the marshes in the area. Pilots hit clouds of bugs that almost completely obscured windshields. Even more dangerous were flocks of waterfowl that flew up out of the marshes. There were so many birds that it was impossible to avoid all of them. Their impact in some cases left damage that looked as though someone had taken a sledgehammer to the aircraft.

Apache fratricide incident, 17 February 1991

One of the more troubling facets of ODS was the incidence of fratricide—the killing of own forces by mistake, sometimes called friendly fire or amicicide. Of 147 U.S. military personnel KIA, 35 died in fratricides. That translated to 24 percent. It is impossible to estimate historical experience because of how losses in prior conflicts were reported. Whatever the historical case, many believed that ODS exceeded any baseline. The difference was more disturbing because people expected that advanced technologies had made the battlefield a much more highly controlled and presumably safer place. The ODS fratricides produced a series of investigations, both official and unofficial, with an eye to preventing similar, future occurrences.

One widely reported and discussed fratricide involved Aviation. On the night of 16–17 February 1991, U.S. ground forces just north of the Saudi border reported sighting Iraqi forces north of their positions. Views differ as to whether any Iraqis forces were actually in the area. The ground commander at the time believed that Iraqis made several forays and that Iraqi hunter-killer teams got very close to his unit. The reconnaissance TF commander, LTC James L. Hillman, anchored his right flank with some scouts. These included a Bradley Fighting Vehicle and M113 APC equipped with special radar to detect ground movement. With his forces so dispersed, Hillman feared being outflanked. He called for Apache backup. About 0100 on 17 February 1991 a team of three Apaches including battalion commander LTC Ralph Hayles found two vehicles. These appeared to be the ones ground forces had described, but the identity was uncertain. Extensive discussion followed among the Apache crews and the ground commander. Eventually Hayles fired two HELLFIRE missiles. These destroyed a Bradley and a M113 APC. Two Soldiers died. Six more were wounded. The next day, the 1ID commander reviewed the gun camera tapes with Hayles, who was later relieved of command. The reason given was that he failed to exercise C2 by becoming personally engaged in the fighting. The same day, the corps commander, LTG Frederick Franks, visited the 1ID's CP. Franks canceled an Apache raid that the division had planned and recalled Hillman's TF partly out of fears of creating conditions for another air-ground fratricide. Shortly after ODS, Hayles retired. He entered private business efforts to get technology into the Army that might prevent the kind of tragedy that had ruined his career and cost the lives of fellow Soldiers.

Several investigations followed. These culminated in a GAO report in June 1993. The GAO report covered not only the incident but also the Army's investigation of the incident. GAO found that human error was the primary cause of the incident. That finding agreed with the Army's internal investigation, leading to Hayles' relief. GAO found no evidence of equipment failure as a cause. The Apaches' navigation systems were apparently working properly. Apache radar warning receivers were known to misidentify ground radar signals, but GAO concluded that condition was not a cause of the incident. In fact, the ground vehicles had turned off their radar specifically because they knew that the signal might cause confusion. GAO, though, found that the Army's internal investigation did not take some factors into consideration or at least did not highlight them as possible contributors. Specifically the Army's investigation did not address the commander's fatigue.

The summary conclusions of the GAO report hid several complexities of the fratricide incident—indeed, of the whole problem of potential fratricides. Key among conditioning factors were the combined capabilities and limitations of the technologies involved. While GAO found no evidence that equipment failure caused the incident, mismatches in capabilities among different types of equipment were clearly involved. The killing range of the guns and missiles was considerably beyond the range of devices that allowed positive identification of possible targets. The thermal imaging systems used on the Bradleys and tanks could acquire "hot spots" beyond 4000 meters, but the systems could not distinguish shape or outline. Things as far off the mark as camels and oil drums were known to produce false targets. A study conducted after ODS concluded that no amount of training could let an Apache gunner positively identify targets at the range of the HELLFIRE.

Technology—or its absence—was also a factor in another way. The Army had been slow to respond to an identifiable need for reliable combat-identification systems—especially ones that worked with night imaging systems, such as the

Apache's FLIR. During Operation Just Cause in 1989 a fratricide incident resulted from a breakdown in air-ground coordination, combined with aggressive leadership in a Ranger platoon and Apaches' inability to detect glint tape on Soldiers' combat gear. Slowness to field adequate IFF systems came at least partly from cost, even though people recognized that means of identification had not kept pace with advances in weapons. Ground vehicle developers had consciously resisted building in transponder-based fratricide prevention. Objections included maintenance complexity, better alternative uses of room, and worries that IFF emissions might reveal a unit's location. No cost and operational effectiveness analysis for any system that had its major combat debut in ODS considered combat identification. After the first fratricide incident with Marines at Khafji, a rush came to get improved means of identification into SWA. Responses included sending 120,000 square feet of thermal-reflective tape, painting black inverted Vs on vehicles, and eventually sending two types of infrared emitters. One emitter was popularly called the DARPA light—named after its sponsor, Defense Advanced Research Project Agency (DARPA). This light was the first product effective with NVG. It reached the theater on 26 February—two days before the ceasefire.

The way the Apache systems displayed data apparently contributed to Hayles' error, although the GAO report did not highlight this. Because of the Apache display's small size, it displayed only selected data at one time. It identified each set of data as a numbered track. There could be up to ten tracks. Hayles became confused between the data that had been entered manually for the target position and the current readout from the navigation system. Thus, he wrongly thought that the vehicles were at the coordinates presumed to be targets. Further, limited capabilities of air-ground systems were a factor. Hayles could not send a visual display to the ground commander. So, the ground commander relied on the information Hayles passed him by radio. On that basis he authorized the Apaches to engage the targets.

Another piece of background was a lack of training together of air and ground elements. This partly reflected the dispersal of different brigades of 1ID. Apaches belonged to the 4th Brigade, based in Kansas. TF 1–41 was a part of the 3d Brigade, based in Germany. This brigade had no Apaches. So TF 1–41 was relatively unfamiliar with the kind of coordination required for effective air-ground integration. Based on expectations that the Apaches would not be part of the counter-reconnaissance mission, Apache crews were left out of mission rehearsals.

Potential for problems was already recognized. Two days before the actual incident, there was a close call. An Apache gunner visually misidentified a Bradley and fired a HELLFIRE at it. This happened in daylight, with clear visibility. The missile missed, apparently only because the gunner made an error in tracking the target. An informal investigation confirmed that the gunner's error, not a malfunction of the equipment, caused this event. The Aviation battalion commander grounded the crew until they received more training, which began immediately.

A marginal factor setting the conditions for the fratricide was a change in the planned use of the Apaches. When the plan changed to include Apaches, Hayles did not object to flying this additional type of mission. He did express his need to understand how the ground troops were to be positioned—explicitly, to prevent the potential for fratricidal engagements. To compensate for earlier lack of training, TF 1–41 and the Apache battalion agreed for Apaches to fly around the tactical assembly area. This would let both air and ground gunners familiarize themselves with what friendlies might look like. However, the rainbow-shaped boundary that existed on the right flank present on 17 February did not apparently enter into either discussions or this familiarization. Hayles presumably received a copy of TF 1–41's graphics showing the rainbow boundary, but he recalled only a concern about a gap on the right flank between 1ID and 1CD. So, lack of prior planning and rehearsal, combined with omissions of information and focuses at the point of execution all helped set up conditions for a tragedy.

The GAO report did not cite weather as a factor, but weather was certainly a factor in the minds of the aviators involved. At the time the ground commander called for Apache backup, the weather was bad. Besides 25-knot winds stirring up the sand, there was no moonlight. Visibility was bad enough that Hayles' driver got lost just going from the commander's tent to the helipad. The combination of factors led Hayles and his brigade commander to try to avoid flying the mission. However, the division headquarters called, demanding to know where the Apaches were. So Hayles and the brigade commander decided to launch the mission.

The Apache incident, combined with a much more lethal ground-to-ground incident, led to more attention to preventing fratricides. Most approaches tended to involve training and doctrine, rather than materiel. Cost was a major deterrent to a materiel solution. In 1993 the estimate was $250 million to equip the vehicles of just one division with a positive combat identification device. By December 1993 the JCS required acquisition reviews for all new systems to consider combat identification but did not dictate inclusion in the final systems.

Postscript to ODS

The formal ceasefire in Iraq did not mean the end of Aviation's involvement. On 24 April 1991, eighteen Apaches from the remaining elements of the 11th Aviation Brigade in Germany began to self-deploy to SWA. These Apaches became part of Operation Provide Comfort. The 6th Squadron, 6th Cavalry, provided aerial security over a 3000-square-kilometer region in Northern Iraq.

Women in Aviation—Entry Through ODS

As with many changes, entry of women into Aviation brought mixed reactions. Many people long opposed the entry of women into the armed forces in any areas role except traditional ones, such as nursing. Women first entered U.S. military service in the Navy during World War I. Women entered into the Army as part of the overall mobilization of American society in World War II. Women's entry into military aviation came more from women pushing than any pull from men. The period following Vietnam, with the All Volunteer Force, brought the first women into Aviation. The road was not altogether smooth. By the end of ODS, though, women had largely become an accepted part of Aviation.

Women's Air Reserve (WAR)

In the period between the world wars, women involved in civil aviation made several efforts within the U.S. to form groups that could make military contributions. In 1931 several prominent aviatrixes organized the Women's Air Reserve (WAR) in California. The main organizer was Florence Lowe "Pancho" Barnes, a granddaughter of Thaddeus Lowe. Several other world record holders, like Bobbi Trout, were founding members. Their purpose was to aid in disasters where only aircraft could provide medical help. Members of the WAR were mostly doctors, nurses, pilots and parachutists who could go directly to the scene of a disaster by air and help. In this respect they foreshadowed the Military Assistance to Safety and Traffic (MAST) that arose after the Korean War. Though a private organization, the WAR's military intent was apparent in its military structure and titles, uniforms, and content of training. Drills included gunnery practice with machine guns. The women who founded the WAR tried to expand this organization into a nationwide one. In 1934 they conducted a national tour, sponsored by an oil company.

An episode during their national tour reflected the kind of obstacles they met. In New York City they ran into trouble when they appeared in uniform, which included trousers, at a cocktail party thrown for them at the St. Moritz Hotel. They were informed they were violating a state law that prohibited women wearing masculine attire in public. The episode baffled Bobbi Trout, who had worn trousers all her life and recently had been touted, along with actress Marlene Dietrich, as being a fashion-setter for the 'slacks' generation. The WAR was disbanded in 1941 when it looked like an official organization would form.

Women in World War II—WAFS and WASPs

By comparison to some nations, the U.S. was slow to use women in military aviation. Through World War II the basic approach in the U.S. was that women's role in the military was to 'free a man to fight.' Three times formal proposals to draft women appeared. Up to 78 percent of Americans believed that single women should be drafted before any more fathers. About 350,000 women did serve in various noncombat roles. By contrast, the Soviet Union, which had a tradition of women in combat, widely used women pilots. There were three all-woman fighter and bomber regiments. One woman commanded a 300-man, long-range bomber squadron. Lily Litvyak became an ace, and 23 women received the Hero of the Soviet Union medal.

In 1941 Jacqueline Cochran, a record-breaking pilot, tried to form a woman's squadron in the U.S. She got help from Eleanor Roosevelt and promises from GEN Hap Arnold. When nothing happened, Cochran led a group of women pilots to England, where they flew with the British.

Once the Women's Army Auxiliary Corps formed in 1942, members became involved in aviation but only in nonflying positions—Link trainer instructors, radio operators, mechanics, photo interpreters and parachute riggers. In 1942 the Navy took a bolder, highly controversial step. It assigned WAVES (Women Appointed for Volunteer Emergency Service) as air traffic control tower operators. Opponents claimed that women could not handle multiple tasks as controller duties required. Women excelled in these duties, hampered only by the fact that the WAVES' long, tight skirt made it hard to climb up and down the tower ladders.

On 10 September 1942 the Army Air Forces finally created the Women's Auxiliary Ferrying Squadron (WAFS) within the Air Transport Command. The WAFS flew planes from factories to military bases in CONUS. Cochran, to whom Arnold earlier had promised command, was furious. Possibly to placate Cochran, Arnold organized the Women's Flying Training Detachment (WFTD). The WFTD set up a school at Sweetwater, Texas, and taught 1074 women to fly while living under a military regimen. In August 1943 the WAFS and WFTD merged into the Women's Air Force Service Pilots (WASPs).

WASPs, who remained civilians, performed a wide range of duties. They flew every airplane in the AAF inventory. They delivered half of all pursuit planes. When the new B-29 Superfortress showed mechanical trouble during testing, some male pilots were afraid to fly it. Two WASPs toured air bases to show the B-29's safety. WASPs towed targets for aerial gunnery practice, simulated strafing, served as flight instructors, and made check flights on repaired aircraft. Ann Baumgartner, a test pilot, flew the YP-59 jet.

By the end of 1944, with the end of war in Europe in sight, male pilots began pushing for duties WASPs performed. On 20 December 1944 the AAF announced the WASPs would deactivate. By then, 38 WASPs had died in their duties and WASPs had flown 60 million miles. GEN Arnold proclaimed the WASPs a success: 'We will not again look upon a woman flying as an experiment.' Still, when Cochran sought a one-day conversion of the WASPs to military status so they could have veteran status and access to the GI Bill, the request was denied. When the Air Force became independent, women were limited to nonflying positions. In November 1977 WASPs finally received veteran status, but they did not receive military honors until June 2002.

The rise of the Cold War led the armed forces to retain women even as the end of World War II and return of millions of male veterans into the civilian workforce pushed many women out of factories and back into home life. On 12 June 1948 the Women's Armed Services Integration Act of 1949 made the Women's Army Corps (WAC) part of the Regular Army. So, women became a regular part of the permanent military establishment just about the same time as the armed forces desegregated racially.

Women's entry in Aviation—1973 and beyond

Women did not gain entry into Aviation until after Vietnam and about the beginning of the All-Volunteer Force. In 1973 the CSA authorized aviation training for women. Women stepped right up. On 11 September 1973, 2LT Sally D. Murphy started the initial entry rotary-wing (IERW) course. In December 1973 Private Linda K. Plock of the Nebraska ARNG graduated as an Army helicopter mechanic. CPT Dolores M. Leon received her wings as a flight surgeon in September 1975. In 1975 CPT Linda McDonald Horan completed the Aviation Maintenance Officers Course. By 1978 women had been in Aviation long enough to move into more skilled and prestigious roles. In April 1978 Deborah Rideout became a Huey IP. On 27 November 1979 2LT Marcella A. Hayes became the first black female Army flight school graduate and reportedly the first black female aviator in the U.S. armed forces. In September 1982 Janet Flowers, a former enlisted air traffic controller, became the Army's first black female WO pilot.

Even so, the numbers of women entering Aviation remained small. Their presence was such a novelty that the graduation of two female Army pilots in the same month, November 1975, seemed newsworthy. Connie Reeves, who graduated from flight school in 1980, learned that she was one of the first 35 female flight school graduates. That included warrant and commissioned officers, AC and RC.

The road for the early women entering Aviation was sometimes rough. In 1975 1LT Murphy's rater noted her exceptional moral strength in dealing with "occasional outward expressions of contempt from aviators reluctant to accept women in a profession heretofore reserved for men." Strict application of regulations not written to consider women could create impediments. For example, nothing in the regulations addressed pregnancy, but interpretation of pregnancy as a medical condition lasting six months or more automatically led to grounding. Reeves received orders that disqualified her from aviation status, removed her aviation MOS, and stopped her flight pay. An accompanying letter said that, if her "medical condition" ended, she could pass a flight physical, and the Army could use her as an aviator again—she might get back her aviation MOS and be reinstated on flight status. After she gave birth, Reeves easily passed a flight physical. The Army reinstated her and even gave her flight pay for all the months she had been disqualified. However, in Reeves' eyes, both she and the Army had lost out unnecessarily, because she was unavailable to perform duties the Army needed and her skills atrophied from being out of the cockpit.

Success for these women depended on superior abilities to learn and get along with others, willingness and ability to take on challenges, and resistance to sometimes-overt discouragement. In 1975 Murphy's rater described her as an "extremely intelligent and persevering officer who is highly motivated and mission oriented." She was then serving as an Operations Officer, a position ordinarily filled by a captain. Another rater noted similar qualities, as well as her willingness to go beyond the required mission. Her first overseas assignment was flying intelligence-collection aircraft with the Army Security Agency. She impressed her superiors by quickly becoming fully mission qualified "in one of the most difficult flying environments in the world." The same rater noted her maturity and quickness in taking on leadership and counseling roles for other women within the command. She had also excelled in her secondary duties in logistics.

Expansion of possible assignments and combat exclusion of women

The legacy of the fact that U.S. did not use women in combat roles during World War II carried on for another half century. Beginning in the late 1970s, about the same time the issue of a separate Aviation Branch was coming to a head, pressure grew to eliminate separation of service members based on sex. Effective 20 October 1978, following Congressional direction, the Army abolished the WACs.

A major issue in all the armed services was what effects broadening assignments for women might have. On 11 May 1981 HQDA established guidelines for a group on the effects that using women might have on combat effectiveness and force readiness. A key concern was physical demands in various MOSs. The expectation was that these demands might require classification by duty position. Another concern was exposure to direct combat. Unlike the Navy and Air Force, no statutes restricted the Army's assignment of women. In 1977 the Army adopted a Combat Exclusion Policy, which kept women from serving in designated combat MOSs. By 1981 TRADOC had the lead for a study covering these issues and tasked each proponent school to help develop recommendations.

By October 1982 the TRADOC study was completed. There were no startling conclusions. Broad concerns related to physical demands in some MOSs and exposure to direct combat. Within Aviation these concerns did not loom large. There were also concerns that exclusions the Army adopted would be challenged in court. Out of the 1982 study the Army in 1983 developed a system of direct combat probability codes (DCPC). The DCPCs restricted assignment of women according to battlefield location.

The issues were not settled. By late 1985 TRADOC was engaged in another major review. This time inquiries went to commanders in the field. A majority thought that the current policy and definitions were hard to manage. The overall sense was that, whatever policies prevailed in peacetime, things would change in wartime. Unit commanders believed that combat effectiveness would suffer as percentages of women increased. At the same time, Army leaders were concerned to use women to their maximum potential and benefit, for both themselves and the Army. Commanders particularly in Europe were torn about restricted assignments because of shortages of men to assign to various positions. GEN William R. Richardson, CG of TRADOC, concluded that female Soldiers were making valuable contributions, but the system needed fine tuning both to relieve commanders' concerns and to enhance equal opportunity.

While the 1986 TRADOC recommendations kept many Aviation assignments closed to women, TRADOC also moved toward selectively coding assignments within most combat-type units. That let women into these units—among them, air troops in reconnaissance squadrons and air cavalry squadrons. TRADOC recommended opening headquarters troops of such units without restriction. Some units, such as the AVUM in combat Aviation squadrons, should open without any restriction. TRADOC also recommended opening additional Aviation MOSs. These included MOS 15B, Combat Aviation—but only with specific additional skill identifiers (ASI). TRADOC recommended keeping closed MOSs for warrant officers associated with scout and attack helicopter pilot, as well as the enlisted MOS for an Aerial Observer (93B).

By 1986, despite restrictions and uncertainties, Aviation had become an attractive option for at least some women. One measure was branch transfers. In 1986 Karen D. (Anderson) Lloyd, who in 1979 became the first female Medical Service Command (MSC) officer to receive Army Aviator wings, transferred into the Aviation Branch. Among 95 women graduating from West Point in 1986, ten indicated Aviation as their first choice. One listed Aviation as second choice. Enough women graduating from ROTC gave Aviation as their first choice to put Aviation fourth highest among the twelve branches open to women. At the same time, the Army could not attract women into Aviation WO positions. There was a quota for 66 women but only 47actual accessions.

By 1986 part of Aviation's attraction for women may have been evidence of challenging command opportunities. In 1986 Sally Murphy returned to Germany to command the 62d Aviation Company. This unit, supporting all of V Corps, gave great breadth of responsibility and high visibility. She was in charge of airfield operations, maintenance of a mixed fleet of aircraft, VIP support, as well as courier and reconnaissance flights.

As during and after World War II, the same notion of filling where men were unavailable, or filling so a man could go to the front, continued. A Defense spokesman in 1988 said the increased percentage of women through the years of the All-Volunteer Force (AVF) had helped the services meet strength goals despite a declining base of youth. A directive from the SECDEF forced the services to open about 24,000 assignments to women. Through the 1980s positions for women in aviation opened considerably across the armed forces, but only a few hundred women were in aviation specialties in 1988.

Women in combat, policy or not

By the late 1980s, while policy might not require women in combat, realities on the ground did. By 1988 there were concerns at the level of the SECDEF about manpower in a major conventional war. A special concern was the situation in the RC, which had higher percentages of women. Either women might have to face combat or units might be severely shorthanded by leaving members behind.

Tinajitas, 20 December 1989—women's Air Medals with "V"

By 1989 the DCPC had lost real meaning for women in Aviation. On 20 December 1989 at least three women pilots were directly involved in a hot combat assault for Operation Just Cause in Panama. CWO Debra Mann was pilot in command (PIC) of one Black Hawk carrying members of the 1st Battalion, 504th Parachute Infantry Regiment (1/504 PIR) into Tinajitas. Another PIC was 1LT Elizabeth Dreiling. Her copilot was 1LT Lisa Kutschera. There was no doubt these women were going into a hostile environment. Apaches had just survived their most severe combat test at Tinajitas, with at least ten heavy mortars—up to 120 millimeter—and a ZPU-4, a 23-millimeter antiaircraft gun. Political conditions made the operation even more hazardous than it might have been otherwise. The Panamanian Defense Forces (PDF) at Tinajitas were known to be especially aggressive. Because of concerns to minimize civilian casualties, there would be no preparatory fires. Moreover, an ice storm delaying departure of the 1/504 PIR meant the assault would occur in daylight, giving up Aviation's advantage in superior night vision capabilities. Enroute to Tinajitas, the Black Hawks took many hits, wounding Infantry in two of these aircraft. Members of the PDF, intermingled with civilians, fired from within crowds. So door gunners could not effectively use their machine guns for suppressive fire. Upon landing, the helicopters immediately came under mortar fire, wounding exiting troops. Before the Black Hawks started the return trip, three aircrew were wounded. One had serious injuries. To complete the insertion took two trips.

Although none of the women at Tinajitas were wounded, there was no way to say they had not been directly exposed to combat. Mann and Kutschera were both nominated for Air Medals with "V" for valor. A third woman pilot, WO Caryl

Newberry, received a similar nomination for actions under small arms fire on a logistics mission on 21 December.

Southwest Asia (SWA), 1990–1991

Despite this apparently slow expansion of women's roles, an unprecedented number of women appeared in many military jobs in a potential war zone following the invasion of Kuwait in August 1990. By November 1990 women comprised 11 percent among more than 220,000 American troops in Saudi Arabia and the Persian Gulf. That was the same ratio as in the armed forces as a whole. Among many aviation-related duties they performed were repairing the engines of fighter jets, piloting supply planes, and tracking ships and planes on radar.

Experiences in ODS for women were remarkable for how little they actually differed from those for men. As one reporter put it, practice in the operational theater made a mockery of the rules and law that forbid females serving in combat. The provision that women could be attached to combat units as long as their duties matched their noncombat specialty took women into places where distinctions were meaningless.

Women in Aviation fell into this kind of situation. For example, CPT Lorelei W. Coplan, 27-year-old commander of an Army aviation company, ferried supplies into and evacuated wounded from hot LZs. In theory she would not be exposed to combat, because her noncombat specialty was as a test pilot and helicopter maintenance officer. When asked about the situation, she replied that she had no strong personal feelings about women serving in combat. 'I just love to fly helicopters, and expect my unit will be operating in a hostile environment.' That probably captured the essence of what other women in Aviation believed. On 14 January 1991 MAJ Marie T. Rossi, a Chinook company commander, told reporters, 'What I am doing is no greater or less than the man who is flying next to me.' Like the vast majority killed in ODS, Rossi died in a noncombat accident. She had flown over fifty miles into the hostile zone before that. The day after the ceasefire, she and three male crewmembers hit an unlit microwave tower. Some, like a female enlisted Army meteorologist assigned to a forward Artillery unit, just laughed. 'When the shells start coming downrange, I will be counting on my flak jacket and foxhole for protection, not my MOS.' What women did notice was the irony of serving to liberate a country that permitted its women very few rights.

The events that led MAJ Rhonda Cornum into a position to become one of two women who were POWs reflected the practical realities that prevailed when conflict became imminent. Cornum was serving in a research position at USAARL at Fort Rucker when Iraq invaded Kuwait. The 2d Battalion, 229th Aviation Regiment, a school support unit, was mobilized to deploy. LTC Bill Bryan, the battalion commander, was told to take anyone he wanted. Cornum wanted to go. Bryan identified her as the person he wanted to take as the unit's flight surgeon. Someone questioned whether a woman should be allowed to go in that capacity because of the Army's policy on possible exposure to combat. When asked, DA responded that the unit should be happy just to have a flight surgeon, and there were more important things to worry about than gender. Once in place in theater, Cornum's duties included being part of a heliborne team supporting Apaches. In case one was shot down, the Black Hawk would grab the pilots before the Iraqis got them. They happened to be in place to be part of an impromptu search and rescue (SAR) response to an Air Force pilot going down. The Black Hawk she was on was shot down in that attempt, putting her in place to become a POW.

A survey conducted within five days of return from ODS to assess possible adverse effects of exposure to combat activities implicitly showed how little the DCPC mattered. Most interesting was the relative percentages of men and women with moderate or high combat exposure. Only 14.7 percent of men fell into that category, while 11.9 percent of women did. For women, who comprised only 11 percent of the population in the theater, their exposure was commensurate to their proportion in theater. For men, it was one-sixth their proportion. By those numbers, women's per-capita combat exposure was six times higher than men's.

The stress survey also implicitly showed how little men and women differed in the impact of exposure. The percentages of those who reported war zone activities as most distressing differed little: 76 percent of men and 80 percent of women. More women than men did describe exposure to potentially life-threatening combat activities as their primary stressor. There were also differences in views of how well prepared they were to go into a war zone. Among men, 75 percent felt "quite or extremely well prepared." Only 61 percent of women reported that way. That difference, though, could have easily reflected actual training levels, based on the Army's expectations of what situations men and women might face. There were differences in satisfaction with personal performance. Eighty-four percent of men reported being "quite or extremely satisfied," while only 78 percent of women reported that same satisfaction. There were also some differences in frequency and level of stress-related symptoms. More women than men exceeded clinical cut-offs on these measures. Against these differences, the analyses noted important differences in the populations. Women were younger in age, less likely to be married, and served at a lower rank at the time of deployment. All of these factors were known, from studies of civilians, to influence adjustment to forms of life trauma. Type of military status—AC or RC—was also a factor in some findings.

One fear within Department of Defense before ODS was that there might be a public opinion backlash if American women were captured or killed in war. Actual events largely disproved that fear. Thirteen U.S. servicewomen were killed—four, by enemy fire. Of those four, three died in one Iraqi Scud missile attack. Twenty-one women were wounded in action. Families of the women killed uniformly expressed pride over their service. At Rossi's interment at the Arlington National Cemetery on 11 March 1991, her husband, CWO John Cayton, expressed the evolving attitude toward women in Aviation. 'I prayed that guidance be given to her so that she could command the company, so she could lead her troops in battle. And I prayed to the Lord to take care of my sweet little wife.' Rossi's death, her earlier statement of how she viewed her place in the military world, and the timing of her death at the peak of what seemed to be national triumph seized the national imagination. Rossi was embraced as a hero and superb representative of the national spirit. There was no backlash.

The concern about women as POWs also drew little attention. The experience in the only two cases was mixed. An Army Transportation Soldier, Specialist Melissa Rathbun-Nealy, testified that the Iraqis treated her well. Cornum said nothing of mistreatment at the time but later said that Iraqis sexually abused her. She explained her delayed disclosure by saying that she feared her mistreatment would be misused by people who want to keep women out of combat.

Perhaps one of the more important but less noted changes that came out of ODS was the experience of men and women simply living and working together routinely in combat or near-combat situations. As former POW Cornum commented in a book about her experiences, the personal bonding that underlies unit cohesion is not gender-specific. During their captivity, MAJ Cornum and Sergeant Troy Dunlap were confined together—probably because the Iraqis realized that the extent of her injuries required someone else present to help her. Their presence and differences both consoled and strengthened each other. As an officer, Cornum realized she was senior and responsible to be in charge; so, she had to maintain a brave appearance. Dunlap, as NCO, felt equally obliged not to show weakness in front of an officer. At the same time, they wanted to be close together through the ordeal. Under far less extreme conditions, service together of men and women fed mutual respect, both personally and professionally.

2LT Sally Murphy at Fort Rucker 1974

Longbow Apache shipboard

Chapter 6: 1990s and Beyond

1990s and Beyond—toward a CONUS-based, expeditionary Army in a Global War on Terror (GWOT)

The years after ODS were turbulent, despite the U.S.'s unchallenged position as the world's sole superpower. Even before ODS ended, events in remote places suggested that a new kind of war with a new set of players and rules would replace the half-century-long Cold War. At the same time, the fact of U.S. military dominance in conventional terms, the traditional preoccupation of Americans with their own affairs, and continuing efforts to adjust for some future superpower rivalry while meeting immediate demands for all sorts of missions around the world largely kept these indicators from having major influence. The Army in general but especially Aviation stayed busy in all directions.

On 11 September 2001, terrorist attacks on the World Trade Center and Pentagon using hijacked airliners instantly brought national focus on the new strategic realities. Aviation, along with the rest of the U.S. armed forces, became decisively engaged in what became called the Global War on Terror (GWOT). This war mixed operations across the spectrum from humanitarian relief through near-mid-intensity combat. Meeting simultaneous demands to reshape the Army and to conduct combat operations became a new, continuous challenge. As much as or more than envisioned in the 1982 Army Aviation Systems Program Review (AASPR), Aviation was the key enabler for ground operations in this new environment. For the first time since the end of Vietnam, flight school graduates could expect to go into combat very soon after reaching their first unit. As before and after Vietnam, much effort went into exploring new, potential missions as well as new ways to conduct old missions better. To prepare and support Aviation Soldiers adequately for these new conditions, Aviation undertook key changes in organization, training, doctrine, and materiel. Only the future would allow assessing the overall successes and failures of these changes.

Increased OPTEMPO

Rather than standing down as projected with the fall of the Berlin Wall, with a brief interruption for ODS—ODS began an astonishing surge of activity for the Army. By a decade later, in January 2001, Army advocates were decrying a grave mismatch between missions and resources. A national strategy of engagement had affected the Army most among the services. Between 1989 and 2001 the Army shrank by more than a third while its mission rates tripled. The pattern also was one of not just going in and out of places but of having some sustaining force over a period of years.

Almost without exception, the Army's worldwide commitments involved Aviation. An example of the ongoing commitments was the Multinational Force and Observer (MFO) in the Sinai. This supported the peace agreement between Egypt and Israel. The MFO required one infantry battalion and one support battalion at all times. This support battalion included Aviation. Domestic antidrug operations involved National Guard and U.S. Army Reserve units. These activities particularly drew on Aviation support, as did similar activities in Central and South America. Operations in Afghanistan and Iraq especially relied on Aviation. At peak of operations, there were more than 600 Army aircraft in Iraq alone.

The situation had an especially large effect on the RC. The mobilization for ODS in 1990–1991 had served as a wake up call that Reservists might actually have to perform occasional active duty. The growing wave of commitments through the 1990s and especially after September 2001 practically erased the meaning of Reserve Components. By 2003 DA projections of forces scheduled to deploy Outside the Continental United States (OCONUS) for ongoing operations expected to use every RC division in the normal rotations. A photograph, circulated widely on the Internet, captured the essence of the situation. On the grimy windshield of a truck was painted "One weekend a month, my ass!" As early as January 2001, well before the GWOT started, Army leaders expressed serious concern about the effects of repeated, extended deployments on Guard and Reserve recruiting and retention because of the special strains on families and difficulties with civilian employers.

The GWOT declared after 11 September 2001 increased both the frequency and duration of many deployments, and sharpened concerns about their effects on the force structure. Conventional military operations to topple regimes in both Afghanistan and Iraq succeeded with startling speed. In both places—but particularly Iraq—conventional combat operations simply flowed into protracted stability and support operations (SASO). In both Afghanistan and Iraq the hunt for key leaders continued for months. Even after Iraqi dictator Saddam Hussein was captured, extreme violence aimed at both foreigners and Iraqis continued with little sign of relief. By 2004 there was a widespread sense that original projections of a 3- to 5-year war had been wildly optimistic. In April an Administration spokesman said that the strategy being pursued was similar to that of Britain's 50-year campaigns against the slave trade and piracy.

Redefining for the contemporary operational environment— LIC to MOOTW to SASO. METT-T to METT-TC

Through this period, people struggled to find concepts to frame changes in the operational environment. Doctrine writers and thinkers went through a succession of terms. In 1981 the Army had published FM 100–20, Low Intensity Conflict. That term gave way in 1993 to Operations Other Than War (OOTW)—also known as military operations other than war (MOOTW). The 1993 revision of FM 100–5, Operations, included a whole chapter on this subject, although the FM did not use the acronym. FM 100–5 said that the Army might "face complex and sensitive situations in a variety of operations," often of long duration. A revision of FM 100–20, Stability and Support Operations, reached final draft stage in April 1996. It was widely accepted that SASO would replace OOTW. In February 2003, under the new Joint numbering system, this became FM 3–07.

An increasing awareness of the importance of noncombat aspects of achieving military objectives led to redefining the factors commanders used to analyze the battlefield. Key in forcing this change was the increasing incidence of military operations in areas with dense civilian populations. As world population increased and more of that total population concentrated in or around cities, odds increased that combat would occur in such settings. In August 1979 the Army published FM 90–10, Military Operations on Urbanized Terrain or MOUT. Aviation's operations in built-up areas included aerial fire support, lift for assaults, relocation and resupply of ground units, observation, and sensor and retransmission operations. Through the years that FM 90–10 had been used, commanders had used mission, enemy, terrain and weather, troops and support available-time available (METT-T) to envision the situations they faced. An increasing awareness of the impact of nonmilitary factors on operations led to a revision of this acronym by adding the letter C for civil considerations. The new acronym METT-TC appeared in a revised capstone manual, FM 3–0, Operations, published on the Army's 226th birthday, 14 June 2001.

Impact of legacies of Vietnam and 1980s build-up, reduced funding, and new technological possibilities

A major obstacle to Aviation in the years after ODS was the legacy of the huge investments the Army had made in Aviation through Vietnam and again during the Defense boom period of the 1980s. Army acquisition of aircraft during Vietnam, despite combat and other losses, left the Army with a huge inventory of serviceable aircraft. In 1970 the Army had 12,652 aircraft. Of those, 82 percent were rotary-wing. Some aircraft were relatively new when the war ended. Acquisition of a new generation of aircraft began in the late 1970s with the Black Hawk. In the early 1980s acquisition of the Apache attack helicopter followed. Through these years the Army also upgraded its fleet of Chinook helicopters to a much more capable D model. The result of these inventories, along with shrinking Defense budgets and then the collapse of the Warsaw Pact, was an inability to acquire new systems. Rising cost to maintain aging airframes undercut further modernization. In 1995 the Congressional Budget Office (CBO) studied the Army's helicopter inventory and plans to modernize the fleets. Despite heavy investments in new combat and utility helicopters during the 1980s, CBO found that more than half of all of the helicopters the Army had in 1995 were Vietnam-era aircraft. Many had exceeded their useful service life. The Army wanted to retire them but could not practically do so. Even scaling down the helicopter fleet to parallel overall force reductions did not help. The Army had too few modern aircraft to fill its requirements. At the very best, U.S. manufacturers of helicopters would have to consolidate to survive. In terms of how well the fleets could do their jobs, the picture was bad. For example, Cobras and Hueys were not equipped to fly at night, had obsolete communications and navigation equipment, and lacked the power needed to fly at altitudes of 4000 feet and higher and in the hot temperatures that prevailed where most operations were occurring. These limitations sometimes also reduced the value of the newer aircraft. Case in point, the OH-58D Kiowa Warrior could not keep up with and thus find targets for the Apache attack helicopters. Finally, having both older and newer types of aircraft in the total fleet created an extra logistics burden for the Army. Each type of aircraft needed different parts, tools, and skills in operators and maintainers. All of these differences added cost that kept the Army from buying newer types that were supposed to replace the aging ones.

Changing the model from alert/train/deploy to train/alert/deploy

Changing conditions changed the ideas about how the Army worked. Under the model that had prevailed through the Cold War, with its emphasis on a massive build-up of forces mobilized to augment those already in place, the Army had presumed that there would be enough warning time to allow alerting units that they would be going to war. Based on that knowledge, which would identify the nature and size of the threat, forces would conduct any special training required. Then units would deploy to fight. The smaller force structure after ODS, along with much greater uncertainty about situations but a premium on rapid response, caused the Army to change its model. In October 2002 FM 7–0, Training the Force, mandated a different sequence—train, alert, deploy, fight.

End of a tiered readiness force—RC integration, end of cascading

Closely related to the change in the training and deployment cycle was a change in ways of posturing AC and RC forces. Under the old model, the Army handled shortages by giving newer, more capable systems and more intensive training to the AC. Priority among AC units went to those, like the 101AB, that were presumed to be the first to go in response to a crisis anywhere. Later-deploying units had some shortages of equipment or manning and lower levels of training. Less capable equipment cascaded from AC units into the RC units, assumed to deploy still later if at all. By late 2003 the Army abandoned tiered unit readiness based on early and late deployers, because "late deployer" merely meant a future deployer.

Symbols of breaking barriers between tooth and tail

There was also a mindset in the Army during this period that generally wanted to erase the distinction between operating and institutional forces. One indicator of this thrust was abandoning wear of the dress uniform in favor of wearing the battle dress uniform throughout most of the institutional Army. CSA Eric K. Shinseki directed wearing a beret to symbolize the entire Army as a deployment- and combat-oriented organization. His successor, GEN Peter J. Schoomaker, went further by ending the practice of wearing distinctive articles, such as the colored hats that had been traditional to basic flight students for almost half a century.

Fusion of simulators and simulations—training, developmental, planning, fighting systems

Advancing technology continued to shape the course of Aviation, as the Army at large. The increasing sophistication of digital systems through the 1990s brought unprecedented value to simulations. At the same time, the complexity of some also made them victims and symptoms of the recurrent challenge of acquiring fully capable systems at an affordable cost. In some cases the capabilities required and complexities to do all that confronted the Army with bad choices: accept a system that lacked all required capabilities or go without any system for some unknown time.

Simulations as vehicles for highlighting Aviation needs

While the most widely recognized use lay in training, simulations played an increasing role in developing doctrine, organizations, and materiel. One role of simulations was in calling attention to areas where there were systemic problems. An illustration of that was in warfighting experiments. From April to September 1997 efforts were made in connection with a simulation called WARSIM 2000 to overcome the long-term failure to include the spectrum of Aviation capabilities in major simulations. Without inclusion, experiments would fail to show what Aviation could and could not do. The importance of this hearkened back to Hamilton Howze's presentation in the 1950s to show how airmobility could transform the battlefield to sell Aviation to Army leadership. Without the ability to show the difference, it was hard to convince leaders about Aviation's value.

Growing sophistication and limits of technology—Aviation Combined Arms Tactical Trainer—Aviation Reconfigurable Manned Simulator (AVCATT-A)

The 1990s saw great advancements in simulations, but also showed how there could be pitfalls in evolving systems. The Aviation Combined Arms Tactical Trainer—Aviation Reconfigurable Manned Simulator (AVCATT-A) illustrated these situations.

Origin and growth of AVCATT-A

AVCATT-A grew out an earlier development—the Aviation Reconfigurable Manned Simulator (ARMS). One of the major questions through the 1990s was, given that the Army would have simulations, how could the Army really use this technology to train an increasingly digital force. The goal became to tie simulations together with actual systems like the Army Battle Command System (ABCS) and train everyone from the brigade commander down to the pilot in the cockpit in a single exercise.

For the Army—especially, Aviation—simulation was nothing new. Between 1983 and 1989 the Simulator Networking (SIMNET) project made a major effort to interconnect simulations over a computer network. SIMNET let several tank simulations collaborate. Its success spurred further research into distributed simulations. Comparable combat simulations for collective training evolved at the Aviation, Armor, and Infantry centers. DARPA sought to see how much of the battlefield could be included within that environment.

The next step was to extend simulation into the digital world. During February 1997 the Task Force XXI Digital Training Exercise (TF XXI DTX) at the Aviation Test Bed at Fort Rucker showed the capability to create a digital, collective training environment. DTX I was designed to prepare the 4th Brigade staff from the Experimental Force at Fort Hood for a major warfighting experiment at the National Training Center. DTX I provided the springboard for several more initiatives at Fort Rucker. These included a series of Aviation Training Exercises (ATX) to prepare Aviation units deploying to Bosnia and elsewhere. A network of three hubs at Forts Benning, Knox and Rucker tied simulations at those locations together over the Distributed Simulation Internet (DSI) and created virtual battlefields. Through the DSI Soldiers at all three locations could move, shoot and communicate with each other. By 1999 the value was proven. The challenge was to get this kind of capability into the rest of the Army and down to the Soldier level at an affordable price.

These challenges turned out to be major. In 1995 USAAVNC had prepared the operational requirements document (ORD) for Aviation Combined Arms Tactical Trainer (AVCATT). The National Guard had also started work to create the ARMS. This would provide company-level training for six different types of aircraft in the ARNG. Each ARMS would have six crew stations. Each station could represent controls, dials, panels, and displays of any airframe.

The first chance to integrate these systems came in 1998 at Fort Hood. On 6 July 1998 a prototype system was completed. Units of the 4ID conducted an exercise linking AVCATT flight simulators with Close Combat Tactical Trainers. Success showed in performance of RC Apache pilots that went to Korea and Bosnia.

Based on this early promise, on 12 February 1999 USAAVNC published the AVCATT-A System Training Plan (STRAP). Requirements defined in the STRAP greatly increased sophistication and complexity of the system. The AVCATT-A would be mobile and trailerized. It would simulate flying under widely varying conditions and provide an AAR where people could go back and replay any point in the events. It could also work across networks with other Joint and Army simulations. At the same time AVCATT-A was not allowed to increase requirements for money or people—including new skills. Finally, the contractor had to deliver the first suite within 15 months after award of the contract.

Bumpy road to acquiring AVCATT-A

Development started well, but the road ahead turned out to be rough. Funding was a chronic matter. By September 2000 nine of 18 systems were unfinanced requirements (UFR), and 18 was always known to be too few to meet needs. Technical problems caused delays. By June 2002, by the nature of a firm-fixed-price contract, the value to the contractor had dropped to 44 cents on every dollar. Worse, delays in meeting milestones jeopardized funding vital to moving forward. The fact that competing businesses had to share key information caused a year's delay while corporate executives and lawyers wrangled.

There were ripple effects. The delay in delivering the AVCATT-A version for the Apache Longbow upset critical work for the Comanche, which was itself a vulnerable program. The Apache Longbow situation also boded ill for versions to support other aircraft. All these conditions endangered Flight School XXI (FS XXI), the new model of flight training, which was an extremely high priority.

Finally, on 19 September 2003 the South Carolina National Guard received the first AVCATT-A. A month later another reached Fort Rucker. By late 2004 the Captains' Career Course (CCC) was using the AVCATT-A. As more suites arrived, reports were mixed. Where commanders directed its use, AVCATT-A was widely and successfully used. Elsewhere it was underused. The Chief Warrant Officer of the Branch observed that use would remain limited until regulations changed to make time in the simulator count toward required flight time.

AVCATT-A acquisition and patterns in Army acquisition practices

The story of acquiring and fielding AVCATT-A reflected the dynamics among ideas and technology—especially how mismatches between new ideas and speed of technological advances could cause trouble.

AVCATT-A's career reflected the recurrent fact of emerging needs—and the Army's persistent goal to be responsive. New demands kept arising. Shortly after a suite first reached Fort Rucker, concerns about training pilots to deal with man-portable air defense systems (MANPADS) led to looking at what AVCATT-A could do to simulate these weapons and teach maneuvering flight. By late 2003 work was also underway to adapt AVCATT-A to meet the needs of SOF operating in Afghanistan and elsewhere. A few months later the idea arose for AVCATT-A to train Kiowa Warrior pilots on Advanced Precision Kill Weapon System (APKWS) rockets. This use could overcome the lack of any provision for these pilots to have the training rockets they needed.

Another aspect of the AVCATT-A story was the Army's way of dealing with recurrent shortages—especially its ways of handling cuts to the budgets of acquisition programs. At one point, MG John M. Curran, CG of USAAVNC, said the Army might have to buy fewer actual Longbows to get the proper simulators. By contrast to the Air Force, which treated each simulator just like a production aircraft, an Army simulator had no such protection. As pressures came to cut nonessential items, simulators tended to fall out of an acquisition program or at the best be delayed. Their absence could seriously impede putting all the pieces of a new system together and making it work.

In the end, a persistent factor in AVCATT-A's bumpy ride was its sheer complexity and the expectations placed on it. The ambitious goals for AARs meant recording and manipulating huge amounts of data. By June 2002 each suite included more than 100 computers. The complexity of the software matched anything the Army had ever developed before.

The cost and difficulty in maintaining currency for some of these systems led to homegrown expedients. CWO David L. Hacker demonstrated a laptop-computer emulation that let Longbow pilots practice pagination for their cockpit displays. The TRADOC System Manager for the Longbow bought three personal computers to run this software for each attack battalion.

Simulations in air traffic control (ATC) training—DATS and ETOS

As with other areas of training, simulations played a key part in supporting the Army's needs for ATS. In less than a decade, these simulations went through a generational change. The rapid obsolescence of technologies and difficulty of maintaining older systems drove the change. This situation mirrored the larger dilemma Aviation faced with rising costs with older systems.

From June through November 1994 USAAVNC received and accepted four Data Automated Tower Systems (DATS) to train ATC students in control tower procedures. While sophisticated for the moment, like all other simulation technology of the 1990s, the DATS rapidly ceased to be state-of-the-art. DATS required a very large room with a huge, wrap-around, concave screen. A bank of high-intensity projectors gave a highly realistic view of specific scenarios from the control tower.

By 2000 the DATS technology was obsolete and urgently needed replacement, even though DATS was scarcely 8 years old. The major problem was substantial downtime for maintenance. This downtime had not adversely affected training only because USAAVNC had a spare radar lab. Adding to maintenance problems, the builder had gone out of business. Parts were increasingly hard to find and expensive. Computer malfunctions reduced training time. The ultimate effect was contributing to the bottleneck in the field.

Meantime work was underway to acquire a more advanced replacement. On 28 March 2000 TRADOC approved the ORD for the Enhanced Tower Operator Simulator (ETOS). Basic requirements were demanding. The system had to provide 360-degree representation of the airfield and environment as viewed from a control tower. The database had to include all current U.S. military and civilian aircraft that controller trainees would see. The displays had to accurately depict aircraft at accurate distances and position. The display also had to accurately simulate all military aircraft maneuvers, profiles, and speeds. Other capabilities included digitized voice and data communications among all participants; display of tower radar information, airport and weather information; monitor and control of radio navigational aids and lighting systems. The device also had to fit into existing space. On 18 August 2003 the ETOS was formally inaugurated with a ribbon cutting ceremony. By then, ETOS had already been in use for ATC training for some time.

Army flying after ODS

As before and even through ODS, Aviation performed a wide array of tasks in its roles within the Army as the servant of the American People. The combinations of skilled people, technology, and culture of responsiveness that had always characterized Aviation often drew Aviation into diverse missions. In some cases, these responses quite literally took Aviation to unprecedented heights.

Non-warfighting roles

As back to the founding of the Republic, the Army during the years after ODS spent most of its time and energy outside combat, often performing tasks that supported civil institutions. Throughout its history, the Army played a special role in government response to civil emergencies, such as storms, floods and other natural disasters. Within the limits imposed by the Posse Comitatus Act of 1878, the Army also played an active role in domestic law enforcement. Beginning in the 1980s and especially after 11 September 2001, the wall between military authorities and civilian law enforcement agencies lowered in the interests of homeland security. The flexibility and adaptability of Aviation made it feature prominently in these areas.

Emergency response missions

National policy provides for DOD to aid civil authorities when disasters exceed the limits of civil resources. This aid includes personnel, equipment and other, unspecified services This aid can occur in any of three categories of emergencies, defined as Major Disaster, in cases where the President declares that an emergency exists, and Imminently Serious Conditions Emergencies. In major disasters and declared emergencies, the Federal Emergency Management Agency (FEMA) requests help through the Army, regardless of what service or services will be involved in the response. The last category covers cases that require prompt response "to save human life, prevent human suffering or reduce great destruction of or damage to property" and where the serious disaster is too imminent to allow getting instructions from higher headquarters. Through the 1990s and beyond Aviation repeatedly played vital parts in responses to civilian emergencies. Among the most common ones were missions from by Military Assistance to Safety and Traffic (MAST) and High Altitude Rescue Team (HART), discussed in Chapter 5.

Storm and Flood Relief/Rescue

Far more common than rescues from glaciers and off mountainsides were Aviation operations to evacuate and sometimes rescue people in the paths of floods. This kind of mission was one where RC Aviation—especially National Guard—was prominent. However, AC units also were involved in these operations.

An example of AC involvement came with Company B, 4th Battalion, 123d Aviation Regiment—nicknamed the Sugarbears—in late August 1994. The Koyukuk River crossing the Arctic Circle rose to flood stage, threatening to drown the village of Allakaket. The governor of Alaska asked the Army for help. On 28 August five Chinooks flew to Allakaket, landed on a hilltop near the village, and loaded all 109 villagers and the belongings they carried. Some wanted to take animals, which were not authorized. After loading everyone, the Chinooks took off for a civilian airport, which was the nearest refueling point. The mission was clearly timely. As the pilots left Allakaket, they noticed that the flagpole at the local sports field was almost entirely under water. At the civilian airport, there was only one fuel truck. So it took some time to refuel all five aircraft. This created an unexpected problem. At Allakaket no alcohol was available. At Bettles, there was as much alcohol as the drinkers could afford. By the time the aircraft were refueled, some of those being evacuated were in almost no condition to go onboard. It was also dark by the time the aircraft left Bettles. This complicated things, because not all the pilots had NVG. The crews compensated by having the NVG pilots fly in the front of the formation. By the other pilots flying at the same altitude, they knew they were safe. The crews involved in this mission received Humanitarian Service ribbons.

Hurricane Floyd, 1999

When major storms hit, Aviation often becomes engaged. In cases where storms with flooding affected wide areas, Aviation was almost always heavily involved. The extent and severity often called for heavy participation of RC Aviation.

In mid-September 1999 Hurricane Floyd—one of the largest storms ever to hit the U.S.—hit the East Coast. Waters from Hurricane Floyd shattered records from floods of 1919. The Federal Emergency Management Agency (FEMA) called on XVIII AB and Fort Bragg for help. Over 10,800 National Guard troops were called out in eight Eastern states to help civil authorities. Because most roads and bridges were impassable, helicopters were the most reliable transportation. A Black Hawk from the Tennessee Army National Guard medical detachment picked up a pregnant woman in labor in Wilmington, North Carolina. The crew, using NVG, helped deliver the baby in the air.

Army helicopters rescued hundreds of people from rooftops and buildings that were surrounded by rising water. The special capabilities to meet the Army's tactical requirements sometimes proved uniquely invaluable in difficult, noncombat situations. Army aviators from the 57th Medical Company (Air Ambulance) at

Fort Bragg rescued 15 people using their high-speed rescue hoist. To reach stranded people, the medic rode down on the Jungle Penetrator hoist, while the crew chief sat in the open door and ran the hoist's controls. Pilots took commands from the crew chief that guided the medic to the victims. Coast Guard and Navy helicopters with seats then took victims stranded on high ground to safer points while the Army aircraft looked for more stranded people on the rooftops.

Simply providing life support during the recovery phase from the storm depended heavily on Aviation. By 21 September 1999 aviators from Fort Bragg delivered more than 150,000 Meals Ready to Eat (MRE) and expected to deliver at least 200,000 more. When asked, SGT Chris Smith, F Company, 130th National Guard Aviation Battalion, said doing this kind of thing was the reason he had joined the National Guard. His crew had evacuated a dialysis patient and a child hurt by a generator. They had delivered insulin and other supplies to the flood shelters. Helicopter crewmembers also showed civilians how to heat MREs. On a single trip one Chinook delivered two tons of MREs and 3000 pounds of water.

Disaster relief abroad

Aviation commonly provided emergency relief in natural disasters in other parts of the world. Often, because of local conditions, helicopters provided the only effective means of providing vital responses. Central and South America were frequent locations for these kinds of operations.

During 6–28 June 1994 Chinooks delivered supplies to survivors of a 6.4 magnitude earthquake in Colombia. A landslide engulfed several remote Indian villages, killing about 250 people. Hard on the heels of Hurricane Floyd, Soldiers from the 160 SOAR were among troops delivering supplies and providing rescue assistance to flood and mudslide survivors in Venezuela. Similar operations occurred in El Salvador. One Salvadoran housewife said, 'All we have is God and the helicopters that bring food.'

Humanitarian aid

Some relief operations, because of their political circumstances, continued to involve Aviation for years. Such was the case with efforts following ODS. In April 1991 Operation Provide Comfort began in northern Iraq to give the Kurdish population a secure environment in a volatile region. Nearly every type of Army aircraft was involved. Apaches and Kiowas provided reconnaissance and security. Chinooks and Black Hawks provided transportation, food and water to the displaced populations. Provide Comfort typified situations that characterized the post-Cold War era for Aviation. The potential for further conflict made Aviation ideal, because Aviation could quickly shift from SASO to operations involving lethal force, if necessary.

Unusual missions providing civilian support—dinosaur rescues

Sometimes, where regulations and resources would ordinarily have kept the Army from responding to civilian needs, the creativity of Army Aviators found ways to meet both military and civilian needs at the same time. An example was cooperative efforts in 2002 between the Sugarbears and the University of Alaska to recover two important fossils in isolated locations but in danger of being pilfered. One was an ichthyosaur fossil about 14 feet long, weighing more than a ton, and lying in remote tundra about 400 miles from Fairbanks. On 29 July 2002, the First Platoon of the Sugarbears flew its Chinooks to northern Alaska. Their military purpose was to enhance tactical skills—specifically navigation and operations in remote sites with unusual, adverse conditions. Aircrews had to launch a boat from a hover. They hovered to unload over an ice shelf that prohibited landing. Thus, while performing invaluable support to the civilian community, the unit practiced skills that might serve especially well in places like Afghanistan and Iraq.

Law enforcement/counterdrug operations

Through the years after ODS the lines became increasingly blurred between conventional military operations and law enforcement. As a result, Aviation played important parts in this gray area. In part this reflected changes in national policy. It also reflected the often-unique capabilities of Aviation, both in the AC and especially in the RC.

With the end of the Cold War, threats to national security from what had previously been considered simple criminal activity increased. The collapse of the Soviet Union and its allied states created a vast potential black market in weapons. These ranged from very low-tech, such as rocket-propelled grenades (RPG), to very high-tech, such as sophisticated fighter aircraft. By mid-1992, anyone with the cash in hand could buy a MiG-21 Fishbed aircraft for $20,000. Such materiel offered great opportunities to wealthy, sophisticated drug traffickers, who all but ran some nations and sometimes tried to topple the government if officials did not cooperate. Examples occurred in both Venezuela and Peru in early 1992. The relationships worked both ways. In Peru, for example, the Shining Path guerrillas, trying to overthrow the government, financed their rebellion with the proceeds from drug trafficking.

In 1989 Congress gave the Department of Defense three missions in this arena. First was to serve as the lead agency to detect and monitor drug smuggling across U.S. borders. Second was to plan a national network for command, control, communication, computers, and intelligence (C4I) aimed at interdicting this traffic. The third was to enhance the role of the National Guard in this area. In April 1990 the Army published its counterdrug plan to support the Department of State, Customs, and the Drug Enforcement Agency (DEA). Many of those things done as part of counterdrug operations were simply application of principles and practices covered by FM 100–20, <u>Military Operations in low-intensity conflict (LIC)</u>. In April 1996 FM 100–20, <u>Stability and Support Operations</u> specifically mentioned counterdrug operations among missions that bridged into the realm of law enforcement. The Secretary of the Army and the CSA specified drug cartels, along with ethnic militias and terrorists, as types of irregular forces that threatened U.S. national interests. By the summer of 1997 the National Guard had more counter-narcotics officers than the Drug Enforcement Agency (DEA) had special officers.

Aviation had key roles in carrying out the national strategy against drugs and their effects. In December 1989 USAAVNC published a draft doctrinal framework, <u>U.S. Army Aviation Employment in Counter-Drug Operations</u>. By 1992 Aviation was directly involved in five Latin American countries. Activities included destroying crops and reconnaissance of drug traffickers. Aviation officers were also training the host nations, helping plan operations, and providing maintenance and flight instruction. The end of the civil war in El Salvador with peace accords signed in January 1992 freed Aviation assets to expand operations against drug traffic.

Counterdrug operations were challenging, because of the environment throughout the region. Pilots often encountered mountain, jungle, and hot-weather conditions within a single flight. Operations also occurred over long distances where there were few navigational aids and few refueling sites. In October 1993 DOD shifted the emphasis from interdiction to eradication. This change had operational ramifications for Aviation. Interdiction occurred in Central America. Eradication meant more operations in South America. Since the operations depended on the 128th Aviation Brigade, headquartered in Panama, the shift meant even greater challenges in dealing with distances and related environmental factors. Closer to home, the Army helped patrol the borders. These activities involved using combat aircraft in nontraditional ways. In September 1991, in Operation Bush Hog, Apaches from the 6th Cavalry Brigade helped identify people and equipment illegally entering the U.S. around Laredo, Texas. The Apaches'

FLIR let them clearly identify people. The Apaches then guided civilian law enforcement officers to an intercept. By the end of 1993, the 33d Aviation Group Counterdrug Task Force at Fort Rucker alone was responsible for eradicating marijuana with a street value exceeding $100 million. This TF, which included both federal and state agencies from Alabama and Georgia, illustrated the advantage Aviation brought. The agent in charge for Georgia estimated that Aviation allowed covering twice the area that would be possible otherwise. As with humanitarian assistance and disaster relief, counterdrug missions tended to fall heavily on Aviation in the RC. Because of restrictions under the 1878 Posse Comitatus law, the National Guard played the major part in these activities.

Law enforcement—notably, counterdrug operations—became an explicit consideration in acquiring new Aviation systems. An example was a proposed Extended Range/Multi Purpose (ER/MP) UAV. Among the overall tasks of the ER/MP were two related to counterdrug operations. One type was to support detection and monitoring of drug shipments. The other was to provide command, control, communication, computers, and intelligence (C4I) support for counterdrug efforts.

Increasing demands for Joint and over water operations

Over the years after Vietnam, Aviation became increasingly involved in operations that were Joint in nature. Some of these operations led to needs for extensive training in overwater operations and related skills that were new to Army aviators.

During 1994 preparations for operations in Haiti led to extensive training and preparations for extended-range, overwater operations by Army helicopters. By 2000 some units were conducting extensive, regular overwater missions. Such missions were usually part of increasingly complex Joint/Combined operations The 6th Cavalry in Korea was an example. Among its other responsibilities, 6th Cavalry had missions for countering SOF and for conducting overwater attacks. Much of this activity occurred at night. This led to a requirement for 60 percent of the training to involve night flying. 6th Cavalry had a LNO onboard the U.S. Navy command ship to help coordinate these operations. Korean operations involve a deep operations concept. As a result, the 6th Cavalry talked directly to the JSTARS and other reconnaissance and communications assets belonging to other services.

Requirements for overwater operations increased. On 25 March 2004, for the first time since the end of the Vietnam era, the Army landed a helicopter aboard an Army vessel, named the Joint Venture. This was an experimental, high-speed vessel—hence, its designation of HSV-X1. The Army, in conjunction with the Navy, leased this wave-piercing catamaran for experiments in projecting ground forces over-the-horizon. During Foal Eagle—a combined, U.S.–Korea exercise—training involving the Joint Venture showed that the Army could use the vessel to support Army, Joint and combined air operations.

Safety as a Force Protection (FP) Issue

Following ODS, safety gained increased emphasis as a major force-protection (FP) and readiness issue. Over almost 25 years, by more than twenty to one, accidents outstripped combat in killing service men and women. Even though aviation deaths were only 15 percent of the total, there was a special importance in Aviation because of its overall importance to operations and its high cost. The period saw what seemed like continuation of great strides, followed by a reversal and increasing incidence of accidents that caused alarm. Strenuous efforts did not seem enough to completely stop the unwanted change.

Efforts to stem the tide

By 2003 senior leadership had undertaken strenuous measures to try to change the pattern. By May the alarming trend made SECDEF Donald Rumsfeld challenge the services to cut by half both numbers and rates of accidents in two years. To oversee this effort DOD created the Defense Safety Oversight Council with an Aviation Safety Improvements Task Force.

The Army undertook several programmatic approaches to improving safety. In November 2001 the Secretary of Army and CSA approved the Army Safety Strategic Plan. The plan established risk management and safety objectives linked to Army Transformation. An Army Safety Campaign Plan, to be published in the late Fiscal Year 2004, was the logical extension. This plan would give DA and major commands implementing guidance. DA had also established a senior-level Army Safety Coordinating Panel.

Aviation in comparison to the other services

The Army did not fare badly in its safety efforts when compared to the other services. In a 1997 report the Defense Science Board (DSB) Task Force on Aviation Safety made three key findings. One was that the long-declining trend in aviation accidents across the services had reached a plateau. Service safety programs had done an excellent job of addressing immediate causes of accidents but often had not addressed basic causes. Finally the lifecycle cost of accidents was rarely addressed. The chairman of the TF said that only making safety an integral part of mission performance would take results closer to the goal of no Class A accidents. The chairman specifically noted the Army had showed how this approach could have a positive effect.

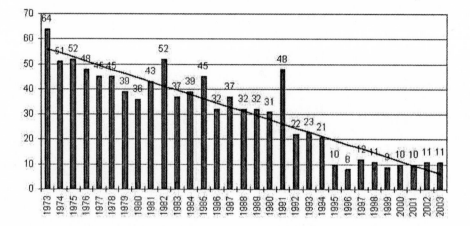

Aviation Accidents per 100K Flying Hours

Good news turns bad

The trend on which the DSB TF lauded the Army failed to hold. Instead, the Army found itself wrestling with a perplexing shift. Although the flying hours did not change drastically during 1997–1999, the rates of Class A accidents climbed to more than double the 1996 level. An intense effort beginning at the very top of the Army's leadership reversed the pattern for Fiscal Year 2000, but the rising trend resumed in Fiscal Year 2001 and continued through 2003. By February 2004, when the Director of Army Safety testified before Congress on the subject, Fiscal Year 2004 was off to a runaway start—a projected rate of 3.3 Class A accidents per 100,000 flying hours. That was more than four times the 1996 rate. The situation for all Aviation accidents showed a similar tendency.

Reasons behind the shift—inexperience and a combat environment

Through the mid-/late 1990s there was an increasing concern about the decline in experience among Army aviators. Beginning at least in Fiscal Year 2002, the Army had become engaged in active combat. As BG Joseph A. Smith, the Director of Army Safety, told a HASC meeting on Aviation safety, "We are an Army at war. From my experiences in Iraq and Afghanistan, I know commanders, aviators, and Soldiers are doing everything in their power to mitigate risk...the high cost of training, combined with the harsh environments we expect our aviators to operate in daily, equals high risk."

The impact of a combat operational flying environment became more apparent in looking at the accident rates by specific types of aircraft. SOA had a much higher rate of Class A accidents than conventional Aviation. Overall the next highest accident rates involved the attack and scout aircraft. Other aircraft had generally lower rates. Among the fixed-wing aircraft, the C-12, which had the highest rate among such aircraft, was still quite low. Rates for the training aircraft—the TH-67 Creek from 1994 onward—were remarkably low. This fact reflected both the expertise of the IP and the extreme care taken to imbed safety controls in training.

Army leadership's efforts to correct—programs and technology

Army leadership was highly sensitive to all these matters. By the late 1990s Army leadership was pressed hard to adopt measures that would reduce accidents and improve survivability of aircraft. Senior Army leaders came to talk of accident avoidance as a key aspect of readiness and force protection (FP). There were several approaches. One was programmatic—which included increasing emphasis on safe practices in training. The other basic approach was to find some technology at hand that could eliminate accidents.

Programmatic approaches—ASIST and MFOQA

The Army undertook several programmatic approaches to improving Aviation safety. For example, in 1999, responding to increasing risks in aviation operations along with proposals from OSD, the Army established the Aviation Safety Investment Strategy Team (ASIST) to "achieve breakthrough gains in aviation safety." The approach was to conduct formal analyses of actual aircraft accidents and recommend the most productive controls to reduce those risks. The Army Safety Strategic Plan, which the Secretary of Army and CSA approved in November 2001, called for a strategy to invest in aviation accident prevention.

A program called the Military Flight Operations Quality Assurance (MFOQA) showed the close ties among Aviation, the Joint community, and civilian industry. MFOQA, which involved installing flight recorders on military aircraft, mirrored a highly beneficial program in the commercial airline industry. A particular focus was to identify hazardous human errors before they become mishaps. Such error was a causal factor in 80 percent of aviation mishaps. Besides identifying possible human error that caused accidents, this monitoring also could reduce excess operating costs. One airline saved millions of dollars just on unnecessary engine inspections.

Military acceptance of MFOQA began in 2000 and differed across the services. On 28 August 2000 the Joint Service Safety Chiefs signed a memorandum of agreement to pursue funding for a MFOQA. It would bring commanders and managers information from flight data recorders to improve flight operations in several key the areas. These included maintenance, training, safety, and mission planning. By 2003 the Navy had tried a prototype program. By February 2004 the Army was conducting pilot programs at Fort Rucker, Fort Campbell, in Korea and Iraq. The South Carolina National Guard was also participating.

As with other programs, competition for funding became an obstacle, especially as wartime commitments squeezed funding. Centralized funding from DOD evaporated. By November 2004 each service would have to fund its own program out of its current operating budget. Faced with uncertainties about the payoff against known needs elsewhere, the Army moved cautiously. The Army believed that enhancements already programmed into Aviation modernization would achieve the goals.

Training as an approach to improving Aviation safety

Improvements in Aviation safety suggested changes in training. A major thrust was Aircrew coordination training.

Lack of effective aircrew coordination was a cause in two-thirds of all Class A accidents. The problem was neither new nor unrecognized. Accident records for 1984–89 revealed that aircrew coordination failures contributed to 147 aviation fatalities at a cost of $292,234,720. The DCSOPS directed TRADOC and USAAVNC to develop a comprehensive program of instruction to correct crew-error accidents. Based on this, in 1989 the ARIARDA began research on training in this area, and a contractor prepared a candidate Aircrew Coordination Exportable Training Package in 1992.

Over the next few years, there were concerted efforts to make this knowledge effective. On 14 June 1995, the Army's birthday, USAAVNC sent a message that required all active Army aircrew members to qualify in aircrew coordination by 31 May 1997. The message allowed National Guard and Army Reserve crewmembers until 31 May 1998. Crewmembers could not progress to Readiness Level 1 (RL1)—full proficiency—until they completed aircrew coordination training. In May 1998 the first of several new, revised aircrew training manuals was fielded. These included specific, clearly defined aircrew coordination skills. Also, a new training package was available by 1 July 2001.

Like many things, the effectiveness of aircrew coordination training depended on leadership. By September 1997 USAAVNC was highlighting the importance of this training in the pre-command course (PCC) for those selected to command Aviation battalions and brigades. In November 2002 the Director of Evaluation and Standardization (DES) reported that the biggest problem with aircrew coordination training was sustainment. Aircrew coordination was a perishable skill. In units where commanders demanded it, aircrew coordination training was great. In units where commanders do not view it as a priority, aircrew coordination training was usually very poor. Out of this recognition came a requirement for refresher training.

Aircrew coordination did not disappear as a factor in accidents, at the same time that senior Army leadership highlighted it as a specific concern. In December 2003 the CSA sent a message to all Army activities on the subject, "PROTECTING OUR COMBAT READINESS." In discussing Aviation, he specifically noted that aircrew coordination was a factor in half of the Aviation accidents in Operation Iraqi Freedom (OIF). As of February 2004 the USASC and USAAVNC were working toward an enhanced aircrew coordination training program.

Technological efforts—Tactile Situational Awareness System (TSAS) and Ground Proximity Warning System (GPWS)

By 2004 Aviation was exploring several technologies to address safety issues. One, already discussed in conjunction with MFOQA, involved flight data recorders. Another technology was a Tactile Situational Awareness System (TSAS). This device used the sense of touch to tell a pilot which direction to move the controls to put the aircraft in the proper position. Such information was especially useful to aircrews during terrain flight, take-offs and landings in conditions of reduced visibility, such as blowing sand and dust. By 2004 there were urgent needs for some such device for operations in SWA. A third area was technology that would prevent pilots from inadvertently flying into the terrain—a situation commonly called controlled flight into terrain (CFIT).

Brownout in SWA

A major factor in operations was bad terrain and bad weather. Both were familiar challenges to Army aviators at least from ODS. The major differences resulted from the fact that operations after ODS often involved much higher altitudes and stretched out over months and into years, rather than weeks. One of the most bothersome conditions was called brownout. This condition commonly arose when an aircraft was landing at low speed in a very dusty area. The wash from the rotor blades blew huge amounts of dust into the air. This dust made a dense could that swirled around the aircraft. The effect could not only blind but also disorient pilots. The problem was serious. In 2003 brownouts caused 39 percent of the Army's Class A aviation accidents and 75 percent in OIF.

Brownout could be especially dangerous under conditions where an emergency arose. An example occurred to CWO 3 Rodney Swanson of the 82AB during a night combat assault in Afghanistan. Flying with NVG, Swanson was making the final approach in a Chinook. Besides the crew, the aircraft had 36 paratroopers onboard. Carrying this number of passengers required removing the seats that were designed to absorb impact and reduce injuries in a crash. So it was an especially dangerous situation. Brownout conditions, causing the crew to lose all visual references to the LZ, made Swanson decide to go around, rather than land immediately. As the Chinook climbed above 60 feet, one of its two engines exploded. Because of the high altitude, the remaining engine lacked enough power to avoid a crash. Fortunately Swanson was an extremely skilled pilot—based, in large part, on his years as a maintenance test pilot (MTP). In the three to five seconds before the aircraft hit the ground, Swanson applied all the right emergency procedures. The aircraft was destroyed but everyone easily could have been killed. Because of Swanson's skill, all 41 people onboard escaped serious injury. For his actions, CW3 Swanson received a Broken Wing Award—awarded to aviators who, through their skill, successfully overcame a serious emergency in flight.

Army leadership recognized that the operating environment would not change. So the focus had to be on improving crews' ability to deal with the environment. By January 2004 the USASC was focused on three initiatives. First was advanced simulators that would allow building a country database within hours and then present visual cues, such as grass moving while at a hover and brownout. Experience in these simulators would let pilots build muscle memory, control, and confidence. Another was the TSAS. Finally the USASC advocated aircrew coordination training.

Congressional interest also pushed technology to prevent CFIT. The most notable of the related technologies was a Ground Proximity Warning System (GPWS). An analysis by the USASC of accident causes for 1993–2003 showed CFIT as the outstanding culprit on every measure—percentages of Class A accidents, fatalities, dollar costs, and aircraft destroyed. While successfully applied to fixed-wing aircraft, helicopters seemed to present some technical challenges. By 2002, at least some Aviation units had acquired technology that helped considerably in some of these conditions. An example was a system called a Radar Altitude Hold on the MH-47E—the SOF variant of the Chinook. The Radar Altitude Hold was a radar altimeter. The radar altimeter was extremely accurate and allowed the pilot to know exactly where he was in reference to the ground, but only a very small number of aircraft had these systems. All other Army aviators had to rely on skill and luck.

Personnel changes

Concerns about personnel management, career progression, and retention of skilled people were key elements in creating the Aviation Branch in 1983. Creation of the Branch and associated changes clearly improved many of the conditions that prevailed before 1983. The years following ODS showed both the successes of the new Branch as part of the Army's system and lingering effects of some bedrock factors. As with all times, what happened within the Army partly reflected the conditions of the American society from which the Army comes. Changes in the environment had major effects. Particularly important were major shifts in the overall economy from unprecedented prosperity to severe recession followed by slow recovery, and from a general sense of security to a state of war after 11 September 2001.

Success of the Aviation Branch—general officer promotions

One consideration in forming the Branch in 1983 was the adverse effect that the existing system had on growing senior leaders with a strong foundation in aviation. Under the pre-1983 system, aviators were part-timers in one of several basic branches. They had to compete for assignments, retention, and promotion against their fulltime contemporaries in that branch. Especially as new technologies brought new capabilities to the battlefield but demanded much more time in aviation to acquire and retain proficiency, the effect was to prevent many aviators from surviving beyond the middle grades. Changes in force structure—creating a career progression through brigade command—after 1982 fixed part of the problem, but many had serious doubts that the Aviation Branch would be truly viable. The real measure of success would come only a decade or more after creating the Branch. It would take that long for young officers to rise through an Aviation career track and compete for general officer selection. The Branch would have proven viable if those truly-Aviation officers began achieving general-officer selection and then promotion in flag grades at rates comparable to their contemporaries from the old combat arms—Infantry, Artillery, and Armor.

One milestone came in 1993, when COL Johnny M. Riggs was promoted to BG. Although several generals had served as Army aviators and worn Aviator wings, Riggs had spent most of his career in Aviation assignments. He was commissioned through OCS and attended the Infantry Officer Basic Course. After six months as a tactical officer in the Infantry School, he completed flight training at Fort Wolters in 1969. He then served in a series of Aviation-related assignments. After two years as an Infantry company commander, 1976–1978, he returned to more Aviation-related assignments through 1991. After a year's assignment in NATO, he became the assistant division commander of 3d Infantry Division (3ID) in Germany. While there he was promoted to BG. After a year as DCG at USAAVNC, he became the Director of Requirements, Office of the Deputy Chief of Staff for Operations. Promoted to MG in July 1996, he became the Assistant Deputy Chief of Staff for Operations and Plans. He commanded Fort Carson, Colorado, and the 7th Infantry Division. In July 1999, promoted to lieutenant general, he took command of First United States Army. In 2001 he became the Director of the Objective Force Task Force (OFTF) He remained there until he retired in 2004.

By the mid-1990s there was more evidence that the Branch had at least not hurt those who had chosen to grow mainly within an Aviation career path. Of special importance were the promotions to the rank of lieutenant general (LTG). In 1998 a breakthrough came when both MG Ronald E. Adams and MG Daniel J. Petrosky were selected for a third star. Both had served as CG of USAAVNC. In July 1998 Adams became Chief of Staff/Deputy Commander of Land Forces Central Europe. In August 1998 MG Petrosky was chosen to command Eighth Army and serve as Chief of Staff, United Nations Command/Combined Forces

Command/United States Forces Korea. Both Adams and Petrosky's assignments were significant as being key components of the Joint warfighting commands.

Equally or more important as a measure of success within the Army were appointments to division command and to the major positions on the Army Staff. These were the various deputy chiefs of staff, the VCSA and ultimately the CSA. Division commands were the plum positions in the warfighting part of the Army and were the usual stepping stones to the key jobs in the senior leadership. The deputy chiefs formed the inner circle of those who made and implemented policy within the Army. They were also the positions that, with the right credentials in combatant command, marked officers for command of one of the Joint combatant commands or for the position of the CSA.

The officer who blazed this trail was Richard A. Cody. After graduating from West Point and being commissioned in 1972, he went into the Transportation Corps. In 1977 he started a long series of Aviation-related assignments—first as a rotary-wing section leader within the aviation brigade of the 2ID in Korea. As with other Transportation aviators, he acquired a strong maintenance background. In 1984 he started a recurrent affiliation with the 101AB and Fort Campbell as executive officer of the 229th Aviation Battalion. During ODS his battalion carried off TF Normandy, taking out the Iraqi radar sites. In 1994 he took command of the Aviation brigade in the 1CD, then commanded the 160th Special Operations Aviation Command (160 SOA). In November 1997 he was promoted to BG. In April 1998 he became the assistant division commander for maneuver of the 4ID. A year later, he went to a one-year assignment as the Director for Operations, Readiness and Mobilization within the DCSOPS. In June 2000. Cody took command of the 101AB. In August 2002 he became the DCSOPS for the Army. This assignment made him the first post-Branch officer to fill one of these key positions. In June 2004 the Senate confirmed his promotion to General and appointment as the VCSA. He thus became the first officer with a career predominantly in Aviation to achieve that level of position.

By 2004 officers with Aviation careers seemed to be competing on equal terms with their contemporaries in the other branches. Officers in Aviation were faring better than their contemporaries Army-wide in promotion through the rank of COL. The differences were most pronounced at the transition from MAJ to LTC. Results of the last boards showed 85 percent of Aviation officers being promoted. The Army-wide average was 79 percent. Other officers had achieved three-star rank. Most notably, by 2003, four successive commanders of USAAVNC—Ronald E. Adams, Daniel J. Petrosky, Anthony R. Jones and John M. Curran—

had all achieved this rank. DCGs had also gone on to positions as divisional deputy commanders and then to operational assignments. Assignment to a school position at the grade of COL, which had long been seen as a terminal assignment, had not proven to be a dead end. Thus, the Aviation Branch seemed to be healthy and to have fulfilled the hopes of those who had fought to establish it in its modern form.

Of at least passing notice was the fact that, in Fiscal Year 2004. for the first time, two Aviation colonels—husband and wife—were selected for BG. COL John A. MacDonald and COL Anne F. MacDonald were both West Point graduates. Both had commanded Aviation brigades in Korea.

Recruiting and retention

The tremendous increases in OPTEMPO after the end of the Cold War threatened the Army, along with the other services, with serious losses of skilled people. An indicator of the changes was a radical change in perception about assignments to some places. Whereas, for many years, many Soldiers had considered Korea a hardship tour and many worked hard to avoid it, the pattern shifted radically. By January 2001, Soldiers were seeking assignments to Korea for stability in a tour. Soldiers already in Korea were extending their tours to have families there. These conditions challenged Aviation, as it did other branches.

The pilot personnel picture across the services

By the late 1990s all services had shortages of pilots. In 1999 the HASC directed GAO to study and report on the situation. DOD reported a shortfall of about 2000 pilots and expected shortages to continue for several years. DOD found the actual shortages hard to assess. Requirements included nonoperational positions, such as providing training, as well as nonflying positions needed to develop pilots' leadership skills for advancement, education, medical treatment, and transfers between assignments. GAO found that no units were deploying without having all of their authorized pilot strength. However, the services met their operational commitments by extending some pilots on deployments and by sending senior pilots to what had traditionally been junior cockpit positions. The services also were deliberately not filling some nonflying positions that called for pilots. Whether these shortages were important or not was uncertain. GAO noted that the Army was unique in using warrant officers as pilots.

One concern GAO expressed about the losses of pilots was the high cost of producing them. DOD estimated it cost about $1 million to provide basic flight training for each pilot. Total costs to achieve full operational readiness could exceed $9 million per pilot, although costs varied widely by type of aircraft. In addition were costs of special aviation pays—commonly called flight pay. That began when pilots started training and, in 1999, could run up to $22,000 per year.

GAO identified several reasons for the shortfalls. One was reduced recruitment during the drawdowns after the end of the Cold War and continuing through the 1990s. Also, problems in coordinating training, spare parts, and other factors had increased training times and reduced numbers of pilots available for first assignments. Third, a booming economy offered many career opportunities in private industry for pilots. Finally, many pilots were dissatisfied with conditions they found within the military. Many were tired of the high OPTEMPO, as well as shortages of spare parts and equipment to do their jobs well. They were also dissatisfied with leadership that seemed too willing to accept unacceptable demands on service personnel. Some also thought that they were being kept in cockpit positions at the expense of serving in other positions that would help their careers. However, some were glad to stay in the cockpit and were dissatisfied with assignments that took them away from flying.

Recruiting of new commissioned officers—Aviation as a branch of choice

While the services overall faced pilot shortages, Aviation enjoyed strong popularity among potential commissioned officers. Success in attracting and obtaining high-quality officer material was not something left to chance. The organization directly responsible, the Aviation Proponency (AP) Office within USAAVNC, made consistent, strenuous efforts to attract and acquire the best candidates available. Efforts included presentations at the service academies, advanced camps for ROTC, and activities targeted specifically to increase representation of minorities. Despite concerted efforts to recruit minorities and women, Aviation saw only modest success.

The success of Aviation and its people were mutually dependent. To succeed Aviation demanded high-quality people. The nature and overall success of Aviation attracted such people. This dynamic was nowhere more evident than in recruiting. It was easiest to see in recruiting for commissioned officers. Aviation stood out from the pack in the expressions of preference from students at West

Point and ROTC. In 2004 Aviation was the only branch that filled all available slots at both West Point and in the ROTC programs.

Exploring ways to get and keep pilots flying—PRK and LASIK

The high cost of producing pilots and difficulty of obtaining enough of them created an ongoing interest in ways to retain them in flying status. The main cause of medically disqualifying flight applicants was their inability to pass an eye test. Moreover, once the Army had invested in a pilot, the normal aging process worked against that person's retaining vision required to fly. The particular conditions of Army flying—especially involving NVG—constrained the use of glasses. The idea of some technology—likely, surgery—that could reduce a pilot's need for corrective lenses appealed. That would reduce problems with such equipment as head-mounted displays and protective masks. At the same time, expanding use of surgical correction among civilians meant more people would enter the military after having these procedures. If people who had already had these procedures could not enter flying, populations of potential recruits could shrink even more. So, in 1999 the USAARL began studies on these surgeries and their effects.

Results of an early phase of the study, completed in 2003, showed promise although there were some concerns, such as complaints about night vision By January 2004 the refractive surgery studies had made real strides. USAARL found that the surgery did enhance combat visual performance. The surgery's effects greatly improved the user's ability to use optical media, such as laser protective devices, ballistic eyewear, and visors. Finally the effects allowed aviators to use advanced-technology imagery.

Personnel effects of restructuring—WO pilots

Aviation generally shared in the same experiences and conditions that GAO found with the other services. However, the Army also had some special challenges of its own. These derived partly from the legacy of build-ups during Vietnam and the 1980s. Challenges also derived partly from the Army's heavy reliance on WOs as a major part of its aviator force structure. In September 2003 Aviation had positions for 5496 WOs. That was 48 percent of the entire WO Corps.

Imbalances and effects through the 1990s

A byproduct of prolonged retention of Vietnam-era aircraft was a difficult, interlocking set of force-manning and personnel management problems. To man the large number of older aircraft, through the 1980s and into the 1990s, the Army had trained a large population of pilots rated in those aircraft. However, efforts began with the ARI in 1995 simultaneously to modernize the Aviation fleets and to reduce excessive costs for both personnel and maintenance. These efforts had the double effect of reducing total numbers of aircraft while requiring an increasing percentage of those pilots remaining to be rated in newer types of aircraft. At the same time, a large percentage of the middle-and senior-grade WOs who wanted to remain were not rated in the aircraft that were left to fly. Because flight school was always operating at maximum capacity, there were too few seats to allow the existing population of pilots to qualify in the newer types of aircraft. So an increasing mismatch grew between the skills available and those required in the middle and senior WO grades. The situation worsened. By 1996, the VCSA directed Aviation to reduce its accessions and retrain the existing pool of aviators to operate modernized aircraft.

The requirement to retrain existing aviators severely squeezed both personnel management and training. With requirements to train new pilots and the large number of middle-grade WOs needing to convert to newer aircraft, there simply were not enough seats in classes to cover everyone. To try to accommodate those WOs already in the system, for almost a decade—from Fiscal Year 1991 through Fiscal Year 2000—the Army reduced the number of new WOs it acquired. This was intended to bring the numbers in balance by natural attrition. However, by the late 1990s, Army aviator populations were badly unbalanced. On paper, the situation was self-correcting. In Fiscal Year 2002 promotion opportunities would increase greatly, but the result was a drain of experienced Army WO aviators, who could not readily be replaced because of the long time it took to develop them. By Fiscal Year 2001 66 percent of all attrition in Aviation was CW2s and CW3s. It took 8–10 years to grow a new WO to that level of experience. The drain of middle-grade WOs also threatened the future Aviation force. Aviation was not getting enough applicants to ensure a quality selection. The shrinking number of in-service applicants also increased the burdens on recruiters to find and attract people who could qualify. Finally there were concerns that a declining level of Aviation experience in the field was one of those factors contributing to the rising accident rates after 1996.

The situation was recognized. On 8 August 2001 USAAVNC submitted a broad strategy aimed at retention to the DCSPER. Among other adjustments this strategy called for several incentives to induce WOs to remain. These included increasing WO opportunities for promotion, extending Aviation continuation pay (ACP) to include every MOS held by AWOs, and offering a measure of security to middle-grade individuals.

Overall the picture seemed to improve. By January 2003, the ratio of fills against requirements had improved even more—reaching an average of 95 percent. However, because units deploying to active operations were being filled beyond 100 percent, lower priority units lived with even greater shortages than the average. There were also worries about backlashes from a policy known as stop loss. Stop loss met urgent needs by involuntarily retaining on active duty individuals who were due to leave the service. In December 2001 the Army applied this measure incidental to increased combat operations, first in Afghanistan and then in Iraq. Stop loss particularly affected Aviation. Fears existed that, once stop-loss lifted, even more people would leave the service than would have otherwise. If that happened, Aviation could see a large drop in numbers within key groups. The result would be big holes in experience levels. Happily for the Army, by February 2003, it seemed that the backlash from stop-loss might not be as bad as feared.

The difference between feared and actual attrition among senior aviators related to stop loss reflected one of the shining fundamentals of the people in Aviation. In hindsight of 2004, it appeared that the causes for many people leaving the service had more to do with uncertainty about how long the Army would commit individual Soldiers into operations in SWA—particularly, Iraq—than unwillingness to serve under difficult conditions. Once the Army announced that rotations would be for one year and families could plan around that situation, attrition dropped. The pattern reaffirmed the basic tenet of Army leadership: Take care of Soldiers.

Favorable changes in the environment after 2000—economic downturn, threats to the nation, and integration of WOs within the Aviation Branch

Two conditions entirely beyond the Army's control largely accounted for improved retention among WOs. One was a drastic change in the economy. Through the 1990s the nation enjoyed the longest boom in its history. When the bubble burst in April 2000, the stock market quickly lost about 30 percent of its value. These huge losses radically changed the civilian employment prospects for many people—among them, Army aviators. This enormous shift in the general economy, with the uncertainties it created, reduced the economic incentives for career pilots to leave the service. Particularly hard-hit in the downturn were the commercial airlines. Some Army aviators who had left the service were returning.

The second major change outside the Army was the nature of the emerging, global threat. The shock of the attacks on 11 September 2001 galvanized the nation. Especially within the armed forces, there was a renewed sense of mission. With that, many of those who might have drifted away during a more benign period felt reaffirmed in their choice to serve the country in uniform. With less incentive to leave and more to stay, the balance shifted.

By the fall of 2003 there were also changes within the Army environment for WOs that made staying more attractive. In 2002 WOs received unprecedented recognition of their importance within the Branch with the appointment of the first Chief Warrant Officer of the Branch (CWOB). The CG of USAAVNC introduced the first incumbent, CWO 5 Stephen T. Knowles, on 5 February as part of the Aviation Leaders Training Conference. Knowles had served in Vietnam as an assault helicopter pilot, including with the 48th Assault Helicopter Company during Lam Son 719. Creating the CWOB gave warrant officers an effective observer, adviser, and spokesman for their special needs, much as the creation of command sergeant major (CSM) positions had for NCOs earlier.

By the end of 2003 there were also other changes affecting WOs. Some disincentives in the personnel management system either had gone away or at least showed signs of improving. Promotion forecasts were good. There were changes related to policy on retention. Among these was a lock-in at 18 years for WOs who had twice failed to be selected for the next higher grade. Also, CW4s who found themselves in this situation would be allowed to continue in service until they had reached 24 years of service. The only apparent downside to this change was that it would slow promotion for CW3s.

A symbolic change for WOs throughout the Army came on 9 July 2004, when they exchanged their 'rising eagle' insignia of the Warrant Officer Corps for the insignia of the branch of which they were a part. While the shift to wearing branch brass was largely symbolic, it came as part of a much larger set of changes shaping the future for Army WOs. The changing of insignia was part of Army Transformation—in this case, intended to strengthen the identity of WOs within their branches and to eliminate the perception of warrant officers as something separate.

The change also reflected changes in the roles of WOs. While they originated as skilled technicians, WOs had increasingly filled positions and borne responsibilities traditionally part of the duties of commissioned officers. For example, in June 2000, the Branch Chief, MG Anthony R. Jones, discussed the initiative to change the Average Grade Distribution Matrix (AGDM) to increase the number in Aviation in grades of CWO 3 and CWO 4. More, experienced, senior warrant officers were critical to a proposed change in force structure—a shift to multi-functional battalions (MFB). These units would routinely conduct complex missions in a Joint/Combined environment. WOs would often serve as flight leads and attack/reconnaissance battle captains. For these reasons, it had become vital to put senior WO experience at battalion level and below. The existing, pyramidal grade structure did not allow that. Senior WOs were also routinely assigned at battalion, brigade and division levels, as well as in higher headquarters and in Joint settings. There they frequently performed senior staff duties.

Along with these changes came changes in how WOs would be managed. Previously WOs were assigned and distributed according to three grade bands. This practice sometimes led to mismatches of skills and duties. In the future, assignment would be by individual grades of CW2 through CW5. There were also new, regulatory guidelines for utilization of WOs. Consolidation of guidance for career management and professional development into a single publication for all officers, including WOs, sought to assure that WOs requirements regularly appeared within the view of commissioned leaders.

There were also efforts to adjust compensation. Of particular concern had been a compression of pay scales that resulted from raises targeted to NCOs in 1999 and 2000. The study found this issue to be the second most important one to WOs in the field.

Noncommissioned officers (NCO)

Aviation faced a similar problem with NCO structures and issues as it did with WOs: Aviation required a kind and level of skill in its operators that took longer to develop than in most branches. The Army's enlisted personnel management system did not readily accommodate Aviation needs. That system expected junior Soldiers to perform detailed, technical tasks. Once Soldiers had served long enough to become NCOs, the Army expected them to supervise and lead, rather than perform technical tasks. This mismatch between years in service/time in grade and skill/experience levels lay at the root of the grade imbalances and concerns with senior WOs. The same problem existed with NCOs.

CINCOS—recognizing differences between NCOs as operators and as supervisors

The nature of the problem came to a head during the mid-1990s as the Army reached the bottom part of its long, post-Cold War drawdown. In June 1996 the DA initiated a program called Change in NCO Structure (CINCOS). The VCSA directed CINCOS to reduce NCOs to 47 percent of total enlisted strength. This reduction in higher grades sought to avoid cutting 20,000 Soldiers. Those cuts would reduce the Army's end strength below 495,000. The real, driving force came from direction to save $170 million in the Army's Military Personnel account for three fiscal years, beginning with 1998. At the Army level, CINCOS offered benefits to both the organization and the individuals in it. Reductions would let the Army return to manning all NCO positions. Moreover, to cushion the impact on those adversely affected, reductions would be spread over three years.

The DCSPER had the overall responsibility for this task. The approach to making these changes was the normal one—to weigh costs in people and functions against risks that the Army would not be able to perform its missions adequately. All reductions were supposed to balance savings from reductions against risks the reductions created. To assess people and functions involved screening each Career Management Field (CMF) across the Army. The DCSPER approach was to apply standard grade changes for certain positions across both TOE and TDA organizations. The Aviation Branch percentage stood at 52 percent. After reviewing the average grades across the Army, the DCSPER produced a target of 45 percent for Aviation. When the AP Office at USAAVNC reviewed the effects of the DCSPER proposals, AP thought risks in TOE units were too high. USAAVNC developed an alternative proposal that would produce a ratio of 47.8 percent NCOs for Aviation.

In the initial rounds of CINCOS, Aviation fared well. In actuality, Aviation emerged with a target of 49 percent. In the end, Aviation's reduction was only one percent of its NCO positions. Through the initial round of CINCOS, Aviation did streamline every enlisted MOS. That scrub achieved a second goal of CINCOS—to eliminate career stagnation for junior enlisted Soldiers and increased promotion opportunity to SGM in CMF 67, Aviation Maintenance, by almost 50 percent. Most importantly, the Branch leadership was satisfied that Aviation maintained its overall warfighting capability. CINCOS preserved having E-8 First Sergeants (1SG) in attack companies and cavalry troops. CINCOS also retained having sergeants first class (SFC) as Facility Chiefs in ATC units. CINCOS also retained more staff sergeants (SSG/E-6) than sergeants (SGT/E-5) in TI positions. In one sense, Aviation units nominally gained out of the new rules. Under CINCOS the first TI position in a unit, which had normally been a SGT, was allowed to become a SSG.

Despite the upward adjustments for Aviation from the original DCSPER proposals, CINCOS still caused squeezes in the field. CINCOS forced Aviation to shift tasks for TIs from SSG to SGT. The difference in grade made a practical difference both in experience and schooling that NCOs would normally have. With the CINCOS changes, units sometimes had trouble finding school-trained TIs. Availability or lack of fully-qualified TIs in the field affected Aviation safety. By mid-2000 the key Aviation initiative regarding NCOs was NCO 'buyback'—trying to regain some of the positions lost.

CINCOS as reflection of the basics—people, technology, and organization

In part CINCOS reflected and tried to take advantage of changes in technology and resulting changes in practices that the structure of Army military occupational specialties (MOS) had changed to keep pace with these new conditions. For example, CINCOS combined several jobs with separate repair and maintenance MOSs into one. MOS 33R was an Aviation Systems Repairer. 33T was a Tactical Systems Repairer. 33Y was a Strategic Systems Repairer. 33Z was an Electronic Warfare/Intercept Systems Maintenance Supervisor. CINCOS combined all these into MOS 33W, Electronic Warfare/Intelligence Systems Repairer. This change reflected the fact that less and less often did Soldiers make repairs at the component level. That fact theoretically made it necessary neither to have the separate, highly-specific skills nor to have so many people available to perform tasks using these skills. At the time CINCOS started, the Aviation NCO fields had not been restructured for 10 years.

CINCOS and the way it unfolded for Aviation also reflected a larger pattern in the Army as related to personnel, practical needs, and perceptions. Aviation constantly ran against the wind to gain acceptance of a need for higher average grade levels—which related directly to years of experience—and to retaining people longer at some grades than was the desired state across the Army. There was a longstanding perception of the Army as a low-technology organization. In part that was a legacy of the Army and public perceptions of it through World War II. Recognition that the Army—especially in Aviation—had changed came only slowly and never completely. As a result, in several areas related to personnel management and force structure, Aviation was at odds with whatever standard framework the Army wanted to apply.

Incentives for retention—Airframe and Powerplant (A&P) license

Aviation sought various incentives to try to retain enlisted Soldiers with vital skills. An example was a program to let Soldiers gain a civilian license while on active duty. That would both enhance their value to the Army and increase their chances of competing successfully once they left the service. A specific license sought was the A&P license. The process was not simple. Aviation started the initiative in March 1999, paralleling work the other services had undertaken with the FAA and some major U.S. airlines. By February 2003 an agreement allowed Soldiers in such a program to take the test at their post education center and without cost. This benefit was considerable. A wide range of the enlisted Aviation MOSs were eligible, and this licensure led to well-paid jobs in civilian industry.

NCO retention in the GWOT

As was true with officers and WOs, the kind of people who comprised the enlisted and NCO ranks of Aviation generally showed a high level of commitment to the nation, the Army, and their chosen paths. That became especially pronounced after 11 September 2001. Despite the increased hardships on individuals and families with the increased deployments, uncertainties of rotation, and higher risks of combat—enlisted and NCO retention rose. Aviation completed Fiscal Year 2003 with an astonishing overall retention rate. The Branch stood at 130 percent of its retention goal. Only one area had significant problems. That was the MOS 67U [which became 15U] for Chinook Helicopter Repairer. This was the one Aviation enlisted MOS that had been subject to stop loss in 2001. The heavy reliance on the Chinooks in the extreme flying conditions of SWA created an exceptional OPTEMPO on these units, even beyond what Aviation as a whole experienced. As always, the OR of every aircraft ultimately rested on the enlisted Soldiers who maintained it. That condition put a special strain on these Soldiers.

Response to new needs—an Aviation Life Support Equipment (ALSE) MOS

Increasing sophistication and complexity of Aviation missions and related equipment drove demands for further specialization with the NCO ranks. Of special note in this era was the push to create a MOS dedicated to caring for Aviation Life Support Equipment (ALSE). This need reflected two facts of life in Aviation after ODS. One was the equipment itself. As the aircraft systems became increasingly complex, there was a parallel development in materiel that the Soldier-Aviator wore. In response, in April 2002, the Army established the Program Executive Office (PEO)-Soldier. This recognized that the acquisition and management of items that went on the Soldier demanded the same level of attention that went into any major weapons system. The other fact driving toward a separate ALSE MOS was the common pattern that units diverted the NCOs who were supposed to take care of this type of equipment to other tasks. As a result,

ALSE was commonly in poor condition and unready to do what it was supposed to when needed. The diversion of people reflected the chronic shortages in people against identified requirements that the Army faced throughout the period.

Attention to ALSE reflected the dramatic changes in Aviation's operating environment after the end of the Cold War. Through the end of the post-Cold War, Aviation's operational environment had allowed getting by with relatively little attention to ALSE. Through World War II, Army Ground Forces (AGF) aviators had no dedicated equipment. Anything they had beyond what was common to the ground Soldier, they scrounged. This situation continued through the Korean War and beyond. During Vietnam the Army finally recognized that rotary-wing crewmembers had unique needs. The main additions were survival vests, fire-retardant clothing, body armor, and helmets that gave some crash and hearing protection. Through the latter years of the Cold War, the complexity of operations dramatically increased crew workloads. Of particular concern were night operations and operations in a nuclear/biological/chemical (NBC) environment. Exposure to chemical and biological threats during ODS, along with experience with the extraction of an Apache crew under fire, heightened awareness of needs for something better. As a result, the Army began to develop requirements for more sophisticated ALSE. Operations through the 1990s forced Aviation into conditions that fell well beyond the limits of previous design. Missions in Afghanistan beginning in 2001 involved operating at altitudes above 10,000 feet. Flying at these altitudes required Soldiers to use oxygen—something that only SOA and the High Altitude Rescue Team (HART) had done until then. Doing this required training and equipment that previously had mainly been worries for the Navy and Air Force flying fast-moving, fixed-wing aircraft. Because of changing employment policies and the OPTEMPO, these requirements would include the RC as well as AC Aviation.

Illustrating the need—the Air Warrior (AW) system

An illustration of the kind of complexity with these new systems was the Air Warrior (AW) ensemble that replaced existing flight gear. The goal of AW was to create a single, integrated set of pieces that would all fit together in a package that would meet all of the aircrew member's needs but without interfering with his ability to enter, exit, or perform tasks within the aircraft. Among many other things, the AW ensemble included an electronic kneeboard, laser protection, helmet-mounted displays, oxygen systems, helmets, and a protective shield for the face. Some parts of this system already existed and were being brought over from the sister services, because these services had long experience in the kinds of operating conditions that the Army now faced. Examples were the Navy's AIRSAVE system. AIRSAVE would let an aircrew member escape an aircraft that went down in the water and then survive once out of that aircraft. Water-survival items required additional training—called Dunker/Helicopter Aircrew Breathing Device (HABD). The AW system also included a new Aircrew Battle Dress Uniform (ABDU). That would replace both the existing ABDU and the one-piece flight suit. The AW ensemble began fielding in 2003. To meet operational needs in OEF and OIF, some parts of operational tests were actually completed in combat units in the field.

UH-60 door gunner wearing Air Warrior ALSE items

Demands for expertise and adequate training

Simply operating in the more extreme environments of post-Cold War operations increased demands for expertise among Soldiers responsible for ALSE. A major concern in these new systems was the cost that came with their capabilities. The Joint Combat Survival Evader Locator cost about $10,000 apiece. If these systems were not properly maintained, their cost would increase and they might still fail when needed. Seemingly minor changes could be important. Simply how something was attached or repaired could mean the difference between an aircrew member coming through a mishap unscathed, injured, or dead. The potential for complexity was always increasing. Civilian industry constantly developed new items that might be useful. Vendors routinely presented these items at military conferences. Every one of these items, if acquired, required someone to know how to use and maintain it so that it could work if needed. Pilots and aircrew members often had little or no experience using ALSE in the conditions where it mattered most. CWO 4 Michael Durant, whose Black Hawk was shot down in Mogadishu on 3 October 1993, noted that he had never used any of his survival gear, other than his weapon, before his life depended on it.

As AW was fielded, ALSE technicians received a huge increase in both quantities and sophistication of materiel to control, maintain, and train users on. The ALSE technician was responsible for rebuilding many of these items and custom-fitting them properly to each aircrew member. Moreover, since AW was designed to be reconfigured according to missions, there was additional workload involved each time an individual had to adjust the combination of modular pieces.

Toward a dedicated ALSE group

To develop the expertise in the Soldiers responsible for ALSE meant training. One of the challenges was how to deliver it. The official position of the Army was that none of the components of AW would require additional people nor a new MOS or ASI. There was a formal school for those assigned to these duties. By October 1996 that school lasted five weeks and two days. At the end, the graduate received an additional skill identifier. By 2002 the Army was trying to make the training available to Soldiers within the units by developing interactive, computer-based training. Beginning in October 2003, USAAVNC added a 6-week resident course for ALSE to a 1-week distance learning (DL) course. The Army used ASIs and SQIs to identify Soldiers with special skills or qualifications closely related to but beyond those expected in a MOS. A graduate of the ALSE course received a Special Qualifications Identifier (SQI) of Q2. Only Soldiers in about ten Aviation MOSs could carry that SQI.

One reason that ALSE did not become a separate MOS, despite the rising demand, was that trends within the Army were running the other direction. With the Army shrinking by a third from September 1990 to September 2000, the Army sought more flexibility in using its remaining Soldiers. As part of implementing Transformation, in October 1999, CSA GEN Erick K. Shinseki ordered creation of a special TF to decide how many WO specialties and enlisted MOSs the Army could manage. The TF concluded that future Army missions would require Soldiers with basic knowledge in two or more skills, rather than a focus on tasks. This change would mean that specialization would occur at unit level, based on function, and would be supported by assignment-oriented training. The TF also foresaw reducing the number of Army MOSs from 241 to 191. This consolidation would reduce redundancies across proponents. The Army would have fewer MOSs but each would be larger. The change would increase predictability and efficiency in supporting training institutions. Leaders would also gain flexibility in using Soldiers. The Army would also gain flexibility in distributing Soldiers.

The need to do something to close the expertise gap for ALSE forced some organizations to adjust without a central solution. By November 2002 some commands were taking steps to provide fulltime people focused entirely on these duties. The Delaware National Guard advertised for a dual-status ALSE technician. This was an approach that the National Guard took to meet many of its ongoing requirements for skilled, fulltime people. The ALSE technician would be a master sergeant (MSG) but also a Wage-Grade 8 civilian employee.

By January 2003, AP was explicitly considering a specific MOS to support the expanding mission related to ALSE. The Director of AP noted that the existing workloads for ALSE were heavy. The advent of AW would create "an even greater need for highly skilled and qualified ALSE specialists and managers." In January 2004 the CG of USAAVNC, told Aviation leaders that people were working hard to establish a MOS for ALSE. The big problem, the CG noted, was that getting someone one place meant giving someone up somewhere else. In January 2004 a briefing to Aviation leaders noted that the new MOS would take Soldiers away from MOS's that were already short of people. There would also be more requirements to qualify for an ALSE position. That reduced the flexibility of local commanders, who could no longer put a grounded crew chief in the ALSE shop. This had been the kind of issue the GEN Shinseki's TF in 1999 had tried to combat. However, for Aviation and for the Army, in this case it looked like the right thing to do.

By September 2004 the training was being developed for a new ALSE MOS, with implementation projected for Fiscal Year 2007. The Branch CSM attributed this change directly to the complexity in AW. AP was working the Manpower and Personnel Integration (MANPRINT) requirements. It looked like the new MOS would involve about 500 Soldiers. Technology and the demands that it made on people were, once again, forcing a change in organization. Constrained by numbers of people, commanders could have expertise or they could have flexibility. They could not have both.

A new kind of professional—the tactical operations (TACOPS) WO

The rising complexity of air-ground operations led to creating a new professional track among WOs. In May 2003 the first class of a new TACOPS course began. Most of the course was devoted to Joint operations and training, and almost half the course dealt strictly with battlefield operations.

This course was a response to a need in the field that the increasing complexity of operations and new technologies had created. Aviation units increasingly needed someone who had a broad grasp of combined-arms operations, good skills in planning, and a good command of the related systems that were coming into the field.

Efforts to create a pipeline to develop people with such skills had begun shortly after ODS. In 1992 the Army approved a Tactical Operations Officer (TACOPS) career track for WOs. It took several years before that approval bore real fruit. When the TACOPS Officer career track was first approved, there were two, alternative, qualifying paths. One was to attend the Air Force Joint Firepower Controller's Course (JFCC). The other was one year of on-the-job training (OJT) as either an assistant Operations Officer (S-3) or Flight Operations Officer. Neither path proved satisfactory. The JFCC, oriented toward Air Force philosophy, focused on fast-moving, fixed-wing aircraft. OJT showed did not produce the skills needed. Meantime, as new equipment went into the field, individual units struggled to meet their needs as best they could. Most field units developed someone as their resident expert to run the new Aviation Mission Planning Station (AMPS).

In 2001, at the same time TRADOC approved the course, it redefined what the TACOPS officer would do. Experience through the 1990s showed that the initial duty description had failed. There was no consistency across types of units nor standardization of duties. In some cases, the position was simply an S-3 position. In others it focused on flight operations.

The revised duty description for the TACOPS warrant officer was highly demanding. This officer was to be qualified to plan, schedule, coordinate and brief Organic, Joint/Combined tactical and non-tactical aviation missions. He could also develop, plan, and coordinate EW operations. The TACOPS officer would also be the qualified, resident expert for a host of new digital systems—among them, ABCS, AMPS, and Advanced Field Artillery Tactical Data System (AFATDS). The TACOPS officer would also integrate courses of action for downed aircrew recovery into operations plans and orders, develop air maneuver TTP, and determine settings for ASE. Among the more important functions was also providing liaison for Interagency, Multi-Service, Joint, and Combined Operations.

To be sure that a student was ready to take on the challenges of this course, there were some fairly stiff prerequisites. These included prior qualifications in Aircraft Survivability Equipment (ASE)/electronic warfare officer (EWO), professional schooling, and rank with time in grade.

The revised standards provided for a career progression from entry level through CW5 and included a Special Qualification Identifier-I (SQI-I). Assignments ranged from company or troop level through brigade and higher levels. TOEs changed accordingly.

By 2004 the TACOPS officer had become a key figure in Aviation, with demands for these specialists increasing. Once again, though, the recognition of a need outran the ability of the system to produce the skilled people who could meet the need. The restructuring of Aviation in connection with the shift from divisions to brigade combat teams (BCT) as the basic tactical unit increased demand for these specialists. A TACOPS officer was one position in the new Brigade Aviation Element (BAE), discussed below. The demands were so high that some WOs might be forced into the career track to fill gaps left by volunteers.

Organization—from capable, affordable to Joint, expeditionary force

In the years after ODS the Army underwent major changes in force structure. Through the 1990s changes were mainly in size, with a series of efforts to adjust to decreased resources after the end of the Cold War. By 2000 the new global environment required more basic changes. The beginning of the GWOT both highlighted and increased the urgency of making these adjustments. By late 2004 the Army was well into a reorganization of its operating forces that was as comprehensive as the AOE in 1983 and possibly unequaled since the ROAD in the 1960s.

Officially the Army Campaign Plan called the change the most extensive since early World War II. The goal was a larger pool of agile, cohesive, deployable units.

Aviation Requirements for the Combat Structure of the Army (ARCSA) V

From the adoption of the AOE design in 1983 until after 2000, the Army wrestled to find a satisfactory solution to a dilemma in Aviation force structure. The Army needed about 8300 spaces across the AC and RC to fix all deficiencies in the AOE. Within this larger problem the trick was to have enough Aviation capability while keeping Aviation within affordable costs. The problem arose out of the huge size of the Cold War forces and the increased density of Aviation in the AOE forces. There was simply not enough Aviation to meet all the requirements. The Army could never find a way to divert enough resources to Aviation to fill the gaps. In part this problem reflected the parochialism inherent in the Army's branch system. As late as 1991 an assumption prevailed that aviation should not exceed about 6 percent of the Army's force structure. That was about the percentage each branch would have based on dividing the whole Army by the number of branches. This figure completely ignored relative contribution to the institution's overall effectiveness. It also reflected an incidental cost of Aviation becoming a separate branch. Aviation had lost the sense of ownership and selfish interest in the leadership of other branches that existed when aviation was part of those branches. That sense of ownership had allowed GEN Herbert Powell to double the amount of aviation in the ROAD, as discussed in Chapter 5.

Relative contribution to the fight was a hard, emotional issue. Even direction from senior Army leadership did not produce broad response. When MG Ostovich took command In October of 1989, Apache battalions were authorized 264 Soldiers. As it was, the Apache battalions did not have enough mechanics or supply specialists. There were no fulltime aviators for the three Black Hawks in the Apache battalion. In November 1989, GEN Robert RisCassi, the VCSA, repeated a decision earlier that year that these battalions should have 35 more people. In USAREUR GEN Saint acted and dismantled an Artillery battalion to pay the structure bill. U.S. Army Forces Command (FORSCOM) did not, leaving its units at 264. FORSCOM also continued to resist any increase through the Army's programming process.

The crumbling of the Warsaw Pact threat that became apparent with the fall of the Berlin Wall in 1989 started to allow movement toward some solution. On 12 July 1990 a modified Aviation System Program Review (ASPR) led to an Aviation

Requirements for the Combat Structure of the Army (ARCSA) V Study on how to organize aviation to support ALB. Increasing resources for Aviation solved some parts of the problem. For example, equipment for a FARP was funded. The ASPR also approved in concept having two pilots for the OH-58D Kiowa Warrior. Door gunners were authorized for assault aircraft in contingency corps. Partly the ASPR solved problems by simply accepting shortages and distributing them unevenly to minimize the likely harm. For example, the ASPR approved the concept of creating an E Company in Apache battalions. E Companies were U.S. Army Reserve units that lacked their primary equipment.

Aviation Restructure Initiative (ARI)

MG John D. Robinson, Ostovich's successor at USAAVNC, made more drastic efforts to adjust the balances. Robinson was dissatisfied with the thrust of the ARCSA study. He saw a basic flaw in focusing on Aviation without similarly considering the other pieces of the combined-arms team. He believed the main thrust of an ARCSA belonged with the proponent at Fort Rucker, rather than at Fort Leavenworth, and urged the Army to undertake similar, concurrent reviews of the other combat arms to address the kinds of imbalance issues that MG Ostovich had noted. Robinson also was worried about the effect of the huge, diverse inventory of Army aircraft. He sought to shed expensive, obsolete aircraft to make room for new, improved equipment. In the process he wanted to drop the number of types from 10 to five for helicopters and about eight to four for fixed-wing. Finally he believed that Aviation worked best if organized into homogenous units. There was a special concern with the assets assigned to cavalry units. In Robinson's view, these needed to be under the Aviation brigade commander. That commander could provide both support and seasoned judgment about matters that easily could escape the view of less experienced, non-Aviation leaders.

The expression of MG Robinson's concerns became the ARI, which the CSA approved on 3 February 1993 to correct the AOE deficiencies. The ARI was supposed to produce a newly-structured Aviation force in both the AC and RC that could support all aspects of warfighting to meet the requirements of a 21st Century Army. ARI forces would be modular and flexible to quickly respond to specific regional crises. Through phased substitution, ARI provided for modernization with reduced numbers of aircraft across the total force. An attack battalion went down from 34 to 24 aircraft. The AOE battalion in a heavy division previously had 13 OH-58A/C Kiowa scout helicopters, 18 Apaches, and three Black Hawks. Under the Interim ARI configuration the same battalion had nine Apache Longbows with radar. These would perform the scout function. There were also 15 Apache Longbow attack aircraft. The ARI Objective configuration substituted nine RAH-66 Comanches for the nine Longbow scouts. Both heavy and light division attack aviation battalions lost their utility/lift aircraft in the conversion from AOE to ARI. The same numbers and changes applied to air assault divisions in the different configurations.

One effect of the ARI was to standardize configurations. The heavy division cavalry squadron would have two Aviation troops. In AOE there were two configurations, depending on the type of aircraft in the unit. One configuration had 21 aircraft. These were 12 OH-58A/CKiowas, eight AH-1 Cobras, and one Black Hawk. The other had a total of 17 aircraft: 16 OH-58D Kiowa Warriors and one Black Hawk. The ARI Interim would have 16 aircraft—either 16 AH-1 Cobras or 16 OH-58D Kiowa Warriors. The ARI Objective, however, would increase to 24 RAH-66 Comanches.

The ARI had some serious ripple effects in several areas. Most of these are discussed elsewhere in this chapter. One example, though, was reducing the average number of flight hours per aviator from more than 180 per year to less than 120 by 1998. On 9 August 1999 the Structure Manning Decision Review (SMDR) for Fiscal Year 2002 prompted discussions about balances of AWOs and lieutenants in Aviation, as well as about funding and aircraft to meet training requirements. If more funds were unavailable, AWOs would be shorted in training, because they were third priority behind students under Foreign Military Sales (FMS) and commissioned officers. This reflected personnel accession patterns. Aviation was taking in the same number of lieutenants as in earlier years but had many fewer aircraft. Also the ARI had put more officers in the battalions than existed before. Results in the field were that WOs were getting more flying time, and lieutenant pilots were spending most of their time in staff work. This effect was creating problems in career progression and retention among junior commissioned officers. Some lieutenants had returned from yearlong assignments in Korea without getting an hour of flying time. Frustration over not being able to fly was leading lieutenants to leave the service. Aviation would have to document the number of captains required to correct the situation.

One sidelight of the ARI illustrates the kinds of conundrums Aviation faced. The ARI identified a requirement for a battalion of Light Utility Helicopters (LUH) to augment corps-level assets in situations that did not require a Black Hawk, which was much more expensive per flight hour. These battalions were put in the National Guard, scattered across 14 states. Budget shortfalls, rising cost of maintaining old aircraft, and emphasis on acquiring attack and reconnaissance aircraft—notably Comanche and Apache Longbow—effectively stifled efforts to acquire a modernized aircraft for the LUH missions. This left the burden on the aging Huey fleet. In 1994, based on direction from TRADOC, USAAVNC conducted two studies related to the LUH. One rejected a commercial off-the-shelf (COTS) alternative to the UH-1 because of the costs related to procurement and the limited number of airframes needed. The total number of aircraft was only 131. Acquisition of a COTS aircraft also ran counter to the ARI goal of reducing the logistics burden by reducing the number of types of aircraft to support. Lacking a viable alternative, the other study pointed toward a service life extension program for the Huey. This approach meant upgrading avionics and making other changes that would make the Huey suitable for the LUH missions. These changes meant additional costs in the aging Huey fleet. In any case, from 1995 onward, repeated safety of flight messages on the Hueys either completely grounded them or severely restricted their use.

Aviation Modernization into Aviation Transformation

By the late 1990s the Army's inability to solve the modernization problem, along with the high OPTEMPO of the post-Cold War military, seriously affected Aviation and its ability to do its jobs. By March 1999 continued budgetary pressures led the Army to trade off Aviation modernization and adopt strategies that fielded aircraft below authorized unit levels. By the beginning of 2000, Aviation was moving toward a new modernization plan, reflecting new direction and priorities. In October 1999, the new CSA, GEN Shinseki, called for a transformation of the Army into a lighter, swifter, and more versatile force. The focus fell on a new Future Combat System (FCS). This would be a networked system of systems. The centerpiece was a family of 20-ton vehicles with the lethality of the M1 Abrams tank but with far greater tactical and strategic mobility. These changes would let the Army quickly place forces anywhere to handle any type of conflict. Some critics zeroed in on Aviation's absence in GEN Shinseki's initial announcement of this initiative. GEN John M. Keane, the VCSA, asserted that Aviation was an integral part of the thrust, and GEN Keane promised a comprehensive aviation plan.

On 4 April 2000 a new Army Aviation Modernization Plan was announced. This plan sought three interrelated objectives. First was to reduce the force to four helicopter types: AH-64D Apaches, RAH-66 Comanches, Black Hawks, and Chinooks. Second was to equip AC and RC units with identical types of aircraft to make these units interchangeable. Third was to reorganize both AC and RC helicopter forces into Multi-Functional Battalions (MFB). Each MFB would have 10 Comanches, 10 Apaches, and 10 Black Hawks. Chinooks would provide support. Aviation force structure was 25 brigade-equivalent organizations and three Regimental Aviation Squadrons (RAS). This excluded SOA, MEDEVAC and SEMA fixed-wing units. In some cases, such as the 6th Cavalry Brigade for III Corps at Camp Humphreys, Korea, the vast bulk of those Aviation assets were in the RC. Even for XVIII AB, over half the Aviation units were RC. There were unique Aviation units in Alaska and U.S. Army South (USARSO) at Soto Cano in Honduras. Over half the total ATS units were RC.

The Multi-Functional Battalion (MFB) concept

The MFB concept was crucial to the new plan in several ways. It made Aviation more deployable, sustainable, and flexible. With this basic building block, Aviation could quickly tailor for different missions—especially Joint/combined contingency operations. Unlike the existing battalions, the modular MFB could detach a company-sized TF to conduct separate operations while the parent unit operated elsewhere. The MFB design made changes to allow 24-hour, split-based operations while reducing the total Aviation force structure. The ARI structure, based on divisional Aviation, required 51 Aviation combat units. The new concept would eventually reduce the total to 40 MFBs. MFB also had important implications for developing leaders. Because the MFB included different aircraft types performing diverse missions, it would grow leaders skilled in many aspects of aviation employment. This was in contrast to the situation under the ARI, where officers had little chance to gain such breadth of knowledge until they reached the brigade level. The plan called for starting conversion to the MFB structure in 2002.

The trick was the transition. The first, critical step was to retire the Cobras and Hueys out of the RC. Divesting these increasingly-unsupportable aircraft would free money to update and procure modern aircraft. Black Hawks would replace the Hueys. OH-58D Kiowa Warriors, Apaches, and eventually RAH-66 Comanches would replace the Cobras. Many Chinooks would also be upgraded. These changes would allow rebalancing of AC and RC forces.

Very quickly the cost implications of both the objective MFB and the costs of retiring and replacing the obsolete, Vietnam-era aircraft stalled the effort. Maintaining readiness was a constant battle. Army leadership soon felt sticker shock. A review for the program objective memorandum (POM) beginning in Fiscal Year 2002 showed a total shortfall of $7.8 billion for Aviation programs, and a special TF the VCSA convened estimated $3 billion more. Implementing the MFB concept also put a huge personnel bill on the table. The new MFB structure required 2106 new aviation spaces, including almost 600 new pilots, each with a training bill exceeding $800,000. Since no other branch would give up spaces, the only way to fill Aviation needs was to increase the Army's overall end strength. The bill just to retrain people converting from the retiring aircraft was $1.7 billion. There were other kinds of objections to the plan. One related to synchronization. Members of the other arms expressed concerns that making major changes in Aviation was unwise. Determining the Aviation force without knowing what the ground force would look like risked a mismatch. Finally the delays in the Comanche program meant the Army risked shorting Aviation units for almost a decade.

On 15 December 2000 the VCSA Aviation TF presented its findings to a general office steering committee (GOSC). As the briefers laid out the various bills, the costs mounted. One general concluded that Aviation was out of balance with the Army. The GOSC adjourned even before hearing everything.

Revised plan

By summer 2001 MG Anthony R. Jones, CG of USAAVNC, announced that Aviation units would not change until 2008. However, senior Army leadership was determined to proceed with some parts of the plan—most notably, retiring Cobras and Hueys. To do this without creating a political crisis required rebalancing the AC and RC Aviation force structures. The obsolete aircraft, marked for retirement, made up the vast majority of Aviation assets in the National Guard. Under the initial plan, cascading modernized aircraft from the AC would have made up at least some of the losses from retirement. Those gains, though, depended on converting the AC to the MFB structure, with the smaller number of units freeing up some modernized aircraft to go into Guard units.

In part, cascading modernized aircraft into the National Guard only reflected prevailing realities. In January 2001, discussing the Aviation modernization plan, MG Joseph Bergantz noted growing demands. As Hueys retired, Black Hawks went to war. Whether the user was AC or RC did not matter. RC aircraft with RC crews were in Bosnia, Kosovo, Kuwait and other places. This fact made obsolete any notion of putting front-line aircraft in the first units to deploy. "'First to deploy is whoever happens to be there. The activity that the Army is engaged in today takes all hands, and we're running out of hands." Beyond that, Bergantz sounded a quiet alarm about where Aviation was headed, barring some major changes. All Apaches, Black Hawks and Chinooks had been around for a long time. The Army had used them hard. If the Army failed to put those fleets into a good recapitalization program, Aviation would face the same problems with them that it had with worn-out Hueys and Cobras.

On 7 September 2001 the Army announced that it would accelerate Aviation Transformation. The way of achieving this was to revise the plan to focus lift assets in reserve forces units and attack assets in active units. By 2004 all of the Hueys and Cobras would be gone. About 240 modernized aircraft would move from the AC to the RC. The chiefs of both the Army National Guard and Army Reserve applauded the change. LTG Roger Schultz, director of the National Guard, noted the value of utility aircraft. While warfighting requirements justified Aviation formations, cargo and utility aircraft in the Guard were used daily responding to local and state emergencies. The accelerated plan also required developing options for the crew ratios to maximize warfighting potential of aircraft. Having more than one crew per aircraft would let units maintain a higher OPTEMPO for longer periods. While this goal was desirable, it also raised concerns about implications for personnel tempo, training, leader development, maintenance structures, and repair parts. Finally the Army had established a goal of a 90-percent OR rate by 2004. That was up from the existing average of 75 percent. To achieve that goal meant several changes. One was to pour more maintenance assets on a smaller number of aircraft. There were two approaches to doing this. One was to keep the same number of maintenance units for a reduced number of aircraft. The other was to increase the number of crewmembers per aircraft in some units to enhance crew-level maintenance. Retiring the old aircraft that dragged down readiness rates was a major step. Remaining aircraft would be restored to zero-hours condition through a recapitalization program. Finally the Army would shorten the time to field Comanche. In January 2002 the Army issued an execution order to proceed, and in April 2002 USAAVNC published a White Paper entitled "Transforming Army Aviation."

On 10 March 2003 USAAVNC published an update to the 2002 white paper reflecting several changes. Modernization of Aviation in the RC had caused an interim restructuring. In September 2002 the CSA had approved the initial draft of the Unit of Action (UA) Operational and Organizational Plan. That embedded both manned and unmanned Aviation in the UA. Primary focus was on the UA and a milestone decision on the FCS due in May 2003. However, U.S. Army Combined Arms Center had published a plan to refine the Unit of Employment (UE) Concept. Aviation was an essential element in that.

Unmanned aerial vehicles (UAV)

A shift with major implications for force structure came in June 2003 when Aviation acquired proponency for Unmanned Aerial Vehicle Systems (UAVS). While the impact was not immediate and obvious, it reflected key changes in thinking and organization across the Army that affected Aviation and that gave Aviation broadened roles.

In January 2003, at the annual Association of the United States Army (AUSA) Aviation Symposium, LTG Johnny Riggs, the director of the OFTF, announced that Army Transformation would include adding a reconnaissance team with UAVs and Comanche helicopters. Aviation would be an important part of the Army's new UA. This organization would be ready and equipped in 2010. At the same time, the Army's Deputy of Staff for Programs (DCSPRO) said that the role of UAVs in UAs posed near-term challenges—everything from surveillance to attack to resupply.

On 6 January 2003 a GOSC decided to incorporate unmanned systems as part of an Aviation priorities list. The GOSC decided that neither UAV being considered addressed Aviation teaming requirements. The only requirements met were Military Intelligence (MI), possibly reflecting a restrictive view within the proponent, which was MI.

Impatience was growing with a restrictive view. Other services and agencies were already demonstrating broader values on the battlefield. During the 1990s DOD had invested over $3 billion in UAV development, procurement, and operations. While reconnaissance, surveillance, and target acquisition (RSTA) were the main uses of UAVs, UAVs were also being developed as weapons platforms and with other uses, such as logistics and resupply. In 2000, when the CIA thought it had the terrorist leader, Osama bin Laden, under live aerial surveillance in Afghanistan, the CIA pressed for a weaponized version of the RQ-1 Predator. In the fall of 2001 a Predator with HELLFIRE missiles grafted on made its first remote-controlled kills. In March 2003 a Predator made history, taking out Iraqi antiaircraft batteries while its operators remained safely away from the battlefield. By 2003 DOD had more than 90 UAVs in the field and had programmed to quadruple that number by 2010.

These concerns to expand uses on the battlefield and to deconflict airspace, along with these trends and events, led to shifting proponency.

Aviation Task Force—modular brigades

The 2003 Army Modernization Plan, published in February 2003, noted some changes in Aviation forces. Still, there were no obvious, dramatic changes. That changed after retired-GEN Peter J. Schoomaker was recalled to become the new CSA in August 2003. Schoomaker's background included Joint and particularly SOF experience. Schoomaker almost immediately identified several key areas of concern and appointed a special TF to report to him on each. Aviation was one of these areas.

By 2004 Aviation was undergoing a major reorganization to align with the Army's new force structures. By 2010 the Army's operational force structure would collapse from four to three levels. Armies would cease to exist. Their functions, as well as some functions previously done by the corps, would devolve to what was designated as Units of Employment (UE). Some functions previously done at corps, as well as some functions previously done at division level, would also migrate to a UE. Letters x and y were added to UE labels to distinguish respectively those performing formerly army/corps functions involving major operations and warfighting and formerly corps/division functions involving theater operational land force and joint support. Below the UEx were organizations designated as Units of Action (UA). Force designers emphasized that these echelons were not merely new labels for the familiar division, corps, and brigades. Both UEx and UEy would be complementary, modular entities designed to employ tailored forces within integrated joint campaigns. Each would have organic combat, combat support (CS) and combat service support (CSS) units assigned. Each could have modular combat Units of Action (UA) attached as required. Aviation force structures would be designed at the UA level. To increase agility and flexibility, the emphasis was on designing as nearly identical units as possible that could be mixed and matched to adjust to different sizes and types of demands without any significant delay in beginning operations or sustaining them once engaged.

Multi-Functional Aviation Brigade (MFAB)

The emphasis on modularity and versatility meant reshaping the Aviation brigade, which was the Aviation UA to augment the UEx. The new Aviation brigade was labeled a Multi-Functional Aviation Brigade (MFAB). The MFAB could task-organize as required for any type of operations.

The change in Aviation structure was as drastic as that with the ROAD in the 1960s. The new MFAB nearly doubled in numbers of both aircraft and people.

This reflected the MFAB having its own aviation support battalion (ASB), ATS company, Signal company, and enhanced headquarters. The changes in the headquarters reflected the expectation that the MFAB would be able to conduct, not just support, mobile strike operations. The increases also reflected the inclusion of assets that had previously been outside the brigade. Both MEDEVAC and Chinook companies became part of the MFAB's general support aviation battalion (GSAB). Each of these types of units now had 12 aircraft. The air ambulance units had previously been autonomous, and the Chinooks had been part of the corps battalions.

One key change in the new MFAB was to address the chronic problem of under support to Aviation maintenance. The bad effects of these shortages were notorious. The normal way of doing business had been to strip the maintenance support and thus render almost useless some battalions to be able to support an Aviation TF deployed in contingency operations. For the MFAB the AVIM structure received additional Shop Equipment Contact Maintenance (SECM) kits. These were mounted on High Mobility Multipurpose Wheeled Vehicles (HMMWV) to provide modular immediate response capability. Additional prime movers greatly increased overall mobility at the unit level. Sustainment at battalion level also increased. A forward support company was added to each, and each AVUM company also received enhancements. These two changes would allow creating tailored mission packages required to support brigade combat teams (BCT).

The composition of the new MFAB Headquarters reflected the changed operational environment as well as the brigade's expanded mission. The special staff included both a two-man public affairs section and a three-man operational law section. The S-2/Intelligence section added a nonlethal effects cell for information operations and EW. The S-2 also had a JSTARS Common Ground Station team and a Geospatial Information and Services (GI&S) topographic engineer element. The JSTARS team allowed the brigade to develop operational, high-payoff, and high-value targets. The G&IS allowed terrain visualization and some terrain analysis. The S-3 similarly grew both in size and scope.

One difference between the proposed structures of the late-1990s and the new one was the level at which multifunctionality operated. In the design from the late 1990s, this came at the battalion level. In the new design, it came at the brigade level—the same as the old structure. Each MFAB had five battalions. Two were reconnaissance/attack. There was also one each of an assault battalion, general support aviation battalion (GSAB), and aviation support battalion (ASB). All battalions were optimized for tactical operations. Battalions had planning, coordination and sustainment elements that allowed them independently or autonomously to conduct combined arms operations. To conduct these operations for extended periods still required support from the MFAB and augmentation from the ASB. In this design the flight company was the basic fighting component. Aviation companies had eight to 12 aircraft based on standard company building blocks. Companies were normally assigned to a functionally pure Aviation battalion for training, safety and standardization, leader development, sustainment operations, and the conduct of combat operations. Individual companies could conduct brief, limited, independent action but normally fought as parts of a battalion. Companies could also be organized into Aviation battalion TFs for small-scale contingencies.

The new design sought to fix the problems of Aviation maintenance and support that had been a perennial problem. Two organizations arose to meet this need. One was the Aviation Support Company. These included maintenance modules focused by aircraft type. The new AVUM design allowed task-organizing into platoons to support of operational companies or troops. The name Aviation Support Company (ASC) for the old AVUM unit made Aviation terminology consistent with the rest of the Army. Importantly, the enhanced modularity of the ASCs was achievable within existing personnel levels, although the changes required more tools and test equipment. The other organization was the Forward Support Company (FSC). The FSC, which was part of each battalion, built from assets that already existed in Aviation battalion headquarters companies (HHC) and in higher echelons through Corps. The FSC was multi-functional. It included a distribution platoon and a maintenance platoon. The FSC commander assumed most of the logistical responsibilities that were previously in the battalion HHC.

From liaison officers (LNO) to Brigade Aviation Element (BAE)

A change in structure easily overlooked but of critical importance in the long view was creation of a Brigade Aviation Element (BAE). For the first time ever, each ground brigade would have its own, dedicated cell to assure that Aviation was integrated into the ground commander's scheme of maneuver. Through the ABCS it also gave Joint capabilities.

The BAE addressed the longstanding, well-recognized need for air-ground synchronization. That need until 2004 was only partly and sporadically addressed through assigning LNOs. The air liaison officer (ALO), usually an Air Force officer, was the most recognized and most consistently present. Insofar as LNOs existed for Aviation, they were often fairly junior officers placed in casual relationships. The absence of an effective Aviation LNO over a span of two years was one of many contributors to the Black Hawk shootdown in 1994 discussed elsewhere. The absence created a gap in an awareness, both in the Joint air coordinating elements and the JTF's command center, of changes in practices. Eventually a sense of even the need to make others aware of friendly helicopters' presence was lost. A new Army LNO had just arrived when the accident occurred, but he was not fully aware of relationships among the different elements in the networks.

To assure responsiveness, the chief of the BAE, who would be an Aviation major, was a permanent part of the brigade combat team (BCT) staff. Other members were an Aviation captain, a CWO 4 TACOPS officer, an Aviation operations sergeant, and two Aviation operations specialists. To integrate aviation into the scheme of maneuver meant working closely with the brigade's S-3/Operations Officer and the commander. The chief of the BAE, also called the brigade Aviation officer (BAO), had to maintain a close relationship with the aviation brigade commander and his staff to assure a good flow of information. The captain, who was the BAE plans officer, together with the major, gave the BAE a 24-hour capability. By September 2004 Training Circular (TC) 1–400, Brigade Aviation Element (BAE) Handbook, was already out to field units, and BAEs were training with deploying units and transforming units.

A major challenge the members of the BAE faced was to be knowledgeable across the spectrum of Aviation operations. The BAE was responsible to work with any Aviation assets that might be supporting the BCT. Two challenges the Branch would face would be to find enough majors to fill all of these positions and to develop the breadth of knowledge in the officers assigned to handle the demands of the positions. The numbers of TACOPS officers required also led to substituting some CWO 3s for CWO 4s in these cells.

What differences made?

A review of force structure changes and efforts through the period after ODS showed several common threads. One was the relentless dominance of limited and mostly declining resources in determining Aviation's course. Another was the persistent effort to find a way to work past these limitations to achieve a more capable force within the resources available. Still another was the need for Aviation largely to stay within its resource box—although that could be a very large box in comparison to the total available to the Army. One other thread was the change in relationships between the AC and RC as shrinking forces met increasing operational commitments. The pressures increased because the kinds of operational commitments did not fit the type of Cold War, big-fight model that the Army and Aviation within that Army preferred to organize to fight. Ultimately all these factors led Army leadership at all levels to break some of the molds. In the process of doing so, the Army leadership in effect had to reverse itself on the importance of the centerpiece of Aviation modernization—the Comanche program. Whether the changes imposed in 2004 would actually answer the mail remained to be seen.

The main importance of the Aviation TF was to give a major push to changes in Aviation structure, partly as a byproduct of the resources freed up by canceling the Comanche program. In effect, in killing the Comanche program, GEN Schoomaker had cut the knot that had held Aviation back from some of the key, persistent goals of the preceding decade. Most specifically, freeing the resources committed to Comanche offered a promise of upgrading the other fleet aircraft and acquiring more Black Hawks, Apache Longbows, and improved Chinooks to fill gaps. In concert with the decision to change the entire force, these changes also offered a hope of achieving the kind of multifunctional organizations that Aviation had sought for so long.

Reorganizations—AVSCOM to AMCOM

Vital to Aviation worldwide was the development of materiel and the logistical support for that materiel. The key agency responsible for those tasks was part of the AMC. Through the years after ODS, the parts of AMC with these responsibilities changed. After July 1997 the major agency overseeing these aspects was AMCOM, headquartered at Redstone Arsenal, Huntsville, Alabama.

The creation of AMCOM reflected the long-term trend within the Army toward consolidations of missions. AMCOM subsumed the missions and organizations of both Army Missile Command (MICOM) and U.S. Army Aviation and Troop Command (ATCOM). Previously each was a major subordinate command of AMC. Two major threads of functions and organizations interwove to create AMCOM. One involved particularly rockets and missiles—the traditional province of the Ordnance Corps. The other involved logistical supply and movement—within that, Aviation. These aspects had tended to belong to the Transportation Corps.

The other major stream of development leading to AMCOM was from the Transportation Corps, which had absorbed the lead for the Army in aviation functions in the early 1950s. Most of these organizations have already been discussed in Chapter 5. By the late 1980s, even before the end of the Cold War, dissatisfaction with the way acquisition and sustainment worked across the Army led to a different concept of organization. In 1987 a new management concept was imposed. These were called program executive offices (PEO). PEOs were supposed to direct and control all aspects of their assigned programs. This responsibility included development, production, fielding, product improvement, and follow-on support. On 1 May 1987 PEOs were created at St, Louis and Huntsville, respectively, for aviation and missile programs. The drawdown following the end of the Cold War began to force further consolidations across the Army. On 8 September 1995 Congressional approval of the Base and Realignment Commission (BRAC) List for 1995 disbanded the commands at St. Louis. Mission and organizations were relocated to Redstone Arsenal. Out of this shuffle stood up AMCOM.

Along with these reorganizations came the development of new facilities to enhance Aviation capabilities. For example, on 1 August 2002 the Redstone Aviation Propulsion Test and Research Facility (RAPTR) officially opened. The facility provided a new capability to test components and engines. During the opening ceremony, the director of the Army Aviation and Missile Research, Development and Engineering Center (AMRDEC) said that the new test site was 'another part of our master plan to convert Redstone real estate to aviation engineering support facilities.' Similar changes occurred at Fort Rucker, where there were major constructions involving advanced simulation facilities that could support both training and experimentation.

Doctrine and training adjustments

The diversity and pace of operations after ODS demanded speed and frequency in changing doctrine and training that outran Cold War systems. At the same time, trends toward increasing complexity of Aviation systems, cuts in people, and higher OPTEMPO squeezed schools to produce competent people faster. Aviation pushed in several directions to address these needs.

Approaching real-time, living doctrine and training

Through the period following ODS one clear trend was the blurring of lines between the operational and institutional parts of the Army—the tooth and the tail, as the distinction was often made.

Breaking barriers between tooth and tail—Aviation Training Exercises (ATX), special courses, and the Aircraft Shoot Down Assessment Team (ASDAT)

In simplest terms, the old Army of World War II and forward had an industrial and training base that prepared and equipped people and units to deploy and conduct operations. While essential to the fight, those institutional elements were seldom directly involved in the fight. A common complaint was that training provided was out of touch with operational realities. A common view was that the first thing a person did upon reaching a field unit was to forget everything learned in school.

Over the decades the Army had tried various efforts to break down the separation and isolation of these parts and functions. In Vietnam the Army developed an elaborate, formal system called operational reports, lessons learned (ORLL). In the 1980s the Center for Army Lessons Learned (CALL) stood up. Both ORLLs and CALL focused on changing TTP. Neither ORLLs nor CALL proved wholly satisfactory. Conditions after ODS drove almost-ongoing collection efforts. Diversity and frequency of events called for almost-real-time exchange between operating units and those in the institutional Army trying to adapt and support the field. Fortunately through the 1990s, the explosion of communication via the Internet and related technological changes allowed that kind of exchange.

The ease of exchange partly offset the shrinkage in the numbers of people and other resources in the institutional Army to process information from the field and convert it into revised training or doctrine. Under the Cold War system, developing doctrine was a complex, laborious process. The TRADOC regulation covering it suggested 18–24 months as the time needed to go through all the steps to produce a final, published item or revision to an existing one. Five years might normally pass before new information or changed practice reached the field. Also, through the 1990s the Army drastically cut the number of people in training and doctrine development in a conscious decision about where to lose people and the capabilities that came with them. By 2003 the state of Army doctrine and training caused concern in Congress, and two Army leadership panels had concluded that TRADOC's training and development standards had fallen.

These same conditions forced Aviation to seek ways to shortcut the normal processes. Several paths emerged. One was to develop special training exercises aimed specifically at units deploying and based on information gained directly from those who were already engaged in those operations or who had recently returned from them. These, first called Aviation Training Exercise (ATX), were initially tailored to operations in Bosnia. Later they were adapted and refined for other operations—notably, in Kosovo, Afghanistan, and Iraq. A second path was to expand use of existing, highly-specialized training programs, such as the High Altitude Army Aviation Training Site (HAATS) of the Colorado National Guard. This trained pilots to operate in the extreme conditions encountered in places like Afghanistan, as well as for missions like the High Altitude Rescue Team (HART). A third path was to develop specialized functional courses meeting specific needs—notably, for unit master gunners, a Black Hawk Nonrated Crewmember Instructor Course (NCIC), and Dunker/Helicopter Aircrew Breathing Device (HABD) training. Still another path, which reflected the pattern of diverting assets to the most urgent needs, was to shift the focus of the DES from assessment to training assistance. The Directorate of Training and Doctrine (DOTD) at USAAVNC also used electronic staffing and publication to expedite turnarounds and get changes into the field. A final approach was the fielding of special teams to deal with specific problems arising in the field. The most notable example of these was the Aircraft Shoot Down Assessment Team (ASDAT).

The ASDAT arose in November 2003 after an unknown enemy weapon system shot down several Army aircraft in Iraq. These incidents showed an urgent needed for outside help to identify the enemy weapon systems involved and to develop countermeasures. The commander of the 12th Aviation Brigade realized that the Army had no standard methods or organization to answer these needs. So he contacted USAAVNC for help. An ad-hoc team formed, including subject matter experts both from within the Army and from private industry. The team reached Iraq within two weeks, received briefings and investigated wreckage from several aircraft, conducted interviews, and analyzed both enemy and friendly TTP. This analysis allowed the team to recommend remedial actions, which also produced briefings to aircrews and writing an urgent mission needs statement for the Combined Joint Task Force (CJTF) 7 commander. The ASDAT's results let field commanders effectively revise their TTP, fed into acquiring improved technology, and led to efforts to create a permanent organization to meet these needs.

Training—providing the field more capable people in less time

During the years following ODS there were major efforts to revise the training and education for Aviation Soldiers. These efforts affected both branch-commissioned officers—lieutenants through colonels—and WOs. There were two major forces driving these efforts. One was the cost—including the time—required to gain and develop basic technical proficiency. The other was change in both technical and professional knowledge and skills necessary to succeed in an evolving operational environment.

Flight School XXI (FS XXI)—producing better graduate pilots faster

An Army-wide officer education system (OES) developed leaders in the combined arms branches, including Aviation. The OES was graduated and progressive, with formal courses in schools that ran from precommissioning through general officer levels. Precommissioning sources—mainly West Point and ROTC—provided a diverse pool of talented people to all branches of the Army. Aviation recruited its junior leaders from that pool. Once chosen for Aviation, the officer went to Fort Rucker for the Officer Basic Course (OBC) and flight school. The model of OBC in the years after ODS had two phases—one preceding and one following IERW. The OBC provided the basic knowledge and skills to prepare lieutenants for their initial assignments as platoon leaders. IERW taught only basic flying skills using training helicopters. After completing the second phase of OBC, the officer went into an Aviator Qualification Course (AQC). That taught the specific aircraft the graduate pilot would fly in the field. WOs started along a path that largely paralleled commissioned officers. The point of entry was Warrant Officer Candidate School (WOCS), part of the Warrant Officer Career Center (WOCC) at Fort Rucker. New WOs chosen for Aviation then went into IERW, followed by the Warrant Officer Basic Course (WOBC). This was a four-week course specifically focused on technical and tactical certification—functional skills needed at platoon level. Like the Branch commissioned officer, the WO then attended AQC. After AQC, both branch-commissioned officers and WOs received their first assignment in Aviation.

Pressures mounted through the 1990s to shorten the amount of time an officer—whether branch-commissioned or WO—spent in schools and, thus, away for primary duties. The amount of time through their careers that Soldiers spent in schools and special courses was part of the huge logistical tail the Army had to confront. As a general rule, at any moment, almost two out of every five Soldiers in the AC of the Army were not deployable. This included about 25 percent assigned to the institutional Army organized under TDAs and another 12 percent in a temporary status as Trainees, Transients, Holdees, and Students (TTHS). For at least 20 years the Army had sought ways to shrink the TTHS account. Especially after ODS, as the total force structure drew down but OPTEMPO increased, finding ways to get more Soldiers off the bench and into the game gained urgency. This was especially so since the alternative to reducing the non-deployable Army was to put more Soldiers on active duty. Having these additional Soldiers meant not buying modernized equipment and not maintaining what already existed. At the same time, the Army—especially Aviation—had to address increasing demands for greater sophistication and proficiency among those in the field.

By the late 1990s, the combination of these pressures led Aviation to seek a radical restructuring of flight school. The result was a concept that came to be called FS XXI. This concept sought to kill two birds with one stone. The first was to shrink the total amount of time from entry into flight school to completing qualification in the aircraft the graduate pilot would fly in the first assignment. The second was to send the new graduate pilot to the first unit at a higher level of proficiency, so that the unit would need to invest less time and other resources in making the new arrival a fully useful member of the team.

As it existed through the 1990s, flight training required students to learn to fly at least three different aircraft from entry into flight school to the time they went to their first assignment. IERW Common Core taught the basic tasks of rotary-wing aviation and ended with instrument qualification. That phase used the TH-67 Creek helicopter. No variant of the TH-67 Creek existed in the field. So the TH-67 had no tactical use. It was an aircraft that the student would learn and forget. The next phase of flight training was basic combat skills (BCS). That phase, which included initial qualification with NVG, used the OH-58C Kiowa or Huey—both, mostly obsolete. At the end of flight training, in AQC, the student learned to fly the aircraft that he would actually use in his first assignment. Just learning each of these aircraft took time and other resources.

FS XXI streamlined the process into two phases. Phase I focused on basic aviator skills in the TH-67 aircraft. Phase II taught the AQC. This eliminated the student having to learn an intermediate aircraft.

One key to FS XXI was a dramatic increase in the use of simulation. Not only was more simulation used but also more of that simulation was specific to the advanced aircraft the new aviator would fly. So, the new pilot left Fort Rucker with fewer total flying hours than in the old IERW but went to his first unit with more hours in the airframe he would actually fly. Thus, the field Army got new pilots faster, while the new arrivals were more prepared to go to work. This created a double value to the Army.

These effects made FS XXI one key to the whole Army Transformation Plan. Changes in the content of simulation experiences also provided the building blocks to new attributes the Army believed leaders in the new operational environment required. This additional experience would let field commanders focus on collective training—bringing aircrews together as a team—rather than spending resources to develop individual skills. That collective training would let a unit deploy more quickly as contingencies arose. The redesign from the old IERW to the new FS XXI model also changed flight instruction to increase the skill levels of graduate pilots. A new basic navigation phase that included more cross-country flights, more solo time, operations in confined areas, and treating the student as the Pilot In Command (PIC) for their final check ride. The new POI also doubled both total time in the aircraft and the time using NVG. Thus, FS XXI promised to give the whole Army a higher level of readiness at less cost than the old system.

By January 2002 Army leadership had embraced the concept and training cycle for FS XXI. By late 2002 senior leadership had linked enhanced skill levels to Aviation safety and promises of reduced costs. In September the CSA had noted that Aviation accidents had cost the Army more than $200 million. The situation seemed to be pay now or pay later—either invest in improved training or replace aircraft. At least partly on that basis the CSA directed two of the deputy chiefs to find funds to effect FS XXI as part of his strategy for Army Safety and overall readiness.

Early experiments toward FS XXI were encouraging. In September 2000, B Company, 1st Battalion, 223d Aviation Regiment (1–223), successfully completed the first test class of FS XXI for the CH-47D Chinook. DES evaluated the results and confirmed that the course produced a more qualified CH-47D pilot. Graduates were tracked to provide feedback for refining the program. Results of four test classes with the Chinooks validated the FS XXI approach. So, on 7 October 2002, 1–223 formally implemented CH-47 FS XXI training.

As with almost everything in Aviation, little about FS XXI was easy. While Army Transformation depended in part on FS XXI, FS XXI also depended on other parts of Army Transformation—especially changes in the Army inventory of aircraft. Implementing FS XXI required putting enough modernized aircraft in the schoolhouse to make up for the loss of obsolete airframes. With the modernized aircraft already in short supply, it was a hard sell to shift aircraft from operational units to the training base. There were no quick fixes for aircraft availability.

FS XXI also required more resources in other areas at Fort Rucker. These included reopening stagefields, with all the attendant ATC equipment and people. The size of the simulation requirement created a need for new facilities. A FS XXI Simulation Program called for TH-67 virtual simulators and advanced aircraft virtual simulators.

The rapid transition to advanced aircraft possibly increased costs of maintenance and repair, simply as a byproduct of student pilots' inexperience. In December 2000 a student in the prototype class ruined the transmission of a Chinook. Armywide there were already 22 Chinook engines without transmissions, including three at Fort Rucker. Because of parts shortage, it would be some time before Fort Rucker had a replacement to get the aircraft flying again.

The critical role of simulation in FS XXI also brought an increased draw on other agencies and businesses. During 2000 the coming of new image-generator technology strengthened the symbiotic relationship between the Army Research Institute and civilian industry—including overseas companies. A key contractor was CAE, International, a Canadian firm. The complexities involved led to creating a Simulation Division team to address issues and to provide an interface with PMs at U.S. Army Simulation, Training and Instrumentation Command (STRICOM).

The cost for bringing in some systems to support full FS XXI was huge. There were needs for new simulators, as well as upgrades to make simulators current with fielded aircraft. Not everything was in the Army's budget nor even the budget requests for Aviation. By the end of September 2002, the CSA had directed the Army Staff to find the funding for FS XXI. Even then there was reluctance, if not resistance, to diverting funds to this program. In many cases, there were no new resources to be had. Meeting the new requirements to bring FS XXI to reality meant the same people doing more with the same or less—taking it out of hide, in Army jargon.

By 27 March 2003 all of these factors had come together to force a decision about how to get to FS XXI. In looking at the options, the most expensive one was to retain the current state with one-third of students in FS XXI and the rest staying under the old program. The CG of USAAVNC directed gradual implementation that would not exceed funding levels being staffed in HQDA but to achieve full implementation by 1 October 2005.

Estimates made years before an event often had important effects. That was true at this point with bridging from the old IERW and AQC programs to FS XXI. Complicating the ability to manage the different student populations through this transition was a surge in demand for seats in the AQCs. This surge reflected a backlog from not having projected enough seats several years earlier. At the same time, a spike in requirements for IPs came from moving advanced aircraft into the RC at the same time the Army was fielding the Apache Longbow. In April 2003, it seemed that no way existed to make the transition as the CG had directed. There were simply too few modernized aircraft, and there was no way to get the necessary simulations.

Outside help broke the bottleneck. On 14 May 2003, when the HASC approved the defense authorization bill for Fiscal Year 2004, it contained $148 million to support FS XXI. This funding allowed progress toward acquiring the vital simulation. In late September 2003 Computer Sciences Corporation (CSC) Federal Sector-Defense Group won the contract for FS XXI Simulation Services. This contract was huge—$1.1 billion over 19–1/2 years. Responsibilities were commensurate.

By late January 2004 the transition to FS XXI had started to smooth. FS XXI had been fully funded for Fiscal Year 2005. Moreover, the results of the changed training model were getting favorable reviews at high levels in the field. LTG Charles C. Campbell, commanding Eighth Army in Korea, had sent message saying that FS XXI was making a difference. Commanders were finding that it took the FS XXI graduates four or five flights to be ready to go on missions. Under the previous system new pilots needed four or five months to reach the same level. Clearly FS XXI was off to a successful start, achieving the goals of reducing the amount of time spent in training and improving readiness in the field.

Apache Longbow pilot qualification

Efforts to compress training also applied to the fielding of newer models of aircraft. An example was the Apache Longbow. In the early stages of fielding the Apache Longbow, it appeared that the amount of time projected for a pilot to master the new systems had been unduly optimistic. By May 2001 the new equipment training team, which was training experienced Apache pilots on the enhanced Longbow version, was finding that it took 20 hours to train a pilot.

The POI for pilots already qualified in the Apache and simply upgrading their qualifications to fly the Longbow allowed only 4.7 hours. It seemed clear at that point that the training program could not succeed.

Much of this problem with this transition came from the sheer complexity of the new Longbow radar system. The TRADOC System Manager for the Longbow noted that the Apache with the Longbow radar was similar in complexity to the Air Force's F-16 Fighting Falcon multi-role fighter aircraft. The Air Force allowed 1–2 years to train an F-16 pilot The Army might allow as little as 18 weeks for someone to learn the basic Apache and then learn the differences in the Apache Longbow.

New training to meet emerging needs, with/without a recognized requirement—Dunker/Helicopter Aircrew Breathing Device (HABD) Training

Over the years after Vietnam, Aviation was increasingly engaged in Joint operations. Such operations increasing put Army aircrews flying over water for extended periods. This pattern was most pronounced within SOA but also applied to conventional units. Examples were long flights over open water as in Operation Urgent Fury in 1983 and air cavalry operations in Korea, as well as ship-based operations from the 1987 Tanker War onward. All such operations raised the prospect of Army aircrews having to ditch aircraft in deep water. By 2003 the rate of accidents involving going into the water had risen to two for every 100,000 hours of flying.

Individual units first undertook to provide both the necessary training and equipment. In March 1994, based on the possible need to conduct operations in Haiti, the 3d Battalion, 229th Aviation Regiment (Attack) (Airborne) began over-water training. The unit found a CWO within the unit who had been a water survival instructor with the 160 SOAR. The unit's training prepared it for training at Norfolk Naval Air Station using the Dunker/Helicopter Emergency Egress Device System (HEEDS). By June 2003 the 6th Cavalry Brigade in Korea was conducting such training with its own facility. Brigade commanders repeatedly stated the needs for such training in their annual conferences.

Besides meeting Army needs, the availability of such training was also a consideration in discussions about consolidating undergraduate helicopter pilot training at Fort Rucker. Its lack was one reason given in July 1999 for the Navy's opposing consolidated training there.

USAAVNC moved toward such training. In July 1998 USAAVNC developed courses of action for an overwater course. On 5 October 2000 MG Anthony R. Jones, the CG of USAAVNC, announced plans to conduct water survival training. On 2 December 2003 the first class in underwater egress procedures started at USAAVNC. Over time this training would remove the burden on field units. A contractor furnished both equipment and training. Students covered hazards of breathing compressed air and hypothermia, ditching, emergency exits. Students also learned how to know their position in relation to the airframe, release their seatbelts, move to and open the door or window, and exit the aircraft.

Dunker training quickly proved to be a great success. By 23 August 2004 over 1200 Soldiers had been trained. A plan would push 3000 students through annually and add a one-day refresher course. Benefits of this training were extended to as many different users as possible, including the precommand course (PCC) and field units.

Survival, Evasion, Resistance and Escape (SERE)

The addition of dunker training paralleled a long-sought goal of giving every Army aircrew member more advanced training in Survival, Evasion, Resistance and Escape (SERE). Both of these programs were integral parts of the revision of the flight school model into FS XXI. The goal was to develop skills and attributes required for the 21st century. Making dunker part of the core training for Army aircrew members reflected the increasingly diverse, complex, and Joint operational environment for Aviation. SERE reflected the increased risk Aviation Soldiers faced of capture, interrogation, and possible exploitation for propaganda purposes.

Experience after ODS showed the need to intensify the training Aviation Soldiers received to survive, resist capture and interrogation if captured, and ideally to escape capture. In 1993 the shootdown of two Black Hawks in Somalia led to extended captivity for one Aviator, CWO Michael Durant. Durant survived and became an advocate for more advanced SERE training. In March 2003 the capture of two Apache Longbow pilots in Iraq reinforced the basic concern.

There were really two threads to the type of training involved. One was survival. By the mid-1960s the services had established basic survival schools. During Vietnam the Army met needs by sending some aircrews to schools that the Navy and Air Force had. Later Fort Wolters conducted SERE training. In 1976 the Army discontinued all such training after abuses appeared in some locally-developed programs. However, in 1982–83 the Army restarted SERE training within constraints of DOD Directive 1300.7. In 1982 USAAVNC asked permission to establish Level C SERE training for Army aviators. This was the most rigorous type of training. The Resistance Training Laboratory (RTL) at Fort Bragg was the Army's only authorized site, but both Fort Bragg and TRADOC recognized that the number of Army aviators pointed toward establishing a second site at Fort Rucker.

The other thread of SERE related to the resistance to an enemy's efforts to extract useful information or induce a captive into actions that might have a propaganda value. This concern especially arose out of collaboration by American POWs in Korea. In 1955 President Dwight D. Eisenhower promulgated the Code of Conduct for members of the armed forces. The Army defined three levels of Code of Conduct training according to how likely a Soldier might face capture and interrogation. Level C was for Soldiers whose position in wartime put them at a high risk of capture and whose position, rank, or seniority also increased their danger of being exploited by captors. Among these were some pilots and flight crewmembers. In 1985 a Peacetime Level C was added. This applied to Soldiers who had a high risk of being taken hostage by terrorists or being detained by a hostile government. The only authorized Level C instruction was at Fort Bragg.

Repeated student staff studies from at least the mid-1970s into the 1990s concluded that Aviation Soldiers needed SERE training that included a resistance element. Even so, in 1994 a staff study showed that less than 16 percent of experienced Army aviators had received formal SERE training. A 1997 staff study noted that the largest numbers of POWs in the preceding 30 years had been aircrew members. That fact had led the Navy and Air Force to require every crew member of any aircraft type to complete Level C SERE training.

During 2002 all IERW students attended a SERE course accredited as Level B. That training included survival skills, land navigation to evade, and resistance methods if an individual were captured. In the fall of 2002 construction began of an Academic Role-Playing Laboratory field site. That lab would allow exposing students to limited resistance training. By December 2002 the projected training load of about 2100 Aviation students per year exceeded Fort Bragg's capacity. The DCSOPS directed USAAVNC to come up with a plan for expansion along with other considerations of a DA action plan for Army Personnel Recovery (PR). By September 2004, USAAVNC was still working to stand up SERE-C training, projected to start in Fiscal Year 2007

Efforts to provide a better SERE training for Aviation Soldiers became a factor in major redesigns of professional courses. TRADOC directed a major revision of basic officer instruction across all branches. Generally this redesign shortened the time available for overall instruction. It particularly shortened time available for branch-specific instruction. However the need for SERE training pushed the opposite direction. In January 2002, USAAVNC added 11 days to course length for SERE.

SERE qualification was also a desired incidental in redesignating enlisted Soldiers and NCOs into the Career Management Field (CMF) 15, Aviation. Besides uniting all members of the Aviation community within the combat arms, this redesignation opened the door to Level C SERE training for enlisted flight crewmembers. In the eyes of the Aviation Branch CSM, Soldiers in the back of aircraft needed this training. They went into harm's way, just as the officers in the front of the aircraft. Vietnam had proven this fact. In February 1968 crew chief Robert Chenoweth's Huey was shot down and he was captured. By the time he was released in March 1973, Chenoweth had spent more than one-fifth of his life as a POW.

Materiel—prolonged fieldings, increasing sophistication and increasing integration

Following the Cold War, acquisition and sustainment of Aviation systems underwent major changes as a result of several, larger trends. One was an increasing pressure to move toward Joint programs. Another was a trend toward large, multiyear contracts that covered not only acquisition of systems but also a wide range of related services. One factor feeding these trends was a drawdown in budgets. Budgets were inadequate to sustain both current readiness and acquisition; but, through most of the period, the Army tried to do both. This meant stretching out programs to acquire new systems. Nominally this approach cost less in early years, but the delays often incurred extra expenses and raised costs for the same systems in later years. In at least some cases this pattern proved fatal. Another effect of trying to do everything with too little was to jeopardize the ability to support systems that the Army did buy. By 2001, every Army acquisition program was buying at levels below the economic threshold to sustain them. This fact jeopardized the industrial base. To offset budget reductions and increase capabilities, the Army undertook service life extension programs under the terms Recapitalization and Reset.

Comanche—a long road to cancellation

The most dramatic example in Aviation of the bad effects of stretching out acquisitions was the Comanche program. The CSA cancelled the Comanche program in February 2004 after two decades of effort and investment. This happened despite the fact that the Army's top leadership had repeatedly ranked Comanche first among the systems the Army needed for the future battlefield. The long delay in fielding the Comanche was both symptom and cause of other flaws in the acquisition system that finally proved fatal. The story of the Comanche, thus, offers useful insights into the Army's experience through this era. Ultimately, as with the AH-56 Cheyenne 30 years earlier, Comanche fell victim to changing demands of the operational environment.

The early program—the LHX family

The Comanche program grew out of very broad ideas in the early 1980s about the Army's future aircraft needs. Aging Vietnam-era fleets were becoming obsolete and needed replacement. The Army would also have a continuing need for a light helicopter. In 1982, the Army Aviation Mission Area Analysis (AAMAA) assessed Aviation capabilities against a projected threat from the Warsaw Pact in the mid-1990s. The AAMAA found many deficiencies in the existing fleet of light aircraft—which included 80 percent of the Army's helicopters.

The AAMAA recommended developing a family of two variants—scout/reconnaissance and attack (SCAT) and utility/observation—to replace existing aircraft. These aircraft would complement the other, newer helicopters. The variants would have extensive commonality and should be fielded by 1995. The program was designated LHX for light helicopter. The X represented the variants.

In January 1983 a LHX Special Workgroup formed. A year later the first LHX program manager (PM) was assigned.

Risk reduction and a vicious cycle of changes to accommodate changes

A major emphasis from the outset was to reduce risks in the program. This concern led to a decision to build a two-pilot aircraft because foreseeable technology would not let one pilot do the job. To further minimize risk, proven managers were put in charge and given a high degree of control.

Efforts to speed fielding and adjust for budget cuts led to a deadly pattern. Parts of the program originally designed to minimize risk were dropped to cut costs. To compensate for increased risk, development timelines stretched. These extensions required reprogramming money, while failures to perform according to plan eroded confidence in the program. To restore confidence, the program restructured several times, either dropping or deferring capabilities in deliverable aircraft. These changes undercut enthusiasm among potential users, led to further losses of funding as pressures mounted on competing programs, and led to further delays. Successive changes also caused the estimated average cost per aircraft to jump, as total numbers of aircraft to be bought declined.

By about 1987, frustrations with this pattern led the Army Acquisition Executive (AAE), Mr. James Ambrose, to declare that the Army would not select an aircraft that weighed a pound over 7500 and cost a dollar over $7.5 million. Much like the 5000-pound limit for Army aircraft that arose in 1952, Ambrose's numbers became sacred beyond any functional or budgetary merit.

A new strategic environment and first restructure

By 1990 signs that the Cold War was ending created a more hostile climate for all large acquisition programs. The Bush Administration sought ways to reap a 'peace dividend.' In June 1990 the SECDEF directed a review to assess both affordability of and needs for several major aircraft systems. Among these was the LH. Also, requirements to consider Joint contributions that arose from the Defense Reorganization Act of 1986 complicated an already twisting path. Based on review by a Joint Requirements Oversight Council (JROC), in August 1990 the SECDEF directed another restructure. That delayed the first aircraft reaching the field from 1996 to 1998, cut the total number of aircraft almost in half again, and made average unit cost leap again.

On 12 April 1991 a joint venture of Boeing and Sikorsky won the contract for the LH. An important part of the contract was features to reduce risks in development. Besides four prototype aircraft, there would be both static and dynamic test beds. In April 1991 the CSA also announced that the Light Helicopter (LH) would be named the Comanche, designated the Reconnaissance/Attack Helicopter (RAH)-66.

As these steps occurred, other events pushed toward more complexity. In January 1991 the Under Secretary of Defense for Acquisition directed integrating the Longbow Radar into the LH. Before the end of 1991 an update to the Soldier

Modernization Plan included completely integrating aircrew clothing and equipment. This meant developing a helmet for the Comanche that was compatible with all other aircraft.

During preparations for the 1992 budget, the Comanche program suffered a further setback. The SECDEF announced that DOD would continue to fund development of new weapons but would not guarantee that they would actually be produced. On this basis, on 29 January 1992, the SECDEF directed a second restructure of the Comanche program. This new guidance had familiar effects.

Meantime DOD changed procedures for developing systems, and there was a major shift in the national strategy to reflect the new global environment. A new SECDEF directed a comprehensive analysis of national defense, called the Bottom Up Review (BUR). The BUR questioned the Comanche program for its risk but confirmed a critical need for the kind of battlefield intelligence the Comanche was meant to provide. So the program continued but with nine new requirements and changes to 23 others.

Through 1993 most effort went into streamlining the Comanche acquisition to reduce costs while expediting the aircraft's reaching the field. On both counts, a high priority was given to finding commercial approaches that might make things go better and faster. The new plan, submitted in April 1994, was unacceptable because it included too much risk. By mid-August 1994 the Deputy Secretary of Defense directed the Army to develop alternatives ending the Comanche program because of its high cost. That was despite the Army describing Comanche as its Number One acquisition priority.

At this point, senior Army leaders became alarmed about the effect canceling the Comanche would have on the industrial base. In 1996 production of the Black Hawk would end. Without Comanche the helicopter industry in the U.S. would have no new military aircraft in production. This concern became interwoven with a complex set of political power struggles involving Congress and the Executive Branch in which adequacy of the overall Defense budget became the focus.

One other element played into the Comanche's fate during this period. That was the level of support Comanche had as an Aviation program when Army leadership faced giving up major programs. In December 1994 the SECDEF cancelled or restructured several defense programs. Modernization programs that could be delayed to pay for readiness and people would be deferred. The intent was to relieve budgetary pressures on the Army, but the cuts forced the Army to choose between a ground and an air system. Facing cancellation of both the Advanced Field Artillery System (AFAS) and Comanche, the Army leadership let Comanche become a program that preserved an industrial and technology base only. Production was indefinitely postponed.

In response COL James Snider, the PM, and key leaders, including the CSA, mapped out a new plan. This rested on a premise that, if the program could give the Army some of the Comanche's capabilities, that fact would attract enough support to carry the program forward. This new plan provided for building six aircraft with reduced capabilities by 2001—within the reduced budgets. On 21 March 1995 a third restructure was approved.

Technical progress

Despite all the turmoil, the Comanche did well technically. On 25 May 1995 the Comanche team conducted a rollout ceremony for the first prototype to world-wide media coverage. Results of early tests permitted an airworthiness release in late 1995. On 30 December 1995, Comanche Aircraft #1 did the first full-up, bladed ground runs. This was less than 10 months from the beginning of final assembly. On 4 January 1996 the first prototype first flew, and its test flights went well. Other systems, such as the XM-301 turreted gun system, did well. Meanwhile other organizations moved ahead with related technology, such as the helmet. Work also moved ahead to show how Comanche could affect operations. In 1995 Comanche Player Station was installed at USAAVNC. This sophisticated cockpit simulator let Comanche participate in computer-based exercises.

Comanche and Longbow Apache

Joint involvement and renewed thrust toward more capable aircraft

By 1996 the Comanche had moved a long way from the original idea of a light scout/attack helicopter to replace the Loach and be in the field by 1995. An increased emphasis on Joint operations gave Comanche a boost. There was a Joint effort to develop, integrate, and demonstrate advanced concepts, technologies and doctrine that would give a JTF commander advanced reconnaissance capabilities. These concepts included linking the Comanche and UAVs within an integrated network that reached from tactical to national levels.

As part of the changing approaches to acquisition, the yardstick used to measure Comanche changed in 1996. In March 1996 the JROC approved key performance parameters (KPP) for the Comanche. These included a vertical rate of climb (VROC) threshold of 500 feet per minute with a goal or objective of 750. Other KPPs included the ability to communicate digitally with combined-arms, Joint and coalition forces.

In late 1997 another restructure began. This reflected concerns about the impact of fielding aircraft with only limited capability. The aircraft under Snider's plan, when fielded, would not represent the production model. BG Joseph Bergantz, the new PM, believed that fielding these less capable aircraft would lose support among users. Of special note was the absence of the Longbow radar. At the same time, Bergantz saw senior leadership within Defense and Congress favorably disposed to the program. On these bases, he proposed the fifth restructure. The tradeoff was that the proposed aircraft would arrive two years later than the less capable aircraft. At the same time, the revised schedule would let Comanche enter the next phase of development four years ahead of the previous schedule. This acceleration was meant to signal everyone—most importantly industry, which was nervous about continuing investments—that the Army was serious. This restructure plan was barely out before criticisms about its cost hit again.

By mid-1999 Aviation in general and Comanche in particular had close congressional scrutiny. On 5 August 1999 the Conference Report on Senate Bill 1059, the National Defense Authorization Act for Fiscal Year 2000, had a separate section on Aviation Modernization. It required the Secretary of the Army to submit a comprehensive plan to modernize the Army's helicopter forces. The Army had to address specific systems, including Comanche. Three weeks later, the GAO officially issued a report that reflected serious doubts about Comanche. Besides risks in the program, Comanche would consume almost two-thirds of the whole Aviation budget by Fiscal Year 2008. That drain forced the Army to retain older aircraft longer.

Adding to these concerns were others arising from Aviation operations in Kosovo in early 1999. Experiences of TF Hawk in Albania fueled attempts at drastic change. The Army began to design a new, highly deployable force. The Kosovo experiences also made Joint and senior leadership lean away from using manned aircraft in the roles initially conceived for Comanche. Comanche, though, might have a future teamed with UAVs. In the spring of 2000, Comanche passed its next review, and the engineering and manufacturing development (EMD) contact was awarded.

The decision to move forward at this point was part of a larger set of decisions about Aviation and concerns about the overall state of the helicopter industry. On 4 April 2000 the Army announced that three of the Army's helicopters would retire in the next four years: Cobras, Hueys, and A and C models of the OH-58 Kiowas. Apache Longbows and eventually the Comanches would replace Cobras and Kiowas. The decision to proceed with building Comanches brought sighs of relief particularly for Sikorsky, where employment and production was the lowest since the end of Vietnam. The Comanche contract, worth $34 billion over its life, was critical. Meantime, with DOD hard-pressed financially and Congress pushing to save taxpayer dollars—foreign-built aircraft threatened domestic firms.

Difficulties continued to dog the program. BG Bergantz, the outgoing PM, believed that the program was on a solid footing and told his successor, COL Robert P. Birmingham, to concentrate on keeping the program on track. Within six months, though, Birmingham realized that objectives were unachievable for several reasons, including basic management structures. The way the weight of the aircraft was tracked was symptomatic. No one could say what the weight really was, because many designs remained unfinished. When Birmingham insisted on closing every item that was overdue, the total weight shot up to over 10,000 pounds. At that weight, the existing engine specifications could not get the aircraft off the ground. An assessment team that Birmingham requested from OSD concluded that the contract as awarded could not work, and the head of the Boeing-Sikorsky joint venture agreed.

The bleak picture that followed posed a dilemma for those responsible for the Comanche program. To expose shortcomings within six months after the contract had been awarded entailed huge risks, because the program had long been weakened so many times in so many ways. Money was taken out of program six times in 10 years. Each time the reduction made the program weaker and harder to defend. Collateral effects of Aviation becoming a separate branch further weakened the chances of defending the program. Even convincing the Army that something was wrong was hard. Birmingham repeatedly had to retell the history of Comanche to various people. Repeatedly he had to explain the sacred numbers of 7500 pounds and $7.5 million. Eventually he convinced senior leaders to accept another restructure, leading to a new contract in November 2002. At that point Birmingham thought the program would succeed.

Although things seemed to go well for the first quarter, the CSA, GEN Shinseki, worried greatly on several counts. One was cost, which was tied to another cut DOD imposed on the number of aircraft to fewer than the Army wanted to meet needs in the force structure. Still, Birmingham had told Shinseki that the right time to cancel the Comanche, if the Army did that, would be after EMD. Then the Army would have proven technology for later use, as well as some things that could go into other programs. Also, Birmingham argued, any savings hardly warranted earlier cancellation because of expenses to close out the program.

Comanche got approval for a sixth restructuring in 2002, but the program was possibly at high political risk. Civilian leadership all the way up to the President was impatient with large, slow programs. During the 2000 campaign, George W. Bush had proclaimed that he would modernize only selectively, skipping a generation of military technology. Conservative watchdog groups monitored President Bush's actions on major weapons programs as indicators of his commitment to their values. Comanche was on a list of five major weapons systems across the services that the Cato Institute singled out for cancellation. By June 2002 Secretary of the Army Thomas White told reporters that either those in charge would get Comanche right or the Army would not wait for OSD to cancel it. The Army would cancel it. There were also many indications that the some in the Administration—most notably, SECDEF Donald Rumsfeld—eyed Army leadership and its performance with suspicion, if not disdain. On 8 March Rumsfeld challenged almost every aspect of the Army's vision for the Objective Force (OF) and publicly denounced Shinseki's estimates of the troop strengths required in Afghanistan and Iraq.

The Aviation TF and decision to cancel

In August 2003, when new CSA Peter J. Schoomaker, took charge, he immediately ordered a review of several key areas, including Aviation. A sequestered TF conducted the review in each area. MG James D. Thurman led the Aviation TF. Not included was MG Bergantz, then PEO-AV. While some industry-watchers read something sinister into this absence, the situation caused Bergantz no special concern. He spoke to members and had representatives from PEO-AV and selected PM offices on the TF.

The Aviation TF seemed to validate much about the Comanche program, but the outcome was otherwise. On 23 February 2004 the Acting Secretary of the Army announced that the Comanche program would end. The SECDEF and President approved this recommendation. Some, such as recently-retired COL Birmingham, were stunned. The shock for Birmingham was less that the program was canceled than the timing and rationale. Bergantz shared that view. During several of the restructure reviews between 1989 and the termination, Bergantz believed, it would have made more sense to cancel the program. Birmingham had gained support to infuse enough funding to make the program solid and executable with low risk.

What neither Birmingham nor Bergantz had been able to see, because of the closed nature of the TF's work, was how Comanche became a central concern within the TF. When Schoomaker formed the TF he told it to take a capabilities-based approach. When the TF looked at future operational capabilities, the fact emerged that the Comanche could not provide all of those capabilities. At the same time, Aviation had several glaring shortfalls, such as needs for lift coming from lessons in Afghanistan and Iraq. Recent combat experience also pointed toward a need for more capabilities in close combat attack (CCA) and less in deep attack, for which the Comanche had been intended. The lists of other needs and Comanche's shortfalls grew. The TF asked the Comanche PM what worried him most. He said software integration. This answer meant that the one area where the Comanche had been most heavily prized—serving as the 'quarterback of the battlefield'—had the greatest chance for failure. At the same time, Comanche consumed over 40 percent of Aviation's budget. The gaps between capabilities and resources made it clear there was a big problem. The question within the TF became how to close the gaps. The TF started to look at what would happen if Comanche were cancelled but Aviation could keep the money. It appeared that this money could fund several of the key needs.

Based on the findings of the TF, the CS formed a second, separate group to look strictly at Comanche. That review resulted in the decision to cancel the Comanche.

Comanche in hindsight

Several aspects of the Comanche story bear noting. Some are obvious—especially those related to the adverse effects of pilfering modernization accounts to meet current expenses. In that sense, the Comanche story was one of death by a thousand cuts. Closely related was the Army's common position as last in line among the services in the priority for funding big, expensive programs.

Related but less obvious was that stretching programs was far more costly than many realize. OSD's Cost Analysis Improvement Group (CAIG) had shown that every dollar redirected in a given year required three dollars in the future. Comanche had at least six such diversions.

Another lesson related to the whole way of managing major programs. In his interview before retiring, MG Bergantz noted that there were good reasons to cancel both the Crusader Advanced Field Artillery System (AFAS) and Comanche and to use the resources elsewhere. Yet the Army found it extremely hard to let them go. He attributed that partly to a defect in educating acquisition executives. The underlying assumption was that any program worthy of starting was worth completing. In some cases, passage of time and changes in the Army's need invalidated that assumption, but the institution was ill equipped to adjust.

One facet worth noting is the extreme complexity of influences operating in any major acquisition. The ultimate goal is putting superior technology in the hands of the Soldier, but that is a wildly complex and highly political process. The interests and people affected reach far beyond the formal organization of the Army into the offices and homes of tens of thousands of contractors, subcontractors, and communities where they work and live. When the Comanche program ended, there were about 10,000 outstanding purchase orders and contracts. Contractors ranged from Boeing and Sikorsky to many, smaller companies in at least 34 states.

Still another facet was the changing needs of the Army itself, especially as other emerging technology offered alternative solutions. When Comanche started, the need for eyes-on tactical reconnaissance was indisputable. Well before the system would reach the field, even if fielded according to its original timelines, the battlefield for which Comanche was designed had grown less probable. By the time the necessary changes in the system had begun to evolve, the operational environment changed again. As with the Cheyenne 30 years earlier, the Comanche could not reach enough maturity to go to the field in time to justify continuing it.

An important element in the Comanche's fate was basic shifts in the way that Defense approached acquisition from the Cold War to the post-Cold War era. The former era relied mainly on developing systems that met standards by incorporating components with known characteristics. The latter era abandoned this level of specification. The transition did not necessarily work smoothly. Comanche fell victim at least partly to garbling in translation.

An aspect easily overlooked was the intense effort and commitment among the people who tried to bring the Comanche to the field. For over two decades people worked to make the program succeed and meet the needs of the national defense. For many people at many levels, in both government and industry, moving Comanche forward was a consuming affair. Most involved were talented, thoughtful people. They dealt with extremely complex, sometimes intractable situations. Many invested huge amounts of emotional capital. In the end, their efforts were overcome by events.

Comanche did not simply die. At the same time the Army ordered a stop on work, on 18 March 2004, contractors were ordered to continue work on several key subsystems. Thus, technology arising out of the Comanche program would probably meet other needs—some, probably not yet foreseen. Beyond that, efforts were underway to acquire an Armed Reconnaissance Helicopter (ARH), based on an OTS aircraft. Production was to begin in Fiscal Year 2006.

Lastly, those who fought hardest for the Comanche over the years also recognized the merits of the course of action taken. MG (ret.) Bergantz noted that, while it was a shame to terminate Comanche in the condition it was, the Army faced huge, near-term spending with on-going operations and maintenance bills. The Army could not afford to carry forward two expensive programs—Comanche and the FCS. At least so far, the Army had kept its word and retained Comanche funds in Aviation. Those funds allowed remanufacturing Apaches, Black Hawks, and Chinooks. These funds also started three new efforts—ARH, LUH, and a fixed-wing Future Cargo Aircraft. In Bergantz's mind, those programs would have greater near-term benefits while exploiting many technologies from Comanche.

Efforts to expedite

Through the years after ODS Aviation, along with the rest of the Army and DOD, tried to find ways to get more capability into Soldiers' hands faster. Two particularly important approaches were spiral development and buying items that already existed in the civilian marketplace. The latter was commonly referred to as commercial off-the-shelf (COTS). Both showed some promise. Each brought some difficulties. Both also showed the trend toward almost-total dependence on the commercial marketplace in contrast to the government-owned, government-operated arsenal system that the Army had used for most of its life.

Spiral development

Rising costs and declining budgets created lower tolerances for errors in major acquisition programs through the 1990s and beyond. As part of the effort to deal with this situation, as well as to speed the movement of technology to the field, the model used to develop systems changed. The older, linear, sequential Concept Based Requirements System (CBRS) gave way in the 1990s to evolutionary approaches. One of these was called spiral development.

Spiral development originated in the mid-1980s to reduce risk on large software projects. Software engineers often designed and built large programs without active input from customers. The result was often programs that failed to meet the user's wants or that unforeseen obstacles delayed. A commercial scientist, Barry Boehm, proposed a cyclical approach. Working this way, customers saw results and engineers found potential troubles earlier. Problems could be fixed more quickly and at less cost. By 2002 DOD had adapted Boehm's ideas to get newer technologies into large platforms faster.

Spiral development required breaking large, long-term projects into phases, called blocks. Each block produced some new, usable military capability. These approaches resembled long-recognized, preplanned product improvements (P3I). The distinction DOD drew was that the newer approaches focused on fielding "an initial capability that may be less than the full requirement as a trade-off for earlier delivery, agility, affordability, and risk reduction." In simple terms, half a loaf now was better than a whole loaf later.

The numbers and frequency of changes with spiral development could create problems. Major systems were so complex that one change in the main system meant many related changes. The time and cost to make all these changes sometimes meant that another change came before all adjustments had been made for the last one. Sometimes there just was not enough money to make all changes in all places.

These kinds of situations appeared in fielding the Apache Longbow, which had several blocks and several upgrades within blocks. At one point the commander of the ATB at Fort Rucker feared that inconsistencies among models and workarounds to accommodate them might lead to students being graduates of no definable course. Also, by May 2000 the costs and difficulties in upgrading the Longbow Crew Trainer (LCT) defied having currency with existing cockpits. Instructors faced doing the same thing with the new aircraft that they were already doing with older ones. An instructor would take a piece of paper to show differences between the simulator and the aircraft the student would try to fly the next day.

Meeting urgent operational needs—COTS and LUH

To bypass many of the hurdles in DOD acquisition that could delay fielding by years and even decades, services, units, and even individual Soldiers often resorted to buying items that already existed in the civilian marketplace to meet immediate military needs. In some cases COTS involved whole systems, and even with this approach delays could arise.

An example was the Light Utility Helicopters (LUH). The LUH derived from the Aviation TF in 2003. The TF found a need for a light utility helicopter that was less costly than the Black Hawk, which was Aviation's main lift helicopter. The necessity stemmed from the Army's retiring both the Huey as well as its OH-58A and OH-58C scout helicopters. The LUH was an expedient to meet two types of needs in general aviation support. One was to give AC TDA units an aircraft for training, testing, and MEDEVAC. The LUH also supported the National Guard needs in homeland security and MEDEVAC. Since the LUH was not intended to deploy into combat environments, the Army sought an aircraft that the FAA had already certified for commercial use. This way, with a decision sometime in late 2004, the Army could field the first lot of aircraft in 2006.

SOF channels—end-runs on the system

Another avenue that brought new materiel into Aviation but bypassed many procurement obstacles was the SOF community. SOF had its own procurement channels and operated under rules that frequently exempted it from many of the bureaucratic requirements that any conventional systems had to go through. As a result, Special Operations Aviation often acquired COTS or nondevelopmental items. Often these items later fed into the wider Aviation community.

Efforts to extend service life—remanufacture, recapitalization and Reset

Long before the Cold War ended, the spiraling cost of acquisition for major weapons forced major changes in how the armed forces acquired, used, and retired individual systems. By the end of the Cold War people accepted in principle that major new aircraft would have very long lives. Rather than advancing capability by replacing whole systems at intervals of about ten years as the Rogers Board had proposed in 1960, the approach was to make major modifications to the basic platform. With these upgrades, a basic platform might have a lifespan of several decades—much as, in reality, had happened unintentionally with the Huey. Two cases where this happened were upgrades to the Vietnam-era Chinooks and the conversion of AH-64A Apaches to the Apache Longbows. While the airframe looked almost unchanged from the outside, the differences in capabilities were huge.

Remanufacture—A-to D-model Apaches and Longbows

In 1997 the first modernized Apaches—the AH-64D—were fielded. These drastically improved on the A-models. Differences included the Longbow fire control radar, a radio-frequency interferometer, fire-and-forget radar HELLFIRE missile, and an integrated glass cockpit. Testing indicated the Apache Longbow had three times greater lethality than the A-model and eight times the survivability. The Longbow model also had no instances of fratricide compared to 34 for the AH-64A.

The manufacturer built some new AH-64Ds for foreign customers, but the Army planned for all Apache Longbows to be remanufactured A-models. Remanufacture only partially fixed some reliability, availability and maintainability (RAM) issues with the Apaches already in service. During remanufacture, all serviceable parts common to both the A and D models remained in the aircraft. By September 2000 the fleet of Apaches used for training at Fort Rucker desperately needed refreshing. However, refreshing this fleet meant bringing newer aircraft from the field into Fort Rucker. That exchange meant feeding the oldest A models into the line for remanufacture. Injecting these oldest aircraft meant that the new Longbows going to the field would have problems based on the old parts in them.

Recapitalization

On 2 May 2001 the Army signed a contract with Sikorsky Aircraft Corporation for design, development, integration, testing and qualification of the new UH-60M Black Hawk. The UH-60M Black Hawk was an upgrade of the Black Hawk UH-60A and UH-60L models. These were fielded in 1978 and 1989, respectively. The contract signed in 2001 provided for the first recapitalization program where the original equipment manufacturer, industry, and government depots were all partners in remanufacturing helicopters.

Reset

Still another initiative to increase the readiness and availability of aircraft was the Reset program. This involved something on the order of a depot-level overhaul of the aircraft, replacing those parts that needed it.

Enhancing readiness by improving reliability, availability and maintainability (RAM)

One area where the Army sought substantial gains, of necessity, was to make a smaller force more effective by having less of it out of use at any time for repairs or maintenance. Part of GEN Shinseki's Transformation initiatives was a specific requirement that all systems would achieve 90 percent availability. This standard applied for every AC and RC unit, in both peace and in war. Moreover, the CSA directed achieving this capability by Fiscal Year 2004. This goal, in the estimates of those involved in the details, was highly ambitious and involved significant risk. In June 2002 the results were briefed to the VCSA and the CSA, and the CSA approved the recommendations.

Two reasons for the increased emphasis on availability were Aviation's criticality for the rest of Army operations and the high cost of Aviation spares and repairs. Feeding frustration with the prevailing state of Aviation RAM were recurrent instances of materiel failures that caused whole fleets to be grounded. For example, on 6 August 1999, the Army grounded all its Chinooks as a precaution after cracked transmission gears showed up in a routine mechanical overhaul in one aircraft of the British Royal Air Force. While the grounding affected specific aircraft, by late August the shortage of aircraft pushed USAAVNC toward having to cancel whole classes. Similar groundings with Apaches and Black Hawks had worldwide impacts on operations.

Working around some of the materiel problems sometimes required wholesale replacement of scarce, expensive parts. Sometimes the problem became self-reinforcing. When new parts were unavailable, parts were sometimes taken from aircraft undergoing other repairs to make another aircraft immediately flyable. This substitution increased workloads on maintainers who were already stretched thin. Sometimes simply removing or reinstalling a part damaged it, worsening the system-wide shortage of serviceable units.

Preventing some of these problems by engineering reliability and maintainability into the systems became a specific part of the acquisition process. An example was with the M-model Black Hawk. Improvements were expected to reduce maintenance costs by one-fourth compared to UH-60As.

While the Army struggled against funding limitations, other factors sometimes obstructed meeting needs for Aviation spares. Some obstacles were not things that most people would expect, such as changes in consumer products. These could drastically affect the availability of key Aviation parts. Industry's responsiveness to the highest bidder—or least-costly customer—could give Defense a back seat. That vulnerability increased with the shift to in the just-in-time-logistics that DOD embraced after ODS. An illustration was the metal titanium, which was a key component in rotor blades of the Black Hawk. Just about the time the nation committed itself to war in 2001, there was a pinch on the supply of Aviation parts using titanium because of an abrupt rise in demand for high-grade sports equipment. Because of the technical difficulty and high cost of producing titanium, barely a handful of companies were in the business. Since non-aerospace items could be produced quickly and involved much lower quality standards, titanium producers eagerly shifted their efforts to producing for consumer markets. The producers also saw some opportunity in the situation to punish the aerospace customers for the treatment received while aerospace had the upper hand as almost the sole customer. Aggravating the situation was a major drop in worldwide production from disruptions in the former Soviet Union, and one of the few major suppliers in the U.S. quit the business. At the same time, other applications for titanium alloys multiplied. These included architecture, food processing, medical implants, automotive springs, eyeglass frames, nuclear waste storage, and petrochemical plants. So, even when the Army had the money to buy parts, they might not be forthcoming as quickly as needed, and Aviation could enter combat operations in harsh environments with shortages in critical stockages and no ready way to fill the gaps.

Army Airspace Command and Control (A2C2) and ATC

A realm of issues that loomed increasingly larger through the years after ODS was management of airspace. The complexity of operations, along with advances in and proliferation of technology, increased strains in an area that senior Army leaders had identified as woefully deficient as early as 1962. The effects of Jointness, technology, and changing operational environments pushed toward changes in organizations, which in turn, reshaped demands on and for people in Aviation.

Distinction between A2C2 and ATC

A2C2 is an overall concept that included four parts—C2, AD, some aspects of fire support coordination, and ATC. Aviation Branch was the proponent for only ATC but had a large interest and played at least some role in all of them.

Airspace management as a longstanding problem—Black Hawk shootdown, 14 April 1994

Concerns about effective control of airspace were almost as old as aviation itself. Deconflicting airspace for aircraft and other users, such as artillerymen, had long been a lethal problem. Two facilities at Fort Rucker—Hunt Stagefield and Murphy Hall—honored aviators killed by a friendly artillery shell in Korea on 21 June 1952. An Air Force fighter pulling up from a strafing run split an artillery observation aircraft from the 24th Division and killed both pilots. Dangers among various users of airspace were well-recognized among senior Army leaders by the time the Army ventured into full-scale development of air assault. In endorsing the Howze Board's report in August 1962 GEN Herbert B. Powell, commanding CONARC, specifically highlighted airspace management, ATC, and friendly recognition among several areas requiring major effort. During Vietnam, midair collisions in tactical operations were among the most demoralizing events for Army aviators. By ODS, despite a smaller overall number of aircraft, the air remained crowded. Joint operations at greater distances increased the demand for coordination.

An incident in the spring of 1994 showed the dangers in Joint operations covering huge areas over extended periods. On the morning of 14 April 1994 two Air Force F-15s shot down two Army Black Hawks in northern Iraq. This incident, killing all 26 on the helicopters, showed serious holes in Joint Combat Airspace Command and Control (J-CACC). The accident occurred while the F-15s were on missions to protect the Kurdish populations in the area of Iraq designated as a security zone (SZ). Both the F-15s and Black Hawks were under simultaneous control by an Air Force Airborne Warning and Control System (AWACS) aircraft.

On 27 May 1994, the board to investigate the shootdown concluded its investigation. The air tasking order (ATO) contained no detailed information on the Black Hawks, and AWACS controllers did not advise the F-15s of the Black Hawks' presence. So the F-15s had no foreknowledge of the Black Hawks. After picking up the Black Hawks on radar and being told by the AWACS controller that the area was clear, the F-15s made a visual pass. The lead aircraft misidentified the Black Hawks as Hinds or Hips. Identification friend or foe (IFF) equipment failed.

On 14 November 1994 the JCS issued Joint Publication 3–56.1, <u>Command and Control for Joint Air Operations</u>. While not specifically mentioning the shootdown, this publication addressed some key issues of interservice coordination. It required all air missions to appear on the ATO/flight plan even if lacking a tail number, using IFF modes and codes, and checking those before a mission started. It also emphasized strict control of flights during peace operations, as well as continual reevaluation of control measures as the environment and mission changed.

The incident raised serious questions about practices to prevent aerial fratricides. In 1998 the GAO noted several flaws in the Air Force's investigation although GAO found nothing actionable. The investigation neglected to address individuals' lack of knowledge about specific procedures and an apparent general lack of discipline among F-15 pilots in Operation Provide Comfort. Other analyses identified characteristics of the operational environment that invited room for error in Joint operations—particularly, those that spread over time. Scott A. Snook, an Army officer and sociologist who had been wounded in an aerial fratricide incident in 1983, proposed a theory of practical drift. Over three years operators changed local practices. Nothing was remarkable about any of these changes. Only their sum of them in the specific conditions caused tragedy. A key element in the outcome was the very complexity of the network that had to work together to prevent an accident. From another viewpoint, an Air Force judge advocate general cautioned about rules that allowed lethal action based solely on presence in an exclusion zone. Such rules justified the pilot's decision to shoot despite lack of urgency and with considerable room for doubt about the targets.

The incident partly reflected ways in which Aviation operated differently from the other services. To retain maximum flexibility to respond to ground commanders' needs, Aviation did not pin down flights with the precision used by the other services—particularly the Air Force. The daily ATO included the schedule for all aircraft operating within the Combined Task Force. Because exact times were uncertain, Black Hawk flights simply carried the comment, 'as required.' Immediately after the incident both DOD and the Air Force conducted analyses that led to corrective actions, including putting Black Hawk flight times into the ATO. This inclusion of more specific information was done to insure greater safety for all in the increasingly complex environment. The challenge for Aviation was to retain its flexibility to respond to ground commanders' needs without sacrificing safety.

Uniqueness of Army ATC and expanding demands

Like Aviation in general, Army ATC had certain characteristics that gave it unique value, not only to the service but to the entire nation.

Much of uniformed Army ATC's focus was on tactical operations. The nature of Army operations and the close relationship with the ground Soldier created situations for controllers that were unusual among the services. The Army was responsible for initial entry operations. Much work involved setting up and providing services in places where there was no permanent, established presence or facility. Moreover, much of Army ATC's expertise was in supporting high-density, very localized movement, rather than handling aircraft enroute over long routes. For example, in Somalia in 1993, after shooting started, Aviation from 10th Mountain Division (10MTN) occupied Mogadishu Airport. Volume of air traffic and flow into a combat zone started to increase. Air Force personnel were not prepared to handle the volume and density of traffic. Army ATC operators, more attuned to these conditions, came in and successfully carried off operations. A similar situation arose in Haiti in 1994. Also, the Air Force did not necessarily provide for instrumented operations that the Army needed in a contingency environment. That was true in SWA in 1990, Somalia in 1993, and Bosnia in 1995.

Field expedient air traffic control tower—Mogadishu

In some cases the Army had capabilities that met needs beyond the service-specific. By 2003 the Army was the only agency that could still conduct flight inspection of a GCA using a theodolite on the ground. The Air Force had dropped this capability years earlier. This capability became important in

Afghanistan. The U.S. Army Air Traffic Control Activity (USAATCA) at Fort Rucker also could go to a site, loiter, land, and help make the adjustments and checks to make a navigational aid (NAVAID) fully functional. The FAA could only conduct a one-time, fly-by inspection.

Demands for people with related skills increased. Internal expansion of pilot training at Fort Rucker created a demand for more controllers there by 1999. Other demands arose from the fielding of new systems like the Tactical Airspace Integration System (TAIS) and changes in the new Stryker Brigade Combat Teams (SBCT). There was also a growing sense that some, if not all Army controllers needed to complete the Joint Force Air Component Commander's Course (JFACC). ATS technicians needed to know who else was operating in the environment and how the relationships worked.

Organizing to meet the new needs—rise of ATSCOM

The Army's ability to meet its need for ATS worldwide was a longstanding concern that extended into the civilian National Airspace System (NAS). On 4 March 1988 an interim operational concept defined Army ATS's primary mission to facilitate airspace use at all Army operational levels in both peace and conflict. ATS supporting en-route and terminal flight operations was a key to the Army Aviation command and control (A2C2) system. To carry out these mandates meant meeting requirements for both civilian airspace and military-specific conditions. So DOD and the FAA agreed to realign some radar approach control jurisdictions during 1995–2000. DOD would be responsible for locations where most air traffic was military, where DOD had the capability to provide services equivalent to the FAA, and where DOD asked to be the provider of ATC. These conditions especially applied around places like Fort Rucker, which also had global responsibilities because of the missions of the U.S. Army Air Traffic Control Activity (USAATCA).

In October 1994 USAAVNC asked the U.S. Army Force Integration Support Agency (USAFISA) to review manpower and organization of the USAATCA. The goal was to ensure that USAAVNC, as the Army's proponent, was effectively using its limited ATC resources in the areas that directly contributed to warfighting. The study concluded that the 1986 ATC Transfer Plan, which shifted responsibility to Aviation, was never fully implemented. As a result, ATC skills and services were eroding to the point of affecting readiness and safety. This study started a chain of events that finally produced a new organization, the Army Air Traffic Services Command (ATSCOM).

A large part of the problem was that downsizing and regulatory changes had forced the USAATCA to support ATC worldwide on a budget only for Fort Rucker. For many years, ATC was an area that the Army would borrow from to pay for higher-priority needs. At the same time, the Army's ATS workload expanded. In June 1996, USAFISA reported that Army ATC was "in distress" and would soon be "unrecoverable." The proposed remedy was centralized management for both tactical units and fixed-base facilities. USAFISA proposed a provisional command at Fort Rucker with the Aviation Branch as the proponent. Joint warfighting commanders opposed this Army Air Traffic Control Redesign Initiative (A2RI). Rather than having assets under their immediate control, regional commanders would get their support for operations by ATS assets sent forward as part of a projected force. This smacked of the pooling concept that had been the basis for disputes between air and ground commanders all the way back before World War II. Pending resolution, HQDA imposed a moratorium on ATC manpower and resources that was supposed to last through 31 July 1997. It lasted far longer, and ATS weakened. By January 2001 the DCSOPS told Congress that Army ATS was funded only to a 55-percent level. Since the nature of the equipment was inherently expensive to maintain, just a few parts ate the entire budget in some years.

The force structure issue was also inseparable from issues of retention and promotion. In 1998 three proposals were being evaluated for restructuring of all Army ATS and ATC units. One eliminated ATS battalions and groups. This proposal increased the number of controller positions, and established organic A2C2 elements in division and higher headquarters. However, resistance came from the field because the proposal eliminated command and CSM positions.

Restructure also ran into manpower barriers. A need for more people was validated, but HQDA delayed implementation until someone found the billpayers. Also, FORSCOM could not find a BG position to command the worldwide organization.

On 18 October 2001 FORSCOM provisionally activated the ATSCOM at Fort McPherson, Georgia, under COL Don M. Adkins. Even so, going beyond provisional status remained doubtful. Finally on 28 August 2003—almost a year after the target date—ATSCOM activated at Fort Rucker as a major subordinate command of FORSCOM.

Developing and retaining people with Air traffic control (ATC) skills

After ODS there were several efforts to raise the level of experience of ATC Soldiers in the field. These efforts reflected changes in grade structures that the Army had imposed across the board in the large post-Cold War drawdowns. In the case of Aviation, the attempt to align force structure with a pyramidal career progression ill-suited the skill and experience requirements to let Aviation operate efficiently and perhaps even safely. The overall competition for high-quality people in a booming economy, as well as the potentially high transfer of skills from uniformed to civilian sectors, added to the challenges of meeting the Army's needs in some key areas.

To try to meet the specialized skill needs, the Army basically took three approaches. One was to create enlisted ATC specialists. Another was to create WO ATC specialists. The third was to have civilian ATC specialists. While efforts concerning the second waxed and waned, the Army consistently used both NCO ATC specialists and civilians throughout the period.

Challenges in growing and retaining ATC skills

One area of special concern during the mid-to late-1990s was retention of enlisted Army air traffic controllers. As with the loss of middle-grade WO pilots, the Army faced a crisis in training and retaining enough air traffic controllers to meet the service's needs. As with WO pilots, changes in the civilian economy and the international security environment, along with positive steps the Army took, largely fixed the problems by 2004.

Some challenges in growing and retaining ATS Soldiers with the right skills and grades were inherent in the nature of the tasks and the skills required. First it was difficult to recruit enough Soldiers to fill the needs in the related MOS. The high OPTEMPO for ATC Soldiers created intense pressures on ATC Soldiers with families to consider leaving the service. Through the 1990s the civilian sector also had shortages of air traffic controllers, and salaries and working hours were generally better for civilian air traffic controllers than for ATC Soldiers. All these factors added up to an intense pressure on Aviation to gain, train, and retain enough ATC Soldiers to meet current needs.

Among efforts to retain highly-skilled Soldiers where their skills could meet critical needs was a restructuring of fields. In 1995, MOS 93P Aviation Operations

Specialist and MOS 93C Air Traffic Control (ATC) Operator were merged at the master sergeant (E-8) level. This action increased promotion opportunities, allowed for more diverse assignments, and retained the knowledge and skills of senior aviation sergeants. The Army also tried to meet some of these critical needs by shifting people from obsolete career paths into ATC. At the school level, a major emphasis was reducing the number of students who failed to graduate from the basic course. One approach was adding three weeks to the length of the initial training for MOS 93C. There were various efforts to find ways to enhance pride, including efforts by January 1999 to create an Air Traffic System (ATS) Skill Badge. The Army also tried straight, economic incentives. By May 1997 selective reenlistment bonuses (SRB) were in effect for several Aviation MOSs including for ATC operators. Special Duty Assignment Pay (SDAP) was also authorized for Soldiers holding MOS 93C.

Through the 1990s the Army stayed short in the ATC MOSs and had no program that could completely close the gap without causing dislocations in other areas. The chronic shortfalls and apparently inability to fix them drew attention and action at the highest Army levels. In June 1998 the chronic shortfalls in enlisted strength in the MOS 93C Air Traffic Controller put that MOS on the list of items for the CSA and Secretary of the Army's monthly review of the most critical issues. By March 1999 development of Soldiers with MOS 93C was part of an Army-level action plan.

By October 2002 the crisis related to MOS 93C was largely past. Strength had risen from 78 percent to 95 percent. In February 2004 strength of 93Cs—which had been redesignated to 15Q—had risen to 109 percent. At least in the eyes of the senior Aviation Branch NCO, authorizing the SDAP had been a powerful help in retention.

Retention of valuable skills versus the Army's personnel system—the ATC WO MOS

The Army's difficulty retaining Soldiers with advanced ATC skills partly reflected the mismatch between skill levels required to perform some types of tasks and the Army's personnel management structure. The Army's personnel structures generally presumed that, by the time a Soldier had spent a few years in the Army, the person should be a supervisor, not a technician actually performing a task. The WO existed partly to address this mismatch, and more than once the Army tried to elevate ATC functions into the WO realm.

Attempts in the 1980s and 1990s to create an ATC WO were unsuccessful. In 1987 the CSA disestablished the MOS 150A WO ATC technician because there were too few to be viable in the AC. In the late 1980s the ATC WO was also not viable for other reasons—most notably, that it could not attract the people success depended upon. The MOS had to attract ATC Soldiers who had several years of experience. By the time a Soldier had that experience, most were senior NCOs. Their NCO pay was high enough to make the transition to entry-level WO rank unattractive. In addition, going from NCO to WO meant going through a Warrant Officer Candidate School (WOCS), which resembled basic training for new recruits. Few senior NCOs would tolerate that. In 1998 the Army again reconsidered but dropped the idea.

By June 2003, for several related reasons, the Army once again considered reestablishing MOS 150A. These WOs could replace some Aviation Branch officers needed in flying positions. Also, existing practices, assigning newly-graduated Aviation lieutenants (LT) went into ATS positions, hurt both flying officers and the Army. The units had no aircraft associated, so lieutenants could not get flying experience they needed for promotion and retention. The ATC WO would also help meet needs in the RC. Despite all these benefits, there was a fear the Army might be creating a requirement it could not fulfill.

Small numbers

Part of the overall ATC problem was that of small numbers within a huge organization. During 1988 the USAAVNC Noncommissioned Officers Academy (NCOA) graduated only 151 MOS 93C students from the Basic Noncommissioned Officer Course (BNCOC). With such small numbers, losing only a few people could have a big impact. Yet Army-wide requirements did not justify producing larger numbers. Additionally, most operators at fixed-bases outside Fort Rucker were civilians, who had to retire at age 56. The FAA could allow waivers, but no one existed to process the waivers. At higher levels the numbers and issue were too small and just got lost.

Competing fixed-base and tactical demands—and training base and certification needs

Further complicating development and management of ATC Soldiers was that Aviation ATC Soldiers might work in two, very different environments—a fluid, mobile tactical setting and a fixed, airport-type setting. Compounding this issue was the certification process for controllers. Besides general qualifications, each controller going to a fixed-base operation had to qualify in that specific location.

It could take months to become fully qualified. This fact added strain when people turned over. The result was that the Army needed some fixed-base operations to let ATC Soldiers gain the general skills but needed to get them out to the field to perform tactically.

Fort Rucker as both an asset and liability in meeting ATC needs

Because of the constant training of helicopter pilots there, the heavy volume of air traffic made Fort Rucker an ideal learning environment and place to get fixed-base experience. The number of aircraft coming and going in the normal training cycles gave ATC Soldiers in the towers experience handling several aircraft in a relatively tight airspace. In 1997 Cairns Army Airfield (CAAF) alone handled more than 175,000 military and civilian aircraft. This maintained CAAF's ranking as the busiest Army airfield in the world. In 2000 CAAF was one of the ten busiest airfields in the United States.

The downside of this heavy traffic was that Fort Rucker also absorbed a large percentage of the total Army ATC population.

Effects of dramatic events—and events overlooked

From the end of ODS up to 2004, the changing operational environment led Aviation and Army aviators through a succession of changes that were probably at least on a par with those of the decades following Vietnam. The focus shifted away from the high-intensity battlefield envisioned during the Cold War to one that was more loosely defined and much more unpredictable, but still highly lethal. As with the rest of the Army, Aviation found itself having to adapt systems designed for high-end conflict to these situations. Several incidents can be used to plot the trajectory of this adjustment, beginning with one that passed all but unnoticed during the time of ODS.

A key element in the changing operational environment was the incidence of failed nation-states as the context for operations. The notable exception was Iraq, where a strong dictator exercised power seen to present a direct threat to the United States. Another characteristic through this period was a gap between the expected threat to Aviation forces going in and the actual threat encountered. In several cases, underestimation of the actual threat played an important part in the course of events. By the end of this period, Aviation had adjusted its expectations to offset this gap. However, the dangers posed by a thinking, adaptive enemy remained, with the possibility of surprise always lurking in the background.

Pickett shootdown, 2 January 1991

For Aviation the first shots in the GWOT may have come on 2 January 1991 in El Salvador. On that day, insurgents of the Communist-backed Farabundo Marti Liberation Front (FMLN) killed three Aviation Soldiers. The insurgents shot down the Huey carrying the commander of the 4th Battalion, 228th Aviation Regiment. The pilot, CWO Daniel Scott, was killed in the crash. The battalion commander, LTC David Pickett, and crew chief PFC Earnest Dawson, were both injured but survived the crash. FMLN insurgents murdered both Pickett and Dawson in cold blood.

As with most of Aviation operations after the Cold War, the background of these events went back some years, involving a bitter civil war. In 1981, with training and materiel from Cuba and Vietnam, the FMLN started one of the most savage civil wars in Latin American history. During the 1980s the FMLN also learned greatly from African insurgencies. The FMLN had learned effective antiaircraft tactics using small arms—especially, AK-47 rifles and RPGs—with a homemade sight that adjusted for different speeds and distances, as well as different attitudes in flight. The FMLN also had well-developed training on how to use these devices to shoot down helicopters, on which the FMLN had a bounty. Part of the FMLN's antiaircraft tactics was to locate spotters near airports to call when an aircraft departed After meetings failed to produce a peace settlement, in November 1990 the FMLN launched another major offensive. Security for American citizens was a concern; the FMLN had also murdered several. To avoid FMLN checkpoints, all movement was by air.

The more immediate background of the shootdown on 2 January 1991 related to efforts to improve security of Aviation operations in El Salvador. Several U.S. Army Hueys had been hit, and several Salvadoran army aircraft had been shot down. SAMs were a special worry. Twice SAMs had shot down aircraft leaving no survivors. The SAM threat made it seem safer to fly low. This practice, though, brought pilots well within the envelope of small arms.

Limitations on aircraft communications increased risk. The radios on the U.S. Hueys did not allow continuous contact while flying NOE. To compensate in case of an emergency, the aircraft flew a route along Highway 1. Pilots had flown the route so many times that, by 2 January 1991, they were not using maps. The specific path took aircraft very close to the ground along a ridgeline. Pickett's aircraft was flying low over that ridgeline, on the same path flown in the morning, when it was shot down.

In one sense, this shootdown was a case of being unlucky. This was the first time the FMLN had shot down a U.S. aircraft using small arms. The insurgents peppered the aircraft. One shot hit the compressor blades, causing a failure. However, the FMLN had contrived the situation to increase the odds of success. They had set up a linear ambush and had good intelligence. Salvadoran military intelligence had intercepted a broadcast when Pickett took off. He crossed the fatal point 15 minutes later. Because the aircraft was flying alone, no one was readily available to pick up the surviving crewmembers when they went down. This gave time for the FMLN to reach the aircraft, murder the survivors, and set the aircraft on fire.

Out of this incident came immediate changes in practices. The battalion went to multiship operations. The unit added Infantry door gunners on six-month rotations—much as had evolved during Vietnam. The battalion also obtained a Salvadoran LNO who checked enemy activity during the 12 hours preceding a mission. This information allowed rerouting or canceling missions, as seemed prudent. Coordination was also established for a QRF. MG Rudolph Ostovich, commanding USAAVNC, arranged for the unit to have AN/ALQ-144 infrared countermeasures sets installed. Additionally the unit mounted commercial, Sabre radios on their aircraft. These let crews talk through their intercom to anyone in the country.

The unit returned to high-altitude flying, because the SAM threat seemed lower than the small-arms one. The FMLN used their SAMs only against attacking aircraft because the missiles were scarce. Also the FMLN did not want the bad publicity that came with a shootdown in a populated area. Finally, Army aircraft began flying out over water, because there was no threat off the coast. This practice led to additional equipment—notably, Navy survival vests and the Helicopter Emergency Egress Device System (HEEDS). With these changes, there were no more incidents.

In hindsight, this shootdown foreshadowed events recognized a decade later as the GWOT. At the heart was a diffuse, international network, sharing lessons and broad goals. Whatever lessons were to be learned were mostly lost in the noise surrounding ODS, which began barely two weeks later.

UH-1 with the ALQ-144 countermeasures on bottom of tail boom

Black Hawk Down—Somalia

The shootdown of two Black Hawks in October 1993 in Somalia in what became known as the Battle of Mogadishu, has been thoroughly covered elsewhere, as in Mark Bowden's <u>Black Hawk Down</u>. It is still important to consider in specific relation to Aviation's experience since the end of the Cold War. As with the downing of Pickett's Huey two years earlier, this incident involved surprise brought about by an enemy exploiting low technology to lethal effect. Much more widely recognized than in El Salvador, the context in Somalia involved a failed state and an apparent climate of near-chaos that brought U.S. forces into play, and then brought those forces into deadly conflict with others there.

The context of 'Black Hawk Down'

The Army's involvement in Somalia began in August 1992 as part of an international effort to provide humanitarian relief after civil war threatened hundreds of thousands of Somalis with starvation. From a small contingent for logistics with Aviation and a QRF for the immediate relief tasks, U.S. forces gradually became engaged in poorly defined nation-building. These activities entangled U.S. forces in power struggles among rival clans. On 3–4 October 1993, an operation to snatch lieutenants of one of the most troublesome warlords went badly awry. In the end, 30 U.S. Soldiers, four Marines, and eight Air Force personnel died. Worldwide broadcast of parts of the event and its aftermath gave an impression of chaos and disaster. Most shocking to the American public was the sight of cheering Somali mobs dragging dead U.S. Soldiers through the streets. These were the same people Americans thought they had just rescued from starvation.

In longer view, the situation in Somalia was a legacy of the Cold War. The Somali civil war grew out of the surrogate conflicts between the Western powers and Soviet Union during the Cold War. Conflicts between Soviet-and U.S.-backed leaders became endemic kidnapping and murder. When the central government collapsed in 1991, regional warlords drew upon clan loyalty to create independent power bases. Food supplies from international organizations became the focus of clan raiding to gain control over the population.

Eventually, unable to explain why the world's sole superpower could not stop starvation, President George H. W. Bush ordered U.S. forces into Somalia. Their mission was to ensure relief supplies reached the people who needed them. That brought U.S. forces into conflict with the warlords. From June 1993 onward events moved toward a state of war between the U.S. and one warlord, Muhammed Farah Aideed. On 22 August the new SECDEF, Les Aspin, created a joint special operations task force (JSOTF), called TF Ranger, to capture Aideed and his key lieutenants.

During August-September 1993 TF Ranger conducted six successful missions, both daytime and nighttime, into Mogadishu. All used both helicopters and ground vehicles to reach their targets. However, on 8 September Somali militia attacked with heavier weapons. Only extensive ground and Aviation fire suppressed the Somalis' fire. This incident marked a growing willingness to engage TF Ranger. That same day a civilian mob also joined in the militia's attack. On 25 September a U.S. Black Hawk was shot down, killing five Soldiers. U.S. and Pakistani forces evacuated the casualties under fire. Most disturbingly, the Somalis shot down the helicopter using RPGs—normally, used to attack armored vehicles.

The Battle of Mogadishu, 3–4 October 1993

On 3 October TF Ranger launched into Aideed's stronghold to capture two of his key lieutenants. Helicopters carrying assault and blocking forces launched from Mogadishu airport. A ground convoy left three minutes later. Ground forces quickly reached the target location. The blocking force quickly set up while the assault force searched. Both took more intense enemy fire than previously encountered. Just after the assault team captured 24 Somalis and was about to load them onto the convoy trucks, a RPG knocked down a Black Hawk circling about three blocks from the target location.

From there, things went downhill rapidly. Almost immediately, six men from the blocking force, a MH-6 assault helicopter, and a Black Hawk with a 15-man CSAR team went to the scene. The MH-6 landed in a narrow alley in the middle of a firefight and evacuated two wounded Soldiers. The six-man blocking element arrived on foot, followed by the CSAR helicopter. As the last two members of the CSAR team were sliding down the fast ropes to the crash site, a RPG hit the helicopter. The pilot kept the helicopter under control until the last two CSAR members reached the ground, then returned to the airport.

The situation worsened. Ground fire struck two more Black Hawks. One crashed within a mile of the first downed helicopter. A Somali mob killed everyone except one pilot that they took prisoner. Trying to defend this location, MSG Gary Gordon and SFC Randall Shughart were killed. Both posthumously received the Medal of Honor for their efforts and were inducted into the Army Aviation Hall of Fame.

After loading their detainees onto the trucks, remaining assault and blocking forces moved on foot to the first crash site. Soldiers took heavy fire, wounding several. They set up defensive positions in buildings, used suppressive fire to hold off the Somalis, and treated their wounded while trying to free the pilot's body from the wreckage. The ground convoy with the detainees also tried to reach the first crash site by a different route. The convoy commander aborted after heavy fire caused many casualties. While returning to the airport, this convoy met the TF's internal QRF enroute to the second crash. The QRF took some of the convoy's casualties, and both convoys returned to base. Meantime the U.S. QRF for the UN also tried to reach the second crash site. Somali fire stopped this group, which finally withdrew to the airport to work with others from the TF to provide a coordinated rescue plan.

Soldiers at the first crash ran short of supplies. RPGs hit a Black Hawk bringing in water and ammunition. That aircraft just reached the airport before breaking down.

After hours of planning and collecting forces, more than 60 vehicles departed the airport with Pakistani tanks in the lead and Aviation support,. Two Malaysian APCs mistakenly turned off the road, were ambushed, and took four hours to be rescued. At 0155 on 4 October 10MTN Soldiers in Malaysian APCs reached the first crash site. Soldiers from the various groups worked throughout the night under heavy fire. SOA AH-6 Little Birds and Cobras using 2.75-inch rockets helped keep the enemy off until daylight. Forces also reached the second crash site but found no trace of those lost there. At dawn all casualties from the first site were loaded onto the APCs. The rest of the force moved rapidly on foot along what became known as the Mogadishu Mile.

At 0542 on 4 October, with helicopter gunships providing suppressive fire, a fighting withdrawal started. About 0630 the main convoy reached a secure area, allowing emergency medical and movement to the hospital or the airfield. Thus ended one of the fiercest firefights since Vietnam.

The Battle of Mogadishu in hindsight

These battles marked a watershed. Conditions largely frustrated the use of technological superiority. Outcomes depended on old, Soldierly qualities. Friendly casualties were heavy. Somali casualties were estimated at between 500 and 1500. The events had huge political-military effects. The event led to the U.S. withdrawing from Somalia and brought down a SECDEF. Even more importantly, the outcome fed a widespread view that the U.S. was so casualty-averse that it could be discounted in international affairs. Results were extreme caution in other situations and possibly increased boldness of terrorist groups wanting to act against U.S. interests.

At a smaller level, the Battle of Mogadishu also highlighted the potentially tight linkages between tactical Aviation and the realm of geopolitics. Aviation was an instrument of choice. It was also a pressure point. Aideed realized that hovering helicopters were vulnerable. He also knew that U.S. forces would risk much to support comrades in trouble. As in Vietnam, where the NVA chased SF on the ground to bring in helicopters to shoot down—Aideed knew knocking down a helicopter could draw Rangers into conditions where he could inflict casualties. Helicopters were also symbols of U.S. superiority. The publicity value of bringing down a helicopter was great. Aideed perhaps could not anticipate the huge effect of the incident; however, he recognized the helicopters' value to the extent that he massed available RPGs to focus on them. Osama bin Laden, the leader of al Qaeda, cited the Battle of Mogadishu and the U.S. withdrawal as proof that the U.S. could be defeated.

Aideed also had received expert advice on tactics against helicopters. Muslim veterans of Afghanistan passed on knowledge that the most vulnerable part of the helicopter was the tail boom. A RPG modified with a timing device to explode in the air, rather than on contact, could bring down a helicopter. The Somalis knew that it was all but suicidal to confront helicopters or even to fire on them from the open. So they used holes or slit trenches dug in the streets, often covered with a small tree. They could lie concealed with the RPG, rise up, and shoot at the aircraft after it passed.

Crash site of CWO Mike Durant's Super 64

The training of the Somalis reflected the convoluted nature of the post-Cold War world. In Afghanistan during the Cold War, the CIA had trained Muslim fighters in how to take down Soviet helicopters. One of those who trained the Somalis was a veteran of these CIA activities. He recruited Arabs for the war in Afghanistan against the Soviets at a center in Brooklyn that also recruited for al Qaeda. In 1993 Canadian police picked him up with an al Qaeda terrorist but released him based on a call to the Federal Bureau of Investigation (FBI). Later he was rearrested in connection with the first bombing of the World Trade Center and then the bombing of the U.S. Embassy in Nairobi in 1998.

In hindsight the tactics used in Mogadishu showed some of the flaws present in the El Salvador shootdown in 1991. While the SOF had undisputed advantages at night because of NVG technology, this operation began in broad daylight. This was also the seventh mission conducted. Thus, the mission abandoned any element of surprise before it began. At least one pilot had serious reservations, but the decision seemed already to have been made. So aircrews executed.

Beyond that, there was a gap between what aviators believed they could do and what the overall commander promised. At the pre-mission brief, pilots objected that conditions precluded extraction by air. Some Rangers expressed concerns about the ground convoy's ability to reach and extract them. The mission commander assured the Rangers that, worst case, Aviation would extract them 'like they always do.' Here Aviation's longstanding tradition of willingness and ability to go beyond seemed to foster inattention to the actual hazards of the mission and realistic contingency planning.

The operation also had a noteworthy human aspect. As many times in Aviation history, this event was rife with examples of personal courage and persistence. Those aspects reflected the qualities of the people involved and did not end with the immediate events. An example was CWO Michael J. Durant, a pilot of the second aircraft shot down who became a captive for nearly two weeks. During that time he was badly injured, including a broken leg and back. Medical treatment was barely basic. Once released, Durant was determined to fly again—partly, to honor those who died to let him survive. He eventually did resume flying in the 160 SOAR. His return to full duty clearly proved the 160th's motto: 'Night Stalkers Don't Quit' (NSDQ).

Uphold Democracy—inherently Joint operations

One event that showed the movement toward Joint and multinational operations in the 1990s was Operation Uphold Democracy in Haiti in 1994. Helicopters from the 10MTN replaced much of a Navy air wing and flew off the carrier USS Eisenhower. This event echoed Organic Army Aviation's first flight into combat in 1942. It was possibly the first time since 1942 that a Navy carrier had been used exclusively for an Aviation operation.

Operation Joint Endeavor—Apaches as power-projection, passive deterrence

Following Somalia and Uphold Democracy, for the first time, Army doctrine specifically addressed the need for attack helicopters and tanks in peace operations. In April 1996 the Army published FM 100–20, <u>Stability and Support Operations</u>, in final draft. This introduced the new term, SASO. Included were operations to combat terrorism, counterdrug operations, arms control, nation assistance and foreign internal defense, as well as support to insurgencies, counterinsurgencies, and diplomacy. Such operations came to dominate the Army's activities for the rest of the decade.

Often overlooked in the course of military operations is the success of combat power not committed to combat. During the 1990s deterrence was one of Aviation's major values. A clear example was the use of Apaches in bringing peace to Bosnia after four years of bloody civil war. This flowed from ripple effects of the Soviet Union's collapse and efforts of old Communist regimes to retain control. After a bitter, internecine struggle and finally NATO intervention, a peace agreement among the warring factions was achieved in November 1995. A formal agreement followed on 14 December 1995. Part of that agreement was that a NATO-led peacekeeping operation, called Operation Joint Endeavor (OJE), would guarantee compliance with the military provisions of the agreements. That became effective 15 December. From then through 20 December 1996 Army, Navy, and Air Force units participated in NATO's first-ever ground force operation, first deployment "out of area," and first time since World War II that Russians served alongside U.S. troops.

The absolute lack of time between signing the agreement and starting the mission put extreme pressure on NATO forces to go into position to carry out their mandate. During the first stages of movement into Bosnia, the 1AD had few ground forces in the area of operations. Apaches were the only combat forces able to provide presence throughout the sector to let the Former Warring Factions (FWF) know that the new Implementation Force (IFOR) was there.

Just deploying the Apaches posed major challenges because of bad weather and limited availability of potential fueling points. Further hampering was the fact that maintenance equipment had been packed for delivery to the operational destination, and the support units expected to move forward any day. Instead, Apaches wound up working from an intermediate base in Hungary. This meant tripling the amount of maintenance. The few aircraft already in Bosnia had difficulty because spare parts were hard to get.

As often in Aviation history, those involved worked past the limits of their systems. Relative inaccuracy of the Apache Doppler Navigation System led members of the 2d Battalion, 227th Aviation Regiment (Attack), to buy hand-held GPSs from mail-order catalogs. To gain the additional time on station for missions in Bosnia, the unit got permission to take auxiliary fuel tanks and plumbing from the Apaches of the sister battalion that had recently inactivated.

The Apaches were invaluable, often using their technology in unorthodox ways to achieve the political-military goals without firing a shot. For example, during the first two months the video recording system on Apaches played a critical role in forcing the former combatants to comply with the peace agreement. The Apaches filmed weapons locations and relayed the information to headquarters. Task force representatives confronted faction leaders with evidence that they had not cleared weapons from areas as required. The faction leaders always removed weapons after being shown this evidence. The TF also used attack helicopters in various security operations: screening, guarding, and escorting lift helicopters. Although doctrine manuals did not address that mission, attack helicopters also provided crowd control. Pilots used rotor wash to move belligerent crowds away from protected persons. In one incident, a crowd beat a Swedish medic going to aid a person wounded in a minefield. The pilot placed the helicopter between the medic and the crowd, saving his life.

AH-64 Apache as force protection

The reputed lethality of the Apaches eliminated the need to use their firepower. 2–227th planned only one attack, and that ended without firing a shot. Serbs moved air defense weapons from a storage site and threatened to shoot down IFOR helicopters. Apaches got into their battle positions, and the Serbs conceded.

One of the greatest dangers the attack pilots encountered was complacency in a noncombat environment. To combat that, 2–227th paired newcomers with veterans to heighten the situational awareness (SA) of the veterans. The high OPTEMPO also required caution as result of fragmenting units. Lieutenants and warrant officers usually led missions that would normally have captains. No formal training existed to prepare young pilots for the increased responsibility. Often junior WOs led responses because they were near an incident. The battalion tried to compensate by careful intelligence preparations, assigning the most experienced pilots to likely trouble spots, and creating a graduated response matrix (GRM). The GRM was so successful that the Combat Maneuver Training Center (CMTC) in Germany adopted it for training follow-on units.

TF Hawk—turning point toward Transformation

A turning point for the Army, with a special focus on Aviation, was another NATO effort, Operation Allied Force, in 1998–1999. This sought to end ethnic cleansing by Serbs in the Kosovo province of Yugoslavia after political pressure on the Yugoslav government failed.

Allied Force was fraught with troubles from before it started. For broad political reasons, this effort devolved into an air-only campaign. Belatedly a ground force, of which the Army part designated TF Hawk, was added. TF Hawk built around 11th Aviation Regiment with Apache Longbows. A last-minute switch shifted operations from Macedonia to Albania. Over 5500 troops began deploying on 8 April 1999. These were directly under the command of LTG Jon W. Hendrix, V Corps commander. Hendrix became both ground force and TF commander.

Almost everything about the conditions of execution was bad. A clear humanitarian crisis in the international spotlight took priority on the only airstrip in Albania. Moreover, the Tirana airport required substantial improvements before it could support combat operations. Tents had water standing so deep that people used two cots. Had pads not been put down first, the Apaches would have sunk into the mud up to their wingstores. So Hendrix personally decided to delay sending in the Apaches. Force protection was a concern because of Serb cross-border forays, banditry, and presence of Muslim extremists. Potential for fratricide, as in the Black Hawk shootdown in April 1994, was another consideration. Altogether it took until 26 May 1999 for TF Hawk to become operationally ready.

During deployment Army aviators arrived in theater and began specific training for their novel mission and flying conditions. On 5 May an Apache crashed while training. Both pilots died. Another Apache also crashed for unknown reasons.

After a 78-day air campaign and with ground forces in Albania, the Yugoslav government signed a technical agreement on 9 June.

The rapid end of hostilities shifted much attention to supposed deficiencies of the Army and particularly to the Apaches' deployment. An article based on an email by BG Richard A. Cody to the incoming CSA caused a sensation. It claimed that pilots sent to fly the mission were undertrained and underequipped to fight the war they never fought in Kosovo. The article catalogued shortcomings. In September 1999 Hendrix responded to criticism about slowness and lack of value in the campaign, but his rebuttal drew little public notice.

In March 2001 the GAO published its report on Kosovo air operations as related to the Apaches. GAO said that 47 of 107 lessons were recommended for closure but it would take years to complete actions. GAO also said "the Army was not always successful in implementing lessons" and suggested that the Congress might want to have the Army report on progress.

In large part, the perceived failures of the Apaches in Kosovo started well before the campaign and had nothing to do with either aircraft or their crews. These reflected intra-NATO conflicts that excluded a ground option. With no ground threat, the Serbs had no need to concentrate. Their dispersal pointed against using the Apaches and let the Serbs survive NATO air strikes largely intact. The early decision to forego a land component commander compounded problems of employing the Apaches in an air-only campaign. The lack of a joint approach created needs to improvise procedures. Finally, faced with sharply conflicting views among senior military advisors, President Clinton agreed to deploy Apaches but withheld final approval to use them. Some concern about employing the Apaches sprang from an understanding that the Serbs were well supplied with MAN-PADS. A very real challenge was the mountainous terrain.

Setting aside criticisms that were either unfounded or exaggerated, TF Hawk revealed some important facts about the match between operational requirements and Aviation capabilities at that time. One issue was the ability of Aviation units to support round-the-clock operations. The conclusion drawn was that the regiment and squadron staffs were undermanned for continuous operations. Planning and mission-rehearsal equipment also had limitations that either made systems unusable or added workloads to compensate.

Possibly of greater importance was the Army's model of training. The impossibility of training for every mission with shrunken resources led to a model, used in Bosnia, of Alert, Train, Deploy, Fight. For TF Hawk, the model was Alert, Deploy, Train, Fight. The fact that the training was done in-theater may have at least exaggerated a sense that crews' overall proficiency was inadequate. Unusually difficult conditions, such as high altitudes and long flights requiring extra fuel, simply highlighted the extremes that Army aviators might encounter. Flying heavy reduced the margins of power available in an emergency. There were also hazards of flying at night in unmapped areas. Weather was a factor. The Apaches were deployed partly because they could operate despite the cloud cover that prevented the Air Force from doing so. Different factions, frequently changing locations, made it critical to track both friendly and enemy forces along the border.

Some of the difficulties encountered in TF Hawk reflected complexities inherent in Joint-Combined operations. The crunch came with the ATO. TF Hawk was responsible for developing potential engagement areas within Kosovo for deep attack missions by Apaches and ATACMS. The combined forces air component commander (CFACC) controlled all airspace. These two facts demanded coordination between TF Hawk and the combined air operations center to prevent fratricides and to give TF Hawk the support it needed for combat missions. Placing Aviation on the ATO cycle was a challenge. Aviation deep attacks required maximum flexibility to adjust for their targets. That flexibility conflicted with 72-hour ATO inputs. TF Hawk overcame this hurdle by identifying a projected F-Hour 72 hours in advance. F-Hour was the time for Army aircraft to cross the FLOT. Still, difficulties arose whenever TF Hawk moved its F-Hour within the ATO cycle less than 24 hours from execution, as happened several times.

Possibly a final consideration about employing the Apaches was Joint suppression of enemy air defenses (JSEAD). Weather caused the Air Force to suspend its operations. That suspension eliminated any JSEAD. NATO ROE prohibited Apaches conducting their own SEAD. So, they could not be committed into action.

Almost completely lost in the noise were two basic facts. First, the operation succeeded. Second, the decision to deploy but not employ the Apaches made good sense. Their presence made Serb defenses spread thinner. Beyond that, it made little sense to risk people and aircraft. So, the Apaches admirably fulfilled the role that had already proven successful in Bosnia.

As often the case, perception was far more powerful than reality. The criticisms of TF Hawk presented the incoming CSA, Eric K. Shinseki, with a serious challenge. Shinseki responded immediately. On 23 June 1999 he signed his "Intent of the Chief of Staff, Army," which said 'The world situation demands an Army that is strategically responsive.' From the principles laid out in this memorandum flowed Army Transformation that was the focus of Shinseki's tenure.

Afghanistan—Operation Enduring Freedom (OEF)

Following the attacks on 11 September 2001, the nation officially responded with military operations designed to clean out key training bases for the terrorist groups identified as responsible. The Al Qaeda network, headed by Osama bin Ladin, had headquarters and training bases in Afghanistan. There it had at least tacit acceptance of a radical, Islamic regime under the Taliban. As a result, in October 2001, Afghanistan became the first theater in what officially became the GWOT.

Special considerations for Aviation in Afghanistan

Combat operations in Afghanistan quickly highlighted features of special importance to Aviation in the post-Cold War operational environment. One feature was ground forces' extremely high reliance on Aviation to enable success. Conditions put a special premium on aerial movement and fire support just as had applied with airmobility in Vietnam. Of special note, as in Vietnam, were the small size of forces relative to the sizes of areas to cover, distances between points, ruggedness of terrain and weather, threats of dispersed enemy forces, and time available to respond. An assessment of lessons learned written in late 2002 noted the great value and relative success of airmobile operations. Anthony H. Cordesman proclaimed that light, highly mobile U.S. and allied ground forces consistently succeeded whenever engaged, even under near-worst-case conditions. Cordesman specifically mentioned the opening engagements in Operation Anaconda as exemplifying those conditions.

Another feature was the need to adapt tactics and missions of different aircraft in light of the extreme environments. High altitudes in Afghanistan combined with hot weather conditions and the desire of the enemy to avoid fighting on terms favorable to U.S. forces. Aircraft designed to Cold War-era parameters were over-stretched. Aviation often used Chinook helicopters for air assaults in place of the Black Hawks. Not accidentally, places that terrorist groups like Al Qaeda chose largely fell outside the Cold War-era parameters. Much of Afghanistan fell at altitudes above 3000 feet. Large parts of the country sat above 10,000 feet. Such isolated, hard-to-reach places made ideal havens for Al Qaeda and were exactly where some of those now opposing U.S. forces had learned and honed their skills fighting Soviet forces, which also used helicopters extensively, during the Cold War. Among the tactics the Mujahideen had developed were mining potential LZs, massing RPG fire against helicopters attempting to land, trying to overrun LZs before troops making an air assault could get established, and hugging forces so that helicopter gunships dared not fire at them for fear of hitting their own troops.

Afghanistan occasioned a definitive answer to a question that had lurked in the background ever since the Aviation Branch had stood up: Was Aviation still firmly committed to supporting the Soldier in the ground fight—or, as those thinking back to the days of the Army Air Corps put it, would Aviation 'fly away from the Army?' Poor intelligence on enemy strengths and capabilities was key in early fighting. Planners consistently underestimated enemy numbers, capabilities, and willingness to stand and fight. The result was that almost everything fell on the shoulders of the troops in the fight. They would discover the situation once they came into contact and either adapt to succeed or fail.

Of special importance, given the conditions of terrain and weather, as well as the nature of the enemy, were Apaches as direct fire support to forces in contact. Despite further development after ODS and great amount of hyperbole, sophisticated aerial munitions launched from fixed-wing aircraft had very limited and largely unknown effects. Even when targeting intelligence—which was often faulty—was good, it often took a direct hit from a large bomb to have any effect. One Al Qaeda CP survived five near misses with 2000-pound bombs and ceased effective operations only when ground forces seized it. Even though the thin air forced changes in tactics, the Apaches were able to operate at the high altitudes. Decisions made prior to deployment, as well as practicalities of lift in the theater and extremely bad weather just as operations were to start, all but took conventional tube artillery out of play. Instead, forces engaged in Operation Anaconda made the combat debut of a 120mm mortar, first fielded in 1994. This weapon, while good, was limited in critical ways—most importantly, that it was, itself, a stationary target. Conditions put a premium on responsive, direct, eyes-on aerial fires. AC-130 gunships supplied much support at night, but AC-130 operations after dawn were prohibited. Moreover, the wide turning radius of the AC-130 made eyes-on fire impossible under some conditions. In one instance, it caused a mission to abort. A-10s were not present for some of the key events.

CAS in the Shahikot—Operation Anaconda, March 2002

All of the strands came together in March 2002, when SOF, troops from the 10MTN, and Afghan allies went into the Shahikot Valley. This goal was to trap and capture or destroy Al Qaeda forces and leadership. Operation Anaconda had special importance for at least two reasons beyond its simple military outcome. The Shahikot Valley had been where Afghan fighters had, practically speaking, defeated Soviet forces during 1979–1982. Like the Ia Drang Valley in Vietnam, where the VC had defeated the French and where the airmobile 1CD got its first real test in combat, Operation Anaconda would test the newer U.S. forces in a place where other major ones had previously met defeat. The second, more immediate reason was that efforts to capture the key leaders of Al Qaeda and large numbers of Al Qaeda troops had failed. Those efforts had relied heavily on Afghan forces, with support by U.S. and other allied forces, to trap and destroy Al Qaeda in the Tora Bora area, which was heavily infested with caves. Unknown but certainly large numbers of leaders and followers had slipped safely across the border into neighboring Pakistan—which, like Cambodia and Laos in the Vietnam era, provided effective, safe haven. So, to a high degree, both military and national prestige were on the line in the Shahikot Valley.

2 March—Apaches of 3d Brigade, 101AB

The situation typified the old adage that no plan survives first contact with the enemy. In this case, mix-ups caused the plan to unravel even before that contact. An AC-130 gunship misidentified and attacked a column of U.S. and Afghan troops during the dark morning hours on 2 March 2002. Besides causing casualties and delay in a ground movement that was already struggling, the incident practically nullified other preparatory air strikes. This mix-up left the forces on the ground and those about to arrive in an air assault on their own against an entrenched enemy.

Events quickly became a test of Aviation—both men and machines—in close combat as happened so often in Vietnam. The troops from the ground column quickly found themselves under observed, preregistered, indirect fire. The U.S. troops called for help from Apaches circling nearby. The camouflage of the enemy, especially in the light conditions, made them almost invisible from the air. The Apaches were able to identify and quickly destroy a key mortar position.

Almost at the same moment, troops that had air-assaulted found themselves under fire. These troops quickly realized that the enemy was going after the helicopters. The technique was to use a focused barrage of small arms, machine guns, and RPGs. These were the same methods developed with marked success against the Soviets 20 years earlier and used against U.S. helicopters in Somalia. None of the Apache pilots had been under fire before. At first, none recognized that rounds were hitting their aircraft. A bullet cut electronics cables that controlled weapons on one Apache. So, that Apache could still fly but not fight.

Another Apache became a casualty through a chain of events related to designed limits. To prevent firing too many rounds, before launching, Apache crews set a limit on the number of 30mm rounds they could fire in a burst. Their ten-round limit was too few. While making a turn just above a ridgeline to make a second run on the enemy, the Apache put itself position for a gunner with a RPG. The RPG hit one of the Apache's rocket pods and caused one or more rocket motors to explode. The explosion damaged key systems. The line-of-sight characteristics of the Apache's radios prevented the wingman, just across the ridgeline, from hearing the distress call.

In the heat of the fight, the Apache crew members adapted to overcome the limits of their machines. The aircraft that could still fly but could not fight changed roles. CWO 4 Jim Hardy had started flying Cobras in teams with OH-58 Kiowa scout helicopters. Hardy and CWO 2 Stanley Pebsworth adopted the role of the unarmed scout in the Vietnam-era Pink Teams. Hardy and Pebsworth flew to draw the attention and fire of the enemy on the ground. The enemy's fire disclosed positions and made them vulnerable to those Apaches able to fire.

The built-in durability of the Apache and courage of the crew were proven when the crew of the damaged Apache landed and found their transmission was completely dry. At that point, the pilots were only about two kilometers out of the fight and deep in hostile territory. Rather than abandon the aircraft, Hardy, the senior maintenance man in the unit, decided to risk flying the Apache back, This meant relying on the design standard of 30 minutes' flight with a dry transmission. No one had actually flown an Apache like that before. To make matters worse, the trip back was over mountains that gave no place for an emergency landing. After 20 minutes of flight, Hardy and Pebsworth successfully landed the Apache in a brownout. Hardy's determination and flying skill led to his receiving

<u>Rotor & Wing</u> magazine's 2003 Helicopter Heroism Award. This award normally went to a crew for an exceptionally hazardous or difficult SAR or emergency-rescue mission.

At the end of the day, when all of the Apaches reassembled at the FARP, none had escaped damage. Many had taken far more hits than their pilots realized. Almost all rotor blades had holes through them. Several drive shafts were similarly shot through. Within 45 minutes, the first Apache out of action was restored and ready to go back into the fight. Post-combat assessment showed extent of damage to the Apaches that would have taken down most other aircraft. Thus, the survivability designed into the Apache had again been proven.

The events in the Shahikot should have provided a clear answer to any questions about Aviation's commitment to Soldiers in the ground fight. The engagements that put Apaches in position to suffer the damage they did directly reflected their role as an integral part of the ground commander's battle. Apaches engaged directly and close enough to be personal. For example, the brigade tactical CP, which landed by Black Hawk during the fight, came under close fire from a squad-size enemy in the rocks. After about 30 minutes of ground fire failed to subdue the enemy, the commander called in two Apaches. These aircraft quickly killed the enemy with rockets and 30mm cannon fire. When the brigade commander called for Air Force CAS, he had to give special authorization to drop bombs within 300 meters—a distance defined as "danger close." To respond to the calls of one commander pinned down by small-arms and RPG fire, an Apache had to attack a position within 150 meters of the friendly troops. When the Apache had used all of his rockets and 30mm ammunition, he had to resort to using a HELLFIRE to finish the job. Because of the closeness of the target and the fact that a HELLFIRE had to travel 500 meters before arming, the pilot had to fly the Apache backwards until he was far enough away to let the HELLFIRE work. When a bullet broke his canopy and cut his face, CPT William A. Ryan and CWO 3 Jody Killburn were firing on a target between 200 and 300 meters in front of them. By the end of the day, the Apaches had fired 540 rounds of 30mm cannon ammunition, several hundred rockets, and the one HELLFIRE.

Soldiers on the ground recognized the value of the Apaches to them that day. The brigade commander, COL Frank Wiercinski, said that the Apaches clearly saved the day for his TF. MG Franklin Hagenbeck, the 10MTN commander, called Ryan and his people 'magnificent' and praised the Apaches as making a key difference. Possibly most significant was a visit to the Apache unit by a 23-year-old, enlisted tactical air controller. He had become separated from the rest of the unit.

A machine gun pinned him down and fire destroyed his satellite radio. A RPG had barely missed him, and an Al Qaeda mortar crew was walking rounds onto his refuge, He had resigned himself to the idea that he was about to die when an Apache swooped in and attacked his attackers. The diversion let him slip away and survive. He wanted to thank the crew that had saved him.

As almost always, success in the air reflected the effort of people on the ground. Ground crews, who expected a humdrum day, leaped into action when reports of an actual fight came back. SSG Chad Bardwell, in charge of maintenance for Ryan's unit, scrambled to get ammunition forward to the FARP. He put together a team with three more Soldiers. They flew to the FARP. They found six Apaches waiting for them. The condition of the Apaches shocked him. The maintainers went to work to make as many flyable as possible. Within an hour they had two Apaches ready, although CPT Ryan decided to send only one back into the fight. Meanwhile the ground crews transferred rockets from the aircraft that were out of the action to those going in.

Hindsight on Apaches in the Shahikot

The fight in the Shahikot Valley provided both answers and questions. It clearly showed the durability of the aircraft and the commitment of Army aviators. To many, the performance of the Apaches in this fight answered doubts about the aircraft and its role that had arisen, fairly or otherwise, out of TF Hawk in 1999. Some, however, questioned the events in terms of the Army's doctrine and tactics. While escort was a defined mission for the Apaches, the kind of close-in firefighting that erupted on 2 March seemed to fall well outside that role as defined. Some questioned whether it really was a good thing to have Apaches engaged in combat that entailed such high risk to both people and aircraft.

One result of the Apaches' success was a renewed emphasis on making them rapidly deployable. MG Richard A. Cody, who commanded the 101AB and had commanded the Apache battalion engaged in TF Normandy during ODS, stressed the importance of mobility for the Apaches. He had become the Army's DCSOPS. In light of Operation Anaconda, he pressed for ways to put several Apaches onto an Air Force C-5 Galaxy. He wanted to deploy the Apaches the same way SOA could deploy its Little Birds.

A revolution in tactics—returning to and relearning high-energy, running and diving firing techniques

Experiences in Afghanistan fostered a change in gunship tactics, much as experiences in Lam Son 719 and at An Loc had changed flying 30 years earlier. Within less than a year and a half, a major shift occurred. That included developing specific training and publishing revised doctrine. The change reflected new demands for providing direct fire extremely close to friendly troops as well as new perceptions of what kinds of weapons most threatened helicopters providing close support. The April 2002 edition of the Apache Longbow team training handbook included diving firing as one of the minimum requirements to be covered in classes. In October 2002 a program to train the trainer on what had become called close combat attack (CCA) started. This training focused on engagement at ranges defined as danger close—defined as very close to friendly troops and varying by the type of munition. "Danger close" was defined in terms of the probability that a weapon hitting at a specific distance from a prone Soldier would incapacitate him for five minutes after the strike. A 500-pound bomb with a laser guidance package might come as close as 200 meters. The types of munitions commonly found on attack helicopters allowed getting closer to friendly troops without creating the same risk. 2.75-inch rockets with various warheads could be targeted as close as 175 meters. A HELLFIRE missile could come as close as 75 meters. By January 2003 the teaching and use of CCA techniques had gained special attention in a master gunnery conference at Fort Rucker and senior Aviation leadership agreed that changes had to occur. MANPADS posed a special hazard to high-flying aircraft. Flying low made good sense against those threats. The conditions in Afghanistan were almost the reverse. In Afghanistan pilots had to provide precision fire support in close fighting where no significant threat from MANPADS existed. Pilots quickly found that the main threat was RPGs and small arms. To get away from those, pilots needed to fly higher. The altitudes forced pilots into using rockets where their 30mm cannon would have been better. The pilots could not use their cannons while flying with the auxiliary fuel tanks, because they did not know how to deal with the extra weight. Pilots then started using tactics that they had not learned and took themselves into situations involving power management that younger crews did not know how to handle. Accidents resulting from inadequate grasp of maneuvering flight fundamentals were increasing.

By the summer of 2003 important decisions had been made and changes were underway. In July 2003 the USAAVNC published a Power Management

Handbook that addressed high-energy techniques. On 21 August 2003 a revised FM 3–04.111, <u>Aviation Brigades</u>, published standardized procedures across the Army. Thus, in response to conditions that almost stood the lessons at the end of the Vietnam War on their head, Aviation had gone through another revolution in flying tactics.

Lift in Afghanistan—Chinooks in adaptive roles and calls for more

In Afghanistan the combinations of rugged terrain, high altitudes, long distances, and sometimes weather conditions put a spotlight on the differing capabilities across the Army's cargo, lift, and utility fleets. Chinooks became the workhorses and led to their being used in all kinds of roles. One Chinook, besides landing troops for the air assault on 2 March 2002, provided MEDEVAC for the wounded from the fratricide incident. Realizing that one wounded WO was barely clinging to life, the pilots pushed their Chinook so fast that they popped out windows.

The combinations of distances, altitude, and lift requirements in Afghanistan also led to renewed emphasis on intra-theater airlift. A partial answer to that deficiency was upgrading the Chinooks from the D to the F-model. That included a new rotor head that required less maintenance, cockpit upgrades, and enhanced air transportability, and a 27 percent increase in power with 3 percent reduction in fuel consumption. Advocates even outside the Army still saw a need for much more capability than even the CH-47F could bring. This call seemed consistent with Army efforts to acquire a much larger, more advanced Air Maneuver Transport.

CH47 Loading Soldiers in Afghanistan

Operation Iraqi Freedom (OIF)

Operations were still ongoing in Afghanistan when a U.S.-led coalition launched a major assault on Iraq that quickly toppled the regime of its longstanding dictator, Saddam Hussein. The major, fighting phase of what some called the Second Gulf War lasted longer than the first one but completely removed the Baathist regime from power. On 20 March 2003 President George W. Bush announced that coalition forces had begun major military operations against Iraq. On 1 May 2003 the President declared major combat operations ended. By then scarcely any evidence of an organized Iraqi military existed. However, restoring order and establishing a new, democratic Iraqi regime proved to be long, hard work against a vicious insurgency. Struggles continued well into 2005 and created expectations that the withdrawal of U.S. forces from Iraq might be several years away.

Special conditions affecting Aviation in Iraq

Aviation played a key part in both the initial and post-combat phases of OIF. With rare exception, Aviation operations in Iraq did not face the challenges of high, rugged terrain of Afghanistan. The severity of the climate, however, was still a factor—most notably, extreme temperatures and sandstorms. Both of these conditions were hard on both people and equipment. The international backdrop to OIF also put a special premium on the kind of mobility that Aviation brought to the battlefield. Unlike the first Gulf War, which had overwhelming international support, many nations did not support military operations in Iraq. As a result, lack of basing and overflight rights added logistical obstacles for this campaign. By 22 March, ground forces had already matched the longest maneuver of the 1991 war in one fourth of the time. The speed of movement and distances covered created at least as great logistics challenges as had driven the 1982 Army Aviation Systems Program Review (AASPR) to envision Aviation lift as a key enabler for the future battlefield.

A key reason given for invading Iraq had been Saddam Hussein's obstruction of UN monitoring Iraq's destruction of its weapons of mass destruction (WMD). This cause of war set some of the battlefield conditions. At least some Aviation units preparing for OIF trained extensively with operating under such conditions. For example, Apache Longbow crews practiced and flew their initial missions all the while wearing chemical protective gear. Technology had improved just since ODS. Rather than finding the gear a major impediment and heat stress becoming a problem, the crews found the extra warmth pleasant. Living in an austere environment, the crews often slept under the aircraft and nights were cool.

Threats to Aviation—ground fire and weather

Because overwhelming air superiority was present from the start, the major threat to coalition aircraft came from ground-based air defenses (AD). By mid-March what remained was a wide dispersal of several thousand small antiaircraft machineguns, thousands of SAMs and MANPADS, and large numbers of small arms and RPGs. In this regard, conditions in OIF devolved toward near-mid-intensity warfare—similar to but much less intense than in Lam Son 719 and the last year of the Vietnam War.

Throughout operations, the environment continued to be a major foe. Every Apache Longbow battalion lost at least one aircraft to an accident in brownout conditions. Dust also forced changes in maintenance practices. These conditions put a huge responsibility on maintenance personnel. In part the success in overcoming the effects of the environment reflected the commitment of the civilian contractors who provided support. With the 1st Battalion, 3d Aviation Brigade, every civilian who provided support volunteered to accompany the unit into action and went forward. That fact, in conjunction with taking available spare parts with the unit, overcame the bad effects of the environment.

Aviation capabilities—near-digital battlefield

Much more than in ODS, air and ground operations were simultaneous and integrated, as opposed to sequential. Advances in technologies connecting 'sensors' to 'shooters'—and, most importantly, to decision makers—made these conditions possible. GEN Tommy Franks, commanding Coalition forces, had four screens in front of his desk that he monitored constantly. One provided outputs from the various news media. Two displayed the locations of ground and air units at the points of contact. The last had the current intelligence estimate.

Great efforts were made before going into combat to provide situational awareness (SA) throughout the forces. The lateness and limitations on systems available meant that these efforts were only partly successful. Rapid insertion of technology called Blue Force Tracker (BFT) into both air and ground units gave unprecedented precision and currency to information on locations down to company level and on many helicopters. This satellite-based system provided both precise location and over-the-horizon communications. BFT contributed to what appeared to be a dramatic decrease in fratricides. A preliminary analysis of the major combat phase of OIF showed fratricide causing about 11 percent of 115 U.S. battle deaths, compared to 24 percent in ODS. Limited resources and the speed to field, however, meant that the picture was one-way. During the 3d Infantry Division (3ID) advance, Apache Longbow units and ground commanders took about 45 minutes to decide with certainty that a company-sized formation of armored vehicles in front of them was not friendly.

Strikes on key C2 complexes, aimed to kill key leaders, coincided with ground operations. Air Force assets—including Hunter UAVs—provided targeting information for Apache Longbows. The quality of intelligence as it passed down to the shooter levels was not always good. In 3ID Apache Longbow crews often provided the key tactical reconnaissance for the division.

The overall goal, largely achieved, was to wage an 'effects-based' campaign. There was high integration between SOF and conventional forces. The latter particularly involved the use of armored forces in urban terrain—quite contrary to conventional thinking. There was little in the way of calculated counterattacks. However, the ferocity of loyalist, Fedayeen fighters impressed U.S. troops. Fedayeen tactics, such as deploying children in front of them as shields against aerial attacks, also made it hard for U.S. forces to fight them.

OIF saw the battlefield debut of new weapons, but older technologies also showed their continuing value. OIF saw the first battlefield use of the radio frequency (RF) HELLFIRE missile. This system was designed to be fire and forget—that is, able to steer itself to the target without further tracking by the launching aircraft. In practice, in the often-severe conditions of dust, the missile proved less beneficial than under its design conditions. Where friendly vehicles were operating close to enemy ones, the possibility that a lost missile might find the wrong target seemed too high to risk. So Apaches often used the older, laser-designated HELLFIREs as a safety precaution. Apaches also used the unguided, 2.75-inch rockets and 30mm gun extensively. In many instances, the target did not justify expending an expensive missile, and unguided rockets could often do the job effectively. The unguided rockets were also quite good for SEAD in a pinch and created an unmistakable reference point for sorting out friend and foe in a close fight. Thus, these rockets became another tool for preventing fratricides.

As in ODS, Apaches fired among the first shots in the campaign. The first mission of the Apache Longbows of the 3ID was to take out the Iraqi observation posts along the border with Kuwait. In this case, the mission was originally planned to be a Joint/combined-arms operation, with Air Force strike aircraft and Tomahawk Land Attack Missiles, as well as ground-based artillery and the Apaches. As events developed, the mission fell entirely to the Apaches and artillery.

Calibrating and bore-sighting an Apache

The overall intent to use armor forces within urban areas led to tactics evolving on the run. There had been some expectation that operations would be somewhat like ODS, with forces in open warfare. That idea proved to be wrong and forced adjustments for the use of attack aircraft in conjunction with tanks. The tanks could go into built-up areas and remain generally survivable, although in some cases Iraqi fighters with RPGs successfully swarmed tanks. Aircraft flying above the fight were not so well protected. Instead of working over-the-shoulder, attack aircraft shifted to moving ahead to work other areas. Once the division crossed into Baghdad on the famous Thunder Run, Apaches flew outside the city, protecting the flanks.

Importance of preparations

Preparations played a large role in Aviation success throughout the initial, combat phase of OIF. 3ID Aviation deployed about 45 days before the first missions. Before leaving home station, 1st Battalion with the Apache Longbows had taken precautions for the harsh environment. That included taping the rotor blades. This prior work proved invaluable. In the conditions that prevailed in the theater, it was almost impossible to tape the blades satisfactorily. The division commander also allowed the unit to put three of its aircraft into a phase overhaul, even though that meant the unit could not meet standards of availability as prescribed by DA. However, this prior work gave the division's aviation a cushion of extra hours these aircraft would be available to fight, once operations actually began. Other units, like the 159th Aviation Brigade in the 101AB, took similar steps. Aviation units also prepared packages of spare parts to cover the contingencies they could foresee. PEOs and PMs made great efforts to find and push as many parts to the deploying units as possible. The DCSOPS, LTG Cody, backed this channeling of resources to the high-priority units, even if that channeling meant shortages elsewhere.

Imbalances in the amount of experience among pilots led to mixing crews to create equal levels across the unit. Units also revised SOPs. Advances in simulation helped greatly. 1st Battalion, 3d Aviation Brigade, used its LCT to train extensively on desert scenarios. 159th Aviation Brigade was able to capitalize on experience with dusty conditions in Afghanistan to help prepare inexperienced pilots for conditions in Iraq.

Combat phase, 19 March—1 May

Even more than during ODS, Iraqi forces could not confront U.S. and allied forces in a standup fight. The strategy for OIF, in fact, called for trapping Republican

Guard forces so that they could be destroyed. Estimates were that other Iraqi forces would quickly fold once the Republican Guard units were destroyed.

As in ODS, actual events tended to outrun the schedule, but not without temporary disruptions that forced important changes. One of these directly affected the goal of trapping and destroying the Republican Guard. The 101AB movement was based on this event. 159th Aviation Brigade was to establish two FARPs and to operate those for 3–4 days. These would provide "lily pads" for aircraft moving forward. Weather intervened. A fierce storm delayed operations briefly. Once the storm lifted, the enemy had withdrawn.

During 22–30 March, events moved rapidly. Since the 4ID could not enter through Turkey, a combination of SOF and Kurdish militia handled the northern front, where preservation of oil fields was vital to the reconstruction of Iraq once fighting ended. In the south, U.S. and British forces occupied Basra against Iraqi resistance that was stronger than expected. V Corps, with 3ID and the 1st Marine Expeditionary Force (1 MEF) moved toward Baghdad.

Having to move all forces from the south made the capture of key bridges across interlacing waterways a high priority. Four bridges at Nasiriyah—two at its north and two at its south end—would aid movement of the 3ID and 1 MEF to Baghdad. The 11th Iraqi Infantry Division was defending the town, on an island about two and a half miles square, composed mostly of one-and two-story cinderblock and mud buildings. Apache Longbows provided CCA to capture a key bridge across the Euphrates. In the process, the Longbows destroyed several T-55 tanks and several other armored vehicles. During 22–23 March, Fedayeen fighters entered the town. Nasiriyah, like Basra, became an occasion for a week of heavy fighting.

On 23 March the 101AB made its first air assault into Iraq. After delay from a violent sandstorm on 25 March, U.S. forces moving toward Baghdad encountered three Republican Guard divisions. Intensive air attacks softened the Guard divisions. On 28 March the 101AB carried off the longest helicopter assault operation to date. More than 200 Kiowa Warriors, Chinooks, Apaches, and Black Hawks flew to FOBs south of Karbala. On 3 April the push to seize Baghdad began. 3ID captured the international airport on the west side of the city. By 9 April, Baghdad was occupied. On 14 April U.S. forces took Tikrit, Saddam Hussein's hometown and the seat of strong support for his regime.

Apache-delivered HELLFIRE as weapon of choice—minimizing collateral damage in the war for hearts and minds

A major goal, throughout the planning and execution of OIF, was minimizing collateral damage from military operations. This concern reflected at least two larger goals. One was to preserve the Iraqi infrastructure as much as possible to speed the recovery of the country once Saddam Hussein's regime was gone. Another was to help win the war for hearts and minds, both of Iraqis and of others watching the course of events around the world. These two goals largely explained the unprecedented use of PGMs. Two-thirds of almost 30,000 munitions dropped were precision-guided. In some cases, Apache helicopters with the HELLFIRE missile became the weapon of choice for specific missions over the PGMs of the other services. Because of its warhead, a HELLFIRE could take out a target with much less damage than that caused by the smallest Air Force PGM.

Reminiscent of Organic Army Aviation in World War II, Apaches provided coordinates for artillery, including the ATACMS.

Ground support for Aviation in OIF

A key to the success in the combat phase of OIF was the speed of logistics support. British observers traveling with U.S. forces were impressed at how quickly resupply could occur in the middle of nowhere. They reported seeing dozens of logistics vehicles of all sorts rush up to combat units when they stopped, quickly refuel and resupply, and vanish again, allowing the combat units to resume the push. The ground support to Aviation units was equally important and impressive. Members of 2d Squadron, 6th Cavalry Regiment, and its sister maintenance battalion, the 7th Battalion, 159th Aviation Regiment, headed north from their base camp days ahead of the battle to set up a FARP. They started on 30 March and stopped that night south of Karbala. The convoy quickly set up and refueled aircraft that first night. They left again at 0500. It took 11 hours to travel 18 miles. They pulled up behind the 3ID's 1st Brigade south of the Karbala Gap. Because of a possible chemical threat, they donned their protective gear. They then followed the 3ID through the Karbala Gap. They stopped about 1100, in the desert, about 40 miles from downtown Baghdad. Within 30 minutes they were receiving aircraft. They then worked eleven hours without a rest. Switching to around-the-clock shifts they worked for three days, supporting both the 2–6 Cavalry and 1–3 Aviation Regiment. After Baghdad International Airport fell, the pilots returned to camp that night. The refuelers returned the next day.

11th Aviation Regiment on 23–24 March 2003

In the early morning hours of 24 March, an incident occurred involving Apache Longbows of the 11th Aviation Regiment that renewed the long-running controversy over Apaches and the whole issue of the Army's employment of armed helicopters.

The basic facts were fairly straightforward. The 11th was supposed to carry out a deep attack against the 2d Armored Brigade of the Medina Division of the Republican Guard near Najaf. While flying over the town, the Apaches were hit by a storm of small-arms fire. Apparently this was part of a well-set ambush. As the Apaches reached the built-up area, all of the lights went off and then came on again—a signal to armed men in the town to fire skyward. Later it was found that an Iraqi major general had used a cell phone to call air defenders in the town that the Apaches were approaching. Fire seemed to be coming at the helicopters from everywhere. The bullets caused damage of varying severity to all the aircraft. One Longbow went down, and its two pilots were captured. Iraq tried to make propaganda capital out of the incident. Iraqi television ran footage of the Longbow sitting in a field, with Iraqis around it waving rifles. The Iraqis even claimed that a farmer had shot the Apache down with an old shotgun. This footage aired widely in the Arab world. It took a month to restore the 11th to full capability.

The incident led to an immediate reassessment of tactics. LTG William Wallace, V Corps commander, immediately said that lessons came from the event. Within about eighteen hours, COL William T. Wolf, the 11th Aviation Regiment commander, set up a telephone conference call with the aviation brigades of the 101AB and 3ID. COL Wolf and his S-3 sat down with squadron commanders, discussed everything, and made recommendations. The squadron commanders, in turn, discussed it at the squadron level, all the way down to the individual pilots. The learning and passage of lessons proved effective. Two nights later, the 101st conducted a similar operation. This time, though, the Apaches operated in smaller teams, took ground-based artillery with them, and used Air Force strike aircraft to shape the fight. As soon as the 101st met resistance, they backed off, bringing in A-10s and F-16s to try to take out the enemy. That worked well, as shown clearly on 31 March 2003. The 101st lost no aircraft and had little or no damage from small-arms fire.

Lessons to be learned may have been fewer than appeared on the surface. The Army's preliminary history of OIF, written by Center for Army Lessons Learned (CALL), said "the failed mission suffered from a classic 'first-battle' dynamic."

CALL noted a chain of events reflecting "the inevitable fog and friction of combat." Among contributors to this chain was the eagerness of members of the 11th to get into the fight. While this eagerness partly reflected egos, it also reflected recognition that the rapid advance left the 3ID with fewer ground combat units. The Apaches wanted to support the ground troops. There was also a matter of timing with weather. The attack battalions were the only assets the corps commander had just then to shape the fight. Extremely bad weather was expected within 24 hours. So the night of 23–24 March was the only chance to shape the battlefield for the 3ID's movement. The weather advanced the plan for the attack by a day, giving less time for logistics vehicles to reach the regiment before needed. This fact strongly shaped events.

Much criticism of the incident focused on the Army's sending the Apaches in without support of more powerful, Air Force aircraft. These criticisms overlooked both the conditions and the plan. First, the threat as known was not as actually encountered. That fact suggested a deficiency in available intelligence more than in the Apaches' employment. The Apaches' mission was meant, in part, to overcome gaps in intelligence about enemy force disposition. The best intelligence came from Hunter UAVs, usually ran about 24 hours behind events, and did not account for current positions of vehicles. Moreover, nothing at the time tracked or disrupted the cellular telephone network that the Iraqis were using to move forces around. Moreover, until the encounter of the 11th, no one fully appreciated that the main fight would be with irregular forces—the Fedayeen—rather than the regular Iraqi armed forces. By contrast, the Iraqis had good, tactical intelligence—human intelligence. After the fact, there was considerable discussion about the lack of security in the assembly area that allowed Iraqi civilian vehicles to drive around close to the aircraft during the preparations and concerns that this allowed alerts to be passed to the enemy. While the movement around the aircraft may have posed an immediate force-protection risk, this close-in movement seems unlikely to have had any significant value for OPSEC. It was relatively easy to track the movement of the Aviation units, because they raised a dust cloud that was visible from as far away as 50 kilometers when they lifted off.

There were clearly serious weaknesses in SEAD. The 11th had no immediate artillery support. The unit augmenting them had ATACMS. Difficulties in timing and accuracy of such long-range, indirect fires were more difficult because knowledge of the exact locations of air defense systems was spotty at best. For this mission, the corps planned to fire 32 ATACMS missiles. The corps also planned for Joint SEAD involving electronic warfare aircraft and air strikes on suspected air defenses. However, the actual time of arrival over the target slipped. The air operations center apparently did not realize that fact. So there was no Joint SEAD for support. The 11th Aviation commander, however, did not know that fact at the time. Possibly complicating this situation further was a decision not to have fixed-wing and rotary-wing in same airspace at the same time. In any case, the types of SEAD available—ATACMS and Joint Direct Attack Munitions—were ineffective against the actual type of threat.

Weather and terrain played a large part in unfolding events. The powdery dust affected preparations. Refueling operations took much longer than usual as refuelers went down the long line of aircraft. Moreover, with less than half of the planned fuel trucks on hand, the regiment could not refuel all aircraft. There was an expenditure of time in deciding which aircraft got fuel, and some swapping of crews and aircraft to adjust for which ones had fuel. In the end, COL Wolf discovered that his C2 helicopter did not have enough fuel. With 31 aircraft refueled the regiment leaders believed they had enough for the mission. Dust conditions were so bad that one aircraft crashed during takeoff.

In hindsight, LTG William S. Wallace, the V Corps commander, saw several aspects of the events that escaped the widespread publicity of the incident. Some had long-term implications for the Army beyond just Aviation. Procedurally nothing was wrong. The go/no-go brief before the 23 March operation was the most rehearsed piece. Everyone voted to go. Even so, several things were not right. These included confidence in the tactical intelligence. Analysis did not recognize adjustments the enemy had made since ODS. Enforcement of the no-fly zone in Iraq had given the enemy a decade to enhance tactics against Coalition aircraft. The fire the Apaches encountered was not random. Interspersed in groups was someone shooting heavy tracers. Intelligence thus under appreciated enemy capabilities in small arms and using cell phones for C2. The experience of the 11th also pointed to limitations in the traditional notion of SEAD. The AD system Apaches encountered was not susceptible to traditional SEAD: There was no radar signature, and the weapons involved were hidden behind someone's bed until needed. The 11th's experience also pointed to the perennial problems in ground logistical support. The shortfall in refueling capability where needed caused a delay. That delay desynchronized the planned SEAD. Compounding these difficulties were deficiencies in long-haul communications that left Wallace without information that would have let him help.

From all these things, Wallace concluded several things of importance for the future. One was that the more asymmetric the battlespace, the less young intelligence officers could detect. That relationship meant that commanders would have to be comfortable operating without much information. It also meant that forces must be so solid in fundamentals that they could react and succeed despite the circumstances. The lack of tactical intelligence preceding the 11th's attack also pointed to a need for more UAVs to provide surveillance and reconnaissance, although how many remained in question. There was also a clear need for increased teaming between air and ground efforts. When both friend and foe might be wearing civilian clothes and carrying an AK-47 rifle, the person on the ground would likely have a better sense of the situation than the person in the cockpit. Operations in urban environments also meant lighting that silhouettes aircraft—an environment very unlike the conditions at the National Training Center. Wallace concluded that every fight would be Joint. If Apaches go deep, there was a question of how far they should go. Wallace believed that more needed to be done with JAATs. If Army aviators fly and shoot long-range, they must know how to read the ATO. The 11th's experiences had clear implications for C2 systems. Commanders need better airborne C2. Every time that Wallace flew, he lost communications at least briefly. Wallace noted the importance of reconnaissance. He saw that as a mission, not an organization. The solution was not having more reconnaissance units but having more units that can do reconnaissance. Finally, the rule of thumb needed to be that, if weather was too bad, don't fly.

While many focused on the extent of damage to the Apache Longbows and the downing of the one crew, the outcome testified to the durability of the Apache helicopter and the quality of its pilots. Some aircraft had upwards of thirty hits by everything from RPGs down to 7.62mm gunfire. Hits were everywhere. Whole weapons systems exploded on the wing, but the aircraft survived. With the FLIR systems unavailable to navigate, the pilot in the front seat—the one with lesser experience—flew these aircraft back using NVG under bad conditions—cloud cover and little or no illumination.

One result of the 11th Aviation Regiment experience was changes in training. The 11th's experience reinforced the need for training on running, diving firing, as well as SERE training for all Army aviators.

Apache shootdown in Karbala

CWOs David S. Williams and Ronald D. Young, Jr., had a new fight on their hands once their Apache Longbow went down. Over the next 22 days their experience showed the need for a kind of training that had not been readily available to Army aviators, although it had been a DOD requirement since 1998. Of the two, only Williams had received this training. He had it as an enlisted member of 160 SOAR. Williams thus became the second Army aviator since the end of the Cold War who had become a POW and also had SERE training—the first being CWO Durant in Somalia.

Iraqis heard the aircraft go down and converged quickly. Only after going some distance did Young and Williams realize, as people were shooting at them, that they still had the lip lights glowing on their helmets. With nothing but their 9mm pistols and Iraqis approaching, the pilots went into a ditch, trying to hide in the water. As they moved along, they grew extremely cold. Fearing hypothermia, they climbed out of the mud. Suddenly angry Iraqis surrounded them. Unsure what to do, they sat with their arms straight out, then got up on their knees with their hands behind their heads. The Iraqis started yelling louder. The pilots thought possibly they needed to stand up. Someone nearby fired at them, and other Iraqis began beating and kicking them. Then the pilots were tied up and put on a road that led into town. A growing crowd followed, kicking and hitting them. Taken inside a house, the pilots were searched thoroughly: Everything but their flight suits and boots was taken. Inside a police station in Karbala, Iraqis questioned the pilots for hours. There, a video was shot and later broadcast. After two days in Karbala, the pilots were driven in separate vehicles to Baghdad. There, during the heavy bombing, the two men were housed in a prison with thick walls and a thin tin roof. For 11 days and nights they heard and felt the bombing, which shook their prison walls. Hearing U.S. tanks roar through the capital encouraged them. By 9 April, when the statue of Saddam was pulled down, guards had rushed the pilots out of the prison and were driving them from place to place. Finally they reached a small village, three hours north of Baghdad. There the prisoners were kept bound, blindfolded and locked inside a house, under constant guard. Marines rescued them. By the time the prisoners were loaded into an American vehicle, Williams and Young had each lost 25 pounds. After a brief stop in Kuwait to see their commanders, they were flown to Germany for medical treatment and counseling. They then returned to Fort Hood, where family was waiting. Next day they met President Bush and were treated as war heroes.

Williams volunteered for assignment to Fort Rucker to help expand SERE training. By early 2005, the decision had been made to implement a full SERE course at Fort Rucker. In fact, the school model was changed to put three weeks of SERE at the beginning of the course. That way, the Army would be assured that anyone going through flight training would have shown the ability to endure the rigors of SERE.

Transition to a new Iraq—a three-block war

Even while fighting continued in Baghdad, conditions developed that called for a different type of military operations. Mixed with celebrations of the fall of the regime was a widespread state of lawlessness. In the first days, it was hard, if not impossible, to distinguish simple disorder from insurgency. Soon it was clear that insurgency was a real presence that required action. Iraq was becoming what former Marine Commandant Charles Krulak had called the 'three block war'—combat operations on one block, constabulary tasks on the next, and humanitarian relief on the third. In this environment, success or failure could easily hinge on what Krulak called 'the Strategic Corporal'—the junior enlisted Soldier or NCO at a critical place and time where a single act could have national or even international results. Such situations had occurred in Somalia and most named military operations since the end of the Cold War, but in Iraq the three-block war became the norm.

The insurgency posed a serious threat to overall success in Iraq. Fighters in this insurgency had various origins and could seldom survive a stand-up fight with regular troops. However, they created a constant climate of uncertainty and fear through attacks on a wide array of people.

Combating the insurgency became an overriding priority for U.S. forces. The task was huge because so much weaponry was loose in Iraq. A large and continuing effort went into raids to collect munitions. Between March and September 2004, the 1ID alone confiscated over 24 million pounds of enemy munitions.

Aviation played several key parts under these conditions. In widely dispersed conditions as existed in Iraq, Aviation was the only thing a commander could move around to deal with uncertainty. One role of Aviation was simply to provide a safer means of movement around the country. Aviation also provided a deterrent to at least some insurgent activities. Helicopters routinely escorted convoys through treacherous areas. Ground troops told pilots that things went better when the helicopters were in the air. Rapid response to a variety of situations was a common mission. Sometimes this kind of action saved lives and led to capturing those intent on doing harm. Other incidental missions included SAR. Sometimes these missions proved dangerous in their own right. On 25 January 2005, a Kiowa Warrior went down in the Tigris River while conducting a search for Soldiers whose watercraft had capsized. Both pilots, 1LT Adam G. Mooney and CWO Patrick Dorff, were lost.

The antiair threat in post-combat Iraq—MANPADS and RPGs

Through the post-combat operations phase, helicopters continued to operate under a serious antiair weapons threat. Between the declared end of major combat on 1 May 2003 and mid-January 2004, more than a dozen U.S. helicopters went down in Iraq. In November 2003 a missile brought down a Chinook and killed 16 onboard. On 2 January 2004 fire shot down an OH-58D Kiowa Warrior, killing CPT Kimberly Hampton, who was the first female Army pilot to die under those circumstances. On 8 January a MEDEVAC Black Hawk went down, possibly to a missile, killing nine. Among the victims was CWO Aaron A. Weaver, who had survived ground combat as a Ranger in Somalia and had become an OH-58D Kiowa Warrior pilot. Weaver was on his way to a routine checkup for cancer, for which he had fought to get a waiver so he could deploy to Iraq with his unit. He had two brothers who were also Army pilots—one whom he had just visited in Baghdad and another who was preparing to deploy to Iraq.

Air Force GEN John W. Handy, commanding U.S. Transportation Command (TRANSCOM), considered missiles the greatest threat. Handy especially worried about MANPADS. Their numbers in Iraq were unknown but presumably large. A related concern was that the harsh environment made the AN/ALQ-144 infrared countermeasures set only marginally effective. The pervasive dust got into bearings, forced extensive maintenance, and sometimes made the systems malfunction.

Others were less convinced of the MANPADS threat and more concerned about small arms and RPGs. COL Andrew Milani, commanding the 160 SOAR, said that the main threat to Aviation was small arms. He noted that small arms were cheap, easily available, and deadly. A fifty-dollar RPG had shot down a $43 million aircraft in Afghanistan. Sometimes crews simply did not know they were being engaged. Milani's first priority was to develop a system that would detect the sound when small arms engaged an aircraft and would alert the aircrews.

Improving the survivability of Army aircraft against these threats assumed a high priority within the Army. Among the key criteria for a new aircraft to replace the OH-58D Kiowa Warrior was survivability. By June 2004 requirements including being able to survive small arms fire up to 7.62mm and having ballistic protection for both the crew and vital components. The aircraft also required ASE to protect against both MANPADS and mobile, radar-directed AD systems. Among the priorities given to the funds salvaged from canceling the Comanche was buying missile avoidance systems.

OH-58D Kiowa Warriors on the line in Iraq

Launching a Raven UAV in Iraq

Postscript—Looking forward

What you have read traced the story of Aviation in its key drivers and dynamics, rather than through a strict chronology, up into 2005. In reading the draft, at least one person asked, "And now where?"

The future of Aviation

Everything about Aviation is on a fast-moving train. By the time this book is printed, some of what it says will already be obsolete. Also, predicting the future is the riskiest of businesses for historians. Futurists talk about cones of plausibility—projecting right and left limits on what seems likely to happen, based on patterns of past events. Even those can break down badly. So what is to say from all that has gone before about where Aviation is going?

Seven themes provided the framework for this overview of Aviation spanning a century and a half—People, Ideas, Technology, Organization, Support to the ground commander, Versatility and Flexibility of Aviation, and the Army Values. It is worth a quick review and a little speculation based on these.

People will necessarily remain the bedrock of Aviation. That fact gives room for great optimism. Aviation has continued to draw and retain high-quality people, despite pulls from outside organizations seeking that talent and pushes from sometimes-difficult conditions of service. The way they get things done reflects the quality of the people. This book is an example. One person did not write it. It was the collective, cumulative effort of dozens of people who gave more or less time, attention, and material support. Some, sad to say, did not live to see the promise fulfilled. Examples are LTG (ret.) James H. Merryman and Mr. Joseph P. Cribbins. In retirement both contributed generously to capturing and passing on the story of all those who made Aviation and made it great, just as both gave generously to Aviation during their careers. The same kind of talent, spirit to collaborate, and will to get things done for the greater good promise to carry Aviation forward, regardless of what lies ahead. Those qualities also largely account for the versatility and flexibility of Aviation, as well as the adherence to Army Values. So none of those aspects seems likely to change much.

Ideas, technology, and organization interweave tightly. All constantly change at the margins but also have remained fairly stable over several decades. The most basic idea has been to use the ability to operate in the air to influence immediate events on the ground. That idea created the emphasis on support to the ground commander. It also underlay the split that led to the Air Force. Technology has changed greatly in some aspects over the past half century. One aspect—the ability to hover, as well as maneuver—has remained consistent, dominant, and essential. The specific technology allowing that capability will surely change. However, that capability lets Aviation provide, either directly or indirectly, an immediate presence that the Army often calls 'boots on the ground.' Only a technology that allows that persistence can achieve the Army's goals. At the same time, technology acquired over 40 years ago meant that the boots might not be in direct contact with the ground at the moment. That fact was the essence of airmobility. Further technological changes will almost surely blur the lines that long ago fed the roles-and-missions debates with the Air Force. Meanwhile, increasing sophistication and costs of technologies have driven all services toward interdependence. There is no reason to expect that trend to reverse. So the future of organization, while likely to preserve distinct services, also means that people within the services will increasingly work as members of a tightly-knit, Joint team—not as members of cooperating services, each performing in its own lane. Whether a separate Aviation Branch will remain, no one can know now. That answer depends on the dynamics among people, ideas, technology, and organization. The same holds for which echelons have unique Aviation units and whether those units have one type of air vehicle or many types under a single commander.

The future of Aviation history

A closing word must be about the future of Aviation history. History is like banking: If no one makes deposits, there can be no withdrawals.

In this aspect, we live in perilous times. Changes in technology and habits work against us. We may soon have a better record of ancient Mesopotamians who wrote on clay tablets than of recent events on the same ground. Digital technology has badly outstripped the ability to capture and preserve information in usable form. Many formats that were universal a dozen years ago are unreadable today. So the record, even if it survives physically, is useless. Both the volume and kind of representations created digitally defy reducing more than a tiny fraction to paper. Much that used to become staff papers and memoranda now exists only in emails. Those are usually deleted when the operator reaches a personal limit of tolerance or gets an automated message that the user has exceeded authorized storage. In theory, most of that could be preserved as text, but that preservation is unlikely to happen. A more complex example is gun camera imagery—never mind, displays of real-time systems by which commanders now make decisions. No one has effectively addressed these issues. So the burden increasingly falls on individuals to use older methods—such as interviews and memoirs—to capture and preserve key information in some form accessible for the future.

There are several ways to fill these gaps. One recent initiative is an option for students in the Captains' Career Course at USAAVNC to write a personal experience monograph—a memoir of their experiences, with insights gained, from recent operations. This project follows a tradition that goes back to World War I at the Infantry School. That tradition has provided rich historical sources for the older combat arms, as well as Transportation, covering World War II to the present. Hopefully many Aviation Soldiers will choose to write something like this, whether in a formal course or not. If so, Aviation will eventually achieve parity with the older combat arms.

A great opportunity exists to address historical needs at a command level—most notably, in Aviation brigades. Especially as the Army reorganizes, making the brigade the basic unit of maneuver, the Aviation brigade commander is the person who can set the tone and provide the thrust to capture and preserve key pieces of history. The brigade commanders' role is doubly important in the long view. When a senior commander shows by actions that something is important, the next generation of leaders grows up thinking and acting that way. The culture changes. So do the outcomes. Opportunities for improvement exist here.

So a look forward must end with a personal appeal. Only you—the individual Aviation Soldier, Army civilian, contractor, or family member—can give Aviation its history. Record your own experiences, much as Soldiers going back to ancient times have done. Equally valuable are compilations of documents and even miniature multimedia productions that many of you are making to share within your unit and with your families. Pass copies of these things to places designated to collect and preserve them. Of special importance are the Army Aviation Museum at Fort Rucker and the Army Military History Institute at Carlisle, Pennsylvania. Encourage others to do likewise.

With your help, Aviation history has a future. Without your help, Aviation history ended yesterday.

Above the Best!

A Short Bibliographic Essay

In full draft, this book had over 3000 endnotes. The number and diversity of references defied condensation into a manageable list. This short essay highlights a very small number of specific items and points to sources in various locations for those wanting to delve deeper.

A handful of sources encapsulate key shifts in basic ideas. The earliest is COL William (Billy) Mitchell's "General Principles Underlying the Use of the Air Service in the Zone of Advance, A.E.F." An actual copy of this document seems to be hard to find. Robert Frank Futrell, <u>Ideas, Concepts, Doctrine: a History of Basic Thinking in the United States Air Force, 1907–1964</u>. (Maxwell AFB: Air University, 1971), discusses it and is extremely valuable for other insights into the period he covers. MAJ William W. Ford's "Wings for Santa Barbara," originally published in the <u>Field Artillery Journal</u>, May 1941 and reprinted in the <u>U.S. Army Aviation Digest</u> in June 1974, marks the next milestone. MG James M. Gavin's "Cavalry—and I Don't Mean Horses," <u>Harper's Magazine</u>, April 1954, is often noted as a major expression underpinning air assault. A broader, possibly even more important vision appears in BG Carl I. Hutton's "An Air Fighting Army?" <u>U.S. Army Aviation Digest</u>, July 1955. Where Gavin spoke of a highly mobile force, Hutton points toward a more powerful, capable, fully integrated air-ground force. Gavin's vision eventuated in the 11th Air Assault Division (Test) and its successors to this day. Hutton's vision ties closer to the Reorganization Objectives Army Division (ROAD) and even more to the Army of the 1980s, with the day/night capabilities and firepower available first with the Apache and including Deep Attack operations. MG Carl I. McNair and CPT Josef Reinsprecht, "Army Aviation Systems Program Review (AASPR) '82," <u>U.S. Army Aviation Digest</u>, June 1982, with companion articles, laid out the logic and the compelling need for the kind of long-range, heavy Aviation capabilities that saw battlefield expression in ODS and later combined-arms operations. BG E.J. Sinclair's "Aviation Transformation: How Far have We Come?" in <u>Army Aviation</u>, 30 November 2004, gives an overview of the thrust of most recent efforts. LTC Robert E. Sanders' companion piece, "Modular, Scalable and Tailorable Aviation Force Structures" highlights key aspects of the basic changes.

No comprehensive overview of Army Aviation's development has appeared since The Army Aviation Story by Richard Tierney with Fred Montgomery (Northport, AL: Colonial Press, 1963). So an interested reader must approach the subject piecemeal. Richard I. Wolf, The U.S. Air Force Basic Documents on Roles and Missions (Washington, DC: Office of Air Force History, 1987), is a vital compendium of key documents. Excellent studies of parts of different periods do exist. Most useful for this writing were Maurer Maurer, Aviation in the U.S. Army, 1919–1939 (Washington, DC: Office of Air Force History, 1987); Edgar F. Raines, Jr. Eyes of the Artillery; the Origins of Modern U.S. Army Aviation in World War II (Washington, DC: Center of Military History, 1999); and Richard P. Weinert, Jr., A History of Army Aviation—1950–1962 (Fort Monroe, VA: TRADOC, 1991). Many works cover separate aspects. COL (ret.) Benjamin S. Silver and Frances Aylette (Bowen) Silver, Ride at a Gallop (Waco, TX: Davis Brothers Publishing Company, Inc., 1990), is essential for anyone wanting to understand the 11th Air Assault Division (Test) and its transition into the 1st Cavalry Division (1CD) in Vietnam. Ronald E. Dolan, A History of the 160th Special Operations Aviation Regiment (Airborne) (Washington, DC: Federal Research Division, Library of Congress, October 2001) treats a key piece of Aviation that is mostly inaccessible. James W. Bradin, From Hot Air to Hellfire; the History of Army Attack Aviation (Novato, CA: Presidio Press, 1994) gives a useful summary through ODS. Edwin C. Fishel, The Secret War for the Union; the Untold Story of Military Intelligence in the Civil War (Boston: Houghton Mifflin Company, 1996), is invaluable on balloons and the Balloon Corps. Frederic A. Bergerson, The Army Gets an Air Force; Tactics of Insurgent Bureaucratic Politics (Baltimore: The Johns Hopkins University Press, 1980) provides many insights—often, hidden in his notes. Howard K. Butler, former historian at U.S. Army Aviation Systems Command (AVSCOM), published many studies. In some cases, these provide the only access to critical sources, such as the personal papers of Mr. Joseph P. Cribbins, that Butler drew into the command history files. All of these files disappeared during the reorganization into U.S. Army Aviation and Missile Command (AMCOM). Among Butler's studies are the Floating Aircraft Maintenance Facility (FAMF) (St. Louis, MO: Headquarters, AVSCOM, June 1976); "The Army Ground Forces and the Helicopter, 1941–1945" (St. Louis, MO: Historical Division, AVSCOM, 1987; History Study No. 1 in "A History of Army Aviation Logistics, 1935–1961"); Army Air Corps Airplanes and Observation, 1935–1941 (St. Louis, MO: Historical Office, AVSCOM, February 1990); Army Aviation Logistics in Vietnam, 1961–1975 (St. Louis, MO: AVSCOM Historical Office, January 1985); and Desert Shield and Desert Storm, an Aviation Logistics History: 1990–1991 (St. Louis: AVSCOM, June 1991). COL (ret.) John A. Bonin, currently completing a Ph.D. dissertation, wrote several helpful studies over a number of years—e.g., "Army Aviation for AirLand Battle: the Development of the Aviation Branch in the U.S. Army from 1971 to 1983" (unpublished manuscript, 20 September 1998). Bonin's notes also identify many additional sources. David A. Brown, <u>The Bell Helicopter Textron Story; Changing the Way the World Flies</u> (Arlington, TX: Aerofax Inc., 1995), gave insights into changes in the industry and their effects. Christopher C.S. Cheng, <u>Air Mobility; the Development of a Doctrine</u> (Westport, CT: Praeger, 1994), is similarly valuable. Peter Dorland and James Nanney, <u>Dust Off: Army Aeromedical Evacuation in Vietnam</u> (Washington, DC: U.S. Army Center of Military History, 1982) is brief but focused on a key area of Aviation. William Edward Fischer, Jr. <u>The Development of Military Night Aviation to 1919</u> (Maxwell AFB, AL: Air University Press, 1998) surprises by the extent of effort and depth of some insights gained during World War I that still apply. Especially valuable on night vision development was Donald L. Dobias, Jr., "Flying by the Beams of the Lesser Light: The Genesis of Image Intensifiers in Aviation, (Thesis, University of Oklahoma, 1992). Harry A. Sheppard, <u>They Also Paid Their Dues; a Tribute to Those Who Also Served</u> (NP: Harry A. Sheppard, 1998), treats an aspect of the black Aviation Soldier experience overshadowed by the attention to the Tuskegee Airmen.

Among studies that include important insight into Aviation incidental to their main focus was John L. Plaster, <u>SOG—the Secret Wars of America's Commandos in Vietnam</u> (New York: Simon & Schuster, 1997). Shelby L. Stanton, <u>Anatomy of a Division; the 1st Cav in Vietnam</u> (Novato, CA: Presidio Press, 1987) gives important insights in context of the broader discussion. LTC (Ret.) James H. Willbanks, <u>Thiet Giap! The Battle of An Loc, April 1972</u> (Fort Leavenworth, KS: Combat Studies Institute/U.S. Army Command and General Staff College, 1993), is invaluable in understanding the evolution of helicopters as tank killers as well as the radical change in the air defense threat in the final stage of Vietnam. Jose Angel Moroni Bracamonte and David E. Spencer, <u>Strategy and Tactics of the Salvadoran FMLN Guerrillas; Last Battle of the Cold War, Blueprint for Future Conflicts</u> (Westport, CT: Praeger, 1995), includes discussion of the transmission of low-technology antiaircraft tactics from Vietnam through the 1980s into El Salvador, leading into the Global War on Terror (GWOT).

Among many useful memoirs: James H. (Jimmy) Doolittle with Carroll V. Glines. <u>I Could Never Be So Lucky Again</u> (New York: Bantam Books, 1992), is both highly readable and full of insights into Aviation through World War II. Especially valuable and almost unknown was BG Carl I. Hutton's unpublished manuscript, <u>Without Trumpets and Drums; Recollections of 36 Months With the Army Aviation School, June 1954–June 1957</u> (undated, bound typescript in Aviation Technical Library). Hamilton H. Howze, <u>A Cavalryman's Story; Memoirs of A Twentieth-Century Army General</u> (Washington and London: Smithsonian Institution Press, 1996), covers a central figure and related events. Among the hundreds of Vietnam-era pieces, a few were especially useful—in some cases, because of direct contact with their authors and additional insights provided. Among these was Hugh L. Mills, Jr., <u>Low Level Hell; a Scout Pilot in the Big Red One</u> (Novato, CA: Presidio Press, 1992/2000). John L. Lowden, <u>Silent Wings at War; Combat Gliders in World War II</u> (Washington, DC: Smithsonian Institution Press, 1992), covers an aspect that is almost completely neglected. Hardy D. Cannon, <u>Box Seat Over Hell</u> (San Antonio, TX: privately published, 1985), gave an Artillery pilot's personal view of World War II and includes valuable tidbits on others and their experiences. Michael J. Novosel, <u>Dustoff; the Memoir of an Army Aviator</u> (Novato, CA: Presidio Press, 1999), gives valuable insights into both World War II and Vietnam. Not a memoir but closely akin is Trent Angers, <u>The Forgotten Hero of My Lai; the Hugh Thompson Story</u> (Lafayette, LA: Acadian House, 1999). Also Rhonda Cornum as told to Peter Copland, <u>She Went to War; the Rhonda Cornum Story</u> (Novato: CA: Presidio Press, 1992). MAJ Kevin P. Smith, <u>United States Army Aviation in the Gulf War; United States Army Aviation During Operations Desert Shield and Desert Storm—Selected Readings.</u> (Fort Rucker: U.S. Army Aviation Center, 20 June 1993), is a compendium of edited interviews. Michael J. Durant, <u>In the Company of Heroes</u> (New York: G. P. Putnam's Sons, 2003) complements Bowden's <u>Black Hawk Down</u>. Of special, related importance are many interviews in the U.S. Army Military History Institute at Carlisle, Pennsylvania. MHI is also a crucial resource for all types of materials. These include especially those with GEN (ret.) Hamilton H. Howze; LTGs Harry W. O. Kinnard, George P. Seneff, John J. Tolson, and Robert R. Williams; BGs O. Glenn Goodhand and Edwin L. Powell; and COL Delbert L. Bristol. Among more recent additions to these holdings was a roundtable discussion involving LTGs John (Jack) Norton and Robert R. Williams, as well as MGs George Beatty and George Putnam, on the Howze Board that includes many insights into earlier people and events. A large number of interviews with both serving and veteran Army aviators are part of the permanent historical collections at USAAVNC—e.g., Interview with LTC Daniel E. Williams, 11 April 2005, subject: Experiences in command of a AH-64D Apache Longbow battalion during OIF. Many are not transcribed. An index of these exists at the Army Aviation Museum, and nearly all appear in a lengthy Reference Index of the Historian's collections. In many cases, handwritten or typed notes exist in a related file in the Historian's Reference Files. Also available at the Army

Aviation Museum are tapes of a series of presentations by Aviation veterans to Initial Entry Rotary Wing (IERW) students, covering a wide range of topics, including Aviation in World War II, the Executive Flight Detachment (EFD), research and development (R&D) of the AH-56 Cheyenne and CH-54 Tarhe (Flying Crane), Caribou operations, development of air assault, and the evolution of the crew chief. Hopes are that the current generation of Aviation Soldiers will take advantage of opportunities to record their experiences and insights for future use. Examples are the Personal Experience Monographs, a writing option in the Captains' Career Course (CCC), and interviews with Aviation brigade commanders planned for 2006.

Somewhere between a study and a memoir lie several key works, including LTG John J. Tolson, Vietnam Studies—Airmobility, 1961–1971 (Washington, DC: Department of the Army, 1999); MG Spurgeon Neel, Vietnam Studies— Medical Support of the U.S. Army in Vietnam 1965–1970 (Washington, DC: United States Army Center of Military History, 1973, 1991)

Among treatments of particular events several stand out. These include LTG (ret.) Harold G. Moore and Joseph L. Galloway, We Were Soldiers Once…And Young (New York: Random House, 1992); Mark Bowden, Black Hawk Down; a Story of Modern War (New York: Atlantic Monthly Press, 1999); Ronald H. Cole, Operation Urgent Fury; The Planning and Execution of Joint Operations in Grenada, 12 October–2 November 1983 (Washington, DC: Joint History Office, Office of the Chairman of the Joint Chiefs of Staff, 1997); Sean Naylor, Not a Good Day to Die; the Untold Story of Operation Anaconda (New York: Berkley Books, 2005), gives extraordinary, close-hand detail into a key, recent operation. Noted for his rigor in corroborating oral testimony makes the work of Keith William Nolan especially useful: Into Laos; the Story of Dewey Canyon II/Lam Son 719; Vietnam 1971 (Novato, CA: Presidio Press, 1986) and Into Cambodia; Spring Campaign, Summer Offensive, 1970 (Novato, CA: Presidio Press, 2000).

A number of theses by military officers were invaluable. Among these were MAJ John C. Burns, "XM-26 TOW: Birth of the Helicopter as a Tank Buster" (Marine Corps Command and Staff College, 2 May 1994); LTC Samuel G. Cockerham, "Huey Cobra—a Case in DOD/DA Decision-making" (Washington, DC: Industrial College of the Armed Forces, March 1967); Jason L. Galindo, "A Case History of the United States Army RAH-66 Comanche Helicopter" (Naval Postgraduate School, Monterey, CA, March 2000); MAJ Robert J. Hamilton, "Green and Blue in the Wild Blue: An Examination of the Evolution of Army and Air Force Airpower Thinking and Doctrine Since the Vietnam War" (Maxwell Air Force Base, Alabama: School of Advanced Airpower Studies, Air University, June 1993); MAJ Stephen C. Smith, USA, "Is There a Role for Attack Helicopters in Peace Operations?" (Fort Leavenworth, KS: U.S. Army Command and General Staff College, 5 June 1998) Also valuable were some doctoral dissertations—notably, Roy Richard Stephenson, Road to Downfall; Lam Son 71/9 and U.S. Airmobility Doctrine (University of Kansas, 1991).

Testimony before Congressional committees and published reports by government agencies were invaluable. Where possible, copies have been captured in the Aviation Technical Library—e.g., "Statement by Major General Ellis D. Parker...before the House Armed Services Committee, Subcommittee on Investigations...Aviation Night Vision Goggles, 21 march 1989." Where these were accessible via the Internet, they were downloaded and saved digitally—e.g., "Statement by BG Joseph A. Smith, Director of Army Safety, Before the Committee on Armed Services, United States House of Representatives on Military Aviation Safety, Second Session, 108th Congress, 11 February 2004" http://armedservices.house.gov/openingstatementsandpressreleases/108thcongre ss/04–02–11smith.pdf. Downloaded 20 October 2004. In Aviation Branch History, Sources, Safety, <Smith statement on Army Aviation safety 11 Feb 04.pdf> The U.S. Government Accounting Office (GAO) has published many reports dealing with military aviation, including many focused on the Army. Illustrative are the Report to the Honorable Peter A. DeFazio, House of Representatives, DEFENSE ACQUISITIONS—Comanche Program Cost, Schedule, and Performance Status (Washington: United States General Accounting Office U.S. Government Accounting Office (GAO), August 1999) [GAO/NSIAD-99–146]; also MILITARY PERSONNEL—Actions Needed to Better Define Pilot Requirements and Promote Retention (Washington, DC: U.S. Government Accounting Office (GAO), August 1999) [GAO/NSIAD-99–211]. Some similar reports contain useful chronologies of programs—e.g., Office of the Inspector General of the Department of Defense [DOD IG], Acquisition Management of the RAH-66 Comanche, Report No. D-2003–087, 12 May 2003, (Project No. D2002AL-0150), Appendix B. Comanche History.

Copies of original studies and reports, where available, are essential. An example is the Final Report, U.S. Army Tactical Mobility Requirements Board, 20 August 1962 [Howze Board]. This report has been digitized in a searchable format and is available in the Aviation Technical Library or Army Aviation Museum. Many, even though old, remain inaccessible to the general reader because they have never been through all the processing required for declassification and public release.

For the period it was published, from 1955 to 1995, articles in the U.S. Army Aviation Digest are invaluable. The journal of the Army Aviation Association of America (AAAA), Army Aviation, is also valuable and provides some carryover of the kind of coverage found in the Digest. Other industry publications, such as those of the American Helicopter Society, are also important. Especially for the period from ODS to the present, much information used in this writing depended on notes, briefing slides, and other items captured in connection with the annual command histories of the USAAVNC. No published volume of these histories has been completed since 1994. However, collected documents—increasingly in digital form only—exist in the files of the Aviation Branch Historian at Fort Rucker.

Key repositories include the Army Transportation Museum, Fort Eustis, VA, U.S. Army Aviation and Missile Command (AMCOM) Historical Function at Redstone Arsenal, AL; the 101st Airborne Division Museum at Fort Campbell, KY; and the Air Force Historical Research Agency at Maxwell AFB, AL. Finally, for the Vietnam period, an invaluable resource is the Vietnam Helicopter Pilots' Association (VHPA) and its various publications, as well as a huge and constantly changing set of websites maintained privately by veterans and other interested people. Hundreds of individual inquiries and responses from people in these networks provided information not readily available elsewhere. The VHPA concluded an arrangement with Texas Tech University to be the permanent repository for its archives, and this will be a key resource for the history of Aviation for that period as the years pass.

Acronym Glossary

1AB	1st Aviation Brigade
1AD	1st Armored Division
1CD	1st Cavalry Division
1LT	First Lieutenant
2ID	2d Infantry Division
2LT	Second Lieutenant
3ACR	3d Armored Cavalry Regiment
3ID	3rd Infantry Division
4ID	4th Infantry Division
7/17 Cav	7th Squadron, 17th Cavalry Regiment
10MTN	10th Mountain Division
24ID	24th Infantry Division
25ID	25th Infantry Division
82AB	82d Airborne Division
101AB	101st Airborne Division
160 SOAR	160th Special Operations Aviation Regiment
A2C2	Army Airspace Command and Control
A&P	Airframe and Powerplant [license]
AAAA	Army Aviation Association of America
AAF	Army Air Forces
AAH	Advanced Attack Helicopter
AAR	after-action review
AASPR	Army Aviation Systems Program Review
ABCS	Army Battle Command System
AC	Active Component
ACCB	air cavalry combat brigade
ACIP	Aviation Career Incentive Pay
AD	air defense
AFB	Air Force Base
AGF	Army Ground Forces

ALB	AirLand Battle
ALSE	Aviation Life Support Equipment
AMC	U.S. Army Materiel Command
AMCOM	U.S. Army Aviation and Missile Command
AOE	Army of Excellence
AOR	area of operational responsibility
AP	Aviation Proponency
APC	armored personnel carrier
AQC	Aviation Qualification Course
ARA	aerial rocket artillery
ARI	Aviation Restructure Initiative
ARIARDA	U.S. Army Research Institute Aviation Research and Development Activity
ARNG	Army National Guard
ARPA	Advanced Research Project Agency
ARVN	Army of the Republic of Vietnam
ASE	aircraft survivability equipment
ASPR	Aviation Systems Program Review
ATA	air-to-air
ATACMS	Army Tactical Missile System
ATB	Aviation Training Brigade
ATC	air traffic control
ATO	air tasking order
ATS	air traffic services
ATX	Aviation Training Exercise
AVCATT-A	Aviation Combined Arms Tactical Trainer—Aviation Reconfigurable Manned Simulator
AVSCOM	Aviation Systems Command
AVIM	Aviation intermediate maintenance [company]
AVUM	Aviation Unit Maintenance [platoon]
AW	Air Warrior
AWO	Aviation warrant officer
BAE	Brigade Aviation Element
BCS	basic combat skills
BG	Brigadier General
C2	command and control

CAAF	Cairns Army Airfield
CAS	close air support
CCA	close combat attack
CFIT	controlled flight into terrain
CG	Commanding General
CIA	Central Intelligence Agency
CJCS	Chairman, Joint Chiefs of Staff
COL	Colonel
COMUSMACV	Commander, U.S. Military Advisory Command Vietnam
CONARC	Continental Army Command
CONUS	Continental United States
COTS	commercial off-the-shelf
CP	command post
CPT	Captain
CPX	command post exercise
CSA	Chief of Staff of the Army
CSAR	combat search and rescue
CSM	Command Sergeant Major
CWO	Chief Warrant Officer
DA	Department of the Army
DARPA	Defense Advanced Research Project Agency
DCPC	Direct Combat Probability Coding
DCSOPS	G-3/Deputy Chief of Staff for Operations
DCSLOG	Deputy Chief of Staff for Logistics
DCSPER	Deputy Chief of Staff for Personnel
DCSPRO	G-8/Office of the Army Deputy of Staff for Programs
DES	Director of Evaluation and Standardization
DISCOM	division support command
DSC	Distinguished Service Cross
DTD	Directorate of Training and Doctrine
DOD	Department of Defense
DOTD	Directorate of Training and Doctrine
DS	direct support
DSB	Defense Science Board
DSC	Distinguished Service Cross

EFD	Executive Flight Detachment
EW	electronic warfare
FAA	Federal Aviation Administration
FARP	forward area refuel/rearm point
FCS	Future Combat System
FLIR	forward looking infrared [radar]
FLOT	forward line of own troops
FM	Field Manual
FM	frequency modulation [communications]
FOB	forward operating base
FORSCOM	U.S. Army Forces Command
FS XXI	Flight School XXI
FUE	first unit equipped
GAO	Government Accounting Office
GCA	ground control approach [radar]
GHQ AF	General Headquarters Air Force
GS	general support
GSE	ground support equipment
HAATS	High Altitude Army Aviation Training Site
HART	High Altitude Rescue Team
HASC	House Armed Services Committee
HELLFIRE	Helicopter Laser Air Defense Suppression and Fire-and-Forget Guided Missile
HQDA	Headquarters, Department of the Army
IERW	Initial Entry Rotary Wing [course]
IFF	identification friend or foe
IFR	instrument flight rules
IP	instructor pilot
IR	infrared
JAAT	Joint air attack team
JCS	Joint Chiefs of Staff
JROC	Joint Requirements Oversight Council
JSTARS	Joint Services Targeting and Reconnaissance System
KIA	killed in action
LCT	Longbow Crew Trainer
LNO	liaison officer

LOH	light observation helicopter—usually the OH-6 Cayuse, nicknamed Loach
LT	Lieutenant
LTC	Lieutenant Colonel
LTG	Lieutenant General
LUH	Light Utility Helicopter
LZ	landing zone
MAA	mission area analysis
MAJ	Major
MANPADS	man-portable air defense system
MG	Major General
MEDEVAC	medical evacuation
MFOQA	Military Flight Operations Quality Assurance
MILPERCEN	U.S. Army Military Personnel Center
MLRS	Multiple Launch Rocket System
MOS	Military Occupational Specialty
MRE	Meal, Ready to Eat
MSG	Master Sergeant
NCO	noncommissioned officer
NOE	nap-of-the-earth
NVA	North Vietnamese Army
NVG	night vision goggles
OCM	On Condition Maintenance
OCS	officer candidate school
ODS	Operation Desert Storm
OFTF	Objective Force Task Force
OPFOR	opposing force
OPMS	Officer Personnel Management System
OPSEC	operational security
OPTEMPO	operational tempo
OR	operational readiness
ORD	operational requirements document
OTS	off-the-shelf
OSD	Office of the Secretary of Defense
PEO-AV	Program Executive Officer for Aviation
PFC	Private First Class

PGM	precision guided munition
PM	program manager/project manager
PNVS	pilot night vision sensor
POI	program of instruction
POW	prisoner of war
QRF	quick reaction force
R&D	research and development
RC	Reserve Components
ROAD	Reorganization Objectives Army Division
ROC	required operational capability
ROE	rules of engagement
ROTC	Reserve Officer Training Corps
RPG	rocket-propelled grenade
S-3	Operations Officer
SAC	Strategic Air Command
SAM	surface-to-air missile
SAR	search and rescue
SATSA	Signal Corps Aviation Test and Support Activity
SEAD	suppression of enemy air defenses
SECDEF	Secretary of Defense
SEMA	Special Electronics Mission Aircraft
SERE	Survival, Evasion, Resistance and Escape
SF	Special Forces
SFC	Sergeant First Class
SFTS	Synthetic Flight Training System
SGT	Sergeant
SGM	Sergeant Major
SIP	standardization instructor pilot
SOA	Special Operations Aviation
SOF	special operations forces
SOG	Military Assistance Command Vietnam—Studies and Observation Group
SOP	standard operating procedures
SP4	Specialist
SP5	Specialist 5
SPR	systems program review

SWA	Southwest Asia
TAC	Tactical Air Command
TACAIR	tactical air
TACOPS	tactical operations
TADS	target acquisition and designation system
TATSA	Transportation Aircraft Test and Support Activity
TC	Training Circular
TDA	table of distribution and allowances
TF	Task Force
TI	technical inspector
TIMS	Tailored Inspection Maintenance System
TOE	table of organization and equipment
TOW	Tube-Launched, Optically Tracked, Wire Guided [missile]
TRADOC	U.S. Army Training and Doctrine Command
TRICAP	Triple Capability [division]
TROAA	TRADOC Review of Army Aviation
TTP	tactics, and techniques and procedures
USAATCA	US Army Air Traffic Control Activity
USAAVNC	U.S. Army Aviation Center
USAFISA	U.S. Army Force Integration Support Agency
USAREUR	U.S. Army Europe
USARV	U.S. Army Vietnam
USAALS	U.S. Army Aviation Logistics School
USAARL	U.S. Army Aeromedical Research Laboratory
USACAC	U.S. Army Combined Arms Center
USASC	U.S. Army Safety Center [renamed U.S. Army Combat Readiness Center (CRC)]
UTT	Utility Tactical Transport
VC	Viet Cong
VCSA	Vice Chief of Staff of the Army
VFR	visual flight rules
VNAF	Vietnamese Air Force
WO	warrant officer
WOCC	Warrant Officer Career Center
XVIII AB	XVIII Airborne Corps